Intrigue and Treason

Intrigue and Treason: The Tudor Court 1547–1558

David Loades

Harlow, England • London • New York • Boston • San Francisco • Toronto
Sydney • Tokyo • Singapore • Hong Kong • Seoul • Taipei • New Delhi
Cape Town • Madrid • Mexico City • Amsterdam • Munich • Paris • Milan

PEARSON EDUCATION LIMITED

Edinburgh Gate
Harlow CM20 2JE
Tel: +44 (0)1279 623623
Fax: +44 (0)1279 431059
Website: www.pearsoned.co.uk

First edition published in Great Britain in 2004

© Pearson Education Limited 2004

ISBN 0 582 77226 5

British Library Cataloguing in Publication Data
A CIP catalogue record for this book can be obtained from the British Library

Library of Congress Cataloging-in-Publication Data
Loades, D.M.
   Intrigue and treason : the Tudor court, 1547–1558 / David Loades.
      p. cm.
   Includes bibliographical references and index.
   ISBN 0-582-77226-5
   1. Great Britain–History–Edward VI, 1547–1553. 2. Great Britain–Court and
courtiers–History–16th century. 3. Great Britain–History–Mary I, 1553–1558. 4. Great
Britain–History–Tudors, 1485–1603. 5. Tudor, House of. I. Title.

DA340.L579 2004
942.05'3'092–dc22

                                                                    2004046541

10 9 8 7 6 5 4 3 2 1
08 07 06 05 04

Set by 3 in 9.5 pt Melior
Printed in Great Britain by Biddles Ltd, Kings Lynn

The Publishers' policy is to use paper manufactured from sustainable forests.

Contents

Acknowledgements

We are grateful to the following for permission to reproduce copyright material:

The National Portrait Gallery, London, for use of the following plate images: Henry VIII, William Paulet, Edward VI, Catherine Parr, William Cecil, Philip II, Mary I, and Elizabeth I; the British Library for use of their image of Henry VIII and Will Somers, from Henry VIII's Psalter copyright © The British Library, Royal 2.A. xvi, f.63v; The Society of Antiquaries of London for use of their image of the Eve-of-Coronation Procession of Edward VI; National Museums and Galleries of Wales for use of their image of The Family of Henry VIII: An Allegory of the Tudor Succession; The Davenant Press and Her Majesty's Stationery Office for use of the Ground Plan of Hampton Court, after p. 131, vol. IV (ii), H.M. Colvin, *The History of the King's Works* (1982). Crown copyright material is reproduced with the permission of the Controller of HMSO and the Queen's Printer for Scotland.

In some instances we have been unable to trace the owners of copyright material, and we would appreciate any information that would enable us to do so.

Preface

The Tudor court continues to fascinate, partly because the Tudors themselves were such compelling personalities, and partly because the period is so relatively well documented. Different as they were in many ways from their modern equivalents, sixteenth-century men and women are alive to us in ways that their thirteenth- or fourteenth-century predecessors are not. There are no renaissance courts in the world today, but the psychology of competition and the dynamics of power which then applied are still recognisable. However, students of Tudor England are usually drawn to the feverish politics of the reign of Henry VIII, with its tantalising threads of sexual intrigue, dramatic reversals of fortune – and sudden death; or alternatively to the glossy achievements of Elizabeth, the world of Shakespeare, Spenser, Byrd and Hakluyt. So far the revival of interest in the 'little Tudors' – Edward VI and Mary – which began in the 1960s has not had very much to say about the court, beyond noticing that the political development of the Privy Chamber, which had been going on from the 1490s, was checked and almost destroyed by its conversion into a female precinct in 1553. However, the court of Edward VI was by no means a political backwater, in spite of the fact that the king's immediate context was the schoolroom. How Edward was trained, and by whom, tells us a lot about what was supposed to happen as well as about what actually did. The king would live surrounded by courtiers, and he had to know how to deal with them – and how to exercise the authority to which he was heir. The reign of Edward VI was the one that got away. Mary was England's first ruling queen, and in court as in council she was feeling her way. Handicapped by a lack of experience, as well as by rigid notions of both behaviour and policy, she struggled. Her husband, Philip, chosen for the best of reasons, also struggled with an unprecedented situation. He had plenty of experience, but it was only partly relevant; and their court was a curious hybrid with no very clear sense of either direction or identity.

Intrigue there was in plenty; treason very little, except in the inflated language of faction. Tudor men were very apt to cry 'Treason!' when things went wrong, or when they scented an opportunity against an enemy. As far as we know, no one plotted to murder Edward, and those who would have liked to dispose of Mary were not within her court. During this period the court provided a protective environment, and surprising continuities. It is, however, no less important for lacking the high-profile conflicts of the earlier and later periods. Neither monarch left a clear-cut legacy. In spite of her religious settlement, Elizabeth's court was not remotely like Edward's, and Mary's tastes and friendships died with her. Nevertheless, the court is central to an understanding of this complex period, no less than to the better-known reigns that preceded and followed it.

This study has grown partly out of a long-standing interest in both the court and the period, and partly out of a desire to answer some questions not hitherto addressed. Some of it is new; much will be familiar to students of Tudor England. But it is hoped that something will be added, even to the understanding of the best informed, and that the general reader will be prompted to want to know more about these brief but pivotal reigns. Although the focus is upon the years 1547–53, the situation at the beginning of Edward's reign requires explanation, and for that reason the first chapter is a 'rolling start', taking some aspects of the story back to 1540. For similar reasons an abrupt finish with Mary's death would fail to reveal the very significant changes that the new queen made, and which are an essential aspect of the story. Consequently I have ended with the peaking of the 'Dudley affair' in 1560 rather than with Mary's departure in 1558. The structure of the court, which can look formidably complex to the uninitiated, is outlined only briefly in the text, and expanded in two appendices, which can usefully be consulted alongside Chapter 1. It needs to be borne in mind throughout that the Privy Council is actually part of the court. Although not all councillors were active courtiers, the council normally met at court, and all its members were rated as staff of the Chamber. When the court moved, a nucleus of councillors moved with it, even during a progress, and letters passed regularly between those councillors who were following the court and those who remained at Westminster. The only exceptions to this rule were when the council met during the minority of Edward VI at Somerset

House or (a very few times) at Durham Place. The tensions which existed during the 1540s between the Privy Council and the Privy Chamber were thus tensions within the court, and not between the court and an outside body.

David Loades
Oxford, February 2004

List of illustrations

Henry VIII
Artist unknown [National Portrait Gallery 157]

William Paulet, 1st Marquess of Winchester
Artist unknown [NPG 65]

Henry VIII and Will Somers, from Henry VIII's Psalter
Artist unknown [British Library]

Edward VI
Studio of William Scrots [NPG 442]

Catherine Parr
Artist unknown [NPG 4618]

William Cecil, 1st Baron Burghley
Attributed to Marcus Gheeraerts the Younger [NPG 362]

The Eve-of-Coronation Procession of Edward VI
Artist unknown [The Society of Antiquaries of London]

Philip II, King of Spain
Artist unknown [NPG 347]

Mary I
Master John [NPG 428]

Ground Plan of Hampton Court
[After H.M. Colvin, The History of the King's Works]

Elizabeth I (The Darnley Portrait)
Artist unknown [NPG 2082]

The Family of Henry VIII: An Allegory of the Tudor Succession
Attributed to Lucas de Heere [National Museums and Galleries of Wales]

CHAPTER 1

* * * * * * * * * * * * * *

The functioning of the court, 1540–7

The fall of Thomas Cromwell in June 1540 was not quite the decisive event it appeared to be at the time. Central as his position had been, and great as his influence had been, he was not the king. He fell because he had lost the confidence of Henry VIII – which means that the king's somewhat inconstant mind had been turned against him by personal and political enemies.[1] The same thing had happened to Cardinal Thomas Wolsey in 1529, and to Henry's second wife, Anne Boleyn, in 1536. Within months of Cromwell's execution the king was lamenting that he had been too hasty in judging his great minister. He had said similar things in 1531, but he seems not to have learned from his mistakes. One of the reasons for this deficiency lay in Henry's own psychology, but another lay in the context within which he was operating – that is, the court. Part of the purpose of a court was to provide the monarch with a lifestyle – both the *maiestas* necessary to his honour, and the service necessary to his daily needs.[2] Another part was to support, and influence, his decision making. The two functions of a renaissance monarch were to provide a magnificent and symbolic focus for loyalty and service, and to make decisions. When it came to the latter process, there were customs but no rules. On every major issue of state the king, and only the king, was empowered to decide. He appointed his servants, called his councillors, and distributed his patronage.[3] Most minor decisions were delegated by custom, but the king could always intervene directly if he chose; and he could not be gainsaid. Even a judicial process over which he had no control could be nullified by the prerogative of pardon.

In sixteenth-century England there was only a minimal central bureaucracy to enforce these decisions. The most important agency was the king's council, and in the localities the various commissions issued in the king's name.[4] However, the king might also use his courtiers, either to supplement or to short-circuit the usual processes, because courtiers were the king's personal servants as distinct from agents of the state. For many purposes the king *was* the state; but not for all. The king, for example, could not make law; nor could he levy direct taxes without formal consent. In these matters the court had no part; but in everything which involved the exercise of the prerogative, it was both an agency and an influence.

The court was a complex, multilayered institution – if, indeed, it can be called an institution at all. The larger part of it, the Household, had virtually no political significance except as a source of routine patronage. It existed to provide food, lodging, cleaning, security, transport and other basic necessities. The structure of its numerous departments is outlined in Appendix I. The officers of the Household might have access to the monarch if the latter so chose, but they had no rights in that connection.[5] The 'White Stick', or gentlemen officers of the Household, were the Lord Great Master (or Lord Steward – the two did not exist at the same time), the Treasurer, the Comptroller and the Cofferer, and they controlled the whole outfit through the Counting House, or Board of Greencloth. All the subordinate departments accounted there, and the whole budget of the Household was centrally controlled. The Household was stable, bureaucratic, and dominated by its own customs and traditions. By contrast, the Chamber, or *Domus Regie Magnificencie* as it was significantly called, was politicised up to a point, and the Privy Chamber, which was closest to the monarch, was highly political. The chief officer of the Chamber was the Lord Chamberlain, who was responsible for all matters of 'staff control', assisted by the Vice-Chamberlain, who usually doubled as the Captain of the Guard, and the Treasurer. The Lord Great Chamberlainship was purely a sinecure, and its occupant was not necessarily present at court at all. There were no departments in the Chamber, but rather distinctions of function among the different staff, such as sewers, cupbearers and waiters. Several categories of specialists, such as physicians and chaplains, were also attached to this section. The council was part of the Chamber (which was why the Lord Chamberlain was a councillor *ex officio*), as were the gentlemen pensioners and the yeomen of the guard – the monarch's personal soldiers. The Chamber was also political in another sense. The innumerable gentleman servants were drawn from the ranks of the county elites, and formed a valuable means of communication between the court and the localities.[6] This was a function which the council had virtually ceased to perform after the reorganisation of 1535–40, which had left it almost entirely a body of major office holders. When there was a royal consort (which there was in 1540–1 and again from 1543 to 1547), that almost doubled the number of servants, and hence the opportunities for both communication and patronage. It also introduced a significant number of women into the court, which otherwise was heavily male dominated, apart from the prostitutes who were a constant nuisance in the lower reaches of the Household.[7] Both Prince Edward and Mary also had their own Chamber establishments at this time, but both were modest in scale, and semi-detached from the court proper. The Privy Chamber was more focused still. In one sense its grooms and gentlemen were the king's most intimate body servants, but in another sense the gentlemen were his chosen companions, and also his confidential agents and messengers. Apart from a few key officers, and the king's chaplains and physicians, these were the only men with guaranteed and unsupervised access to the monarch. Their influence was therefore potentially very great, and on at least two occasions, in 1519 and 1526, the council had been sufficiently worried to persuade the king to carry out purges of the membership.[8] By 1540 the political, although not the administrative, influence of the Privy Council and the Privy Chamber were approximately equal. There was no comparison between the public functions of the two, but because the monarch was the political decision maker, the weight of the one and the intimacy of the other had created an approximate equipoise.

This was important in 1540 because Thomas Cromwell, like Wolsey before him, had succeeded in planting some of his own clients in the Privy Chamber – men such as Ralf Sadler and Anthony Denny. Cromwell fell because he lost control of the Privy Council, and the insinuations of powerful enemies such as the Duke of Norfolk and Stephen Gardiner, the Bishop of Winchester, carried more weight with Henry than the voices of

his friends. But his death did not dislodge his friends, and the rather curious result was that for several years the council was dominated by religious and political conservatives, while the Privy Chamber was
dominated by reformers.[9] These men were not protestants, because
Henry continued to detest Luther's ideas on justification and the
eucharistic presence, but they were definitely of the New Learning, and
favoured such Cromwellian developments as the English bible and the
erosion of purgatory. Cromwell's fall did not, therefore, represent the end
of the 'reforming party', as some contemporaries on both sides expected.
Rather, it set up the tug of war between conservatives and reformers
which dominated the domestic politics of the 1540s. This should not be
seen as a battle for control, because until the very last days of his life the
king was in control; but it was a battle for influence. As Henry's health
deteriorated, and his temper became increasingly uncertain, these two
groups struggled to gain his ear; and the main battlefield, inevitably, was
the court which was Henry's personal and political context.

For some time after Cromwell's departure, there was no contest. The
Cleves marriage had been a disaster. In terms of foreign policy it made
sense, but it had left the king offended, furious, and feeling thoroughly
misused.[10] It had been one, but only one, of the factors which had broken
his faith in his chief minister. Moreover, even before the unfortunate
Anne had been bundled into retirement, Henry's fancy had settled upon
one of her ladies-in-waiting, the young and eminently nubile Catherine
Howard. Catherine was the Duke of Norfolk's niece, and had been
brought up in the household of his stepmother the dowager duchess
before joining the court.[11] By the spring of 1540 she was a talented and
experienced flirt, and Norfolk (one of whose ambitions was to break the
Cleves marriage) lost no opportunity of drawing her to the king's attention. The latter's infatuation was already the subject of court gossip
before he finally gave up on Anne, and it came as no surprise to anyone
when, on 28 July 1540, less than three weeks after his hasty divorce, he
married her. Ironically, this was the same day that Thomas Cromwell
went to the block – a symbolic piece of punctuation which seemed to
herald a major shift in royal policy. But it was not so. In the first place,
Norfolk and Gardiner were allies only to the extent of their common
hatred of Cromwell. Once he was gone, they went their separate ways.[12]
Gardiner was recalled to the council after a period of rustication in

August 1540, and his pro-imperial predilections were bound to clash, sooner or later, with Norfolk's Francophilia. For the time being the field belonged to the duke, but neither Cranmer's nor Cromwell's Privy Chamber clients had gone away. It was unlikely that either would make common cause with Gardiner; but, as soon became apparent, Norfolk's ascendancy was far too dependent upon the 'feel good factor' induced in Henry by his latest bride.

Neither Norfolk, nor Gardiner, nor the Duke of Suffolk could take Cromwell's place. None of them had anything like his comprehensive grasp of affairs, and his departure left the king himself as the only person with the necessary experience. This revealed with great clarity what the positions of Wolsey and Cromwell had partly concealed – that the king was the director of policy. Now he was not only the decision maker but also the constructive strategist. In the summer of 1541 he made a progress to the north, which had been promised since 1537. There were two reasons for this: to overawe any residual discontent which might have been left behind after the Pilgrimage of Grace, and to reach an understanding with James V of Scotland.[13] James was Henry's nephew, and Henry was very anxious to persuade him to embark upon an ecclesiastical policy similar to that of the Royal Supremacy. Such a course would break the 'auld alliance' with France, and turn the Scots from potential enemies into allies. In return, it was hinted, James could be included in the English succession, after Edward, of course, and in default of further sons.[14] In one respect the progress was a great success: everywhere the king's enormous and splendid train was received with ostentatious loyalty and enthusiasm. But the second objective made no progress at all. Henry thought that he had persuaded James to meet him at York, but when it came to the point a combination of French influence, orthodox catholic sympathies and natural suspicion caused the Scottish council to discourage their king from taking the risk. Henry waited seven days at York and then, feeling angry and humiliated, he returned to the south.

While this magnificent cavalcade was rolling north, the queen was pursuing her own agenda. Henry was the very antithesis of the virile and exciting lover that such a highly sexed youngster needed. It was not that he was impotent, but his performance was highly erratic, and had been for years. He was elderly, corpulent and in uncertain health. In fact he was more interested in admiring his dashing bride than in using her, a situation which she quickly found boring and frustrating. With a daring which was either desperate or stupid, she renewed an old association with Francis Dereham, a former admirer to whom she had given a position in her household, and began a serious intrigue with Thomas Culpepper, a junior member of the king's Privy Chamber.[15] Every time the court halted, there were secret assignations, backstairs visits and surreptitious infidelity. Catherine may have calculated that the sooner she became pregnant the more secure her position would be, and that Henry's infatuation was such that he would not have doubted how this had come about. However, if that was her thinking, she miscalculated. She did not become pregnant, and enemies of the Howard ascendancy got wind of what was going on. The immediate cause of her downfall was John Lascelles, a minor member of the Household and a strong protestant who was eventually to die for his convictions.[16] His sister, Mary Hall, had been in the service of the Dowager Duchess of Norfolk, and knew most of what there was to know about Catherine's pre-nuptial liaisons. She was not the only one, but Francis Dereham had in effect been bought off, as had one Joan Bulmer, another of her former 'bedfellows', who had demanded, and been given, a place at court less than a month after Catherine's wedding. Whether Mary Hall had attempted blackmail and been rebuffed, or whether she shared her brother's convictions, we do not know, but at some point during 1541 she told Lascelles what she knew.

To him the course of duty was clear. On 1 November, while Henry was still celebrating his joy in his wife's fidelity, he sought out Archbishop Cranmer and told him what he had heard. In spite of his eclipse by Norfolk, Cranmer was still trusted by the king, and was not at all reluctant to strike a blow against the conservative ascendancy which was such a threat to him. Of course, what Lascelles knew was over and done with: it did not touch Catherine since her marriage. On the other hand, Henry had made such a fuss about his pure and innocent bride that the humiliation of such revelations would be almost as bad. It appeared that, in spite of all his sexual experience, the king did not know whether the woman who had come to his bed was a virgin or not. Cranmer passed the king a note while he was at mass, and the latter's first reaction was surprising: he shrugged the stories off as mere calumny.[17] However, Norfolk's enemies were not to be deterred. Cranmer had already confided in two of his allies in the council, the Lord Chancellor, Sir Thomas

Audley, and the Earl of Hertford; and they shared his conviction that these colourful tales were substantially true. In spite of his scepticism, Henry could not afford to ignore Cranmer's note, and he instructed the Earl of Southampton to carry out a secret investigation. Fitzwilliam duly interviewed both Lascelles and Mary Hall, and found their testimony to be consistent.[18] Meanwhile, Dereham and another of Catherine's old flames, Henry Mannox, had been arrested, ostensibly for other reasons. Once in custody, they were questioned about their relations with the queen, and both confessed having 'had to do' with her before her marriage. Dereham, however, alleged a betrothal which, if true, would have exonerated him and annulled the king's marriage.[19] Henry was now disturbed, but still not quite convinced. Worse was to come, because Norfolk's enemies were now hot on the scent. Several of Catherine's ladies were arrested and interrogated with threats; and Dereham, confronted with accusations of more recent misdemeanours, implicated Thomas Culpepper. The charges now escalated from inchastity and possible bigamy to actual adultery. Catherine was placed under house arrest, and the Privy Council went into emergency session.[20]

The queen at first denied everything with copious tears, but on 8 November Cranmer got the whole story out of her, interspersed with fits of hysterics. At the same time she denied categorically that she had ever been contracted to Dereham, the one circumstance which might have saved her life. His delusions now finally shattered, Henry was at first beside himself with fury, threatening to torture her to death, and then collapsed into an orgy of self-pity.[21] By 12 November Culpepper had been arrested, and had confessed to a sexual relationship with the queen since her marriage. Catherine's familiar, Lady Jane Rochford, also arrested, confirmed his story in the hope of saving her own skin. On 13 November Catherine was removed to imprisonment at Syon, the former abbey and now a minor royal residence. Her household was dismissed and her jewellery inventoried. On the 22nd she was deprived of her style and title, and on 1 December Culpepper and Dereham were both convicted of treason on the grounds that they had 'by craft imagined' the bodily harm of the queen. Their conviction spelled the end of all hope for Catherine, because she had been guilty of conspiring her own bodily harm, and had endangered the royal succession by her infidelity. On 10 December Culpepper and Dereham were executed at Tyburn, and the Dowager

Duchess of Norfolk was arrested. On the 22nd the entire Howard family, with the exception of the duke, were found guilty of misprision for concealing Catherine's misdeeds, and Norfolk himself, his influence at court completely destroyed, withdrew in disgrace to his estates.[22] The family was eventually pardoned, and the dowager released in May 1542, but the shock had been temporarily paralysing. Catherine and Jane Rochford were condemned by Act of Attainder on 11 February, and died by the axe at Tower Green on the morning of the 13th. As well as being a personal tragedy, her fate also marked a significant shift in the balance of power within the court. The Howards were now powerless, and although the conservative party within the council remained strong, the initiative passed back to the reformers.

By March 1542 the king had largely recovered. In spite of the anguish of the initial shock, he was actually less affected by the death of Catherine than he had been by that of Jane Seymour four and a half years earlier. However, he wasted no time in removing those male members of Catherine's connection whom he had naturally appointed to the Privy Chamber in the wake of his marriage. Both her uncle Lord William Howard and her brother Charles were removed. Robert Radcliffe, Earl of Sussex, a close ally of Norfolk who had succeeded Cromwell as Lord Great Chamberlain (and Nobleman of the Privy Chamber) in 1540, similarly lost his position in 1542, to be replaced in turn by Edward Seymour, Earl of Hertford.[23] The Privy Chamber, therefore, which had showed some signs of being moved in a conservative direction, reverted to the situation that Cromwell had left. This was aptly signalled by the rise of Anthony Denny. A Cambridge graduate of strong humanist/evangelical leanings, Denny had entered the service of Sir Francis Bryan, then Chief Gentleman of the Privy Chamber, and under his patronage had become a groom in 1536. When Bryan fell from favour in 1539, Cromwell engineered Denny's appointment as his replacement, and he thus became the second most important officer of the Privy Chamber, under Sir Thomas Heneage, the Groom of the Stool.[24] As Heneage had also been a Cromwell client, the removal of the Howard nominees in 1542 left the reforming party almost unchallenged. Denny was not a *mignon*: he had nothing of the earlier favourite's athleticism and high spirits. Instead he was a scholar, and a man of deep piety with a consuming interest in the scriptures – a fit companion, it may be said, for an ageing and anxious king.

The extent to which appointments to court offices followed the vicissi-
tudes of politics throughout the period can be traced through Appendix
II. Apart from the Privy Chamber, it was the higher offices that were most
likely to reflect political pressures, particularly the Chamber appointments and the 'White Stick' offices of the Household.

Denny's close relationship with Henry, which lasted unobtrusively
from 1539 until the latter's death, was significant in a number of ways. It
survived the fall of Cromwell, the Howard ascendancy of 1540–42, and
the numerous attempts by conservative clergy to nail their opponents in
the court on charges of heresy. This demonstrates that it did not survive
because of any dependence upon a victorious evangelical party or faction. It survived because the king so willed it. Henry could be manipulated, but only up to a point, and it was never safe to count on it. He was
most vulnerable when his emotions were aroused, and particularly if a
woman was involved. His desire for Catherine Howard in the spring and
summer of 1540 forced the issue over the Cleves marriage, and helped to
bring about the fall of Cromwell. His revulsion against her infidelity led
directly to the downfall of the Howards; and both of these developments
altered to some extent the composition of the groups around him.
However, it should not be assumed that they led to major shifts of policy.
In 1540 the king wanted to rebuild his relations with the emperor, and it
was that rather than any 'conservative ascendancy' that led to the recall
of Stephen Gardiner to the council in August.[25] Henry's foreign policy
was consistently pro-imperial from 1540 to 1544, and led to war with
both Scotland and France, but none of this had anything to do with the
shifting politics of the court. Rather, it was the other way round, because
it was their success in the field and at sea that built up his confidence in
the Earl of Hertford and Lord Lisle, and caused the promotion of the latter
as Lord Admiral and Privy Councillor early in 1543.[26] There were
undoubtedly conflicts within the council, but the outcome was determined not by the relative strengths of the parties, but always by the will
of the king. Henry might discuss issues of policy privately with Lord
Chancellor Wriothesley or the Bishop of Winchester, but then he did the
same thing with Anthony Denny and one or two other favoured gentlemen. The inconsistencies, particularly of religious policy, which emerge
during these years were therefore less the result of fluctuating factional
conflict than of the genuine doubts and uncertainties in Henry's own

mind. Thus he drove forward legislation to restrict access to the bible, but took no steps to inhibit new editions. He avowed his faith in the mass, and in prayers for the dead; yet he banned discussion of purgatory, encouraged Cranmer to experiment with English liturgy, and apparently spoke seriously of replacing the traditional Eucharist with a communion of the people.[27] In 1545 he even approved a statute confiscating the property of intercessory foundations, although admittedly not on doctrinal grounds.

For several months after the demise of Catherine Howard there was no talk of a new royal marriage. It was a dangerous subject, and the king busied himself with diplomacy and war. However, by February 1543 Henry's eye had been caught by Catherine Neville, Lady Latimer. She had no position at court, but a house in Charterhouse Yard, and a number of friends in useful positions. She was particularly close to the Earl of Hertford and his brother, Sir Thomas Seymour. Her husband, John Neville, Lord Latimer, had been ill for some time, and had moved his residence to London to obtain better medical advice than was available in Yorkshire. By the beginning of 1543 he was believed (correctly) to be close to death, and it was thought that Thomas Seymour was waiting for his widow. However, someone in the Privy Chamber (it may have been Edward Seymour) spotted a better option. Catherine was handsome, and bore herself with a conspicuous calm and dignity. If she was shortly to be a widow, would the king be interested? Henry was interested. Lord Latimer died at the beginning of March, and Catherine may well have been introduced to the king at a minor court function shortly afterwards.[28] By the middle of June she and her sister, Anne Herbert, were sufficiently conspicuous at court for the fact to be commented on, and on 12 July Catherine and Henry were quietly married. This was a completely different kind of matrimony from the last venture. The king's fires were finally extinguished, and for the first time in his life he was looking for a companion rather than a bedfellow. This was bad news for Catherine, who at the age of 31 had already endured two virtually sexless marriages, and now had to suffer a third.[29] Correct noises continued to be made about the prospects of issue, but in truth they were remote: very soon Henry's wife would be more a nurse than a lover.

However, there were compensations in being queen. Catherine was the daughter of Sir Thomas Parr of Kendal. Thomas's father had died young and his mother's second marriage, to Sir Nicholas Vaux, had brought him south and on to the fringes of the court. He was knighted at Henry VIII's coronation, and married shortly thereafter an heiress with a modest estate in Northamptonshire. Thomas might have made a good career in the royal service, but he died in 1517, leaving his widow with three young children. Maude Parr never remarried, and Catherine was brought up in the country, probably in the household of one of Maude's kinsmen. She was an intelligent child, but her education seems to have been rudimentary, and her mother's main efforts were directed to securing a suitable marriage for her. In 1529, at the age of about seventeen, she wedded Edward Borough, the son of Thomas, Lord Borough, who was later to be Queen Anne's chamberlain. In terms of status Edward was a satisfactory husband, but his health was poor and he died in 1533, leaving Catherine a childless widow at the age of 21. By this time her mother had also died, but the family rallied round and secured a second husband for her in the person of Lord Latimer. Latimer was about 40, with grown children, and his new wife was quickly put on her mettle as a stepmother, a role in which she seems to have been conspicuously successful.[30] Latimer's health, however, was seriously undermined by the stresses of the Pilgrimage of Grace, which he narrowly survived, with the consequence that he moved almost permanently to London. It was at this point that Catherine began to learn Latin, and to acquire a taste for humanist piety. By the time she married the king, she was a scholar of some promise, although a relative beginner.[31] More important, her religious convictions were settled and distinctly evangelical.

Catherine's role in the court over the next three and a half years was to be critical, but should not be misunderstood. She was not a factional leader, and her direct influence over Henry was non-existent. On the other hand, the network of her friendships spread throughout the Privy Chamber, and her access to her husband was unique. She was also an experienced stepmother, and this skill was soon put to good use. Edward, who was six, needed a mother; and Mary, who was 27, needed a friend. With the latter, who was an abrasive, frustrated young woman, she was conspicuously successful. In return for a calming and sympathetic relationship, Mary helped her with her Latin and encouraged her humanist reading. Time was to show that their convictions were far apart, but Mary had learned caution from the rough handling she had earlier endured, and Catherine was wise enough not to ask searching questions.[32] Her rapport with Denny and his Cambridge circle was immediate, and it was through him that she made the acquaintance of such scholars as Richard Cox, John Cheke and John Ascham, whom the king at about the same time appointed to be his son's tutors. She did not manage these appointments, let alone make them, but it was through her and Denny that these learned evangelicals were brought to Henry's attention.

Whether Catherine's developing convictions influenced her friends the Seymour brothers is less clear. During their sister's brief reign as queen (1536–7), they had shown no particular sympathy with reform, and they had been untouched by the demise of Thomas Cromwell, but hostility to the Howard ascendancy had pushed them in that direction, and by 1543 they were clearly identified as political opponents of such councillors as Gardiner and Wriothesley.[33] It may, or may not, have been at Catherine's suggestion that her putative suitor, Thomas Seymour, was appointed to the council in 1544.

Conservative councillors considered the queen to be a malign influence, almost as bad as their *bête noire*, Archbishop Cranmer, and the main evidence for the factional strife of the period that is so much emphasised lies in their attempts, or alleged attempts, to convince the king that he was harbouring heretics. The heresy hunting orchestrated by Stephen Gardiner and such zealots as Dr John London, the Dean of Windsor, resulted in a number of strikes which ended in executions.[34] London tried with some success to purge the Chapel of St George at Windsor, but when he tried to implicate members of the Privy Chamber such as Philip Hoby and George Blage, he found that the king would not tolerate such interference with his choice of familiars.[35] That there was an evangelical network of a sort is clear, because although Cranmer had little to do in public with the Privy Chamber reformers, a line of communication ran through his secretary Ralph Morice to Anthony Denny and William Butts, the king's physician; and it is highly likely that Henry knew about that.[36] The king's attitude was paradoxical. Within a fortnight of his marriage to Catherine Parr, which was rightly welcomed by evangelicals, three Windor protestants were burned alive. He would not tolerate heresy charges against his favoured servants, but he was keen to demonstrate his orthodox zeal at the expense of the unfortunate John Lambert.[37]

In no case was this paradox better demonstrated than in the so-called

Prebendaries Plot of 1543. As recent research has demonstrated, this was an ambitious scheme, orchestrated by Gardiner, to destroy Cranmer and the entire evangelical network that he had built up in Kent and London.[38] The intention was to construct a comprehensive set of complaints of false teaching, starting with a number of named evangelical preachers, and leading up to the archbishop himself. A substantial number not only of conservative clergy but also of Kentish gentry were involved; and although the articulated complaints were doctrinal, a wide range of other grievances against the archbishop and his administration lay behind the movement. Gardiner was well aware that both the episcopate and the court were deeply divided, with a majority of the former strongly opposed to the archbishop's doctrinal and liturgical eccentricities. He must have judged not only that the evidence that he and John London had assembled was convincing, but that the complaint represented such a powerful body of opinion that the king could not possibly ignore it. Henry was also known to be particularly sensitive to eucharistic heresies. Such a combination of factors would surely overcome the king's well-known affection for his archbishop.

The complaints reached the king in April, and he did nothing. This was not necessarily bad news for the conservatives, and they went on assiduously collecting evidence, not only in Kent, but right across the south of England. It looked as though a nationwide purge of heretics was about to take place. Meanwhile, proceedings against the Windsor evangelicals were going ahead as expected, and for those accustomed to reading the runes, the fact that it was Gardiner rather than Cranmer who married Catherine and Henry in July must have seemed significant. In fact, it may have been the king's idea of a joke, because about two weeks later, just as the Windsor heretics were meeting their expected fate, Henry confronted Cranmer with the complaints that had been made against him – and told him to investigate them himself![39]

Whatever Gardiner and London may have been expecting the king to do, it was certainly not that. Over the following weeks, their tide of complaint was turned back, or directed aside into harmless channels. Conservative anger and frustration knew no bounds as the exposed leaders of the plot headed for cover, or took refuge in explanations. Why Gardiner, of all people, should have so misjudged his royal master in this situation is a mystery, but it is quite possible that he and his whole following were blinded by their own righteousness. Astonishingly, an even worse miscalculation was to follow before the end of the year. The council, whose judgement must have been seriously undermined by anger at what had happened, decided to arrest Cranmer on their own authority, apparently believing that once he was in custody enough evidence would be forthcoming to change the king's mind. After all, something of the kind had happened to Cromwell. The cases, however, were not alike. Henry's confidence in Cromwell had already been seriously undermined before the latter's dramatic arrest, whereas it had only been a few months since the king had rescued Cranmer from the Prebendaries Plot. In the light of that event, what now transpired was predictable. One of the reforming minority on the council alerted Henry to what was about to happen, and he gave the archbishop a signet ring wherewith to appeal directly from the council to himself. Having been ritually humiliated by being kept waiting at the door of the council chamber, Cranmer exploded his bombshell, and sent his persecutors cringing to their master for forgiveness.[40] It was a debacle which Henry found both amusing and highly gratifying. Superficially, these well-known stories do not tell us very much about the court, being mainly a revelation of the king's determination to retain full control of everyone around him. However, it must be remembered that Henry was receiving overwhelmingly conservative advice on religious matters from both his council and his bishops, and not even he considered it to be wise to reject consensual advice. So it is important to remember that he was hearing very different things from those closest to him.

The victor of these clashes in 1543 was not so much Cranmer as the evangelical Privy Chamber. It may have been an understanding of this that prompted the story of Gardiner's last attempt to strike at the root of his enemies' power, Queen Catherine herself. These events are supposed to have taken place in 1546, but whereas there is plenty of evidence for the conflicts of 1543, what happened on this occasion is overwhelmingly dependent upon a single source – John Foxe – who was writing years later and with his own agenda.[41] What is firmly established is that the Yorkshire radical Anne Askew was imprisoned, interrogated, tortured and finally executed as a heretic. During this process conservative councillors, led by Lord Chancellor Wriothesley, did their best to force her to incriminate several prominent ladies of the queen's Privy Chamber, and by implication the queen herself. It could be demonstrated that some of them had sent her money and other comforts during her imprisonment, but Askew herself would say nothing, and the extent of their sympathy could never be demonstrated. However, according to Foxe, Gardiner set out to sow doubts in Henry's mind about the queen. Her bible study, her suspect friends, and her tendency to lecture her husband about disputed points of theology were all represented as a presumptuous attempt on Catherine's part to offer advice on ecclesiastical policy. Henry, it is alleged, was more than half convinced, and actually had a set of articles drawn up with which to charge his wife. Some careless servant, however, left a copy lying about, and it was brought to Catherine's attention. Mastering her panic, she sought out the king and made a dignified and humble submission, which completely mollified him and caused him to administer a stinging rebuke to the Lord Chancellor when he arrived, by prior arrangement, to escort the queen to the Tower.[42]

It is a persuasive story, with some resemblances to the sequence of events that had actually involved Cranmer. However, as Gardiner's latest biographer has pointed out, there is virtually no corroboration from contemporary sources, and no evidence at all that the bishop was behind it.[43] What is verifiable is that there was some diplomatic comment in the spring of 1546 about a cooling of relations between the king and queen, and that Gardiner was excluded from both the council and the court not very long after. If, however, the story is a myth created to explain the final victory of the evangelical party at court, which certainly occurred during the summer and autumn of 1546, then it is a highly significant one. It attributes that victory to the queen and her Privy Chamber friends – the Dennys, the Hobys, Sir William Herbert, William Butts, and others who had so nearly come to grief over Anne Askew. In other words, it represents a victory of the Privy Chamber over the Privy Council, and the final settling of Henry's vacillating mind. As narrated by Foxe, the story makes the king appear suggestible almost to the point of whimsicality. This was the only way in which the martyrologist could make sense of the behaviour of a man who on the one hand could break with the papacy, dissolve the monasteries, abolish purgatory and authorise the English bible, and yet at the same time could burn Robert Barnes, John Lambert, Anne Askew and many others for heresy, and impose the Act of Six Articles.[44] If good councillors like Cromwell and Cranmer were about him, then his behaviour was godly; if he was listening to evil councillors like Gardiner, then it was the opposite.

It was an obvious route to take with such a complex person, but it was not true. Henry's inconsistencies were within himself, and the factional conflicts that are the standard history of the period reflect his own uncertainties. The so-called faction leaders, such as Gardiner and the Earl of Hertford, or even Sir Anthony Denny, may have had agendas of their own, but their importance was due to the fact that they reflected different aspects of the king's personality. Henry's agenda in the last few years of his life is not difficult to reconstruct. He wanted a successful war in France, partly for his own 'honour' and partly to expand the English bridgehead and put pressure upon his rival, Francis. He wanted to secure English control over Scotland by marrying her infant queen to his own son and heir. He wanted to ensure that the English nobility without exception recognised themselves as his servants, and did not attempt to impose conditions upon their allegiance; and he wanted to ensure the future of his distinctive ecclesiastical settlement.[45] The first of these aims he largely achieved by winning Boulogne in 1544, and holding on to it by the peace two years later; the second totally failed. It was the third and fourth, however, that principally affected the court. The second and final fall of the Howards in 1546 came about not because they were maligned and outmanoeuvred by their enemies, but because the Earl of Surrey chose to place his pride in his ancient lineage ahead of service to his king.[46] There were other factors, but Henry Howard's fondness for the mores of the ancient aristocracy, and the suggestion that there was royal blood in his veins, convinced the ailing king that he was an unacceptable threat to the minority government which was clearly looming. Henry was quite willing to create peers for his own purposes, but deeply suspicious of those who claimed a status outside his control.[47] Similarly, Henry was intensely proud of the *Ecclesia Anglicana*, and was determined to take whatever steps he could to secure its future during the uncertain days ahead. It is that fact which largely explains the paradox of a king who went on burning heretics while he patronised and promoted their more discreet fellow travellers. He may simply not have seen Catherine, Denny, Hertford and his son's tutors as crypto-protestants, believing them to be reformers in his own image, but he clearly recognised their antagonism to Gardiner, Tunstall and Wriothesley. When it became obvious that he would have to make a choice between these rival groups, it is not surprising that he came down on the side of the reformers. Not only were they closer to him personally than their rivals, he also judged them (rightly) to be much more trustworthy defenders of the Royal Supremacy. He probably did not think consciously that heresy was an acceptable price to pay for continued independence, but that is what his decision amounted to. The main casualty of this decision was not Norfolk but Gardiner. It may be true that the actual occasion for his rustication was an ill-judged dispute over a land exchange with his increasingly irascible monarch, rather than a failed attempt to dislodge the queen, but the effect was the same.[48] He was excluded (again) from the council, and cut out of Henry's will. So it could be said that the reformers won their battle for influence over the king in the last weeks of his life; but that would be misleading. It would be more accurate to say that Henry decided that they represented the lesser of two evils, because no one fully shared his unique blend of traditional and reforming convictions.

The Privy Chamber therefore turned out to be more important than the Privy Council when it came to shaping future policy. It also encroached upon, but did not usurp, the executive functions of the council, and of other central institutions such as the Exchequer. This was partly because administrative boundaries were not clear cut. When Thomas Cromwell stood down from the Secretaryship, two successors were appointed. One, Sir Thomas Wriothesley, continued to serve under Cromwell as Lord Privy Seal – that is, he served the council. The other, Ralph Sadler, served the king personally as a member of the Privy Chamber.[49] This continued until April 1543 when Sadler was replaced by William Paget, who was not appointed to the Privy Chamber. Thereafter, the king's personal correspondence was handled by the Chief Gentleman, Anthony Denny. It was not until William Cecil became both Private Secretary and Secretary of State to Elizabeth in 1558 that the two functions were reunited. More significantly, as the king became less and less willing to write even his name, what was in effect a Sign Manual office was created within the Privy Chamber. In September 1545 a dry stamp of Henry's signature was made, and that was applied thereafter to all documents requiring the royal signature. The provision of this essential, and often sensitive, authentication was again the responsibility of Denny, although his fellow gentleman and brother-in-law John Gates was responsible for the physical security of the stamp itself.[50] This meant that a lot of official papers were processed in the Privy Chamber, and an 'office manager' was appointed in the person of William Clerk, who was not a member of the Privy Chamber but rather the Clerk of the Sign Manual. What happened in terms of government was that by the end of Henry VIII's reign the Privy Chamber had replaced the Great Chamber as that had functioned during the reign of Henry VII and before the rise of Wolsey. After 1543 the office of Secretary went 'out of court', and the Secretary served the king through the council, but that did not diminish the need of the king for a private office, and that need was supplied by the Chief Gentleman. Once the dry stamp had been created, that need increased, and security also became a problem.[51]

Similar developments took place in the management of money. The Treasury of the Chamber had replaced the Exchequer as the king's immediate spending department in the reign of Edward IV, and had been replaced in turn by Cromwell's new financial courts in the 1530s, most particularly by the Court of Augmentations. By 1540 the Treasury of the Chamber was handling little beyond Chamber wages and diets.[52] However, the king needed 'secret' money, even if it was only for his gambling debts, and there had always been a Privy Purse which stood apart from the normal accounting procedures. Under Henry VII this had been small, but his son quickly expanded it. In 1520 Wolsey succeeded in cutting it back to £10,000 a year, so it had presumably been substantially greater than that for a while.[53] After Wolsey's fall it escalated again, spending an average of over £16,000 a year from 1529 to 1532 on everything from jewels and building to the expenses of ambassadors.[54] By that time the Privy Purse had overtaken the Treasury of the Chamber, but the Groom of the Stool who held it was answerable only to the king, and was not subjected to normal audit. This has been described as 'bonanza finance' because it was topped up from windfalls such as the French pension and the confiscation of Wolsey's property. All such monies were channelled into a rather obscure fund called the King's Coffers, which seems to have paid out only to the Privy Purse, which was effectively its spending arm.[55] Cromwell gained control over the Coffers, but seems to have done little to reduce Privy Purse expenditure – perhaps he was warned that that was off limits.

By 1540 there were two 'secret' funds, both in the Palace of

Westminster: one (the Coffers proper) held by Denny in his capacity as Keeper of the Palace; the other, in the Secret Jewel House, held by the king himself. Money from all sorts of sources was channelled into these funds, probably in excess of half a million pounds between 1542 and 1546, which was equivalent to about 65 per cent of the declared ordinary revenue of the crown.[56] Denny eventually accounted for some £241,000, but the king accounted to no one and the scale of his operation can only be guessed at. This did not mean that Henry was rich, because almost every penny was spent on war or on his 'magnificence'; but it did mean that the Privy Chamber was running a financial operation on a similar scale to the Exchequer, and far in excess of the Treasury of the Chamber. The king was effectively running two sorts of government, one through his council and his institutions and offices of state, the other through his Privy Chamber. Apart from Henry himself, only a handful of very important people held positions in both structures by being both councillors and members of the Privy Chamber. In 1546 three key men were in that position: the Earl of Hertford as Lord Great Chamberlain, Viscount Lisle, the Lord Admiral, and Sir Anthony Denny, by then the Groom of the Stool. They were allies, and members of the reforming party.

In the course of a long reign and a fairly long life, Henry changed in a number of ways. The self-confidence of his early years evaporated, leaving nagging doubts which help to explain many of his later actions.[57] The simple faith of his youth was replaced by a more thoughtful and discriminating understanding, which frequently appeared paradoxical both at the time and since. Some of these changes were simply the result of time, and natural wear and tear. It is difficult to see the genial and chivalrous giant of 1510 in the irascible and corpulent invalid of 1545. The expanding girth of his surviving suits of armour provide the most eloquent testimony to his physical deterioration. This was not the result of overindulgence, but rather of athleticism run to seed. He stopped jousting in 1527 at the sensible age of 35, but innumerable heavy falls over nearly 20 years had left him with injuries which made him increasingly immobile after 1540 and contributed significantly to his obesity.[58] After a crashing fall in the hunting field in 1536, he curtailed his activity in that direction as well, with similar consequences. The effect of this upon the court was almost as great as it was on the king's body. Whereas 39 jousts or other combats were staged between 1509 and 1527, there were just five between 1528 and 1540, and none at all during the last seven years of the reign.[59] When the young Henry went to war, particularly in 1512, it was with a head full of heroic ideals and images. When the old Henry went to war in 1543, it was with the specific and limited objective of securing a bridgehead town to hold as a bargaining counter. The ardent and (as far as we can tell) effective lover of 1509 became first the passionate but erratic performer of 1533, and then the exhausted volcano of 1541. Even by the standards of the time, Henry did not wear particularly well, and the mood changes of his later years, which could have such devastating effects on those about him, were often the result of one or more of his painful afflictions.

The ageing of the king, as we have seen, changed the nature of the Privy Chamber. The light-hearted sporting companionship of 1518, more than a little touched with irresponsibility, became increasingly politicised and earnest. Henry's tastes also changed in other ways. A youthful enthusiasm for 'big bangs' – experiments with guns – had been replaced by 1540 with a more sober interest in fortifications and cosmography. The French cartographer Jean Rotz became Cosmographer Royal in 1543.[60] Above all, Henry's attitude towards his realm had changed. In his youth his own honour and the honour of England had seemed indistinguishable, and had been seen mainly in terms of victory on the field of battle. Although he showed an early anxiety to escape from the theoretical suzerainty of the pope – an issue which had nothing to do with the 'Great Matter' – he was the most conventional of renaissance monarchs. Thirty years later that had all changed. He was under the ban of the church; and it had been revealed that that once dreaded sanction meant remarkably little either at home or abroad.[61] He had also invented a new method of declaring policy. By using the traditional institution of parliament in unprecedented ways, he had not only solved the succession question, he had also resolved the dual allegiance of the clergy, and particularly the episcopate, and added vastly to his wealth by dissolving the monasteries. It is not surprising that by 1540 he regarded the Royal Supremacy as the jewel in his crown; nor is it surprising that he should have explained this to himself in terms of the will of God.

By the end of his reign Henry was not a traditional king. Ecclesiastically he was answerable to no one except God, a position which he shared only with the Lutheran rulers of Scandinavia.

Temporally, however, he had circumscribed himself with a mechanism of consent. By expanding the function of parliament to embrace business which had traditionally been none of its concern, he had inadvertently focused the consent of the realm in a new way.[62] In a sense parliament now was the realm of England, something which could not be said of the Estates General, the Cortes or the Reichstag. Henry benefited greatly from these changes, and not only in his treasury. Although individual members of parliament asked awkward questions, neither the Lords nor the Commons challenged him on any issue of importance; and this parliamentary endorsement strengthened his hand in both domestic and foreign policy. By 1547 allegiance to the crown was stronger than ever. As a result, Henry did not have to worry about noble affinities. The Pilgrimage of Grace was the last chance for a disgruntled aristocracy to turn against the king, and they did not take it.[63] Policy could not be constrained, let alone made, from Alnwick or Kenninghall, but only at court.

There was, of course, a lighter side to all this, although equally an aspect of the king's magnificence. Henry had always been extremely fond of maskings and 'disguisings', and elaborate pageants almost invariably accompanied the jousts and tournaments of the early years.[64] These entertainments survived the decline in the king's athleticism (and appetite for flirtation), but they probably changed their nature. Records of some twenty of these events between 1540 and 1547 survive in the accounts of John Bridges, Yeoman of the Revels, several of them connected to the ratification of the peace with France in July 1546.[65] It is not always clear who the performers were, but the role of professionals – the gentlemen and children of the Chapel Royal, and the musicians of the King's Music – seems to have increased as the participation of the courtiers themselves declined. When the king had personally led every dance, and was always liable to pop up in some paper-thin disguise, the gentlemen of the Privy Chamber and the queen's ladies joined in with every appearance of enthusiasm. When he became a spectator, they followed that example also. Just as the last tournaments in 1540 had been conducted largely by the gentlemen pensioners, who were at least supposed to be soldiers, so these revels seem to have resembled the plays and concerts of later years more closely than the lively team games of an earlier generation.[66] Henry also kept a succession of fools, or jesters, the last of whom, Will Somers, had been appointed (if that is the right word) in 1535. Somers became close to the king in the last years of his life, and was a prominent figure at court. Whether he was considered to be a 'natural' or innocent is not quite clear. He seems to have been paid no money, and after Henry's death he had a 'minder', but that may have been mainly the result of Henry's death.[67] On the other hand, he is credited with a range of saws and witticisms which indicate great perspicacity – or at least a reputation for it. He twice appeared in portraits of the king, and accompanied him in his restless moves from place to place, so he was very much a personal attendant, but why Henry was so fond of his company is not entirely clear.[68]

As a young man the king had aspired to be *uomo universale*, the all-round man beloved of renaissance idealists: scholar, soldier and lover. In fact he had been a competent Latinist, a moderate theologian, and a general of no particular skill or vision. By comparison with Francis I, or even the sober Charles V, he was not a promiscuous womaniser. He must have been the only king in English history to have had more wives than mistresses, and he fathered only one acknowledged bastard – Henry Fitzroy. He was, and continued to be, a patron of scholars, but his concentration span was never sufficient to acquire much scholarship of his own. He was quick-witted, had a retentive memory, and a consuming vanity to appear more learned than he was. There were, however, two areas in which his talents were genuine and conspicuous – sport and music. Despite the hyperbole he was a jouster of genuine power and skill, a gifted tennis player, and an enthusiastic amateur of other games, such as wrestling. He had a good singing voice, a good ear for music, and was a competent performer on several instruments. His musical compositions are more remarkable for the fact that they happened than for any particular gift displayed.[69] His sense of humour is more elusive, but that may have been because such an attribute was less valued at that time than because he did not have one. As a young man he played practical jokes on his wife, and took a rather childish delight in donning disguises, which were normally transparent because of his exceptional stature, but if he made jokes they do not seem to have been memorable. After 1540, as his physical prowess ebbed away, both his theology and his political skills improved, and he widened the range of his patronage to include not only traditional scholars but mathematicians, astrologers and artists such as Hans Holbein.[70] Whether we should consider his treatment of

Cranmer's enemies – and possibly Catherine's – as evidence of a sardonic sense of humour is a matter of opinion, but at least he continued to appreciate the whimsicality of Will Somers. Ill health, bad temper and political anxiety marred the 1540s, but Henry was the architect of his environment, both cultural and political, and it must have been hard for anyone – most of all for those close to him – to envisage how this enormous burden could be borne by the child who seemed bound to inherit it.

Notes and references

1 G.R. Elton, *Thomas Cromwell* (Bangor, 1991); Susan Brigden, *London and the Reformation* (Oxford, 1989), pp.208–16; D. MacCulloch, *Thomas Cranmer* (London and New York, 1996), pp.269–72.

2 See the various regulations printed in the *Household Ordinances* (Society of Antiquaries, 1790); D.M. Loades, *The Tudor Court* (London, 1986), pp.38–73.

3 D.M. Loades, *Tudor Government* (Oxford, 1997), pp.17–37; D. Starkey, 'The Development of the Privy Chamber, 1485–1547', Ph.D thesis, University of Cambridge, 1973.

4 Commissions were instruments issued under the Privy Seal, authorising named individuals to carry out certain functions on the king's behalf. The most important was the commission of the peace, issued county by county. Penry Williams, *The Tudor Regime* (Oxford, 1979), pp.410–20.

5 Richard Hill, the Sergeant of the Cellar, was a frequent gambling companion of Henry's, but that was by the king's choice. Loades, *Tudor Court*, p.65.

6 R.C. Braddock, 'The Royal Household, 1540–1560', Ph.D thesis, Northwestern University, 1971.

7 Ibid. Attempts were always being made to exclude such undesirables: *Household Ordinances*, p.150.

8 Peter Gwyn, *The King's Cardinal* (London, 1990), pp.559–60; Greg Walker, 'The "Expulsion of the Minions" of 1519 Reconsidered', *Historical Journal*, 32 (1989), pp.1–16.

9 David Starkey, 'Intimacy and Innovation: The Rise of the Privy Chamber, 1485–1547', in *The English Court from the Wars of the Roses to the Civil War* (London, 1987), pp.71–118.

10 Retha M. Warnicke, *The Marrying of Anne of Cleves* (Cambridge, 2000), pp.187–228.

11 PRO, SP1/167, fols.135–6; *Letters and Papers* vol.16, no.1321.

12 Glyn Redworth, *In Defence of the Church Catholic: The Life of Stephen Gardiner* (Oxford, 1990), pp.96–7.

13 *Letters and Papers*, vol.16, no.766; J. Scarisbrick, *Henry VIII* (London, 1968), pp.426–8.

14 *Letters and Papers*, vol.15, no.136. James was the son of Henry's elder sister, Margaret, who had married James IV in 1503, and the father of Mary, Queen of Scots.

15 L.B. Smith, *A Tudor Tragedy: the Life of Catherine Howard* (London, 1961), pp.188–92.

16 *Proceedings and Ordinances of the Privy Council of England*, ed. H. Nicolas, vol.7, pp.352–5; MacCulloch, *Cranmer*, pp.287–8, 354. Lascelles was one of those burned with Anne Askew in 1546. J. Foxe, *Acts and Monuments* (London, 1583), p.1238.

17 D.M. Loades, *Henry VIII and his Wives* (Stroud, 1994), p.129.

18 Smith, *A Tudor Tragedy*, pp.181–2.

19 Ibid. A betrothal would have constituted a pre-contract, which would have barred any subsequent marriage unless it had been formally annulled.

20 Loades, *Henry VIII*, p.129.

21 *HMC*, Marquis of Bath MSS, vol.2 (1907), pp.8–9.

22 Loades, *Henry VIII*, pp.130–31. The Act of Attainder against Catherine was 33 Henry VIII, c.21, which also made it treason for any unchaste woman to marry the king.

23 D. Starkey, *The Reign of Henry VIII: Personalities and Politics* (London, 1985), pp.128–9.

24 *Letters and Papers*, vol.14, pt1, no.144; Starkey, 'Intimacy and Innovation', p.115.

25 Redworth, *In Defence of the Church Catholic*, pp.126–9.

26 D.M. Loades, *John Dudley, Duke of Northumberland* (Oxford, 1996), pp.57–8.

27 Foxe, *Actes and Monuments* (1583), p.1245. The story comes originally from Cranmer's secretary, Ralph Morice, and may be based on a misunderstanding, as the conversation cited was in French.

28 Loades, *Henry VIII*, pp.136–7. His first gift was a little before that, in February, but it is not clear that they had met.

29 It is not clear that her first marriage was consummated at all. When she finally married Thomas Seymour in the spring of 1547, she became pregnant within a few months. Susan James, *Kateryn Parr: The Making of a Queen* (Stroud, 1999), p.35.

30 Loades, *Henry VIII*, pp.136–7.

31 James, *Kateryn Parr*. Lord Latimer's stressful role in the Pilgrimage is discussed in R.W. Hoyle, *The Pilgrimage of Grace and the Politics of the 1530s* (Oxford, 2001), *passim*.

32 Catherine's connection with Mary originated in her mother's service to Catherine of Aragon, who never forgot an obligation of that kind. Antonia Fraser, *The Six Wives of Henry VIII* (London, 1993), p.366.

33 Starkey, *Henry VIII*, p.128.

34 Foxe, *Actes and Monuments* (1583), pp.1212–13, 1230.

35 Ibid., pp.1245–6.

36 MacCulloch, *Cranmer*, pp.319–20.

37 Foxe, *Actes and Monuments* (1583), pp.1122–4. In spite of this sympathetic account, it appears that Lambert deliberately went out of his way to annoy the king, who presided personally over his trial.

38 M. Zell, 'The Prebendaries Plot of 1543: A Reconsideration', *Journal of Ecclesiastical History*, 27 (1976), pp.241–53; MacCulloch, *Cranmer*, pp.295–323.

39 *Narratives of the Days of the Reformation*, ed. J.G. Nichols (Camden Society, 1859), p.252.

40 Ibid., pp.255–7.

41 Foxe, *Actes and Monuments* (1583), pp.1242–4. Foxe's deliberate intention was to magnify the queen's role as a promoter of the Gospel, in the context of the Elizabethan settlement.

42 Ibid.

43 Redworth, *In Defence of the Church Catholic*, pp.233–7.

44 D.M. Loades, 'John Foxe and Henry VIII', *John Foxe Bulletin*, 1/1, (2002), pp.5–12.

45 Scarisbrick, *Henry VIII*, pp.472–97; H. Miller, *Henry VIII and the Nobility* (Oxford, 1986).

46 *Letters and Papers*, vol.21, pt2. no.555. Howard had been dismissed from his command in Boulogne the previous January for incompetence, and had had a number of other brushes with authority before being nailed for quartering his arms with those of Edward the Confessor. Scarisbrick, *Henry VIII*, pp.482–3.

47 By 1547 the majority of Henry's peers held titles of his own creation. Miller, *Henry VIII and the Nobility*.

48 Redworth, *In Defence of the Church Catholic*, pp.239–41.

49 Starkey, 'Intimacy and Innovation', pp.99–100.

50 *Letters and Papers*, Addenda I, ii, no.705; vol.17, no.1154/9. Starkey, 'Intimacy and Innovation', p.100.

51 Starkey, 'Intimacy and Innovation', p.100.

52 Loades, *Tudor Court*, pp.73–7.

53 BL, Cotton MS Titus B I, fols.188 *et seq.*; Starkey, 'Privy Chamber', pp.372–5.

54 Starkey, 'Privy Chamber', pp.384–5.

55 Starkey, 'Intimacy and Innovation', pp.96–7.

56 The ordinary revenue of the crown at this time was about £150,000 a year, exclusive of income derived from the sale of land. F.C. Dietz, *English Government Finance, 1485–1558* (London, 1964), pp.137–43.

57 For a psychological profile of Henry at this stage of his life, see L.B. Smith, *The Mask of Royalty* (London, 1971).

58 Ibid.

59 Alan Young, *Tudor and Jacobean Tournaments* (London, 1987), pp.197–200.

60 E.G.R. Taylor, *The Haven Finding Art: A History of Navigation* (London, 1967).

61 To seek to implement the ban within England was, of course, high treason, but no foreign ruler (except the pope himself) refused to do business with Henry, as they should have done, on the grounds that he was excommunicate.

62 Loades, *Tudor Government*, pp.37–52; G.R. Elton, *The Tudor Constitution* (Cambridge, 1982), pp.233–45.

63 Hoyle, *The Pilgrimage of Grace*, pp.339–65.

64 Edward Hall, *The Union of the Two Noble and Illustre Famelies of Lancastre and York* (London, 1809), is full of descriptions of these entertainments: see e.g. pp.518–19 on the jousts of 1511.

65 Guildford Muniment Room, MS 59, nos.50, 98, 142, 143, 144.

66 A.W. Reed, *Early Tudor Drama* (London, 1926).

67 John Southworth, *Fools and Jesters at the English Court* (Stroud, 1998), p.71. See also below, p.73.

68 Ibid., pp.70–5.

69 J. Stevens, *Music and Poetry in the Early Tudor Court* (London, 1961).

70 For a brief discussion of Henry's artistic patronage, see Loades, *Tudor Court*, pp.127–30.

CHAPTER 2

The court during the Protectorate, 1547–9

When Henry VIII died in the early hours of 28 January 1547, the court was in one sense devastated. He had been king for 38 years, longer than almost any of them could remember, and his personality had been totally dominant, even in his declining years. Yet in another sense his death made very little difference. The only senior officer to lose his place as a result was Lord St John, who was replaced as Lord Great Chamberlain by the newly created Earl of Warwick.[1] The reason for this was political, because the office was largely ornamental and some honourable compensation had to be offered to Warwick for surrendering the office of Lord Admiral to the Earl of Hertford's brother, Thomas Seymour. Sir Edmund Peckham was replaced as Cofferer of the Household by John Ryther, who had performed the same service in Edward's princely establishment, and a few other less senior officers were similarly absorbed, but this would have involved very little disruption.[2] More significantly, three men who had been listed as gentlemen of the prince's Privy Chamber, John Fowler, John Philpot and Robert Maddox, were now taken into the king's Privy Chamber as grooms. The boy apparently found them – and particularly Fowler – especially congenial. In most parts of the court a groom, who performed manual services, ranked as a yeoman, but these men were clearly gentlemen, reflecting the superior status of the Privy Chamber as a whole. In other respects the establishment seems to have remained for the time being untouched, with Sir Anthony Denny as

Groom of the Stool. In the short term even the virtually redundant royal barbers retained their positions. This was partly because the schoolroom took the place of the Privy Chamber as the new king's immediate environment. John Cheke, the 'scholemaster', was transferred from Edward's princely household to the Royal Household proper with the same title; Jean Belmain (who taught Edward French) similarly continued to be styled 'secretary for the French tongue', while Richard Cox was 'recycled' as Almoner.[3]

The identity of the king's schoolfellows is somewhat harder to establish. Of the five listed in the coronation livery list as 'Young Lords and Gentlemen', only Barnaby Fitzpatrick was certainly a fellow pupil. The Earl of Ormonde, Thomas Butler, and Lord Strange, Henry Stanley, who were both sixteen, would have been rather too old. Henry Brandon, the twelve-year-old Duke of Suffolk, who received a special livery and also acted with the king in the masques which followed the coronation, is a more likely candidate; and it seems that the fourteen-year-old Robert Dudley, a younger son of the Earl of Warwick, was also a member of the group. Robert was not especially bright, so the age difference would not have mattered very much. Princess Elizabeth, who was also fourteen, had shared some of her brother's lessons before he came to the throne, and may well have continued to do so. She was certainly being taught by the same people, but as she was exceedingly bright the cooperation may have been less appropriate.[4] Thomas Cotton, who like Barnaby Fitzpatrick subsequently became a gentleman of the Privy Chamber, is another possibility, as is Jane Grey, the daughter of the Marquis of Dorset, who was the same age as the king, and of a similar level of ability.

In the days which immediately followed Henry's death, everyone's normal routines were disrupted. Edward was at Hertford on 28 January, and when the Earl of Hertford arrived unexpectedly on the morning of the 29th to escort him to London, he thought at first that it was in connection with his impending creation as Prince of Wales. Instead he was taken first to Enfield, where his sister Elizabeth was located, and the earl then broke to both of them the news of their father's death. Tradition has it that they wept copiously, but no eyewitness actually says so. There was then a brief lull until the 31st, when the late king's decease was announced in London, and Edward proclaimed. With excellent timing, he arrived at the royal lodgings in the Tower later the same day.[5] No sinister

construction should be placed either upon the delay or upon the reloca-
tion of the court. The first was rendered necessary by the need to put the
appropriate procedures in place, and the second was part of the traditional *cursus honorem* which preceded a coronation. Acting with the
help and advice of Sir William Paget, the late king's secretary, and probably of Denny, Hertford had issued the necessary instructions for the
move before setting off to secure the person of the new king. At the time
of his fall in 1549 he was accused of using this move as a cover for seiz-
ing the king's treasure for his own use:

> he hath robbed and embezzled from the king's majesty the treasure and
> jewels left by his majesty's father of noble memory King Henry the 8th
> not appointing commissioners for the view of the same until 2 months
> after the decease of the said king, which they found to be so small and
> slender as it might be well said (even as he had made it to be bruited)
> that King Henry died a very poor Prince ... where indeed his treasure
> and jewels were not unknown to have been not long before his decease
> an inestimable riches.[6]

However, such a charge reflects the circumstances of October 1549, not
those of January 1547, and if the account referred to was ever actually
taken, it does not appear to have survived.[7] What Hertford did do, and
which may be the foundation for this somewhat sweeping accusation,
was to seize the jewels which Henry had bestowed upon his last queen,
Catherine Parr, on the grounds that they were the property of the crown.
That triggered a long-running and bitter dispute with the queen dowager,
and his action might have been more favourably interpreted if he had not
allowed his wife to wear some of them at the coronation on 20 February.
Apart from this, there is no hard evidence that Hertford acted in any way
improperly in respect of Henry's residual wealth. The manner in which
the late king had handled his Privy Coffers in the last few months of his
life inevitably meant that there were cash sums secreted in all sorts of
places. For some of these Sir Anthony Denny as Keeper of the Palace of
Westminster was responsible, and he eventually rendered account in
March 1548.[8] At that point it was recorded that several chests had been
removed to 'the secret jewel house in the Tower of London' immediately
after Henry's death, and that those chests had contained £11,435 9s. 6d.
in gold angels, sovereigns and Spanish reals. Given the enormous cost of

the recent wars, and the scale of Henry's debts at Antwerp and elsewhere, it is entirely likely that this was all the cash that Henry had left. On the other hand, there may well have been sums for which no one was responsible except the king himself, and since he did not account to anyone we have no means of knowing their scale, or what became of them.

After Edward's proclamation, the most urgent need was to establish a form of government. On 31 January the only group with any status in that respect was the executors of the late king's will. The manner in which they conducted themselves has been much debated and disputed, but the basic fact is that the wishes of a dead king had no force in law, and whatever Henry may have envisaged, his executors' first responsibility was to establish a viable government for Edward VI.[9] This they did immediately after Hertford's return to London, adding Thomas Seymour to their number and redesignating themselves as the Privy Council. At the same time they elected Hertford, who was the king's maternal uncle, to be Lord Protector and Governor of the King's Person. Although this offended Thomas Seymour, who pointed out that he was equally the king's uncle, the decision appears to have been unanimous, and was undertaken for the sensible reason that it was necessary that the executive should be headed by one identifiable person.[10] During Henry's last illness the struggles which had accompanied the final stages of will making had taken place around the king's bed, but these decisions were taken outside the court for the simple reason that a child had no input to make. Nevertheless there was only one way in which to make such decisions lawful, and that was to obtain the personal sanction of the king, however young he might be. Consequently, on 1 February Edward sat in state, surrounded by his peers, and received his new council. They kissed hands, Henry's will was read out, and the king formally endorsed the decisions that had been made on his behalf. Hertford made a brief speech of acceptance, and the new government was in being.[11]

Over the next few days, the council then turned to what has been unfairly described as 'the division of the spoils'. The usual perception of this process is that it was one of more or less fraudulent plundering of the king's resources of honours and land. Sir William Paget testified that the late king had intended to make certain peerage promotions and creations, and to support them with land grants, but that his deteriorating health, and eventual death, had overtaken his good intentions. This may well have been true, although whether the largesse would have been on the scale eventually realised is another matter.[12] However, in the circumstances of a new reign a 'coronation honours list' on this scale was not unreasonable. The Earl of Hertford became Duke of Somerset, the Earl of Essex (the queen dowager's brother) Marquis of Northampton, Sir Thomas Wriothesley Earl of Southampton, and Viscount Lisle Earl of Warwick. Among some half-dozen barons created was Thomas Seymour, the Protector's brother. If this distribution was intended to ensure a smooth transition from one reign to the next, then it did not work, but at least it prevented dissension in the run-up to the coronation, which was fixed for Sunday 20 February. This ceremony followed strictly traditional lines, so traditional indeed that the City of London recycled pageants for Edward's ceremonial entry on 19 February which had last been used to greet the twelve-year-old Henry VI on his return from France in 1432.[13] This was not the result of parsimony, or even of lack of imagination, but in appreciation of the appropriateness of the material. The whole entry took over four hours, but Edward appears to have enjoyed himself, or at least he was well enough trained to put a brave face on it. From his point of view the high spot was the descent of a trapeze artist on a wire from the top of St Paul's steeple, a feat which provoked general admiration. Although the ceremony itself was cut short, in respect of 'his majesty's tender years', it contained all the traditional ingredients. This was, however, the first coronation to take place after the Royal Supremacy had been recognised, and Thomas Cranmer felt obliged to inject some appropriate observations into his address:

> Being bound by my function to lay these things [exhortations to godly rule] before your royal highness, the one as a reward if you fulfil, the other as a judgement from God if you neglect them; yet I openly declare before the living God and before the nobles of the land, that I have no commission to denounce your majesty deprived if your highness miss in part, or in whole, of these performances, much less to draw up indentures between God and your majesty, or to say that you forfeit your crown with a clause . . .[14]

No one who was permitted to be active in politics at that time would have disagreed with these sentiments, but the natural corollary, which followed immediately after, was the issuing of new commissions in

Edward's name to the bench of bishops, a move which horrified some conservatives, notably Stephen Gardiner.[15] The crowning was followed by the customary banquet, of which the king's main memory was that he was constrained to wear his crown, which must have been a sore trial, in spite of the fact that a specially light one had been made.

Edward also remembered with more enjoyment the formal entry and challenge of his champion, Sir John Dymocke, and the barriers and jousts which followed the banquet.[16] Throughout his short life he was to be a keen spectator at martial displays of all kinds, although his own partici-pation was confined to archery, and to 'running at the ring'. Two days later, on Shrove Tuesday, 22 February, we learn (although not from the king's own testimony) that he took part with the Duke of Suffolk and Lord Strange in a 'masque of Orpheus', in which the other actors were the gentlemen and children of the Chapel Royal.[17] King Henry had been laid to rest at Windsor with suitable obsequies four days before the coronation, and these two events constituted the formal gestures of the handover of power. By custom, the young king was not present at Windsor, and even the widowed queen was only permitted to watch the ceremony from a distance. The chief mourner was Henry Grey, Marquis of Dorset, not one of the power brokers of the new regime. Although the Household officers broke their white staves of office into the old king's grave, the great majority of them had already been reappointed to serve the new king, and there can have been little apprehension about the future within the court.

However, difficulties of various kinds lurked beneath the harmonious façade which had so far been maintained. François Van der Delft, the imperial ambassador, did not attend the coronation, not because, in Jennifer Loach's words, he was 'feeling very peevish' and refused the invitation, but because his master, Charles V, had not yet made up his mind about Edward, and instructed his representative not to make any gesture which might be construed as recognition.[18] From his point of view Edward was a bastard, having been born while the realm was in schism and no marriage could be lawfully celebrated. Henry's true heir should therefore have been Mary, and Charles refrained from acknowl-edging the greetings sent to him in the name of Edward VI in case she should make her claim. It was only when it had become clear that Mary had no intention of challenging her brother – and that was well after 20 February – that he reluctantly concluded that he must do business with the new regime. It is not, therefore, surprising that while Odet de Selve, the French ambassador, praised the lavish ceremonies of Edward's crowning, Van der Delft wrote sourly that there was 'no very memorable show of triumph or magnificence', an observation which has been given more credit than it deserves.[19] Like all ambassadors, François was pursuing his own agenda, carrying out his master's wishes and telling him what he thought he wanted to hear. Historians have generally been inclined to take these chatty and self-interested diplomatic letters too seriously, because they are often the only sources of information, particularly for the court, but they should always be judiciously discounted. The contrast between de Selve and Van der Delft on this occasion represented more than different points of view about the ceremonies: it represented the contrasting policies of France and the Empire. It should also be remembered that ambassadors frequently 'padded' their despatches with trivia and unsubstantiated rumours because they were expected to report frequently, and might not have much of substance to say. They also had to justify their existence, unless they were agitating for recall, which sometimes happened.

After the Shrovetide revels other problems also began to surface. Protector Somerset was not satisfied with the powers he had been given, and began to press for a wider commission. The international situation was tense. Not only was the emperor hostile, but the problem of enforcing the Treaty of Greenwich of 1543 with the Scots had not been resolved, and no one believed that the French would not, sooner or later, try to recover Boulogne.[20] There was a need for a chief executive capable of making swift and authoritative decisions, without having to negotiate for the support of his colleagues. Somerset therefore wished to remove the constraint of being obliged to seek the consent of the council for all important decisions. He did not mind being bound to consult it, but felt that decisions should be up to him – as they would have been to the king if he had been of age. The majority of his fellow councillors were sympathetic, but the Lord Chancellor, the Earl of Southampton, was not. The fact that he was a religious conservative was probably irrelevant as the ecclesiastical colour of the regime had hardly begun to emerge in March 1547, but he was definitely obstructive of Somerset's ambitions, fearing a quasi-monarchy. Early in that month Southampton was removed from office. Whether he was the victim of a technical trick, or let off lightly for a serious abuse of his position, is still a matter for discussion.[21] He put his office into commission in a manner which Somerset and most of the council claimed was illegal, and whatever the truth of the matter, he had given his enemies a weapon which they were able to use against him. On 12 March Somerset got his new commission, which also included the right to appoint new councillors, and it is at that point that his effective Protectorate begins.[22] The same day the council was slightly but significantly remodelled. Wriothesley was dropped, along with Sir Thomas Bromley and Nicholas Wotton. In their place came the Marquis of Northampton, William Parr, the Earl of Arundel (Lord Chamberlain), Sir Thomas Cheyney (Treasurer of the Household), Sir John Gage (Comptroller), Sir Anthony Wingfield (Vice-Chamberlain) and Sir William Petre (Secretary). What might be described as the court element of the council was thus significantly enhanced, and the risk of a separate political focus developing there was proportionally reduced.[23]

This was just as well, because there was a worm in the bud of the Privy Chamber. Catherine Parr, the queen dowager, was 36 and in need of a new husband. There were well-founded rumours that she had been intending to marry Thomas Seymour on the death of her second husband, Lord Latimer, in 1543, but that the king had pre-empted her choice. Now that she was again available Seymour wasted no time in renewing his suit. Whether he found her attractive, or coveted the extensive estates with which she was endowed, we do not know, but she certainly found him attractive, and responded to his advances eagerly.[24] The marriage of the king's stepmother, however, was an affair of state, and required the consent of the Protector and the council. In the circumstances, and because Thomas Seymour had already made no secret of his jealousy of his brother's success, there was no chance of that permission being given. Seymour therefore decided upon a subterfuge. As a gentleman of the Privy Chamber he had the right of access to the royal apartments, but he was not intimate with the king. He therefore either cultivated or renewed a friendship with one of Edward's favourites, the groom John Fowler. Fowler later recalled:

> At St. James, where the king was, the lord admiral called me to his chamber. After dismissing his servants he enquired after the king and asked if he lacked anything. I said not. He asked if the king ever asked

for or about him: I said he would sometimes ask for him, but nothing
else. I asked him what the king should ask, and he said nothing unless
why he did not marry. I said I never heard him ask such questions.
He paused and asked me, if I had communication with the king soon,
to ask him if he would be content that he should marry, and if so,
whom . . .[25]

Fowler was as good as his word, and after some prompting Edward
agreed that it would be a good idea if Seymour married. When asked for
suggestions, he became facetious and suggested 'my Lady Anne of Cleves'
(his father's discarded fourth wife), or 'my sister Mary, to turn her opinions'.[26] Having attracted the king's attention to his desire, a few days later
Seymour returned to the charge. This time he asked Fowler to ask the
king directly whether he would be content that he should marry the
queen, and if so, whether he would write to her in his support. He then
approached Edward directly, and came away with the desired letter.
Seymour had no need of the king to put in a good word for him with the
lady, but what he had done was to obtain the boy's explicit consent to the
marriage, thus circumventing the Protector. These conversations must
have taken place during March, because the couple were secretly married
in April. The Duke of Somerset was furious. Not only did he consider
that Catherine had acted with indecent haste, but he had been outwitted.
Technically he could have overridden the authorisation of a king who
was a minor and under his care, but Edward was quite old enough to
have a long memory for such a humiliation, and the Protector did not
venture to do so. He accepted the *fait accompli* with a very bad grace, and
his temper was not improved when he found Thomas vigorously espous-
ing his wife's cause over the question of her jewels.[27] Preoccupied with
other affairs, Somerset had neglected to keep a close eye on the Privy
Chamber, and Denny had simply not been paying attention to what went
on under his nose. According to his own account, Fowler attempted to
reconcile the brothers over the issue of the jewels, but it was hardly his
place to do so, and he had no success.

In August 1547, long after this particular horse had bolted, Somerset
attempted to lock the stable door by replacing Denny as Groom of the
Stool. The new groom was his brother-in-law, Sir Michael Stanhope, but
Stanhope appears to have had no more success than his predecessor in

checking the activities of Thomas Seymour. Seymour had begun passing sums of money to Fowler immediately after the coronation. At first these were probably intended as sweeteners for the groom himself, although his pointed questions about whether the king 'lacked anything' suggests that he was already thinking more ambitiously.[28] At some indeterminate date, but after Stanhope had taken over, Seymour told the king to his face 'Ye are but a very beggarly king now; ye have not to play, or to give to your servants.' According to his own testimony, Edward had replied correctly that 'Mr. Stanhope had for him', but that did not prevent a clandestine relationship growing up, based upon surreptitious pocket money.[29] Most of this money was sent via Fowler, and acknowledged by the king in smuggled notes, but some was given to Belmain, some to an unnamed music tutor, a little to Barnaby Fitzpatrick, and on one occasion the substantial sum of £40 to John Cheke, half for himself and half for Edward. Being in most respects a perfectly normal boy, the king probably enjoyed the conspiratorial air which surrounded these transactions as much as he did having the extra money. Seymour undoubtedly had a slightly raffish charm which appealed particularly to women, but it also worked on Edward, on Fowler, and probably on others. There is no reason to suppose that the king was really short of money. Stanhope may not have been a very congenial character – at least by comparison with Seymour – but his surviving Privy Purse account, which runs from August 1547 to March 1549, shows him giving Edward over £80 for gaming and wagers, as well as spending £411 on rewards at the king's instruction.[30] Such sums compare favourably with the £180 or so which we know reached Edward via Seymour; so his attempt to persuade the boy of his poverty was mendacious, but probably irrelevant. It was more fun to spend money which you were not supposed to have.

Seymour also had a streak of recklessness in him, which may have added to his sex appeal but made him politically dangerous. On one occasion when he arrived to see the king, accompanied by a number of servants, he remarked casually to Fowler that the security of the court was so poor that he could have abducted Edward then and there. This was no doubt mainly intended as a criticism of Stanhope, but it was dangerous talk, particularly given his known hostility to the Protector.[31] He tried unsuccessfully to persuade Edward to intervene personally in the affair of the queen's jewels, and on another occasion told him that he should take power into his own hands 'within this two year at least', because then he would be able to favour his own men – by which he clearly meant himself.[32] By the time action was eventually taken to curb him, Somerset was not the only person to have been alienated by the Lord Admiral's proceedings. John Cheke was distinctly apprehensive, and on one occasion congratulated his charge for having resisted some of Seymour's more politically loaded blandishments. At the same time that the latter was seeking the back stairs to favour at court, he was also flirting surreptitiously with the king's sister Elizabeth, who in the autumn of 1547 had just turned fourteen. Catherine was fond of her precocious stepdaughter, and Elizabeth had been living in the queen's household for some time when Henry died. Although her father had made independent provision for her in his will, the council was in no hurry to implement the decision, and for the time being the princess remained where she was. This arrangement continued after Catherine remarried, and the Protector did not mind, because it saved both trouble and money to leave her where she was. At first Seymour trod a fine line between propriety and impropriety. There was horseplay with clear sexual implications, but scandal was avoided because Catherine herself was often involved, and because Kate Ashley, Elizabeth's chaperone, saw no harm in it.[33] At what point this intrigue turned serious (if it ever did) we do not know, but in the summer of 1548, when Catherine was about six months pregnant, she came upon her husband and their ward in a most compromising embrace. There was a furious row, and Elizabeth was sent away in disgrace. As proper provision had still not been made for her, she retired to Cheshunt to live with the Dennys, Lady Denny being Kate Ashley's sister.[34]

There the matter might have rested, because although Elizabeth had been exhilarated by her sexual awakening, she had also been alarmed, and the Dennys knew enough of the ways of the court to keep an eye on her. However, in September 1548 Catherine died in childbirth. Elizabeth wanted to write to Seymour to commiserate with him on his loss, but did not do so 'lest she be thought to woo him'. The widower himself was less delicate, and rapidly resumed his attentions. Although the Dennys ensured that they did not actually meet, messages passed and the magic word 'marriage' was mentioned. According to their own accounts, both Elizabeth and Kate Ashley were sympathetic to these advances, but always with the proviso 'if the council permits'.[35] There was not the slightest chance that the council would permit. Elizabeth's marriage was a far more important and sensitive issue than Catherine's had been, and Somerset, having been circumvented once, was determined not to be caught again. For about three or four months a clandestine intrigue went on, with Seymour manoeuvring unsuccessfully to gain access to Elizabeth, and then in January 1549 the council acted to put a stop to it. Seymour was arrested on a variety of charges, and both Kate Ashley and Elizabeth's cofferer, Thomas Parry, found themselves in serious trouble.[36]

Exactly what the Lord Admiral was trying to achieve is a matter of some dispute, and much of what was reported of him may have been no more than indiscreet bluster. He had not distinguished himself as Lord Admiral, having remained in London during the Scottish campaign of September 1547. This he had done with the Protector's agreement, so it was hardly improper, but it was rumoured at the time that his real motive had been to take advantage of his brother's absence to ingratiate himself further at court, rather than to conduct the business which he alleged. He was also reported to have entered into secret agreements with some of the pirates whom he was supposed to be bringing to justice, looking the other way in return for a cut of the spoils. However, that was an easy charge to make, and was never proved.[37] More substantially, Catherine's death had hit his finances very hard, and should have led to an immediate scaling down of the large establishment which they had maintained. However, loss of *manred* would have meant loss of political clout, and Seymour continued to maintain a retinue that he could no longer afford. In order to support this he entered into a corrupt understanding with Sir William Sharrington, the Treasurer of the Bristol Mint. In his subsequent testimony Sharrington claimed that he had borrowed money from Seymour to the sum of £2,300, and that the money he had handed over in return was repayment with interest.[38] This may have been true, but it was not the whole truth, and it seems that the pair plotted to take at least £10,000 out of the Mint, and share it between them. The Treasurer professed ignorance, which may well have been genuine, as to Seymour's purposes, but admitted that he was always boasting about how many men he could raise, and enquired on one occasion how much it would cost to pay 10,000 for a month.[39] The implication was that the Lord Admiral was plotting a rebellion of some kind, but the rumour that he was stockpiling

arms seems to have been unfounded, and the substance behind it all may
have been no more than his urgent desire to maintain his 'estimation' by
keeping up an overlarge household. He certainly set great store by his
office, but whether this was because of the honour it conferred, or the
opportunities for profit it gave, is not clear. They were not necessarily
alternatives. He did not know the meaning of discretion, and although he
denied that he was plotting to marry Elizabeth in the autumn of 1548, he
admitted urging the council that she should be married within England,
and speculated about how much income she would have in a manner
which was bound to confirm the rumours of his intentions which were
abounding by that time.[40]

The substance behind Seymour's restless intrigues was a campaign to
have his brother's patent of office annulled by parliament. That patent
had been renewed and further extended in December 1547, and by the
summer of 1548 the Protector was ruling in an autocratic style which was
beginning to make him enemies.[41] He had also arranged for himself to be
paid the very large salary of 8,000 marks a year out of the king's revenues,
over and above the profits of his extensive estates.[42] Seymour was not the
only man to be bitterly jealous, but for the time being the Protector was
in a strong position. Although the advantages of his victory over the Scots
the previous September had been largely negated by continuing Scottish
resistance and French intervention, it was not yet clear that his policy
had collapsed. There were stirrings of discontent in the countryside, particularly in Cornwall, and disquiet over the direction of his religious
policy; but none of this had yet come to a head. Between April and June
1548 he tinkered with the membership of the council, dropping Sir John
Gage, Sir Anthony Browne, Sir Edward Montague and Sir Edward
Wotton. It was no coincidence that all these were religious conservatives.
They were replaced by Sir Thomas Smith, who became an additional secretary in April, Sir John Baker and Sir Ralph Sadler.[43] Of these, Smith and
Sadler were reformers, Baker more ambiguous. Gage was replaced by
Paget as Comptroller of the Household at the end of June, but otherwise
the court was unaffected by these changes. It may be that this shuffling
was connected with the preparation of the first Act of Uniformity, which
went through parliament in December, because no sooner had that passed
into law than another shuffle brought back not only Montague and
Wotton, but also the Earl of Southampton. The Marquis of Northampton

was recalled later, and Francis Talbot, Earl of Shrewsbury, and Lord Wentworth were recruited.[44] Thomas Seymour lost his place with his arrest on 18 January. These changes took place over several months, and were obviously intended to strengthen the Protector's hand in dealing with different situations, so although it may be true that Somerset was frequently bypassing the council and making decisions himself, he was not indifferent to the support which it could offer in certain circumstances.

He needed that support in dealing with his brother, because although the latter's indiscreet behaviour had given enough grounds to justify his arrest, it was at first by no means clear what kind of a case could be assembled against him. It was not treason to question the Protector's position through the House of Lords, although it would have been to arm or assemble men for the purpose of overthrowing him. Similarly, it was not treason to talk vaguely about the desirability of Elizabeth's marriage, but it would have been to take any overt steps to marry her himself. Lord Clinton testified that Seymour had canvassed his support for a bill in parliament, which, as he supposed, was intended to make him Governor of the King's Person, and asserted that he had spoken darkly about making it 'a black parliament'.[45] The young Earl of Rutland, only just out of his minority, had been similarly approached, and had been given gratuitous advice about how to make himself 'strong in his country'. To him Seymour had claimed that the council feared him, implying that this was on account of the size of his following.[46] About a year before, the Marquis of Northampton had been given similar advice, and after Catherine's death Seymour had approached him for assistance in pressing his claim to his late wife's jewellery. He had also told Parr that the Marquis of Dorset had 'wholely entrusted' his daughter Jane to him (which was not quite true), and how there would be 'much ado' over her marriage.[47] Other testimony alleged that he had boasted how he would marry Jane to the king, and the Marquis of Dorset himself alleged that Seymour had advised him to strengthen his retinue in Warwickshire against the Earl of Warwick.

On 17 January 1549 the council assembled to determine how to deal with 'the great attemptates and disloyall practises of the lord Seymour of Sudeley, Admirall of England, tending to the daunger of the Kings Maiestie and the lord protector and Counsaille, and the subversion of the whole state of the realme'.[48] Seymour was arrested, and his goods inventoried, but in spite of all the efforts that followed, the evidence remained circumstantial. He had behaved improperly with Elizabeth when she was in his household, and had certainly conspired to marry her, but he had made no tangible progress in that direction. He had spoken repeatedly of unseating his brother, and had canvassed the support of other peers – particularly those like Southampton who could be reasonably expected to share his sense of grievance. But he had not actually done anything, apart from his corrupt financial dealings with Sharrington. Having decided to act, however, the Protector could not afford to be thwarted, and Thomas did himself no favours by refusing to answer most of the charges that were brought against him. He would admit only to having passed money to Fowler and others for the king's use, and that was not an offence at all, let alone treason.[49] The question was, and has remained since, did Seymour's wild and irresponsible talk add up to sufficient evidence of conspiracy? Although ostensibly to spare the Protector's feelings, it was probably because of these doubts that his case did not come to trial by the common law in the usual way. On 4 March he was condemned by Act of Attainder, and executed on the 20th.[50]

The king himself was one of those who had testified during the investigation, but it is impossible to deduce what he thought about his uncle or his fate. He knew that Somerset was 'much offended' with the marriage which he had facilitated, and he was fond of his stepmother, but most of his evidence was about the pocket money he received, and was simply factual.[51] Nor is it entirely clear how other contemporaries reacted. Years later John Hayward wrote:

> Many of the nobles cried out upon the Protector, calling him a
> bloodsucker, a murderer, a parricide and a villain, declaring that it was
> not fit the king should be under the protection of such a ravenous
> wolf.[52]

However, at the time it appears that Somerset had not only the full support of the council, but also their sympathy. Paradoxically, the 'black legend' about Seymour's death did not arise from any desire to denigrate the Protector, but was rather part of an elaborate explanation of his own fall later in 1549. According to that story he was betrayed into an act of parricide by a scheming rival intending to destroy the whole house of Seymour, and that rival was John Dudley, Earl of Warwick.

Warwick later developed his own black legend, because he took power after Somerset's fall and was responsible both for the subsequent death of the duke and for the failed attempt to put Jane Grey on the throne after Edward's death. To historians such as Hayward, this was all part of a Machiavellian scheme to get the crown into his own hands. It started with a concealed rivalry for the favour of Henry VIII between the Lord Admiral (as Dudley then was) and the Earl of Hertford. When it became clear that Hertford was ahead in that contest, Dudley feigned friendship with him, and after Henry's death was reckoned one of his closest allies. However, in alliance with the Duchess of Somerset he then worked secretly to develop bad blood between the brothers, encouraging Seymour in all those schemes which he knew the Protector most disliked and mistrusted. Having tricked Somerset into ruining his own reputation by having his brother murdered, he then conspired his overthrow, afterwards feigning friendship again in order to tempt the ex-Protector into another snare; whereupon he had him executed on fabricated evidence.[53] When it became obvious that Edward was seriously ill, in the spring of 1553, he contrived to marry Jane Grey to his youngest son, Guildford, and bullied the dying king into naming Jane as his successor in defiance of the lawful heir, Mary. At that point his schemes fell apart, because Mary secured the throne and promptly consigned him to a thoroughly deserved death. The only merit of this story is its simplicity, and the desire of readers to have their history in black and white. It is always good to have a thoroughly evil villain to hiss.

There is no conclusive evidence one way or the other for the relationship between Warwick and Somerset before 1547, beyond the fact that they worked together, along with Paget and Denny, to secure control of the minority government, through both the council and the Privy Chamber. Dudley was not pleased at having to give up the Admiralty to Thomas Seymour, and Van der Delft, who for obvious reasons was not close to the court, picked up some rumour of this when he wrote that Dudley was 'splendid and haughty by nature' and would not take subordination to the Protector patiently.[54] By July of the same year, however, when he was rather closer to affairs, he changed his mind and wrote that Warwick and Paget were the Protector's closest allies. Even when the ambassador was most suspicious of Dudley, however, he did not believe that he was fomenting trouble between the brothers. At some point in the summer of 1547 he reported that Dudley, perturbed by the bad blood which was developing between the brothers, had set out to reconcile them, admonishing Seymour 'to be content ... with the honour done to you for your brother's sake, and with your office of Lord Admiral which I gave up to you for the same motive'.[55] It may be that Van der Delft was fed these lines by Dudley himself, in which case they only tell us about the impression he wished to create, and the ambassador's willingness to be misled. However, early in 1549 both Sharrington and the Marquis of Dorset testified that Seymour had used words to them which clearly implied that he regarded Warwick as a close ally of the Protector, rather than as a rival.[56] In fact, it seems that Somerset's resolute handling of the threat presented by his brother strengthened his position rather than weakened it. His fall was due rather to the crisis which developed in the summer of 1549 than to any long-running conspiracy, either by Thomas Seymour or by the Earl of Warwick.

Somerset in fact was his own worst enemy. By not being frank with his colleagues, and by brushing aside well-intentioned advice with disdain, he alienated men whose support he needed, as the affair of Thomas Seymour had demonstrated. The root of the problem seems to have been that the Protector took himself too seriously, and often forgot that he was not actually the king. A century ago historians tended to represent him as an idealist, with a social programme far ahead of his time.[57] In fact there was nothing innovative about his social policy, which aimed to discharge the traditional royal responsibility of protecting the weak against the strong. The core of it was the prevention of what was called 'depopulating enclosure', by which powerful landlords dispossessed their tenants and turned the land to other uses. This was a problem, not because of the frequency with which it happened but because a steady growth in population had put pressure on the availability of tenancies, and because redress, when it was sought, was available only through the lords' own courts.[58] Somerset's remedies did not at first go beyond those which had been attempted by Cardinal Wolsey 30 years before. He set up commissions of enquiry, and passed anti-enclosure legislation through parliament. However, it was one thing to pass laws and another to get them enforced, and, as one observer wrote, 'it pricketh them most which be chosen to be burgesses'. Sitting in the House of Commons they were not prepared to defy the Protector, but when they sat at home as justices of the peace it was relatively easy to make sure that nothing much happened. Wolsey, who had been more or less going through the motions, had not been prepared to do much about this obstructiveness, but Somerset gave the impression that he was in earnest about overcoming it.[59] The aggrieved were encouraged to testify before the commissioners, and both preachers and balladmongers inveighed with more enthusiasm than discretion against 'step lords ... unnatural lords'. A climate of expectation was created, and towards the end of 1548 Sir William Paget wrote a careful letter to Somerset, warning him of the dangers of this course of action. The Protector had erred in trying to make all men content. Under Henry 'all things were too straight, and now they are too loose; then it was dangerous to do or speak though the meaning were not evil, and now every man hath liberty to do or speak'. Paget went on to point out that the stability of society depended upon the nobility and gentry, and that to alienate them, even in the discharge of a royal responsibility for social justice, was a risk which a minority government could not afford to take.[60] However, on 1 June 1548 a proclamation had announced that 'his highness is greatly moved both with a pitiful and tender zeal towards his most loving subjects, and especially to the poor which is minded to labour and travail for their living',[61] and had gone on to declare that the realm must be defended with men and not with 'flocks of sheep and herds of beasts'. The main purpose of the proclamation was to announce the establishment of the commissions of enquiry, and it contained explicit warnings against the aggrieved taking the law into their own hands, but the intention was clear, and Paget was not the only councillor who was alarmed by the implications.

Early in 1549 Somerset's difficulties were compounded by the fact that he was struggling to control a deteriorating situation in Scotland, and also to impose a highly controversial religious policy. It appears to have been his intention to send the Earl of Warwick to the north, supported by the Earl of Rutland and some 6,000 men, about half of them German mercenaries; but on 12 July Warwick wrote to Sir John Thynne, Somerset's familiar, urging him to persuade the Protector to abandon his plans against Scotland, and to use his troops to put down the risings which by then were spreading all over the Midlands and the south of England.[62]

The earl was thoroughly alarmed by the stories coming out of Warwickshire, of 'gentlemens servants going from their masters to the rebels' (which was seen as a fundamental violation of trust), and uncertain whether his friends would be able to hold Warwick Castle. However, there was no hint in this letter, or in any other written at that time, that Warwick held the Protector to blame for the crisis. He was rather concerned to reassure him of his loyalty.[63] Another proclamation on 23 May had denounced the troublemakers, and at the end of June the council had summoned as many justices as they had been able to get hold of, and urged them to do their duty rigorously.[64] Then, with totally unjustified optimism, Somerset had allowed the enclosure commissioners to resume their work. The result was summed up succinctly in the king's journal:

> the people began to rise in Wiltshire, where Sir William Herbert did put
> them down, overrun and slay them. Then they rose in Sussex,
> Hampshire, Kent, Gloucestershire, Suffolk, Warwickshire, Essex,
> Hertfordshire, a piece of Leicestershire, Worcestershire and
> Rutlandshire, where by fair persuasions, partly of honest men among
> themselves, and partly by gentlemen, they were often appeased, and
> again because certain commissions were sent to pluck down enclosures,
> then [they] did rise again . . .[65]

We do not know exactly when these words were written, so perhaps he was being wise after the event, but Edward certainly became convinced that the troubles and the commissions were effect and cause. By 16 July Warwick was back at court, making arrangements for the fortification of the Tower, but after the 12th there were no more friendly letters to Thynne. At about the same time watches were organised in London, and martial law was proclaimed. Although he remained in post, Somerset was losing the initiative because of his extreme reluctance to recognise the extent to which the risings were the result of his own 'conviction politics'. In the event, remedial action was forced upon him by his council colleagues, but they had every reason to doubt whether he had at last accepted their advice willingly.[66]

Lord Rich, the chancellor, contained the situation in Essex by vigorous action, while in Sussex the Earl of Arundel called upon all the resources of his ancient lordship to appease the rebels without bloodshed.[67] Lord Russell was sent to Devon and Cornwall, where the trouble was about the Prayer Book rather than enclosures, and he was later re-inforced by Lord Grey and Sir William Herbert. Grey dealt with Oxfordshire on the way; Warwick went down to his own 'country'; and the Marquis of Northampton was sent to deal with the camping move-ment in East Anglia. Of these, only the last was unsuccessful, Northampton being repulsed from Norwich with loss. By the middle of August, apart from East Anglia, the situation was under control. There the rebel victory had solved nothing, because Robert Kett, the local leader, had only a negative agenda, and had no idea what to do next. He simply awaited the arrival of the Earl of Warwick, who retook Norwich on 24 August and defeated the rebels with considerable slaughter outside the city the following day.[68] By the end of August all open resistance had been crushed, but those who benefited from the victories were Russell and Warwick rather than the Protector. The reluctance of his resort to force had been clear, but while these events had been in progress he had also lost control of the Scottish borders, and suffered a declaration of war by the French, who had taken advantage of his troubles to renew their attempts to recover Boulogne.[69]

Exactly how and when a majority of the council decided that he would have to go is not clear. The black legend which was already received wisdom by the 1560s made the Earl of Warwick the leader, and linked it to the long-standing animosity that we have already noticed. However, there is no contemporary evidence of anything more than rou-tine disagreements over patronage before August 1549.[70] Then, during the Norfolk campaign, an eyewitness alleges that there was an acrimo-nious exchange of letters, and that Warwick denounced the Protector to his close associates as 'a coward, a breaker of promises, a niggard, cov-etous and ambitious'. However, the writer was a former servant of Somerset's, and he was writing after Elizabeth's accession, so his testi-mony may be taken with a pinch of salt.[71] The acrimonious letters, if they were ever written, have not survived. More reliable than this somewhat dubious memoir is a letter written by Van der Delft on 15 September. According to Princess Mary, with whom he was in regular contact, trouble was brewing over the Protector's plan for the formation of 'a new council'. This might mean that Somerset was planning to dispense with the existing royal council altogether, and to rely in future upon his per-sonal or 'household' council, or it might mean that he was simply intending to get rid of those who he felt were obstructing him, and to replace them with more amenable advisers. In any case, why should Mary, who was not at court and was on distant terms with her brother, be well informed on such a matter? She had, she claimed, been approached by a group of councillors, and she named Warwick, Southampton, Arundel and St John, who had solicited her assistance in removing the Protector. She had told them that she had no desire to be involved. As this was not particularly good news for the emperor, it is likely that on this occasion the ambassador may be trusted.[72] Mary was not specific about what kind of assistance they had solicited, but it could only have been some kind of figurehead to a reconstituted regency council. Neither Mary nor Van der Delft had any motive for deception in this matter, so it is reasonable to conclude that a conspiracy to remove Somerset was in place by the middle of September. How extensive it was, who was the real leader, and what was the positive thrust of its political intentions, are, however, difficult to determine.

A few days later Van der Delft received a visit from Sir William Paget. This seems to have been intended as a broad hint that one of the conspirators' aims would be to repair England's relations with the Empire. Specifically, he solicited the ambassador's good offices to bring the Earl of Warwick to 'a better disposition regarding religion'.[73] Paget was a trimmer in ecclesiastical matters, who had gone along with all the changes so far, but Warwick had the reputation of being a strong reformer. The move may have been prompted by anxiety lest the conspirators should divide along confessional lines, or it may simply have been Paget's way of letting the emperor know that his heart was in the right place. Between 15 and 23 September Warwick also visited Van der Delft. He was ostensibly frank about his dislike of the Protector's government, but blamed much of what had gone wrong upon the pride and vindictiveness of the duchess. He said nothing about religion, but also indicated a rapprochement with the emperor.[74] The ambassador in response claimed to have been vaguely supportive, but offered nothing more. It seems likely that there was no single leader of this conspiracy, but rather that a number of councillors had independently come to the same conclusion at about the same time, and that the basis of their cooperation did not reach beyond the negative purpose of getting rid of Somerset. The Earl of Warwick was important, partly because he had always been seen as the Protector's

right-hand man, and partly because he had carefully refrained from dis-
banding his troops at the end of the Norfolk campaign. He thus had several thousand men at his bidding not very far from the capital. By the end
of September, Southampton, Warwick and Arundel were certainly working together, and if Warwick was the leader it was by virtue of these
resources, rather than because the whole coup was his idea.[75]

There is no sign in the surviving records that Somerset had any idea
of what was afoot. During September a rather thinly attended council
went about its normal business, and Cecil's correspondence shows no
sign of alarm. The first suggestion of trouble is a proclamation of 30
September ordering all mustered soldiers to depart from London and its
suburbs.[76] The Protector must have known that they were there, but had
previously accepted that the uncertain security situation in the aftermath
of the risings justified their presence. Now he seems to have realised that
he had no control over them. Edward and Somerset were at Hampton
Court at the beginning of October, and at the same time the opposition
began to gather in the City. As late as 4 October there is no sign of alarm
in the records of the business being transacted at Hampton Court, but by
that time, as the London-based chronicler Richard Grafton recalled,

> many of the Lordes of the Realme, as well counsaylors as others
> myslyking the goouvernment of the Protector, began to withdrawe
> themselves from the Courte, and resorting to London, fell to secret
> consultation for redresse of things, but namely for the displacing of the
> sayde Lorde Protector, and sodainely of what occasion many marvelled
> and fewe knewe everye lorde and counsaylor went thorowe the Citie
> weaponed, and had their servants likewise weaponed . . .[77]

By the following day, 5 October, Somerset had at last awoken to the true
significance of what was afoot, and issued a proclamation over the king's
sign manual commanding all subjects to gather, armed and in haste, at
Hampton Court to protect the king's person against 'a most dangerous
conspiracy'.[78] This measure, strongly suggestive of panic, was of far
greater value to his enemies than it was to the Protector. The only person
of substance to respond positively was Archbishop Cranmer, who arrived
the next day with 60 men. This demonstrated that he was not a party to
the plot, but little more. The several hundred untrained and virtually
unarmed commoners who also responded were far more of a liability

than an asset. Somerset had perhaps 500 of his own and the king's servants around the court, whom he could and did arm, but he could not hope to withstand a determined attack if one should be made. The 'London Lords', on the other hand, were now in a dilemma. Hampton Court was barely defensible, even with the last-minute efforts which the Protector was now making, and 1,000 amateur soldiers would have been no match for Warwick's German mercenaries. However, a military solution was almost out of the question because of the danger to the king.[79] Moreover, however much they might bluster about the iniquities of the Protestor's government, Edward was with him and not with them. They could not issue instructions over the sign manual, and the longer the crisis continued, the more that would matter.[80]

The only other military force in being was that which Lord Russell and Sir William Herbert were leading back from the West Country campaign, and both sides solicited their support. It was in that connection that Somerset's proclamation was most damaging, because it could be used to make it appear that the Protector was now appealing to those very men against whom Russell, Grey and Warwick had recently been in arms. In other words, he was appealing to the commons against their natural lords.[81] On 6 October the lords, now calling themselves the Privy Council, met at the Earl of Warwick's London residence, Ely Place in Holborn, and issued a public denunciation of the Protector's misgovernment, justifying their own action as being in the king's true service.[82] On the same day they secured control of the Tower, and Somerset hastily moved the king and the court to the greater security of Windsor Castle. By the following day all sorts of rumours were flying round the capital: the king had been abducted; the Protector was planning to take him out of the country; he had sent a massive bribe to the King of France for his assistance – and so on.[83] Sir William Petre, sent from Hampton Court to negotiate with the lords, joined them, and on the 8th Russell sent word that he would stand with his colleagues rather than with the Protector. By the 9th Edward was Somerset's only card, and he was beginning to look increasingly like a hostage. However, any attack on Windsor had been ruled out, and the longer the stalemate continued, the more chance there was that the Protector's widespread popular support might begin to mobilise.

On the 8th and the 9th letters were exchanged, and Cranmer and

Paget, who remained with the Protector, were used to apply leverage to him.[84] We do not know quite how it was achieved, but somehow behind the scenes a deal was done, using the diplomat Sir Philip Hoby as the intermediary. Most likely an agreement was reached between Cranmer and Warwick that Somerset would stand down in return for some kind of immunity and the continuation of his religious reform programme. No documents prove this, but the behaviour of all parties subsequently is consistent with it.[85] What we do know is that sometime on 10 October, a charade was acted out at Windsor in order to preserve the political and courtly proprieties. Hoby 'told a good tale' in the king's presence against the Protector, and the king then ordered the latter to be taken into custody, and his servants were removed from the royal presence.[86] Of course, this could only have been done with Somerset's connivance. If Edward had really been capable of resolving the whole situation himself in such a simple and direct way, there is no reason why he should not have done so before; nor any reason why he should have allowed himself to be taken to Windsor like a piece of fragile and expensive luggage. On 11 October Sir Anthony Wingfield, the Vice-Chamberlain, arrived to resume his command of the guard and to supervise the custody of Somerset and some of his more conspicuous servants, and on the 12th the whole body of the council presented themselves to receive Edward's 'most harty thanks'.[87] Sir Thomas Smith, Sir Michael Stanhope, Sir John Thynne and William Cecil were among those removed from office and incarcerated in the Tower. Theoretically, both Smith and Stanhope were the king's servants rather than the Protector's, but both were clearly (and rightly) seen as Somerset's men. The Privy Chamber was now without a Groom of the Stool, and the time was felt to be right for a drastic reorganisation. Edward recorded the events of these traumatic days in his journal, briefly and factually. We cannot tell from his own words what he thought about them, but other evidence suggests that he had found the whole experience frightening and deeply disturbing. More important, if he had ever felt any genuine affection for his 'entirely beloved uncle', the events of these days killed it, a change which Somerset himself never accepted or came to terms with.

As the fallen Protector was removed to the Tower, his fate itself became a political issue. If there was an agreement between Somerset and Warwick, it seems clear that no one else except Cranmer knew about it.

Van der Delft expected a reversal of religious policy, and became first puzzled and then dismayed as it failed to emerge, and Cranmer retained his place on the council.[88] There were also those who began to assemble arguments of malpractice which went far beyond arrogance and maladministration. As we have seen, Somerset was accused of peculation and fraud on an enormous scale, in a document which commenced:

> *If any man doubt whether Edward, Duke of Somerset be worthy to be deposed of that rule and name of protector which he usurpeth, and not a traitor worthie to suffer shamfull death, let him but indifferently consider these four matters gathered together of a multitude of mischiefs by him practiced and attempted.*[89]

The author then went on to enumerate Somerset's faults: that he had 'disdayned and refused the right sage counsel of wise men', being ruled instead by 'that imperious and insolent woman his wife'; that he had 'made havoc of the kings landes and inheritance'. He had aspired to the crown by taking the royal title of Somerset, and set out to deprive the king of the affection of his subjects, 'following therein K.Richard the tyrant', suborning preachers to praise his government. Having the king in his custody, he had conspired to seize the crown. Most of this bile need not be taken seriously. There is not the slightest reason to suppose that he ever had designs upon the crown, and the charge that he squandered the king's inheritance is at best wildly exaggerated. He did, however, build lavishly (one of the minor charges), and bypassed the council when he should have taken it seriously. The demonisation of his duchess, Anne Stanhope, is little more than a trope, although she certainly had a capacity for making enemies.[90] But what of his alleged financial abuses? The £11,000 transferred to the Tower at the end of January 1547 was still there when Somerset fell from power, when most of it was immediately spent by the council.[91] Denny continued to be responsible for the Privy Coffers, at least until he accounted in March 1548, and although a lot of money – over £246,000 – passed through his hands between April 1542 and February 1548, the great bulk of it had been spent before January 1547 on the personal instructions of the king. Apart from £4,000 which was paid over to Stanhope in August 1547, it is not clear how much of the balance was spent on Somerset's orders.[92] If money had been spirited away, of course it would not show up in the accounts, and it is not at all clear what use was being made of the Privy Coffers during the Protectorate.

A general inventory of Henry VIII's possessions was commissioned in September 1547, but the commissioners did not report until January 1550.[93] They recorded the removal of the Coffers to the Tower, but did not find any other cash, and there is a gap between Denny's account of March 1548 and their own report, so it is possible that money may have disappeared during that interval. There is, however, not a scrap of evidence that it did. Denny's account showed only a small credit balance, and that may have remained in limbo until the Privy Coffers were reconstituted after Somerset's fall. The most telling piece of evidence is surely the fact that the contents of the identified coffer were still untouched in October 1549. The substance behind the colourful charges of peculation lay partly in Somerset's seizure of Catherine's jewellery, and partly in the fact that he gave himself an income of over £5,000 a year – a sum well in excess of all peerage incomes, including his own.[94] However, both of these were matters of record, and were well known. The Protector did not fall because he was secretly plundering the royal revenues. He fell because he refused to take advice, a prerogative which only a lawful king could enjoy. On 7 July 1549, just before the crisis closed over his head, William Paget, who had been one of his earliest and strongest supporters, told him frankly that the whole council had disliked his proceedings over the mounting social unrest: 'you may say you alone are answerable to the king; but so must be those who first consented to your authority'.[95] He himself had given advice, both in public and in private, 'and seen little fruit come of it'. Whatever his enemies might claim, Somerset had not acted unlawfully, because the power to act without consent had been formally granted to him, but the expectation that he would use that authority with restraint and discretion had not been fulfilled.

The court was rather more significant in these political manoeuvres than has generally been recognised. It is usually said that Somerset simply neglected his charge there, and paid the price, but that is not quite true. Both Denny and Cheke, who were responsible for different aspects of Edward's life, were trustworthy allies, and certainly brought the king up to be an enthusiastic supporter of his uncle's controversial religious policies, which was a matter of great importance. The Protector probably did not spend as much time as he should have done with his nephew, and it was that, rather than financial stringency, that opened the door for Thomas Seymour. Both Denny and Stanhope were negligent in that respect, but Seymour was guilty of a breach of trust in behaving as he did. He had his own key to the Privy Apartments, and claimed that he did not know what he had done with it,[96] which was a dangerous abuse even by sixteenth-century standards of security! Edward was also beginning to grow up. By the summer of 1549 he was approaching his twelfth birthday, and beginning to feel his identity and his dignity. This is something which his tutors would have encouraged, but which Somerset failed to recognise. Consequently, when he found himself in a tight corner in October 1549, he simply used the boy as a shield, and appears to have paid no attention to his wishes, if they were ever expressed. This was worse than an insult, it was a mistake, and Edward seems to have played his part in the *denouement* willingly enough. The only change of officer that Somerset effected was to replace Denny with Stanhope. Whether this was because the former was thought to have been negligent, or because his health was declining, is not clear. He appears to have surrendered his last office, that of Keeper of the Palace of Westminster, in March 1548, and he died in August 1549. Somerset's successors were to show themselves much more aware of the young king's development, and no sooner had he fallen from power than major changes began to be carried out.

Notes and references

1 *CPR, Edward VI*, vol.1, p.180.

2 PRO, LC2/3/ii, fol.13; LC2/4/I, fol.19.

3 PRO, LC2/3/I, fols.85–92.

4 Ibid., fols.46, 48, 49; D.M. Loades, *Elizabeth I* (London, 2003), pp.71–3.

5 The Earl of Hertford and Sir Anthony Brown to the council, 30 January 1547, PRO, SP10/1, no.2.

6 BL, Add. MS 48126, fols.1–4. 'Against Edward Duke of Somerset, now falslie usurping the name of protector'. A late sixteenth-century copy, described as 'Out of a booke by Sir Thomas Smithe', but not written by him.

7 A commission was appointed to make an inventory, but not until September 1547, and it did not report until February 1550, long after this paper was written.

8 BL, Lansdowne Charter 14. For a discussion of this account, and of the use

of the Privy Coffers in general, see D.E. Hoak, 'The Secret History of the Tudor Court: the King's Coffers and the King's Purse, 1542–1553', *Journal of British Studies*, 26 (1987), pp.208–31.

9 For a recent summary of the debate on Henry VIII's will and its interpretation, see Stephen Alford, *Kingship and Politics in the Reign of Edward VI* (Cambridge, 2002), pp.66–71.

10 'it shuld be more than necessarie aswel for thonour, suretie and government of the most royal person of the King our Souvereign Lorde that nowe is, as for the more certaine and assured order and direction of his affayres, that some special man of the nombre and company aforesaide shuld be preferred in name and place before others, to whome as to the state and hedde of the reste all strangers and others might have accesse'. *APC*, vol.2, pp.3–4.

11 Society of Antiquaries, MS 123, fols.317–18; J. Loach, *Edward VI* (London, 1999), p.29.

12 Helen Miller, 'Henry VIII's Unwritten Will; Grants of Lands and Honours in 1547', in *Wealth and Power in Tudor England*, ed. E.W. Ives, R.J. Knecht and J.J. Scarisbrick (London, 1978), pp.88–91. For the draft list, subsequently much changed, see PRO, SP10/1, no.11.

13 S.Anglo, *Spectacle, Pageantry and Early Tudor Policy*, 2nd edn (Oxford, 1997), pp.283–94; Loach, *Edward VI*, p.33 and n. A version of this pageant sequence had been published in 1542.

14 *The Works of Thomas Cranmer*, ed. J.E. Cox, 2 vols. (London, 1844, 1846), vol.2, p.146. Although the traditional format of the coronation was retained, the symbolism was modified in a number of ways to emphasise the new level of dignity and splendour which the king derived from his functions as Supreme Head of the church. For a full discussion of the significance of this, see Dale Hoak, 'The Coronations of Edward VI, Mary I and Elizabeth I, and the Transformation of Tudor Monarchy', in *Westminster Abbey Reformed, 1540–1640*, ed. C.S. Knighton and R. Mortimer (Aldershot 2003), pp.114–51.

15 Stephen Gardiner to William Paget, 1st March 1547, in *The Letters of Stephen Gardiner*, ed. J.A. Muller (Cambridge, 1933), pp.268–9.

16 *The Chronicle and Political Papers of King Edward VI*, ed. W.K. Jordan (London, 1966), p.5. The position of King's Champion was hereditary in the Dymocke family; Sir John was the third generation.

17 A. Feuillerat, *Documents Relating to the Office of the Revels under Edward VI and Mary* (Louvain, 1914), p.xxii.

18 Loach, *Edward VI*, p.33; Mary of Hungary to Van der Delft, 6th February 1547, *CSP, Spanish*, vol.9, p.15.

19 *Correspondence politique de Odet de Selve, ambassadeur de France en*

Angleterre (1546–1549), ed. G. Lefevre-Pontalis (Paris, 1888), no.121, 105; *CSP Spanish*, vol.9, p.47.

20 M.L. Bush, *The Government Policy of Protector Somerset* (Manchester, 1975), pp.2, 9. The risk of attack from France was greatly increased by the death of Francis I in April 1547 because his successor, Henry II, was a notorious Anglophobe, who had never accepted his father's treaty of 1546.

21 W.K. Jordan, *Edward VI: The Young King* (London, 1968), pp.69–72; Dale Hoak, *The King's Council in the Reign of Edward VI* (Cambridge, 1976), pp.43–5; Alford, *Kingship and Politics*, p.14.

22 *APC*, vol.2, pp.63, 522–33; *CPR, Edward VI*, vol.1, p.97.

23 These changes strengthened both the courtier element and the protestant element. Hoak, *King's Council*, pp.42, 47.

24 Susan James, *Kateryn Parr: The Making of a Queen* (Stroud, 1999).

25 PRO, SP10/6, no.10; *CSP, Domestic, Edward VI*, no.185.

26 Ibid. Mary was notoriously conservative in her views.

27 Deposition of William Parr, Marquis of Northampton, January 1549, PRO, SP10/6, no.14.

28 Testimony of John Fowler, PRO, SP10/6, no.10.

29 HMC, *Salisbury MSS*, vol.1, pp.65–6; *A Collection of State Papers ... left by William Cecil, Lord Burghley*, ed. S.Haynes and W.Murdin (London, 1740–59), vol.1, p.74.

30 Accounts of Sir Michael Stanhope, Groom of the Stool, PRO, E351/2932, showing a total expenditure of £1,448 9s. 2d.

31 Deposition of John Fowler: 'When the king was at St. James'.

32 *HMC, Salisbury MSS*, vol.1, pp.65–6; *State Papers*, ed. Haynes and Murdin, vol.1, p.74.

33 Confessions of Catherine Ashley and Thomas Parry, HMC, *Salisbury MSS*, vol.1, pp.72–3.

34 Joan Denny had been born Joan Champernowne, and had married Denny in about 1540.

35 Final deposition of Kate Ashley [4th February 1549], PRO, SP10/6, no.22. 'I told her that she would not refuse it if the protector and Council bade her, and she said yes ...'

36 The depositions cited above were taken in the Tower.

37 For the articles with which Seymour was formally charged, see *APC*, vol.2, pp.248–56. The known facts of the case are set out fully in Jordan, *Edward VI: The Young King*, pp.368–85.

38 Deposition of Sir William Sharrington, PRO SP10/6, no.13.

39 Ibid.

40 Loades, *Elizabeth I*, pp.67–70.

41 *CPR, Edward VI*, vol.2, p.96. He was now to hold office during the king's pleasure rather than for the duration of the minority.

42 *CPR, Edward VI*, vol.1, p.184; PRO, E315/258, fol.49. This translates as £5,333, and probably raised his total income above £10,000 – the largest for any minister since Wolsey.

43 Hoak, *King's Council*, p.47.

44 Ibid., p.51.

45 PRO, SP10/6, no.11.

46 Ibid., no.12.

47 Ibid., no.14. Jane Grey had been withdrawn from the Seymour household following the scandal over Elizabeth's departure, but Thomas later persuaded the marquis to allow her to return, apparently by dangling the prospect of a marriage with the king, which he was in no position to arrange.

48 *APC*, vol.2, pp.236–8.

49 'Answers of the Lord Admiral . . .', 24th February 1549, PRO, SP10/6, no.27.

50 *Journals of the House of Commons* (London, 1803–52), vol.1, p.9; *APC*, vol.2, p.262.

51 HMC, *Salisbury MSS*, vol.1, p.65. The words used in the formal record in *APC* were clearly not his own.

52 *The Life and Raigne of King Edward the Sixth by John Hayward*, ed. B.L. Beer (Kent, Ohio, 1993), p.100. None of these peers had, however, voted against the Act of Attainder.

53 Ibid., pp.101, 137–46.

54 Van der Delft to the emperor, 10th July 1547; *CSP Spanish*, vol.9, p.122, D.M. Loades, *John Dudley, Duke of Northumberland* (Oxford, 1996), p.115.

55 Van der Delft to the emperor, 8th February 1549, *CSP Spanish*, vol.9, p.340.

56 PRO, SP10/6, no.13, no.7. Seymour warned Dorset 'to keep my house in Warwickshire, as it is a county full of men, chiefly to match Lord Warwick . . .'.

57 Notably R.H.Tawney, *The Agrarian Problem in the Sixteenth Century* (London, 1912). For the historiography of Somerset, see G.J.R. Parry, 'Inventing the Good Duke of Somerset', *Journal of Ecclesiastical History*, 40 (1989), pp.370–80.

58 For a full discussion of the legal implications of tenure and the resolution of disputes, see Eric Kerridge, *The Agrarian Problem in the Sixteenth Century and After* (London, 1969).

59 For a recent and full discussion of the Protector's professions, and their honesty, see Ethan Shagan, 'Protector Somerset and the 1549 Rebellions: New Sources and New Perspectives', *English Historical Review*, 114 (1999), pp.34–63.

60 Jordan, *Edward VI*, pp.351–2, citing Paget Letter Book 8, among the Fitzwilliam MSS in the Northampton Record Office.

61 *Tudor Royal Proclamations*, ed. P.L. Hughes and J.F. Larkin, vol.1 (London, 1964), pp.427–9.

62 HMC, *Bath MSS at Longleat*, Seymour Papers, vol.2, De Lisle and Dudley Papers, vol.1, fol.20; Loades, *John Dudley*, pp.118–19.

63 'for my meaning towards his Grace, I would his Grace knew it as God doth.' Loades, *John Dudley*, p.119.

64 *Tudor Royal Proclamations*, ed. Hughes and Larkin, vol.1, pp.461–2.

65 *Chronicle*, ed. Jordan, p.12.

66 Loades, *John Dudley*, pp.119–22; Shagan, 'Protector Somerset and the 1549 Rebellions'.

67 For a discussion of Arundel's successful tactic in Sussex, see Andrew Boyle, 'Henry FitzAlan, 12th Earl of Arundel: Politics and Culture in the Tudor nobility', DPhil thesis, University of Oxford, 2002, pp.28–9.

68 Beer, *Life and Raigne*, pp.92–4. 'Dussindale', the alleged site of the battle, has never been identified.

69 PRO, SP10/8, no.38; Jordan, *Edward VI*, pp.302–4.

70 For example, in March 1548 Warwick had written to Thynne: 'I perceive by your said letters that his grace will not condescend to my request [for the manor of Ardingley] ... but seeing his grace esteemeth it to be such a thing, it becometh not me to sue further for it'. De Lisle and Dudley Papers, vol.1, pp.11. Warwick obtained a lot of his requests, and too much should not be read into such rebuffs.

71 BL, Add. MS 48126, fols.6–16; partly published by A.J.A. Malkiewicz as 'An Eyewitness Account of the *coup d'etat* of October 1549', *English Historical Review*, 70 (1955), pp.600–9.

72 Van der Delft to the emperor, 15th September 1549, *CSP Spanish*, vol.9, p.248.

73 Ibid., pp.445–8.

74 Ibid., p.454. Loades, *John Dudley*, p.130.

75 Loades, *John Dudley*, pp.129–31; Hoak, *King's Council*, pp.241–5.

76 *Tudor Royal Proclamations*, ed. Hughes and Larkin, vol.2, p.483.

77 Richard Grafton, *A Chronicle at Large* ... (London, 1568), ed. H.Ellis (London, 1809), pp.521–2.

78 PRO, SP10/9, nos.1–9, copies directed to various persons.

79 Loades, *John Dudley*, pp.132–4.

80 The extent of Somerset's potential support is very difficult to assess. In spite of the events of the summer he remained very popular. As many as 4,000 men were said to have answered his original call, and the longer the situation remained unresolved, the more likely it was that more would follow. Several pamphlets were spread around London, urging the citizens to support the Protector. PRO, SP10/9, nos.11–13.

81 Council to Princesses Mary and Elizabeth, 9th October 1549, PRO, SP10/9, no.33.

82 PRO, SP10/9, no.10; *APC*, vol.2, pp.330–2.

83 PRO, SP10/9, no.14; 'Memoranda of recent events'.

84 PRO, SP10/9, nos. 22, 24, 26, 27; Jordan, *Edward VI*, pp.515–19.

85 For the presentation of a case to this effect, see Loades, *John Dudley*, pp.135–8; also PRO, SP10/9, no.24(i).

86 Grafton, *Chronicle*, p.523.

87 PRO, SP10/9, no.42; Loades, *John Dudley*, p.139.

88 On 17 October, the ambassador wrote: 'The archbishop of Canterbury still holds his place in the council, but I do not believe they will leave him there unless he improves, and it is probable that they are now tolerating him merely that all may be done in proper order.' *CSP Spanish*, vol.9, pp.462–3.

89 BL, Add. MS 48126, fol.1.

90 Hayward was particularly severe, calling her 'a woman for many imperfections intolerable, but for pride monstrous [and] she was exceeding both subtle and violent in accomplishing her ends'. *The Life and Raigne*, p.98.

91 Hoak, 'The Secret History', p.218.

92 BL, Lansdowne Charter 14. Although this sum is recorded as having been paid to Stanhope as Groom of the Stool, it does not appear in his Privy Purse accounts (E351/2932), and he may therefore have spent it in another capacity.

93 Hoak, 'The Secret History', p.217.

94 In 1559 only two peers (Howard and Talbot) had incomes of over £5,000 a year, and that was after a decade of high inflation. According to one surviving account, Somerset spent £14,235 between 1548 and 1551, but that probably does not represent the full total. BL, Egerton MS 2815; L. Stone, *The Crisis of the Aristocracy, 1558–1640* (Oxford, 1965), Appendices VIII, XXIII.

95 PRO, SP10/8, no.4.

96 G.W. Bernard, 'The Downfall of Sir Thomas Seymour', in G.W. Bernard (ed.), *The Tudor Nobility* (Manchester, 1992), pp.212–40

CHAPTER 3

. . . .

Educating and entertaining a prince

Edward recorded the early stages of his own education in the briefest and most formal fashion:

> At the sixth year of his age he was brought up in learning by Mr. Dr. [Richard] Cox, who was after[ward] his Almoner, and John Cheke, Master of Arts, two well learned men, who sought to bring him up in learning of tongues, of the scripture, of philosophy and all liberal sciences. Also John Belmain [a] Frenchman, did teach him the French language . . .[1]

Cox had been one of the first fellows of Wolsey's aborted foundation in Oxford, and both Provost of Eton and one of Cranmer's chaplains before becoming Almoner to the infant prince in 1538. He was apparently named as Edward's tutor in 1540, but according to the king's own testimony cannot have begun to operate as such for about another two years.[2] In 1544 Cheke, the Regius Professor of Greek at Cambridge, was appointed 'as a supplement to Mr. Cox', and probably took over the main daily task of teaching the boy when Cox became Dean of Christ Church in 1546. Roger Ascham, who was primarily Elizabeth's tutor, taught Edward to write, being called thereto 'by Mr. Cheke's means'.[3] The correspondence of Cheke and Ascham is filled with references to the progress of their royal charge, which suggests that they were not often both on duty at the same time, although beyond the fact that he was taught for so many hours every day, we know very little about how their work was scheduled. Jean Belmain, officially his French Secretary, began his teaching duties in 1546, and it is possible that several other men were involved with the royal schoolroom: William Grindal, another of Elizabeth's tutors, Walter Haddon, Sir Anthony Cooke and John Dee.[4] The latter two were not recruited until after his accession, and Dee's role (if it existed at all) seems to have been confined to astronomy – a fringe subject in the curriculum. All those appointed before 1547 were, of course, named by Henry, and apart from their learning they all had one thing in common. They were humanists of the evangelical persuasion, and all of them (except Grindal, who died young) were to emerge after Henry's death as strong protestants. Their progress along that line was so similar to that of Queen Catherine that some scholars have been tempted to see her influence behind their appointment. However, that is very unlikely. Cox was in post well before Henry married Catherine, and the old king was notoriously touchy over attempts to influence him, especially on so important an issue.

We do not know what sort of religious instruction Edward received before he became king, although we can deduce from what happened thereafter that it was at least broadly evangelical. Henry was concerned that his heir, no less than his heir's political mentors, should respect and promote the royal ecclesiastical supremacy, and for that reason strong conservatives were kept away from the schoolroom no less than from the council chamber in the last days of his life.[5] It is likely that the adviser whom the king consulted about such matters was Cranmer – hence the early promotion of Cox – and therefore equally likely that Edward was introduced to vernacular prayers, and the English bible, before he was old enough to use the Latin varieties.

Just when Edward began to learn Latin again has to be deduced. We know that he began French lessons in the autumn of 1546, and by December had progressed sufficiently to write to his sister Elizabeth in that language. However, when he met the French ambassador in February 1547 he chose to converse in Latin, suggesting that he had a longer familiarity with it.[6] He probably began soon after Cheke's appointment in 1544, when he would have been about seven, and by the age of nine was reasonably confident. The earliest of his surviving exercises dates from

June 1549, when he should be classed as an advanced learner. He commenced learning Greek towards the end of 1550, and may not have advanced much beyond the elementary stage before Cheke returned to Cambridge in 1552, and the whole emphasis of the king's studies changed. He did not exaggerate when he claimed to have been brought up with philosophy and the scriptures, and his exercises are very revealing of Cheke's methods, but, as with Elizabeth, languages formed the main content of his studies. Latin, French and Greek are firmly attested by his own letters and exercises, and a visitor to the court in 1550 also referred to his competence in Spanish and Italian.[7] If that was accurate, and not mere flattery, we do not know who taught him, or how far he progressed. By 1550 Elizabeth was certainly competent in Italian, although her Spanish may well have come later; so tuition in those languages was available, and it was desirable for a king to be able to converse with as many ambassadors as possible in their own tongues – it never failed to impress them.

Edward took himself and his duties seriously from a very early age, far more seriously than most of his schoolfellows, it would seem, but that was also the aspect of his personality that was for public consumption. We know from his brushes with Thomas Seymour that he had an impish sense of humour, and that he was inclined to spend more money than his minders thought proper on gambling and wagers. He seems to have betted continuously on the outcome of his own skill or fortune, whether at cards, tennis, archery, chess or whatever, and lost the sizeable sum of £140 in one year.[8] Either he was not very good, or he played a great deal – probably a bit of both. In one sense Cheke was a severe disciplinarian: he insisted on the boy's exercises being completed and done thoroughly. But he was also a humane man who believed that learning should be enjoyable, and that a spirited boy needed ways of letting off steam.[9] Perhaps the most obvious thing about the non-academic side of Edward's upbringing is his enthusiasm for war – not something which he would have learned from his humanist tutors. No sooner had he completed the meagre story of his own coronation, than he was off after Sir Andrew Dudley, and the battle of the *Pauncey* and the *Lion*.[10] His stepmother's marriage merits two lines, but the Scottish campaign of September 1547 gets two pages of his journal, and many circumstantial details. His narrative of the second year of his reign makes only a passing reference to the religious debates in the December parliament, being mainly concerned with the siege of Haddington and the Earl of Shrewsbury's incursion into Scotland. There are passing references to rebellion in Ireland and to the execution of Thomas Seymour, but an incongruous emphasis upon a 'triumph' at Greenwich, 'where six gentlemen did challenge all comers at barriers, jousts and tourney'.[11] If we can trust the evidence of the journal (which, after all, was a school exercise), Edward's priorities appear somewhat different from those usually attributed to him. So who was encouraging these legitimate but unscholarly interests? His father may well have been responsible for the initial impulse. At the age of eight Edward can hardly have been unaware of the immense pride which Henry took in the capture of Boulogne; later it was probably members of his own Privy Chamber who had served in the wars. We cannot be sure, because no one commented upon such matters at the time – the emphasis was always upon the boy's progress in his studies, or in piety – but the fact is that Edward had all the rumbustious tastes and warlike aspirations of a normal aristocratic child of that period, and this was a factor of increasing importance as he advanced into adolescence.

In terms of formal entertainments, the records do not suggest a high level of activity at this time. There was a coronation tournament, and shortly afterwards, on Shrove Tuesday, as we have seen, a 'Masque of Orpheus' in which the king took part. He also seems to have participated in another play at Greenwich in April 1547, but we do not know the subject matter.[12] There is then a prolonged silence until Christmas, when there was a flurry of activity at Hampton Court. Several plays or masques were performed, including one about Prester John, but we do not know who the actors were. Late in the holiday, perhaps on Twelfth Night, there was a play 'of the Tower of Babylon', but nothing else is known about it.[13] Shrovetide (February), which was a traditional revels season, saw no fewer than three masques and plays. The latter were performed by the King's Players (confirming that there was such a group), and two of the masques were for women, but we do not know the subject matter. At about the same time, or a little after, there was a 'Masque of Young Moors', acted by Edward and his schoolfellows. Christmas 1548 saw at least two further masques at Westminster, one of them 'of Almains', and Shrovetide 1549 another performance by the King's Players.[14] 'Challenges' and other martial exercises were not organised by the Revels

Office, and we know about them only from the king's journal or from references in chatty diplomatic correspondence. It seems that Edward himself was much more interested in combats than he was in masques or plays, because even when we know he took part in them, he never refers to the latter in his journal. Perhaps such matters were considered too frivolous to be worthy of record, but it seems more likely that they were akin to school plays in Edward's mind, and he was not particularly proud of his appearances. There is no suggestion at this time that theatrical performances were being used for propaganda purposes, or combats either. Henry had once famously upended a boatload of popish cardinals for the entertainment of his guests, and Edward would have loved that, but nothing so exciting, or pointed, seems to have happened while the Duke of Somerset was in command.

As we shall see, the 'regime change' in October 1549 led to major reorganisation in the Privy Chamber, but it does not seem to have disturbed the schoolroom routine. The king's surviving exercises run without any obvious break from June 1549 to June 1552, when Cheke surrendered his charge and went back to the university.[15] As he approached his twelfth birthday, Edward was studying Cicero, particularly *De Officiis* and *The Tusculum Questions*, by the standard technique of translating passages from Latin into English, and then (after a lapse of time) translating them back again. However, that was only the start, because each text had to be analysed, both for its rhetorical structure and also for its ethical content.[16] Important as the language undoubtedly was, it was the subject matter that had to be considered and analysed, and always with an eye on the royal responsibilities the pupil would shortly be discharging. The general theme remained the same throughout – how do we identify and practise virtue? It was moral philosophy, or *mens humana,* which constituted the contribution of the pagan authors to the understanding of human goodness – the interaction of the Ciceronian cardinal virtues of *Prudentia, Justitia, Fortitudo et Temperentia*. Of course a Christian prince needed more, because no scheme of justice could be complete without recognising and practising the honour owed to God. That was where the study of the scriptures, and particularly the New Testament, came in, to create a due sense of the *beneficia Christi*.[17] None of Edward's surviving exercises are pieces of biblical exegesis, so it may well be that this instruction was given verbally and in English. Cheke was not a theologian, and it may have been either Cox or some other scholar nominated by Cranmer who undertook that responsibility. The court sermons, which the king is alleged to have taken such pleasure in, were a public aspect of that instruction, and the notes which he is known to have taken may have been intended to lead to analytical discussions with his teacher, or teachers.[18] From May 1551 Greek exercises begin to alternate with Latin ones in Edward's schoolbook, and we find him commenting upon quotations from Plato, and from Aristotle's *Ethics* and *Politics*. Always these quotations are to do with the nature of virtue, or of true nobility, and with the duty of rulers and governors to promote such sentiments and practices among their subjects.[19]

Cheke was pragmatic only up to a point. In the autumn of 1551 England was enduring an epidemic of that mysterious illness which has gone down in history as 'the English sweat'. Among many others, this epidemic carried off Edward's close friend, the sixteen-year-old Duke of Suffolk, and his fourteen-year-old brother, Charles Brandon, who were both at Cambridge at the time. On the 1 September the king meditated (in Latin) on the proposition *Ti mortem si cognescent ... sed potius gaudere et agere gratias deo qui eum ex his calamitatibisque liberavit* (If one knows death ... yet to believe and to give thanks to God will free him from these calamities). On another occasion he invoked the memory of his grandfather Henry VII as an example of a virtuous king who had freed his people from the tyranny and cruelty of Richard III.[20] However, by and large Cheke was not interested in modern history, or in contemporary politics. Ancient history, such as Xenophon's *Cyropaedia*, he was prepared to countenance, but when Ascham tried to convince him in December 1550 that the time had come for such a study, he replied that his young charge needed to acquire more judgement before tackling such a complex examination of human vice and virtue.[21] He might have added, but did not, that Edward's Greek was not yet up to such a test. It was partly the Earl of Warwick's conviction that the king needed a more practical regime of instruction, and above all some education in the daily arts of government and decision making, that brought the schoolroom to an end. It is perhaps significant that in the early part of 1552 Edward, now aged fourteen, began to sign his school exercises emphatically 'E.Rex' or 'Eduardus Rex', and after the last wrote 'Deo Gratia'. This may have been no more than a pious formality, but it looks suspiciously like a heartfelt expression of relief.[22]

The new regime was different in several important ways. As far as we know, Protector Somerset had never shown much interest in the king's schooling. He had trusted Cheke and Cox to get on with it, and although they probably gave him progress reports from time to time, there is no evidence that he interfered. The boy was instructed in music, and taught to ride and to fly his hawk, but his yearning for robust physical exercise was never particularly encouraged. The Earl of Warwick began to develop a much more 'hands on' approach, particularly after the young king turned thirteen in September 1550. Warwick was a soldier by training, and believed in encouraging Edward's interest in the martial arts. In March 1551 the king's journal records 'a challenge made by me that I, with sixteen of my chamber, should run at base, shoot and run at ring with any seventeen of my servants, gentlemen of the court',[23] and two days later, 'The first day of the challenge at base, or running, the King won.' On 6 April the same source records: 'I lost the challenge of shooting at rounds and won at rovers.' Such a challenge, involving nearly 40 men and four or five events, would have required a fair amount of organising, and no doubt reflected a victory for Warwick over the declining power of the king's tutor. However, it was eventually government rather than the tilt yard that brought Edward's academic instruction to a halt.

William Thomas was an Oxford graduate of minor Welsh gentry origin. His original patron had been Sir Anthony Browne, but like John Foxe at about the same time, he picked up some radical protestant ideas in Oxford in the early 1540s. As a result he fell out with his patron, and in 1545 took himself off to Italy. Unlike some Englishmen in a similar predicament, he seems to have made good use of his time there, writing an Italian panegyric on the death of Henry VIII, an Italian/English dictionary, and a history of Italy in English.[24] He seems to have returned to England in the summer of 1549, perhaps reassured by the progress of the reformation, and the history was published in London in September. Thomas was almost certainly in need of a new patron at this time, and astutely dedicated his work to the Earl of Warwick. We do not know if there had been any earlier connection between the two men, but in the latter part of 1549 the relationship developed rapidly, and Thomas was soon accepted as a prominent member of the Dudley affinity. In 1550 his dictionary was published at the suggestion of Sir Walter Mildmay, and in April of that year he was appointed as one of the Clerks to the Privy Council.[25] At some uncertain date, but before the end of 1551, Thomas began to write 'position papers' for the king on subjects of topical interest. These were almost certainly connected with the decision which Edward recorded in his journal under the date 14 August 1551, when he noted that it had been 'appointed that I should come to, and sit at, Council when great matters were in debating, or when I would'.[26] It seems that some meetings of the council thereafter were specifically intended to train the young king in the methods of royal business, although whether they were staged especially for that purpose (as has been suggested) is less certain.[27] Whether the Earl of Warwick had this idea, or whether it was suggested to him, either by Thomas himself, or by Nicholas Throgmorton, who has also been credited with establishing the contact between Thomas and the king, we do not know. However, the earl was clearly the moving force behind it. So Thomas's papers, which seem to have come at the rate of about one a week for a while, were part of a new educational strategy, directly aimed at preparing Edward for his public responsibilities. For about nine months this programme ran alongside the existing academic one, and according to the Venetian ambassador the boy never neglected his formal studies. However, there is no doubt that the emphasis had shifted substantially, and as Warwick increasingly encouraged Edward to 'play the king', his schoolroom became obsolete. At about the same time, in late 1551, Barnaby Fitzpatrick also went to the French court to acquire the necessary polish, and who was sharing the king's Greek studies early in 1552 is not apparent.[28]

As Edward's 'politics tutor', Thomas was indefatigable. He had a naturally didactic turn of mind, and wrote a dialogue on the proprieties (and otherwise) of female fashion, and an educational treatise of John of Sacro Bosco, as well as the various things he wrote for the king. At some uncertain date during 1552 he drew up a list of no fewer than 85 questions on matters political, ethical and military, drawn, as he says, from his current reading, which clearly included both *The Prince* and the *Discourses* of Machiavelli.[29] These questions ranged from the nature of political authority, and where it should be located, through the desirability of religious uniformity, to the nature of fortune, justice and virtue. It seems likely that the surviving document is a summary or list of questions posed over a period of time, probably in the regular essays which he was writing for Edward, as it would have been an extremely indigestible lump for a fourteen-year-old to have tackled in one go. In one sense, the subject matter is obvious enough, but it is interesting in the light of other things we know about the king and his training. The list ends up with the sweeping question: 'What is virtue, and when is it more esteemed?' This is almost exactly the same question as that posed by Cheke in his perambulations around Plato and Aristotle, and raises the natural suspicion that the two programmes were carefully integrated, and designed to provide answers from both ancient and modern authorities.[30] At the same time no fewer than eighteen questions relate to the waging of war, varying from 'What is the cause?' (q.42), through the conduct of war (43–50), logistics (51–6), and tactics (57–60), to the prince's personal armour (61). All these are recognisably drawn from Machiavelli, but they also reflect a keen awareness of Edward's consuming interest in things military. In addition, Thomas's five surviving position papers (we do not know how many he wrote) cover such practical matters as reform of the coinage, the dangers of inflation, how to negotiate with the French, and how much power should be allowed to the nobility.[31]

In all Thomas's work there is a recurring thread of moral relativism, clearly derived from Machiavelli. When is it legitimate for a prince to dissemble? Is the appearance of virtue more important than the substance? To what extent can virtue be adjusted to time and events? This is the antithesis of Cheke's approach, and it seems that the integration of the two programmes was the Earl of Warwick's idea, not the tutor's. In May 1552 Cheke appears to have been sufficiently concerned to write to his charge, urging him to turn back to the fundamentals set out in Aristotle's *Politics* and the New Testament.[32] Whether this disagreement had anything to do with his final return to Cambridge in the following month, or whether that had been long planned, we do not know. Nor is it entirely clear which of his two mentors had the most influence on the boy as he turned his back on childhood. Cheke's approach was much more integrated with his developing religious convictions, the reality of which should not be underestimated. On the other hand, Thomas (or Machiavelli) must often have seemed more directly relevant. Thomas also developed a conspiratorial tactic in dealing with the king, which showed an intelligent appreciation of his character. When proposing his scheme of weekly essays, he wrote to Edward that he would send these secretly,

> *that no creature living is or shalbe privy either to this or any of the rest*
> *through me, which I do keep so secret to this end, that your majesty may*
> *utter these matters as of your own study, whereby it shall have greater*
> *credit with your council.*[33]

Surprise your friends . . .! This was almost certainly disingenuous. A man in Thomas's relatively humble position (his only appointment was as Clerk to the Council) would not have ventured such a proposition without encouragement. It was a part of Warwick's educational strategy, not only for giving the king a firmer grasp of the realities of politics, but also to encourage him to play a more prominent role. How far Edward himself understood this, and how far he was deceived as to the substance of his own input into discussions and decision making, is not easy to determine. He certainly wrote his own papers, and six of these survive. One consists of notes on the English occupation of France in the reign of Henry VI, and whether that had any practical application is not clear, but the other five are specific – directed to the reform of abuses and the conduct of the council's business.[34] They range in date from the spring of 1551 to January 1553, the last being the most specific. Probably, like his journal, these were chiefly schoolroom exercises on his new modern syllabus; but the council at least pretended to take them seriously, and in the case of the last may actually have done so.

It is against this background that Edward's notorious 'Device for the succession' must be seen. It was written early in 1553, when Edward was already unwell, but not thought to be in any danger of his life.[35] Perhaps it was a companion piece to 'Certain Articles devised and Delivered' for the reform of council business, but whatever the circumstances of its composition, it was little more than speculation; as though Thomas had posed him the question, what would happen if you were to die without heirs? The answer should have been that his father's succession act would be adhered to, and that his half-sister Mary would succeed. However, that would then prompt the further question, can a statute determine legitimacy? And what would happen to the godly reformation? Edward had been brought up to regard both his half-sisters as illegitimate, not by the law of England but by the laws of God. In fact that was highly dubious, and could not in any case apply to both of them, but that is not the point.[36] The point is what the king thought when he was writing his memorandum. The other point is that Edward had an adolescent boy's contempt for the female of the species. There was no Salic Law in England, but he was determined that no woman should succeed – perhaps because he was aware of the lengths to which his father had gone in order to avoid such a contingency. So he starts his tour through the royal family tree with any son who might be born to Frances Grey, Duchess of Suffolk. Frances was the surviving daughter of Edward's aunt Mary, who had died in 1536. Her daughters were already adolescents and she had not conceived for years, so such a birth was hardly a real prospect. Edward then proceeded to the sons of the three daughters, Jane, Catherine and Mary, the eldest of whom was sixteen, and none of whom was married. He was clearly looking at a timescale of many years, and covered this by proposing that if he died before any son was born to these girls, then their mother should enjoy some kind of ill-defined regency until the magic feat was performed![37] His Scottish cousin Mary, the daughter of his older aunt, Margaret, was simply ignored. This was not real politics, and had it not been for the events of July 1553, no one would have taken it seriously. It is not even certain that anyone knew about it until much later, because it was not men-tioned in the parliament of March, by which time Edward's health was giving cause for concern. In short, it was a speculative doodle, arising from the fact that the young king was being encouraged to think about all manner of political issues as a part of his practical training in state-craft. Whether the Duke of Northumberland (as the Earl of Warwick had by then become) played any role in its drafting seems highly unlikely. If anyone saw it and commented upon it, it was William Thomas. Someone certainly knew of it, and drew it to Northumberland's attention later, probably in June when the king's declining condition made the succession not only a real problem, but an urgent one.[38] Either that person was Edward himself, or it was William Thomas.

The king's education was eventually altered significantly by the regime change of October 1549, but we do not know to what extent this was simply the result of Edward's development, and to what extent it was due to the different priorities the Earl of Warwick brought to his charge.

The same is true of the greatly increased level of activity visible in the Revels Office from 1551 onward. It is sometimes said that Warwick deliberately used the revels to distract the boy's attention from unpleasant realities, such as the execution of the Duke of Somerset, or his own rapacious plundering of the royal resources.[39] However, such a thesis is not consistent with what we know of his concern that Edward should be trained in dealing with real issues and real people. We also know that Warwick's alleged rapacity was greatly exaggerated by the creators of his black legend after his fall. So it may well be that the increasing incidence of masques, plays and tournaments was more connected with the need to teach a young monarch the meaning of *maiestas*, and his proper role as a master of revels, than with any more sinister intention.

The Christmas of 1549, and the Shrovetide that followed, were unremarkable. There were several masques and plays during the main holiday period, but not very much is known about them, beyond the fact that they were staged at Westminster. The Shrovetide play was provided by the king's own company, but we do not know what it was about.[40] The chances are that these were all 'in-house' entertainments, written and performed by members of the Household. A tense battle of wills within the council had been resolved only about a week before Christmas, and it may well be that all the main officers had other things to think about.[41] The time had not yet come when Edward's own wishes would count for very much. The following year was rather more lively. The Christmas saw no fewer than five masques, together with an unknown number of plays and other unidentified 'pastimes', performed both at Greenwich and at Westminster. The king and his 'young lords' took part, but we have no idea what roles they played, and no mention of the entertainment appears in the king's journal. Shrovetide 1551 saw a play of some kind at Westminster, but nothing else is known about it.[42] In March and early April the king staged his 'challenge', and in June Edward was elected to the French Order of St Michael, an honour which pleased him hugely. It may well have been some kind of entertainment provided especially for the French ambassador who came to present the Order that accounted for the revels at Hampton Court during July.[43] Edward reciprocated by conferring the Garter on Henry II, but those celebrations took place in France. This was a period of intense Anglo-French diplomatic activity, and a special banquet was provided at Hampton Court on 19 July. The ambassador, the Maréchal de St André, was a great success with Edward, who entertained him the whole of the next day with hunting, shooting matches, and a guided tour of the palace.[44] The king was learning the political uses of ceremony and festivity, and enjoying himself a good deal in the process. St André was entertained again on 23 July, and from the 26th to the 28th. He left on 3 August, well rewarded and with Edward's agreement to a marriage treaty with Henry's daughter Elizabeth.

At the end of October Mary of Guise, the Queen Dowager of Scotland, paid a state visit, and was lavishly entertained at the court, being received by a large company of noblemen and ladies, as was appropriate to her rank, and a 'great presence of gentlemen'. She stayed several days, at least one of which was consumed with 'dancing and pastime', but none of this appeared in the Revels' accounts, and it is not clear to what extent the king himself was involved.[45] This rising tempo was continued into the Christmas holidays, and it was the almost frenetic level of activity that prompted speculation about distracting Edward's attention. If that was the intention, it did not work, because the king's journal devotes far more space to the misdeeds of the Duke of Somerset than to any of the entertainments, except the tournament challenge which was eventually run on 3 January.[46] We know, however, that the King's Players performed on Christmas Day, and that no fewer than four masques were presented on Twelfth Night – a dialogue of riches and youth, a masque of Moors and Amazons, and two others, plus an interlude of unspecified content. This year, for the first time in the reign, there was a Lord of Misrule, George Ferrers being appointed to that essentially anarchic function. Ferrers apparently wrote the 'Drunken masque' which was presented on 2 January, and paid a ceremonial visit to the City of London on 4 January, accompanied by a substantial retinue. Ferrers had begun his court career as a page, and in his more sober moments was member of parliament for Plymouth, but he is best known for his antics at this time, which included making a ceremonial entry (within the court) out of an artificial moon.[47] One of the Twelfth Night entertainments clearly caught Edward's attention far more than the rest, because he described it at some length. This was the debate or 'talk' between youth and riches 'whether of them was better', which was followed (much more to the point) by the entry of 'six champions of either side [who] fought two to two at barriers in the hall ...'. This, he noted regretfully, was the end of Christmas.[48]

If there were Shrovetide revels in 1552, they are not recorded. From July to September Edward was on progress, and although he was undoubtedly entertained by towns and noblemen as he passed by, no record of such celebrations survives. The king's journal runs out at the end of November, but the Christmas celebrations of that year seem to have exceeded even the achievements of 1551.[49] There was another 'combat' of some kind early in the holidays, followed by hawking and hunting, and a burlesque 'Embassy to the King' organised by the Lord of Misrule on Christmas Day. Ferrers then made his own entry as Lord of Misrule on 26 December, accompanied by his full retinue, which cost a fortune for costumes.[50] On 1 January Ferrers was again in action, this time in a 'joust of the hobby horses', which was presumably a burlesque tournament of some kind, and on 4 January he made an entry into London, as he had the previous year. The holiday period altogether witnessed no fewer than six masques, four for men (Covetous men, 'Babions', Polanders and Soldiers) and two for women (Matrons and Women of Diana). All these took place at Greenwich, but we do not know who performed them. When professionals were employed, the fact was usually noted, so these were presumably the courtiers entertaining themselves. There is no reference to participation by either the king or his 'young lords'. The season concluded on Twelfth Night with a triumph, or play, of Cupid, Venus and Mars, again provided by the Lord of Misrule and his satellites, so this was probably also a burlesque.

There are a number of features of this last Christmas of the reign which call for comment. The first is their lavish scale. In 1551 there had been seven masques, two plays, two tournaments, an interlude and an entry. In 1552 there were at least six masques, and probably more, a triumph, three entries, two combats (one of them a burlesque), and a 'hunting'. These festivities were expensive, costing hundreds of pounds at a time when the council was making strenuous attempts to economise in other directions.[51] The second feature is the high profile – almost dominance – of George Ferrers, the Lord of Misrule. In 1551 he had appeared just once; in 1552 he appeared in one way or another in no fewer than nine entertainments. If the king was melancholic and in need of distraction, we have no direct evidence of the fact. In 1551 his uncle the Duke of Somerset was under sentence of death and awaiting execution, but Edward had never been particularly close to his Protector, and in any case seems to have been convinced of the genuineness of his guilt.[52] In 1552 he was beginning to ail, but nobody at that early stage knew that his illness was serious, and it was not until parliament opened on 1 March that his health required any significant change in the performance of his public duties.[53] Although he took part in both plays and masques, Edward never expressed any particular interest in them – unlike his detailed descriptions of combats and 'barriers' – so the answer is probably that he was learning how to preside over jollities of this kind, how to lead the applause and be gracious to the performers – all important parts of being a renaissance prince. In other words, the connection between education and entertainment was much closer than might be supposed. Whatever the reality may have been, all these festivities were deemed to have taken place at the king's command and for his own amusement, so he was learning how to be a king on holiday.

Apart from Ferrers, another name also occurs in connection with these entertainments which is worth a mention – that of Will Somers. Somers is best known as Henry VIII's favourite jester, and he first appears in the records of the court in 1535. He was paid no fee or wage, but all his personal requirements, down to his hose and buskins, his shaving and laundry, were met out of the Chamber accounts. In 1551 a warrant of Edward VI authorised a payment of 40s. to a certain William Seyton, 'whom his majesty hath appointed to keep William Somer'.[54] Such a statement would appear to be conclusive evidence of his status as an 'innocent', because no one was 'kept' who was deemed capable of keeping themselves. On the other hand, his reputation for apposite comment, both at the time and subsequently, suggests a personality which was eccentric or whimsical rather than deficient. He was close to Henry during the last years of his life, travelling regularly with the court, because he seems to have known instinctively how to avoid upsetting his volatile master.[55] Nothing is known of his activities while Somerset was in power, but he clearly remained at court, because he reappeared at Christmas 1550, the first festive season after the Protector's overthrow. He was then provided with a painted costume to take part in one or more of the masques, perhaps that for which the 'yrishe swordes' were prepared, which suggests his casting as a wild Irishman. In 1551 Will was cast as an attendant on the Lord of Misrule, and provided with several elaborate costumes of rich brocaded silk and satin, in addition to a gilded mace and chain.[56] During the same festivities the king apparently singled him out to take part in a mock combat, which Edward had devised himself. For this Will was provided with a 'harniss of paper boordes'; but whether this was a mark of favour or a piece of rather cruel mockery is not apparent.[57] He may well have played a similar part in 1552, but there are no specific references to his doing so. He remained at court during Mary's reign, and attended Elizabeth's coronation, but we have no idea what he was doing. He died on 15 June 1560 and was buried in St Leonard's Church, Shoreditch.

Unlike his father, and unlike Mary, Edward seems to have kept no other fools, or jesters, but whether this was a conscious decision (and if so, whose) is not clear. The Shrovetide festivities prepared for 1553 did not take place, but this does not seem to have been connected with Edward's declining health, because they were postponed and not cancelled. They took place instead at Easter and on May Day. This was an unusual season for revels, and they were again very elaborate, consisting of five masques and at least two plays. A masque of Greek worthies was fairly orthodox, but others of Bagpipes, Cats and Tumblers, to say nothing of 'Medioxes', look more unusual and imaginative. One of the plays was written by John Heywood and was performed by the Children of the Chapel; another, by William Baldwin, was about the state of Ireland – presumably a satire, given the context.[58] By the time these shows were staged, the king was seriously unwell, and whether he even saw them is not certain. They may have been intended to raise his spirits, but it seems more likely that they were a determined attempt to present a façade of 'business as usual'. If there was any educational purpose behind them, they came too late. Easter Day was on 2 April in 1553, and three months later Edward was dead.

It is not to be expected that a boy of his age, whose parents were dead and who lived surrounded by calculating adults, would have an easy personality to read. His words were almost always reported for a purpose, and he was trained from an early age not to disclose his real feelings about anything. Everyone flattered him for their own purposes, except his sister Mary, for whom he retained a grudging respect. The most revealing document, as far as it goes, is his journal, or chronicle, which he started keeping in March 1550 and ended in November 1552. This was almost certainly a deliberate product of the Warwick/Thomas phase of his education, and was intended to be a practical *aide-memoire* rather than an intimate personal record. The original manuscript consists of 68 carefully written folios in the king's immaculate italic hand, and is probably a fair copy made from notes kept day by day.[59] As Professor Jordan, its most recent editor, observes, the record of events before March 1550 was probably compiled in one (or two) sections once the decision had been taken to keep such a record, and represents Edward's prompted memory, while the rest is more authentically his own reaction to events as they happened.[60] Not too much should be read into its rather detached tone, because Edward had been taught a stoical attitude towards his own feelings and emotions. Events which touched him personally, like the death of his grandmother in October 1550, go unnoticed, and his brief dismissal of the executions of both his Seymour uncles has often been commented upon. Apart from a brief reference to his friend Barnaby Fitzpatrick, whose return from France was hardly a matter of public concern, the whole document is a disciplined statement of events and deliberations. It is much more useful as a source for the history of the reign than for any analysis of Edward's personality. Events at court are described, but only when they were of an official nature, such as the restructuring of the Privy Chamber in October 1549, or the regular movements from place to place, which are meticulously recorded.

Edward's chronicle is therefore more a reflection of his training than of his character, and does not help us to answer the critical question of how important the king had become in the statecraft of his own reign by the time of his premature death. In one respect at least there is a clear answer. The uncompromising nature of Edward's protestant faith can be clearly seen throughout. At first it could be represented as no more than a reflection of ideas being regularly instilled by his tutors, but by the summer of 1550 a personal note was beginning to creep into his exchanges with Mary which the latter persistently failed to recognise. Her declared position was that she would obey the king in all things once he achieved his majority, but until then he could not be expected to understand the mysteries of the faith, and she would take his religious policy as being that of the council and not of himself. An attitude more calculated to anger a young Tudor who was just beginning to seek ways of asserting himself would be hard to imagine.[61]

The creation of the image of a godly prince is a theme which runs persistently through the reign. It was built up by court preachers and official propagandists alike. These sermons are a subject in themselves. The identity of most of the preachers is known, and some of their efforts became deservedly famous. Hugh Latimer was a favourite, and his sermons were lovingly collected and published. John Foxe's *Actes and Monuments* was later embellished with a woodcut of him preaching before the young king, a tableau which made a major contribution to the boy's godly credentials. The lack of reference to these sermons in the journal might be thought suspicious, but we have it on Nicholas Ridley's testimony that it was after one of his own efforts that Edward was so moved by his description of the plight of the London poor that he summoned the lord mayor, and ordered that the old royal palace of Bridewell should be converted into a workhouse and correction centre.[62] It would be unwise to construe the king's own lack of direct comment as evidence of what would now be known as 'spin'. The ideas would have been totally familiar to him: a commonwealth flourished when the righteous reigned (Proverbs 28:12); subjects should honour their king (1 Peter 2:17); disastrous consequences would follow if a king countenanced idolatry (2 Kings 17:18–23); and so on. This arose partly from the need, which all Tudor governments felt, to instil habits of obedience, and partly from a desire to consolidate the Royal Supremacy. However, it also arose from genuine religious convictions about the nature of kingship which it is quite clear that Edward himself shared. The clearest evidence that we have begins with the Lenten sermons of 1550, and it is impossible to separate the ideals of kingship which the boy was learning from the classical moralism of John Cheke from the vision of a godly commonwealth which was being promoted by these preachers.[63]

Consequently, one of the most important aspects of the Earl of Warwick's regime as president of the council was his promotion of a strong protestantism, and that depended less upon his own convictions than upon his reading of the king's mind. He knew his young master as well as anyone, and was as sure as he could be that if he wished to retain the favour of the adult king, it could only be by that means.[64] Events were to show that his own professions of godliness would not stand up to pressure, but in this respect the real Edward and the promoted image are one. How such convictions might have stood up to the temptations of a Machiavellian *realpolitik* must remain an unanswerable question, but the reality of the young king's commitment to them should not be doubted.[65]

Notes and references

1 *The Chronicle and Political Papers of King Edward VI*, ed. W.K. Jordan (London, 1966), p.3.

2 *Dictionary of National Biography*.

3 L.V. Ryan, *Roger Ascham* (Stanford, CA, 1963), p.303. Ascham had presented Edward with a copy of his *Toxophilus* (treatise on archery) in 1545.

4 M.Dowling, *Humanism in the Age of Henry VIII* (London, 1986), pp.212, 218.

5 J. Loach, *Edward VI* (London, 1999), pp.17–28.

6 'pour ce qu'il n'entend encores bien francoys et ne faict que commencer a l'apprendre'. *Correspondance politique de Odet de Selve, ambassadeur de France en Angleterre (1546–1549)*, ed. G. Lefevre-Pontalis (Paris, 1888), p.105.

7 This was François de Scepeaux: *Memoires de la vie de Francois de Scepeaux, sieur de Vielleville*, pp.xxvi–xxvii, in *Collection complète de memoires relative à l'histoire de France*, ed. C.B. Petitot (Paris, 1822). There is some evidence that Edward either knew, or was expecting to learn, some Spanish, because Sir William Pickering presented him with a popular Spanish book in 1550. Loach, *Edward VI*, p.13.

8 PRO, E101/426/8, m.4.

9 T.W. Baldwin, *William Shakespeare's Small Latin and Less Greek* (London, 1944), vol.1, pp.237–56.

10 *Chronicle*, ed. Jordan, pp.5–6.

11 Ibid., pp.7–9.

12 *Documents Relating to the Office of the Revels*, ed. A. Feuillerat, vol.1 (1914), p.xii.

13 Ibid.

14 *Documents*, ed. Feuillerat, vol.1, pp.35–43.

15 Edward's exercises survive in a number of manuscripts: BL, Harley MS 5087, Add. MS 4724, Arundel MS 510; also Bodley MS 899. On Cheke's role in Edward's education, see Dowling, *Humanism in the Age of Henry VIII*, *passim*.

16 Dowling, *Humanism in the Age of Henry VIII*, pp.112–23; *The Literary*

Remains of King Edward VI, ed. J.G. Nichols (Roxburgh Club, 1857), vol.1, pp.cli–clii.

17 BL, Add. MS 4724, fol.6.

18 For some doubts about Edward's alleged enthusiasm for sermons, see Loach, *Edward VI*, p.181. The absence of references to them in his chronicle suggests that attendance may have been prescribed by his tutors, rather than *sua sponte*.

19 Baldwin, *Small Latin*, vol.1, p.247.

20 BL, Add. MS 4724, fol.34. For Henry VII, see ibid., fols.74–5.

21 *Literary Remains*, ed. Nichols, I, pp.cli–clii.

22 BL, Add. MS 4724, fol.75; Baldwin, *Small Latin*, vol.1, p.243.

23 *Chronicle*, ed. Jordan, p.57. For Dudley's approach to Edward's education, see D.M. Loades, *John Dudley, Duke of Northumberland* (Oxford, 1996), pp.191–5.

24 *Chronicle*, ed. Jordan, pp.xx–xxi. The date of Thomas's return to England is highly uncertain, as he seems to have acted as a courier for Sir Philip Hoby. Susan Brigden, 'Letters of Richard Scudamore to Sir Philip Hoby', *Camden Miscellany*, 30 (1990), pp.39, 124.

25 *RSTC* 24020; *Chronicle*, ed. Jordan, p.25.

26 *Chronicle*, ed. Jordan, p.76.

27 D.E. Hoak, *The King's Council in the Reign of Edward VI* (1976), pp.154–5; Loades, *John Dudley*, pp.191–5.

28 Barnaby was admitted as a gentleman of the Privy Chamber on 15 August, which signalled the end of any involvement in the schoolroom. On 7 October he was appointed to go on a diplomatic mission to France, and on 6 December was accepted into the French king's Privy Chamber. *Chronicle*, ed. Jordan, pp.77, 82, 102.

29 BL, Cotton MS Titus B ii, fol.84. Printed by J. Strype, *Ecclesiastical Memorials*, 3 vols. (Oxford, 1822), vol.2, pt1, p.156. The 'Book of John de Sacro Bosco on the Sphere' survives as BL, Egerton MS 857, fols.2–4.

30 For the king's meditations on the Ciceronian virtues, see BL, Add. MS 4724, fol.14. The congruence of the two schemes on this point is inescapable.

31 BL, Cotton MS Vespasian D xviii, fols.2–45. Printed by Strype, *Ecclesiastical Memorials*, vol.2, pt1, pp.372–93.

32 Baldwin, *Small Latin*, vol.1, p.239.

33 BL, Cotton MS Vespasian D xviii, fols.2–45; Loades, *John Dudley*, p.201.

34 Printed in *Chronicle*, ed. Jordan, pp.159–90.

35 Loades, *John Dudley*, pp.231–3. The original MS is Inner Temple Petyt xlvii, fol.316 *et seq*. It is printed in full in *Literary Remains*, ed. Nichols, vol.2, pp.571–2.

36 Mary was alleged to be illegitimate because Henry's marriage to Catherine of Aragon was judged to be contrary to the scriptural prohibition laid down in Leviticus. If that judgement was upheld, then Elizabeth was legitimate. If it was rejected, then Mary was legitimate, and Elizabeth was a bastard born in a bigamous marriage.

37 *Literary Remains*, ed. Nichols, vol.2, p.572: 'If I died wtout issu, and there was none heire masle, then the L.Fraunces to be govvernes ...' This would have been a position unknown to English law or custom.

38 Loades, *John Dudley*, pp.238–41.

39 *The Life and Raigne of King Edward the Sixth by John Hayward*, ed. B.L. Beer (Kent, Ohio, 1993), pp.144–5.

40 Fueillerat, ed. *Documents*, vol.1, 40. The cost was a meagre £8 2s. 1d.

41 There was alleged to have been a plot by conservative councillors, led by the Earl of Southampton, to implicate the Earl of Warwick in Somerset's misdeeds, and to get rid of both of them. See below, pp.86–7.

42 Feuillerat, ed., *Documents*, vol.1, p.xii.

43 *Chronicle*, ed. Jordan, pp.71–3; *Documents*, ed. Feuillerat, vol.1, p.55.

44 *Chronicle*, ed. Jordan, p.73; Loach, *Edward VI*, pp.107–8.

45 *Chronicle*, ed. Jordan, pp.91–2. The main task of hosting seems to have fallen to the Marquis and Marchioness of Northampton.

46 Ibid., pp. 97–100, 103–4.

47 *Documents*, ed. Feuillerat, vol.1, p.89.

48 *Chronicle*, ed. Jordan, p.105.

49 *Documents*, ed. Feuillerat, vol.1, pp.76–83.

50 The total cost of the 1551 Christmas ran to nearly £900, of which the Lord of Misrule spent £299 5s. 5d. Christmas 1550 had cost just £14 17s. 2d.

51 *Documents*, ed. Feuillerat, vol.1, pp.114–25. Christmas 1552 cost a staggering £1,120, of which the Lord of Misrule accounted for £717 10s. 9d.

52 Loach, *Edward VI*, pp.102–5.

53 Loades, *John Dudley*, p.237. The ceremony was held in the royal apartments at Whitehall, instead of the Palace of Westminster.

54 *Literary Remains*, ed. Nichols, vol.1, pp.xliv–v. For a full discussion of Somers and his role at court, see John Southworth, *Fools and Jesters at the English Court* (Stroud, 1998), pp.70–80.

55 Ibid.

56 *Documents*, ed. Feuillerat, vol.1, pp.67, 73, 77.

57 Ibid., p.73; Southworth, *Fools and Jesters*, pp.76–7.

58 *Documents*, ed. Feuillerat, vol.1, pp.xiv, 144–5.

59 *Chronicle*, ed. Jordan, pp.xiii–xxiii.

60 Ibid.

61 For slightly different discussions of Mary's confrontations with her brother and his council, see D.M. Loades, *Mary Tudor: A Life* (Oxford, 1989), pp.158–9, 162–3, and Loach, *Edward VI*, pp.130–4.

62 *Literary Remains*, ed. Nichols, vol.1, p.clxxx. For a testimony to the effect that Edward was personally inviting some preachers with extreme views, see *CSP Spanish*, 1550–52, p.63.

63 Loach, *Edward VI*, pp.180–4

64 Loades, *John Dudley*, pp.200–2.

65 For one (well-informed) opinion on this point, that of Jennifer Loach, see *Edward VI*, pp.180–4.

CHAPTER 4

. . . .

The politics of the court, 1550–3

S ir Michael Stanhope fell with his brother-in-law and patron. He was one of a dozen or more adherents of the Protector who were arrested at Windsor on 10 October. On the 22nd he was in the Tower, along with William Gray, Sir Thomas Smith and Sir John Thynne. All were shortly after released, and William Cecil, who seems to have been held in separate custody for a while, was soon in favour with the new regime.[1] Although there were early signs that some of his allies were after Somerset's blood, Warwick had no intention of proceeding to extremities, and it may be deduced that this was part of the terms upon which the Protector had surrendered. However, the Privy Chamber now required urgent attention, and on 14 October, when Edward returned from Windsor to Hampton Court, a new structure was immediately put in place, 'by my consent' as the king primly recorded. The Groomship of the Stool and the office of Principal Gentleman were abolished, and in their place six Lords of the Council and four knights were appointed to 'be in attendance'.[2] The lords were to work a shift system, two on and four off, but the knights seem to have been expected to be there all the time unless their absence was licensed. The names of those appointed are an indication of Warwick's determination to control access to the Privy Chamber, and to have no more nonsense of the kind that had been wrought by Thomas Seymour. The six lords were headed by the earl himself, who was already Lord Great Chamberlain, and he was joined by the Marquis of Northampton, the Earl of Arundel (Lord Chamberlain), and Lords Russell, St John and Wentworth. The four knights were his brother Andrew, Sir Edward Rogers, Sir Thomas Darcy and Sir Thomas Wroth.[3] The changes that subsequently took place in this team were to be a barometer of court politics over the next two years.

In January 1550 there was a major reshuffle, when Arundel was dismissed from both the court and the council and spent some time under house arrest. Lord Wentworth briefly replaced him as Chamberlain, and Lord Clinton (probably) as a lord attendant when he returned from Boulogne.[4] At about the same time Rogers was replaced as one of the knights by Warwick's close adherent Sir John Gates. Sir William Paget had played an important part in negotiating the settlement of October, but had been too close to Somerset for Warwick's liking. He was raised to the peerage in November 1549, and consequently lost the relatively humble office of Comptroller of the Household. It was generally thought that he was destined for the chamberlainship, but that did not happen and instead he lost his foothold in the court altogether. In April 1551 Darcy moved up from Vice-Chamberlain to Chamberlain, replacing Wentworth, who had died in March, and Gates took over his former office.[5] Whether Gates was then replaced as a knight attendant is not clear, because the structure established in October 1549 seems to have been abandoned by the end of the reign, although no decision to that effect is recorded.

Most of these changes arose from the power struggle within the council which succeeded the coup of October. There had at first been a considerable nervousness among the victors, as if they did not fully trust Somerset's surrender. Their anxiety was not without foundation, because although the Protector had no intention of going back on his word, and there was no armed force immediately available to challenge the council victory, nevertheless wheels had been set in motion which could have led to a repetition of the events of the summer.[6] Consequently the council which met at Windsor on 13 October was almost uniquely complete. Twenty-four members attended, including the four who had been recruited on the immediate eve of the confrontation, on 6 October. This was intended, and understood, as a demonstration of unity, and the despatch of Somerset and his henchmen to the Tower on the following day eased the immediate tension. It was, however, by no means clear what form the new government would take. The offices of Lord Protector and Lord Treasurer were now vacant, but neither had been abolished.[7] It was possible that a new incumbent might emerge, and there seems to have been some talk (again) of offering the regency to Princess Mary. Neither of these solutions was very likely to be acceptable. In theory the *de facto* annulment of the Protector's patent meant that the executive power had reverted to the fourteen surviving executors of Henry VIII's will, but in practice it was vested in the council as that assembled at Windsor on 13 October. There was no clear individual leader, and no obvious agenda beyond the need to defend Boulogne against French assault and repress any further signs of civil unrest. The late Protector's pleas for mobilisation were cancelled, and everyone was instructed to remain peaceably at home, but even the immediate appointments to the Privy Chamber did not send out any very clear signals. Northampton, Wentworth, Sir Andrew Dudley and Sir Thomas Darcy were adherents of the Earl of Warwick; but that was certainly not true of Arundel and Rogers, and not at this point of St John, Russell and Wroth.[8] The touchstone of policy was religion. Diplomatic observers generally believed that one of the main reasons for Somerset's downfall had been the unpopularity of his protestant policies. Van der Delft, the imperial ambassador, in particular, was certain that 'the restoration of true religion' had been one of the main purposes of the coup. On 17 October he reported optimistically:

> *every man among them [the council] is now devoted to the old faith, except the earl of Warwick, who is none the less taking up the old observances again day by day, and it seems probable that he will reform himself entirely, as he says he hopes his elder son may obtain some post in your majesties court . . .*[9]

Cranmer, he believed, was only being tolerated until he could be got rid of in a seemly manner. Whether intentionally or accidentally, Van der Delft had been completely misled. There was no enthusiasm for what he would have regarded as 'true religion'. Some councillors, notably the Earls of Arundel and Southampton, would probably have preferred a return to the Henrician settlement, but (unlike Mary) neither had made their conservatism very conspicuous. Warwick may well have dropped a few sweet words into the ambassador's ear, because he was still hoping for the emperor's assistance to defend Boulogne, but whoever detected a return to the old ways in religion appears to have been deceived. Whether the earl was biding his time, or still hoping for the preservation of consensus, is not clear. Edward was now twelve, and the strength and direction of his religious convictions were emerging more clearly by the day. Moreover, it is probable that Warwick's bargain with Somerset, which had been brokered by Cranmer, had included an undertaking that the reformation would continue. Most of the council had not been privy to this deal, for obvious reasons, but it was a promise that would mean the end of the consensus of 14 October.

The calm was eventually disrupted by a political storm which began to blow at the beginning of November. The focus of this disruption was Sir Thomas Arundel. Arundel appears to have been a client of the Earl of Southampton, but whether he was acting as the earl's agent or on his own behalf is not clear. He set out quietly to broker a deal between the council and Princess Mary, but since he was neither a member of the council nor of the princess's household, the status of his negotiation must be in doubt.[10] Van der Delft heard at one point that he was trying to enter Mary's service, and at another that there was a move afoot to make him a councillor. Although neither Southampton nor the Earl of Arundel were catholics in the Roman sense, they certainly regarded Cranmer and his reforming ideas with distaste, and had probably hoped that Somerset's fall would put the brake on his activities. Sir Thomas Arundel was a stronger conservative than either of them, and his appointment to the council would probably have signalled a campaign against the archbishop. Whether it would also have led to a Marian regency is much more doubtful. The case for having an identifiable head of the executive was as strong as ever, given the king's age, and now that the Protector had gone there was no question of the princess soiling her hands with conspiracy. However, Edward's reaction would probably have been unrepeatable, and Mary herself allegedly disclaimed all interest in such a position, as she had done before.[11] The moves in this opening skirmish have to be reconstructed because the evidence is indirect, but it seems that Warwick and his allies became suspicious of Sir Thomas and his activities. In the words of an Elizabethan commentator, at the beginning of November Warwick 'procured by the means of the Archbishop of Canterbury, great friends about the king'.[12] No one was more 'about the king' than Warwick himself, so this is somewhat misleading, but it probably reflects the fact that Dudley and Cranmer, perceiving a threat, decided to strengthen their hold on the council. Sir Thomas's promotion was blocked, and on 6 November Thomas Goodrich, Bishop of Ely, was sworn instead. Goodrich was a protestant, and his promotion not only strengthened the reforming party within the council, it also sent a signal to the conservatives that their manoeuvres had been observed.[13]

Van der Delft, as usual, was a little behind the game. As late as 7 November he still believed that the Earl of Southampton was 'head' of the council, and was increasingly puzzled by the absence of any decisive action against the 'heretics'. At the same time protestants outside the council, who had been fearing precisely the reaction for which Van der Delft had been hoping, began to pick up the same signals. John Hooper noted with cautious optimism that there had as yet been no 'alteration'; and Richard Hilles wrote to Henry Bullinger on 17 November, 'we are hoping that Christ may yet remain with us'.[14] There were no fireworks, and no open hostility, but as November advanced it became increasingly clear that whatever agreement the conservatives thought they had with the Earl of Warwick, it was not delivering according to their expectations, and they were steadily losing control of the situation. Southampton ceased to attend meetings after 21 October, allegedly for reasons of poor health, and Sir Edmund Peckham, another conservative, disappeared after 30 October, no reason being given. Towards the end of November the Earl of Warwick was also indisposed, with 'a rume yn the hedd', but far from suspending his attendance, he had the council wait upon him, as it did at Ely Place on 27 November. Two days later Henry Grey, Marquis of Dorset, another protestant ally of Warwick's, was sworn, and his recruitment gave the council that slight but critical further tilt which meant that Dudley was now clearly in control.[15]

There was as yet no open rift, and according to one well-informed source as late as 5 December Warwick was still planning to work with the conservatives. The intention at that date was that he would take the vacant Lord Treasurership himself, move the Earl of Arundel into the Great Chamberlainship, and promote the newly created Lord Paget as Lord Chamberlain. However, the fact that this was Warwick's plan, and we have no idea what Arundel or Southampton thought of it, should inject a note of caution. It may indicate no more than that Dudley was taking his ascendancy a bit for granted.[16] The crisis which then followed again has to be largely reconstructed from later (and not entirely disinterested) testimony. Early in December the Earl of Southampton, who had clearly recovered from whatever indisposition had afflicted him during November, was pressing hard for the imprisoned Duke of Somerset to be executed, 'being hote to be rewenged . . . for old groges paste whan he lost his office'. Van der Delft, who clearly got his information from the conservative group at court, believed that the former Protector was certain to lose his head.[17] Nor did the former chancellor's intentions stop at that. Before they had fallen out in the summer of 1549, the Earl of Warwick had been one of Somerset's closest adherents, so if the former Protector could be successfully accused of treason for the misuse of his office, Dudley would also be heavily compromised. According to the source already cited, Southampton had delivered himself of the verdict that he 'thoughte ever we sholde fynde them traytors both, and both worthy for to dye by my advyse'. We should, however, beware of taking this at face value. Even if the Earl of Southampton was as consumed by the desire for revenge as is stated, he can hardly have expected to overturn Warwick's majority in the council so dramatically.[18] Unaware of Dudley's understanding with the duke, Southampton and his allies (because several other councillors, including the Earl of Arundel, were parties to the scheme) probably intended to discredit Warwick by association, and clip his political wings. Once the plot had failed, he was of course wide open to accusations of seeking the deaths of both his enemies, but it is by no means certain that he intended to go so far – or could realistically have expected to do so.

In the event, his scheme was betrayed by Lord St John, who was also a conservative, but one with a keen sense of political survival. As soon as he was approached, he made his way to Ely Place and told Warwick what was afoot.[19] The timing of these moves is highly uncertain, and several different attempts have been made to reconstruct them, but it seems likely that St John acted about 9 or 10 December. According to the same source, Warwick then staged a dramatic showdown. On a date which can be tentatively established as 11 or 12 December, he summoned the council to meet at his London home, again on the pretext of ill health, but probably to put his adversaries at a disadvantage. Southampton allegedly walked straight into the trap by openly proposing Somerset's trial 'for so many high treasons'. Whereupon the Earl of Warwick, 'with a warlike wisage and a long fachell by his side, laye his hand thereof, and said: my lord you seek his bloude, and he that seekethe his bloude woulde have myne also'.[20] We need not take this high drama at face value, but there was clearly a confrontation of some kind in which Warwick made it clear that he would not countenance extreme measures against the late Protector, and knew that he was strong enough in council to prevent them. On 13 December Somerset signed a list of 31 articles of submission, and this signified that the crisis over his fate (if there had ever been one) had been resolved. On the 19th Van der Delft noted that it was now generally believed that the duke's life would be spared, although he makes no reference to any dramatic confrontation, and nor does the usually well-informed Richard Scudamore, writing on the 26th.[21]

Whatever drama may have taken place behind the scenes, the public outcome of these moves was decisive. On 25 December the council issued a proclamation affirming its commitment to the Act of Uniformity, because certain 'evil disposed persons' had been spreading reports that 'they should have again their old latin service, their conjured bread and water, and suchlike vain and superstitious ceremonies'.[22] On 14 January an Act for Somerset's 'fine and ransom' passed its final stages. He made his own formal submission on the 27th, and was released a few days later. On 19 January Lords St John and Russell were advanced to the earldoms of Wiltshire and Bedford respectively, and at about the same time Arundel and Southampton were ordered to vacate their chambers at court, and were placed under house arrest in London.[23] The king, having noted Somerset's submission, recorded laconically: 'The earl of Arundel committed to his house for certain crimes of suspicion against him, as plucking down bolts and locks at Westminster, giving of my stuff away etc.' – in other words, abusing his office as Lord Chamberlain.

If that is what Edward was really told, it is clear that he was still a long way from understanding what was going on around him.[24] On 16 January Sir Thomas Darcy was sworn of the council, followed ten days later by Walter Devereux, Lord Ferrers, another protestant. On the 30th Sir Thomas Arundel and his brother Sir John were committed to the Tower 'for conspiracies in the west parts', and at about the same time Sir Richard Southwell 'for certain bills of sedition written with his hand'. Southwell, one of the conservatives who had been introduced in October, lost his place on the council, and Arundel and Southampton were formally expelled on 2 February.[25] At the same time Warwick assumed the presidency of the council, and it is clear that, whatever lay behind it, a second coup had been staged, less dramatic than the first, but equally decisive. By January 1550 Edward had a new protector, in fact although not in name. The fact that Warwick chose not to assume the obvious titles available to him is indicative of the approach he was already adopting to the exercise of power. The Lord Treasurership was granted to the new Earl of Wiltshire on 3 February 1550; the Lord Great Chamberlainship, which he had held since February 1547, was passed to the Marquis of Northampton. The office of Lord Admiral, which he had resumed on 28 October 1549, was vacated in favour of Edward, Lord Clinton, on 14 May 1550. The offices of Lord Protector and Governor of the King's Person were abolished. Warwick chose instead to exercise his political power through the undefined (and hitherto fairly obscure) office of Lord President, and to control the court through the rather more obvious position of Lord Great Master, which William Paulet vacated on becoming Lord Treasurer.[26]

In spite of the fact that Edward was still a schoolboy, Warwick was not anxious to draw attention to his tutelage. As we have already seen in connection with his educational strategy, his policy was to encourage the king to take an active interest in public affairs, and to make it appear that the boy was exercising a personal influence well before he was actually doing so.[27] His intention seems to have been to effect a seamless transition from Regent to Chief Minister when Edward attained his majority in September 1555. Any formal protectorate would obviously have come to an end at that point, but the presidency and the Lord Great Mastership would continue, unless the king chose otherwise. No one was deceived as to where power really lay in 1550 or 1551, and some very interesting observations recorded by Boisdauphin, the French ambassador, late in 1551 or during 1552 reflect the perception that prevailed at court. Edward, he declared,

> revered him as if he were himself one of his subjects – so much so that the things which he knew to be desired by Northumberland he himself decreed in order to please the Duke, and also to prevent the envy which would have been produced had it been known that it was he who had suggested these things to the king.[28]

This ascendancy, the account went on, was preserved partly by placing his own familiars about the king (Sir John Gates, Vice-Chamberlain in 1551, was named), and partly by constant visits to the Privy Chamber, even to the king's bedroom during the night. If there was anything of particular importance that he wanted Edward to do or say, he would resort to this latter tactic 'unseen by anyone'. The last statement suggests exaggeration. There were supposed to be two gentlemen of the Privy Chamber sleeping on pallets in the royal bedchamber, and if the duke did succeed in removing them for his own purposes, how did Boisdauphin's informant come by his information? We should probably gloss this report as 'well-informed rumour'; but that a close, and even affectionate, relationship really existed is likely enough.[29]

John Dudley used his personal influence over the young king in a number of ways. He steered his education, as we have seen. He also manipulated the court in the same way that he did the council. The comings and goings within the Privy Chamber, for example, although not without regard to the king's wishes, were authorised by the Lord Great Master. The Duke of Somerset returned to court at the end of March 1550, and was readmitted to the Privy Chamber on 15 May, at the same time as Lord Clinton, who was a close ally of Warwick's.[30] There seems to have been, on the earl's part at least, a genuine attempt at reconciliation. A few days later, on 3 June, Warwick's eldest son, Lord Lisle, married Anne Seymour, the duke's daughter, with seemly celebrations which included a masque and the inevitable 'course of the field'. Just three days later the seventeen-year-old Robert Dudley, no longer the king's schoolfellow, wedded Amy, the daughter of Sir John Robsart of Norfolk, again to the accompaniment of tilts, without which, it is clear, Edward did not believe any celebration to be complete.[31] Meanwhile, on 18 April Henry Sidney and Henry Neville were admitted as 'ordinary' gentlemen, and two days later significant steps were taken to prevent unauthorised access to the king: 'Order taken', Edward noted,

> that three of the outer Privy Chamber gentlemen should always be here, and two lie in the palat [truckle beds in the king's bedchamber] and fill the room of one of the four knights; that the esquires should be diligent

in their office, and five grooms should be always present, of which one
to watch in the bedchamber.[32]

This may have been intended to relieve the knights of some part of a bur-
densome task, but the impression given is one of heightened security. At
this stage there seem to have been six lords, and the four knights decreed
in October 1549 had metamorphosed into four principal gentlemen, but
the number of ordinary and extraordinary gentlemen and grooms is
unclear. By the time of the king's death three years later there were thirteen grooms, but the number of gentlemen was still uncertain.[33]

The next change was a purely natural one, occasioned by the death of
Lord Wentworth, the Lord Chamberlain, on 3 March 1551. A month later
Sir Thomas Darcy was created Lord Darcy of Chiche, and promoted to fill
the vacant office; Sir John Gates stepped up as Vice-Chamberlain a few
days later, as we have seen. Both Darcy and Gates were close associates
of the Earl of Warwick.[34] On 22 July Henry Sidney was promoted to be
one of the four principal gentlemen, although it is not clear whom he
replaced, and about a fortnight later Sir Robert Dudley and Barnaby
Fitzpatrick were sworn as 'two of the six' ordinary gentlemen. This is the
only reference to the latter being specifically limited in number; certainly
by the end of the reign the group was considerably larger.[35]

Although such gentlemen were selected to form an harmonious
group, and one of their duties was to protect the king from the rough and
tumble of the court at large, this did not always work. In March 1552
there was an altercation in the Presence Chamber, and Lord Abergavenny
was imprisoned for striking the Earl of Oxford, an offence which could
have cost him his right hand, so seriously was violence in the royal presence taken.[36] Nor were the gentlemen necessarily confined to service at
court. Sir Anthony St Leger served no fewer than five terms as Lord
Deputy of Ireland, two of these during Edward's reign, when he was also
on the Privy Chamber list.[37] In December 1551, between his fourth and
fifth tours of duty, he was actually suspended from his Privy Chamber
position because of a complaint laid against him by the Archbishop of
Dublin. The complaint was not eventually upheld, and he was reinstated
in April 1552.[38] Several of the most senior members of the Privy Chamber
were also councillors, and the reforms of October 1549 had been partly
designed to strengthen that link, so it is clear that the Earl of Warwick's

intention was for the two teams to overlap, and for their work to be closely integrated. He had no desire to see the Privy Council and the Privy Chamber pulling in opposite directions, as had happened in the early 1540s. In October 1551 Henry Neville and Barnaby Fitzpatrick were sent with Lord Clinton on a diplomatic mission to France. This was partly to signal the king's personal endorsement, which was thought to be desirable since Clinton was actually being sent by the council, and partly to give them the benefit of the experience. Henry VIII had often used his gentlemen as personal envoys, and although that was not quite what was being done here, the effect was rather similar.[39] Barnaby remained behind when the mission returned, and was admitted, almost certainly at Edward's request, as an extraordinary gentleman of Henry II's Privy Chamber. He was recalled eventually in September 1552, no doubt having acquired some of the gloss for which the French court was famous.[40] It may well be that Edward was missing his company, because, as we have seen, the schoolroom had come to an end in the summer, and on 27 September the Young Lords' table in the Chamber was wound up. This was represented (to the king at least) as an economy measure, but seems rather to have been another piece of symbolic punctuation as Edward progressed towards his majority.[41]

Although the secondment of Barnaby Fitzpatrick was a minor matter to everyone except the king, the more general role of the court in the diplomacy of the period was of the highest importance. The war which Henry II had launched for the recovery of Boulogne in August 1549 had not succeeded according to his expectations because the English remained strong at sea, but once he was securely in power, the Earl of Warwick decided to cut his losses. Being resolved to continue with the protestant reformation, he rightly judged that friendship with the emperor was not a realistic option. The war was also cripplingly expensive. Therefore, by a treaty of 24 March 1550, Warwick sold Boulogne back to the French, and set out to establish an *entente cordiale*. Henry endorsed the treaty on 10 May, and regular diplomatic contact was resumed. On 25 May a French embassy arrived in London to witness Edward's ratification, and was sumptuously entertained for five days with banquets, tilts and hunting trips. There were fireworks and 'many pretty conceits', as the king noted.[42]

Relations continued to improve. In July Henry released the Scottish prisoners taken at St Andrews Castle in 1547, 'for my sake' as he claimed to Edward, and in April 1551 he accepted election to the Order of the Garter. In the following month the compliment was returned with the Order of St Michel, and while an English mission was in France during June, carrying out the Garter investiture, the question of Edward's marriage was raised for the first time.[43] The Marquis of Northampton, who was leading the English mission, started out by inviting French assistance to secure the union with Mary of Scotland that had originally been agreed in 1543. This was rejected, as he must have known it would be, on the grounds that Mary had been betrothed to the dauphin since 1548. He then followed this by requesting the hand of Elizabeth, Henry's eldest daughter, 'to which they did most cheerfully assent'. There was obviously a lot more to it than that, and a prolonged haggle over the dowry then followed; however, an agreement in principle had been reached.[44] In July the high watermark of Anglo-French amity was reached in the visit of the Maréchal de St André. The official purpose of the visit was to invest Edward with the Order of St Michel, a ceremony which pleased the young king very much, but St André was an amiable soul and a most accomplished courtier, and he made a far bigger personal impact than his formal instructions might have suggested. He remained from 6 July to 3 August, and Edward's chronicle records his entertainment, and the conversations between them, in surprising detail. So charmed was the king that his generosity knew no bounds, and when the maréchal departed he was richer to the tune of £3,000, while his entourage absorbed another £2,500.[45] There was clearly more to this than a personal charm offensive upon a thirteen-year-old boy, but the involvement of Edward in these diplomatic exchanges should not be underestimated. He believed, and was encouraged to believe, that his activities as a host made a real contribution to the establishment of the alliance, and up to a point that was true. While he was wining and dining the Maréchal de St André in and around London, in France the Marquis of Northampton was settling his matrimonial destiny, and on 19 July came away with 'a treaty sealed'.[46]

That was the end of important business for the time being, but in order not to lose the momentum of the amity that had been established, at the beginning of September the resident French ambassador sought audience to explain the worsening relations between his master and the emperor, and to seek English protection for Mary of Guise, the Queen

Mother of Scotland, on her return from France to that country.[47] All this was in marked contrast with the visits of the imperial ambassadors, first Van der Delft and then Scheyfve, who kept up an endless litany of threats and complaints about the king's treatment of his sister Mary. Mary, as we shall see, was a serious embarrassment to the council and a great source of irritation to her brother. Her visits to the court were few, and extremely reluctant, because she totally rejected the religious changes that were not only the policy of the council, but also the personal objectives of the king.[48] However, the renewal of war between Henry and Charles in the middle of September took some of the sting out of the emperor's threats. However hostile he may have been to the English council, he had no desire to acquire another enemy. At the end of October Mary of Guise, perhaps 'driven by storms' as she claimed, or perhaps not quite trusting English and French naval protection, landed at Portsmouth to take advantage of the safe conduct issued earlier, and to return to the north overland. Her journey was granted the status of a royal visit, and as she gently moved northward during October, the gentlemen of each county dutifully turned out to escort her. On the 31st she reached Hampton Court, where the nobility of England turned out in strength. Edward was not there, but on 4 November he received her as his guest at Westminster, and recorded the ceremonial in some detail:

> At the gate there received her the Duke of Northumberland, Great
> Master, and the Treasurer and Controller and the earl of Pembroke, with
> all the sewers and carvers and cupbearers to the number of thirty. In the
> hall I met her with all the rest of the Lords of my Council ... and from
> the outer gate up to the presence chamber on both sides stood the
> guard. The court, the hall and the stairs were full of serving-men; the
> presence chamber, great chamber and her presence chamber, of
> gentlemen; and so, having brought her to her chamber, I retired to mine.
> I went to her to dinner ...[49]

Mary obviously brought her own retinue with her on a similar scale, because her *maitre d'hôtel* presided over her service, and 'In her great chamber dined at three boards the ladies only'; and she wasn't even staying overnight! Mary was no particular friend of the English, and there was unresolved business in Scotland, but this is an excellent example of the political use of protocol, and of the kind of honour which only the king could provide. It was *maiestas* in the service of the state. It was also the last occasion upon which this tactic was deployed. The marriage treaty with France was ratified in France at the beginning of December, but never took effect. On 28 March 1552 Edward recorded: 'I did deny after a sort the request to enter into war'. This was a council decision, based upon economic realism, but it appears to have chilled relations sufficiently to have frustrated the marriage.[50] Relations with France remained friendly, not least because of the threat which the emperor posed to both, but there was no repetition of the joyful scenes which had greeted the Maréchal de St André, and no royal wedding.

Like every other Tudor, Edward moved his court restlessly, seldom remaining in one place for more than a month, and often for only a week or so. In the autumn of 1550, for example, he moved from Oatlands to Nonesuch on 8 September, and then returned to Oatlands on the 15th. On 4 October he went to Richmond, and on the 16th to Westminster, remaining there until he went to Greenwich for Christmas on 21 December.[51] The reasons for this were mainly practical. The palaces needed to be cleaned and aired, particularly in the summer, because the full court numbered some 600 or 700 people. Sanitation was rudimentary, and hygiene unknown. There was also the question of provisioning. Even at Westminster, which was 'headquarters', too long a stay could place a strain upon the commissariat; and smaller palaces, like Oatlands, were difficult of access, although the court resident there would inevitably be much smaller. There was also the matter of showing the king to his people. Edward was too young to go on long hunting trips, and not sufficiently independent to 'take off' occasionally, as his father had been wont to do. So, except for those living close to one of the main palaces, 'moving days' offered their best chance for a glimpse of their young sovereign. Edward had a total of over 60 houses, the most distant of which was in Newcastle-upon-Tyne, but he visited only a small proportion of them, most of which were in a tight circle around London, Westminster, Windsor, Richmond, Greenwich and Hampton Court being the most frequented.[52] He went twice on progress, in 1550 and in 1552. If the 'gestes' set out for the former on 8 June were followed, it would hardly have been noticed as a progress, because apart from a brief visit to Guildford, and possibly Woking, it simply padded round the familiar circuit: Greenwich, Westminster, Hampton Court, Windsor, Oatlands, Richmond.[53] How long this tour lasted, or was supposed to last, is not clear from the king's chronicle, which is less meticulous than usual about recording moves, but a visit to Guildford is noted on 12 August, after which the court returned to Oatlands.

What seems to have been the most memorable event of the summer had nothing to do with any progress, but consisted of a visit to Deptford on 19 June, where the Lord Admiral provided a supper and entertainment. Edward's description was almost breathless with excitement:

> After supper there was a fort made upon a great lighter on the Thames, which had three walls and a watchtower in the midst of which Mr [William] Winter was captain, with forty or fifty other soldiers in yellow and black. To the fort also appertained a galley of yellow colour with men and munition in it for the defence of the castle. Wherefore there came four pinnaces with their men in white handsomely dressed, which, intending to give assault to the castle first drove away the yellow pinnace, and after with clods, squibs, canes of fire, darts made for the nonce, and bombards, assaulted the castle; and at length came with their pieces and burst the outer walls of the castle, beating them of the castle into the second ward, who after issued out and drove away the pinnaces, sinking one of them, out of which all the men in it, being more than twenty, leaped out and swam in the Thames . . .[54]

and so on until the castle was eventually taken. The fact that he described this relatively trivial scene with such gusto, and recorded the executions of each of his Seymour uncles in a single line, raises some interesting questions, about both the king and his chronicle.

The progress of 1552 was quite different, and much more purposeful. Edward had never been more than 30 miles from London, and this tour was intended to be the first of a series which would introduce him to different parts of the realm. The idea was to travel by easy stages to Portsmouth, and to return by way of Poole and Salisbury.[55] He set out from Hampton Court on 15 July, and went to Guildford. From there on the 21st he removed to Petworth, at that time also in the hands of the crown, and by the time the royal party arrived there it was clear that a problem was developing. The king's enormous retinue required almost 4,000 horses, and there was simply not enough provender along the route that had been chosen.[56] Nearly 350 men-at-arms, in fourteen separate 'bands', had originally been appointed to provide the escort. Whether this had been the result of genuine fears for the king's safety, or simply competitive display among his nobles, is not clear, but on 23 July it was decided to dispense with all but 150 of these men, and four 'bands' were sent home.[57] Which noblemen suffered this affront to their dignity is not clear, but the problem seems to have been resolved. The following day the court moved on to Cowdray, where Sir Anthony Browne provided hospitality so lavish that even the king considered it excessive. From Cowdray Edward wrote to his friend Barnaby, describing this magnificent reception.[58] Two days later he moved on to Halnaker, Lord La Warr's seat near Chichester, but we know nothing of his stay there, although it lasted until 2 August. He then set off again, travelling fairly swiftly by way of Sir Richard Cotton's house at Warblington, and one of the Lord Treasurer's residences at Bishop's Waltham, reaching Portsmouth on 8 August.[59]

In spite of the town's acknowledged importance as a naval base, Edward spent only one full day in Portsmouth, inspecting the fortifications, and on the 10th moved on to Titchfield, a new house at that time belonging to the seven-year-old Henry Wriothesley, Earl of Southampton, who had succeeded his father two years before and was a ward of the crown. On the 14th Edward removed to Southampton itself, although it is not clear where he stayed. Appropriately, it was at Southampton that the French ambassador caught up with the court, with news of the latest developments concerning commercial disputes at issue.[60] On the 16th Edward proceeded to Beaulieu, another Wriothesley property, where the ambassador again sought audience to deliver good news of his master's wars in Italy. At this stage the court was moving regularly, every two or three days; on 18 August it was at Christchurch, and on the 21st at Sir Edward Willoughby's seat at Woodlands in Dorset. The projected visit to Poole seems not to have taken place, because on the 24th the king moved on to Salisbury. En route the Duke of Suffolk abandoned the progress, having received urgent and disturbing news of his wife's health, as he explained in a hasty note to William Cecil a couple of days later.[61] The city fathers of Salisbury did their best to make their sovereign welcome, but did not make enough impression to merit a mention in the chronicle. On the 28th the court reached the Earl of Pembroke's converted abbey at Wilton, and on 2 September Lord Sandys' house at Mottisfont in

Hampshire. Over the next two weeks a similar schedule was maintained: Winchester on the 5th, Basing House on the 7th, and Donnington Castle near Newbury on the 10th. The king had a house of his own in the converted monastery at Reading, which he reached on the 12th, and the whole journey concluded at Windsor, which was reached on the 15th.[62]

Whether this considerable effort and expenditure had been in any sense worthwhile is hard to judge. We do not even know whether the king was greeted with loyal rejoicings or sullen indifference. There seem to have been no incidents to alarm Edward's diminished escort, and as far as the councillors accompanying the court were concerned, it was business as usual. Apart from Cowdray, and a brief description of Portsmouth, the king recorded no impressions, favourable or otherwise. It seems reasonable to suppose that he was not entertained with jousts or other war games, because these he would almost invariably comment upon. He may simply have been bored by the endless gatherings of obsequious country gentlemen, but he had at least been put on show. Hundreds of men and women who would never go anywhere near the court now knew what their monarch looked like, and may even have overheard a few of the things he said. For his part, he had seen a great tract of England which he had never seen before, and that was a benefit, even if he was not particularly impressed. It was his only chance, because by the following summer he was far too ill for such journeys.

During the whole of John Dudley's ascendancy, both as Earl of Warwick and as Duke of Northumberland, the issue of security was never far below the surface. Thomas Seymour had mocked the Protector's efforts, such as they were, and even during the disturbed summer of 1549 no additional precautions seem to have been taken, although both the guard and the pensioners were placed on full alert.[63] Somerset probably perceived that whatever threat the insurrections may have posed to the council, or to individual gentlemen, there was no danger of an assault on the court. In this respect, as in others, the October coup took him by surprise. He took 500 harnesses from the armoury at Hampton Court 'to arm both his and my men withal', and when the royal party reached Windsor 'there was watch and ward kept every night'. Interestingly, the council seems to have been more concerned for the king's personal safety in that crisis than the Protector was. They encouraged some of the guard, who had not been with the court on 6 October, to go to Windsor 'fearing the rage of the people so lately quieted', in spite of the fact that this might result in some strengthening of Somerset's position.[64] Of course it was also consistent with their own propaganda position, which represented the risings as being directed against all authority, and they may well have believed that there was tension within the castle between the king's men and the duke's. After Somerset's surrender his men were banished from the king's presence, and presumably disarmed.

During the winter of 1549–50 no further precautions were deemed to be necessary. The forces which had still been in existence at the time of the coup were either demobilised or, like the German mercenaries, despatched to other theatres of operation – the north, Calais or Boulogne.[65] How many men the Earl of Warwick may have retained, and whether they were a factor in his success during November and December, is not at all clear. However, in April 1550 there was a dramatic new development, when licences of retainer were issued to all members of the Privy Council, and 'certain of the Privy Chamber' who were not councillors, to retain between them 2,340 men. This was a new strategy, and in some ways harked back to the previous century, because Henry VIII had set his face firmly against relying on private bands of this kind except in time of war. Some 30 individuals were involved, so the bands would not have been very large, but their existence placed a heavy premium upon the continued unity of the council, and that may have been the point.[66] It was an important aspect of Warwick's strategy to rebuild aristocratic solidarity as the best means of safeguarding the regime against any repetition of the 1549 troubles. He believed that these had arisen because the government was sending out ambiguous signals, and that this had encouraged troublemakers to take the law into their own hands. He was therefore very keen that parliament, the council, the court and the pulpit should all send out the same message: no matter what the pretext, no defiance of authority would be tolerated. There is no suggestion that all these bands would have been mobilised at once, except in an emergency, and the conditions which were attached to their existence are not clear, so the perception that the court would have resembled an armed camp is probably an exaggeration.[67] They should rather be seen as a contingent reserve which could be quickly and easily mobilised should the circumstances require it. Nor is there any reason to suppose that the scheme was linked in any way with the return of the Duke of Somerset to the council, which took place the next day. He would not have been rehabilitated if he had been thought to pose any threat at this stage, and he was to be frequently deployed over the next two years in support of the council's security programme.[68]

In other words, the scheme of retaining was a precaution against the possibility of another long, hot summer, along the lines suggested by Sir Thomas Wyatt in his memorandum of 1549.[69] On 20 June the watches in London were strengthened, and an alderman put in charge each night 'because of the great frays'. Two days later a search was made in Sussex for all 'vagabonds, gypsies, conspirators, prophets, ill players and such like', and on the 24th a conspiracy (nature unspecified) was broken up at Romford in Essex.[70] On 13 July Sir John Gates was sent into Essex, presumably with some support, 'to stop the going away of the lady Mary', a somewhat bizarre adventure which had already been abandoned before the council got wind of it. The idea, which had been blessed by the regent of the Netherlands, Mary of Hungary, rather than the emperor himself, was that an imperial warship should lie off Malden on the pretext of chasing pirates, and that Jehan Dubois, the ambassador's secretary, should contrive the princess's escape from nearby Woodham Walter, and ferry her out to the ship. At the very last minute Mary changed her mind and the idea was abandoned on 1 or 2 July.[71] The council was informed swiftly, but not swiftly enough to have stopped it had it gone ahead, and the incident set up an alarm which rumbled on for some time. On 16 July 800 men under the leadership of Somerset, Bedford and St Leger were sent 'to the seacoast', presumably to support Gates's efforts and to prevent any fresh attempt. Neither the people of Essex, nor Mary herself, could have had any doubt about the seriousness of the council's intentions.[72] Whether these troops were part of the 'household reserve', or raised specially for this purpose is not clear. There is a lot of uncertainty about these limited deployments. On 8 July Edward had noted: 'It is agreed that the two hundred [men] that were with me, and two hundred with Mr. Herbert, should be sent into Ireland'; the 'two hundred with Mr. Herbert' were presumably his share of the 'household reserve', but who the king's 200 may have been is not clear.[73] They cannot have been the ordinary yeomen of the guard, who never numbered more than 180, and were not deployed away from the court. That they were 'semi-professional horse', as Professor Jordan claims, is little more than guesswork.

Still concerned about lurking imperial warships, on 27 July some of the king's ships were 'put in readiness', but the birds had long since flown. Mary herself, 'after long communication', was persuaded to visit Leighs to discuss her situation with the Lord Chancellor, but 'utterly denied' to come to the court, perhaps because she feared that she would not be allowed to leave.[74] There was still tension in the air, and at the end of July the Duke of Somerset 'went to set order' in Oxfordshire, Sussex, Wiltshire and Hampshire. It must have been a hasty tour, because he was back at court before 6 August, when he was sent to Reading on a similar mission.[75] Whether he could actually have accomplished anything in so short a space of time, or whether these 'missions' were merely intended to demonstrate his commitment to the new order is not clear.

There was no further excitement that summer, although the magistrates in Norwich were still picking over the detritus of the previous 'camping' movement with more than a little anxiety, and no doubt their colleagues elsewhere were doing the same.[76] Virtually nothing had been done to address the grievances that had caused such disruption in 1549, and discontent still simmered. Some 2,500 aristocratic retainers could have done little to contain the situation if it had again been allowed to get out of hand, but they did constitute a demonstration of intent, and the show of solidarity which Warwick managed to orchestrate successfully did the rest. Mary continued to be a nuisance, and in December several of her chaplains were arrested for saying mass, presumably in her absence because that was not covered by her unofficial dispensation, but there was no further confrontation until the following year. On 20 December, however, a further 'band' was authorised, this time of 700 horsemen. The basis was the same as for the retainers licensed in the spring: 100 for the Duke of Somerset, and 50 each for twelve other named councillors and members of the Privy Chamber.[77] These appear to have been replacements for the earlier retainers rather than additional to them, and it is probable that the cost was borne from the first by the crown. Someone, probably the Earl of Warwick, had decided that a much smaller number of properly equipped men-at-arms would be more effective than the rather amateurish retainers, and that control was better concentrated in fewer hands. This band seems to have constituted the 'gendarmerie' later referred to.

The problem of Mary and her mass did not go away, and in a sense it got worse. Attempts had continued to be made, both by direct persuasion and by the harassment of her chaplains, to induce her to abandon her high-profile opposition. Nothing worked, and in March 1551 she was summoned to Westminster. This time she came, but did not, apparently, see her brother. The council told her that they were not interested in her conscience, but that as a subject she must obey the king's laws – the more so since she was a very prominent subject.[78] Mary clearly did what she had done before, and complained immediately to the imperial ambassador. The next day Scheyve appeared, threatening war on the emperor's behalf 'if I would not suffer his cousin the princess to use her mass'. The council consulted Cranmer and Ridley, who advised them that whereas to license sin was also sin, 'to suffer and wink at it for a time might be borne'.[79] On the strength of this advice an embassy was sent to Brussels 'to win some time', not least because some important commercial transactions were going on with Flanders, including the purchase of gunpowder and harness for the gendarmerie. In fact Scheyve, having been put on the spot by Mary, had exceeded his instructions, and Charles was by no means ready to launch instant war. The uneasy stand-off was allowed to continue, although to save face the council did clamp down on others who were defying the Act of Uniformity, including Sir Anthony Browne, who ended up in the Fleet prison.[80] By this time the new gendarmerie was taking shape. The Marquis of Dorset, having been appointed Warden General of the Northern Marches, handed over his band to the Lord Treasurer, and the Earl of Rutland took over the 50 men who had 'belonged' to the recently deceased Lord Wentworth.[81] On 5 May a muster of the whole force was commanded which took place on 1 June, by which time presumably the armour ordered in Flanders had arrived.

Apart from some rather obscure alarms in Essex and London during May, which came to nothing, there was no need to deploy it at this time; but a further brush with Mary during June over the arrest of one of her chaplains created a fear that her escape attempt of the previous year might be repeated. On 1 July there was an alarm that imperial ships were at sea off the east coast, and six ships and four pinnaces which had earlier been prepared against such an eventuality were ordered to sea.[82] It turned out to be a false alarm. However, the confrontation with Mary continued. During August Robert Rochester and other of her household officers were sent to the Tower for refusing to support the council's pressure on their mistress, and on the 29th the naval patrols off the east coast were re-instated. On the same day the Lord Chancellor and other members of the council visited the princess at Copthall, armed with personal letters from the king. Mary professed to treat the letters with great respect, but dismissed the councillors with angry and contemptuous words, refusing to accept that her brother was any party to their proceedings.[83]

On 4 September Scheyve called again, but this time he met with an interestingly different response. Having heard him out, the Earl of Warwick declared that on a matter of such importance the king would have to be consulted, and bade him return for an answer the next day. When he came back, he found the council far from intimidated. He had spoken, he was informed, without commission (again), as was clear from the shortness of the time that had elapsed, and in any case it was none of the emperor's business how the king dealt with his sister. 'He was willed no more to move these piques ...'[84] Scheyve's own report glossed over this rebuff. He was told, he reported, that the king was insisting that his laws be obeyed. Edward had just turned fourteen, and the ambassador must have allowed his scepticism at this display of engagement to become visible. The king, Warwick told him sharply, had as much authority as if he were 40, whereupon Scheyve wisely responded that he had no commission to discuss the limits of the king's power, and gracefully withdrew. He had, however, provoked a most interesting comment on Warwick's methods, a clear articulation of what can otherwise only be deduced from his manner of handling the later stages of the boy's education.[85]

The alarms over Mary's (and the emperor's) intentions in the summer of 1551 thus came to nothing, as they had done the previous year. However, by October a fresh crisis was looming, and this had nothing to do with the princess. On the 8th a letter was sent out to all the captains of the gendarmerie to muster on 8 November, and on the 11th there was a major batch of peerage promotions.[86] The Marquis of Dorset became Duke of Suffolk, the Earl of Warwick Duke of Northumberland, and the Earl of Wiltshire Marquis of Winchester. Three members of the Privy Chamber, Henry Sidney, Henry Neville and John Cheke, were also knighted, as was William Cecil. At the same time a conspiracy was declared. There was to be what can only be described as a mass assault on the gendarmerie at their planned muster. Two thousand men led by

Sir Ralph Vane, Sir Thomas Arundel and Sir Miles Partridge, supported by an unknown number of Londoners, were planning to launch a surprise attack, 'and all the horse of the gendarmerie should be slain'. The beneficiary of this slaughter, and the man alleged to be behind the plot, would be the Duke of Somerset.[87] Somerset, it was claimed, had been hankering and scheming to recover power, deceiving himself that he still enjoyed the king's confidence and affection. As we shall see, all this was highly specious, and the reality seems to have been that Warwick was determined to be finally rid of the man whom he continued to regard, for whatever reason, as a serious threat. In this context the peerage and other promotions look like an attempt by Warwick to strengthen his position at the last moment before striking. Somerset and his alleged accomplices were rounded up on 16 and 17 October and consigned to the Tower.[88] The musters were put back to 7 December, when the king reviewed about 1,000 horsemen in St James's Field, including 'the [gentlemen] pensioners and their bands, with the old men of arms, all well armed men', and admired their great horses. The yeomen of the guard, being footmen, were not mustered, but this array included all the rest of the 'household troops' as they existed at that point.[89] There was no attack, possibly because the ringleaders were already in prison, but more likely because one had never been intended.

Some rearrangement of the gendarmerie followed over the next few months. The band of 100 that had belonged to the Duke of Somerset was reassigned to the Duke of Suffolk. Interestingly, no doubt seems to have been cast on their loyalty. The Duke of Northumberland handed over 50 of his 200 to his son the Earl of Warwick. In February 1552 an additional band of 50 was assigned to Sir Ralph Sadler.[90] On surrendering his office as Master of the Horse to the Earl of Warwick in April, the Earl of Pembroke also handed over 50 of his band of 120, 25 being allocated to Sir John Gates and 25 to Sir Philip Hoby. A fresh muster was held on 16 May 1552 which excluded these last three bands, and also the pensioners who had appeared in December.[91] This was clearly a less impressive display, but then the Duke of Somerset had been executed in the meantime, and not even Northumberland pretended that there was any longer a major domestic threat. Partly for that reason, and partly because of the cost – all these men-at-arms were paid for by the king – when Edward returned from his progress in September it was decided to dispense with the gendarmerie. On the 26th letters were sent out, discharging them with effect from Michaelmas, just three days later.[92] This looks like a sudden decision, but it may not have been given that it coincided with a number of other cost-cutting operations around the court. Neither the guard nor the pensioners were affected, so from the beginning of October the court reverted to the traditional security arrangements. Trusted councillors and courtiers continued to receive licences to retain, but these were no longer specifically linked with any need to provide protection for the king. Anxiety about the royal debt was acute in the autumn of 1552, and although it was recognised that both the navy and the garrisons of Calais and Berwick needed to be properly maintained, the expensive bands of German and Italian mercenaries were discharged at the same time as the gendarmerie.[93] One consequence of this was that when the next crisis came in July 1553, after the king's death, the Duke of Northumberland had only his own retainers to rely on, because neither the retainers of his allies nor the remaining Household troops could be trusted to serve his purposes.

For whatever reasons the enhanced security measures of 1550–2 were put in place, they were never tested in any real emergency. During the 'camping summer' of 1549 and the conspiracy that followed it, when the court could easily have come under attack, only the pensioners and the normal guard were in place. By the time that Northumberland was attempting to install Queen Jane, the gendarmerie had been long since disbanded. Perhaps the success of the provision can be measured precisely by the fact that there were no large-scale disturbances in the summers of 1550–2. If the council could deploy nearly 3,000 of its own retainers, plus some 900 professional men-at arms, that may well have been sufficient to deter any rising within reach of London. It would also have demonstrated a unity and strength of purpose which would have had the same effect. In other words, the gendarmerie was a successful deterrent.

The other specific reason which has been adduced for these precautions is much more problematic, and that is the threat allegedly presented by the Duke of Somerset.[94] As we have seen, Somerset had been released early in 1550, and the bulk of his estates had been returned to him. He had been readmitted both to the council and to the Privy Chamber, and on 3 June 1550 his daughter Anne had married Warwick's eldest son.

This was far more generous treatment than the Earls of Arundel or Southampton had received, and indicates that at least in the first half of 1550 the Earl of Warwick was seeking reconciliation and cooperation. However, barely eighteen months later he set up what can only be described as a cynical plot to bring his rival to execution. At first, the duke was treated as a reliable ally. He was given 200 men to lead, and he was used in the late summer of 1550 to 'set an order' in several counties which seemed to threaten trouble.[95] He was appointed Lord-Lieutenant of Berkshire and Buckinghamshire, and as late as August 1551 was executing (apparently by martial law) those who 'began a new conspiracy for the destruction of the gentlemen at Wokingham'.[96]

The reasons why Warwick changed his mind have to be reconstructed from miscellaneous pieces of evidence. It may be that at first he was doing no more than honouring the undertakings he had made in October 1549, although it is unlikely that the reassurances he offered at that stage would have extended beyond personal safety and some return of land. More likely, in 1550 he was looking for a genuine collaboration, but on his own terms. Somerset was given no major office, either in the state or in the court, and the main features of his policy as Protector were slighted. He had done his best, against the odds, to maintain friendly relations with the emperor, seeing the principal threat as coming from France. In this connection he had dealt gently with Mary, and although refusing her any official licence to flout the law, had been prepared to make private undertakings. Mary had not responded to his restraint, causing mass to be celebrated with especial (and very public) splendour on the day when its use became illegal.[97] The Protector had also taken very seriously the complaints of the 'commonwealth men', with their endless accusations of greed and self-interest against just about everybody upon whom the functions of government depended. This sympathy had earned him the title of 'the Good Duke' among the protesters and malcontents, and had been one of the principal causes of his downfall.

Warwick reversed all these priorities. Having made peace with France over Boulogne, he courted the friendship of Henry II, a policy which enabled him to adopt a much more cavalier line with Charles V. This was immediately reflected in a hardening of attitudes towards Mary, who came under severe pressure and twice contemplated running away. Although he had no desire to get drawn into a war, or to attract a trade embargo in the Netherlands, he rightly judged that Charles did not wish to use those sanctions either, and eventually, in an acrimonious exchange over the princess's continued defiance, told the emperor to mind his own business. Charles's reaction was to advise his protégé to make some concessions in order to preserve the core of her freedom, and that – reluctantly – she did.[98] Above all, Warwick withdrew from the Protector's hazardous social policies. There was no dramatic reversal – no wholesale repeal of the traditional anti-enclosure legislation – but he caused parliament to cancel Somerset's controversial sheep tax, and conceded limited rights of enclosure in certain circumstances.[99] These signals were sufficient to indicate that Warwick was running a 'gentleman's government', and that his predecessor's attempts to implement a policy of social justice in accordance with his own vision were at an end.

Understandably, Somerset was not happy. Only Warwick's continued support for the protestant reformation pleased him, and even there he began to share Cranmer's misgivings as the earl moved closer to such radicals as Hooper and Knox. What he did about it, however, is a different matter. The testimony later taken against him is so obviously flawed that it is hard to know whether there was any truth in it at all. The duke was accused of plotting to marry his younger daughter to the king, to overthrow the rule of Warwick and his friends, and even to have some of them murdered. He was going to raise the City of London in his own interest, even to usurp the throne.[100] In fact he probably did talk to some whom he judged to be his friends about the possibility of reversing the coup of 1549, and even of taking advantage of Warwick's growing unpopularity to place him under arrest. If so, it was hardly serious politics, given the way in which the earl had reshaped both the council and the Privy Chamber to reflect his own control. A violent assassination might have been feasible, but could hardly have had the looked-for results. He may very well have harboured ambitions for a return to power, and talked illadvisedly, but the real reason for his second and fatal fall was the profound suspicion and hostility which he succeeded in arousing in Warwick. After the spring of 1550 relations between the two men (and their committed adherents) declined steadily.

The first move seems to have been made on 7 October 1551 when Sir Thomas Palmer (it was later alleged) went to the Earl of Warwick and 'declared a conspiracy':

How at St George's Day last [23rd April], my Lord of Somerset (who was then going to the North if the Master of the Horse, Sir William Herbert, had not assured him on his honour that he should have no hurt) went to raise the people, and the Lord Grey before, to know who were his friends ...[101]

In the same statement Palmer also alleged that Somerset had plotted to kill Warwick and Northampton at a banquet, although neither date nor place were mentioned. Four days later, on 11 October, the duke took his proper place in the courtly ceremonials surrounding the elevation of Henry Grey and John Dudley to the dukedoms of Suffolk and Northumberland respectively. Palmer apparently made a further statement on the same day, embellishing his charges with accusations of a planned attack on the gendarmerie musters, which we have noticed. There was no immediate reaction to these charges. They leaked into court gossip, although by what means we do not know. On the 14th this gossip reached Somerset himself, who tried unsuccessfully to find out what was going on, and Palmer apparently retracted his charges.[102] That did not defuse the mounting tension, and on the 15th the court removed to Westminster 'because it was thought this matter might easilier and surelier be dispatched there'.

The following day Warwick and his agents moved. Somerset came to court as usual, worried but no doubt thinking that absence would be taken as evidence of guilt, and was arrested after dinner. In a concerted operation, about a dozen of his adherents were taken in as well, including Palmer 'on the terrace walking there', and Lord Grey 'coming out of the country'. Sir Ralph Vane was found lurking under the straw 'in a stable of his man's at Lambeth'.[103] It was an efficient swoop, and over the next few days netted a further dozen, including the Duchess of Somerset, Sir Miles Partridge and Sir Michael Stanhope. On the 19th Palmer embroidered his original testimony about an attack on the gendarmerie, claiming that if he (presumably Somerset, although this is not clear) were overthrown in that attack, he would run through London crying 'Liberty, liberty to raise the prentices', adding rather inconsequentially that if he could he would go to the Isle of Wight or Poole.[104]

This whole farrago comes from the king's journal, and no doubt reflects what he was told, but we cannot even be sure that Palmer made the original charges attributed to him, because he denied them later under cross-examination. In fact, it appears from the details of some of the confessions elicited that the driving force was not Somerset himself but the Earl of Arundel. Arundel admitted conferring with the duke, and expressing his dissatisfaction with Warwick's policies, but nothing more.[105] The most sweeping accusations were made by William Crane, in his examination of 26 October. According to him, Warwick and Northampton were to have been ambushed at Lord Paget's house, 'and had their heads stricken off'. He elaborated. Stanhope was the main intermediary between Somerset and Arundel; efforts were still being made as late as August 1551 to stir up support for the duke; and others of Somerset's servants had been keeping 'watch and ward' in the hope of a chance for action.[106] Crane was almost certainly lying in an effort to save his skin, and the assassination attempt was never pressed as a formal charge. However, Lord Strange deserves to be taken rather more seriously. Strange was something of a favourite with Edward, and was handled with kid gloves. So when he said that Somerset had urged him to press a marriage between the king and his younger daughter, he probably spoke the truth, although what he admitted was mere presumption, not a crime – much less treason. More revealing was his further admission that Somerset had willed him to be his 'spy' in the court, reporting (among other things) the private conferences which the king had with members of his council.[107] Although himself a member of the Privy Chamber, the duke knew well enough that this did not mean that he could come and go as he pleased, and in any case he was far too conspicuous for clandestine eavesdropping.

What emerges from these confessions and examinations is the picture of a disappointed statesman hovering on the fringes of a political life to which he believed he should be central, disgruntled at having his advice ignored, and increasingly paranoid about his own security. He had no doubt spoken indiscreetly about abuses of power, and about the country going to rack and ruin, and he may well have proposed a parliamentary campaign to unseat Warwick and place him under arrest. He was, in short, about as guilty of treason as the Marquis of Exeter had been in 1538, or the Duke of Norfolk in 1546; but he was seen to constitute a threat. The real danger which he represented was more subtle than anything that was alleged. The danger of his staging a counter-coup was minimal, but he still had a substantial following, not only among the commons but among the aristocracy, and because of that he could have sabotaged the united front that Warwick was taking such pains to present to the outside world.[108] Open divisions within the council could have been a disaster to the fragile minority government, and rather than risk having his work undermined, Warwick decided to strike his opponent down with a battery of largely fictitious charges.

A very brief announcement of the duke's arrest was sent out to justices of the peace, probably on 17 October, with strict instructions to prevent any 'stirs' or demonstrations.[109] At the same time an official explanation was issued for the benefit of the ambassadors. This made much of the assassination plot, and of the scheme to seize control of London. When some incredulity was expressed, Northumberland blandly admitted that he could not understand it himself. Somerset was one of the richest subjects of the crown, so what could he be hoping to gain?[110] According to Scheyfve, the moves against the former Protector were very badly received; no one believed in his guilt. However, Scheyfve had come to regard Somerset as something of an ally, because of his hostility to Northumberland's pro-French stance. Also most of his contacts were disaffected conservatives, who would have hated Northumberland anyway, even if he had not given them this pretext. So his testimony is not altogether reliable, either. There are some independent accounts of Somerset's arrest, and more particularly of his trial, which suggest that the ingredients of serious trouble did exist; but there was no real breach of the peace anywhere on his account, and the strength of popular feeling, if not its orientation, may perhaps be doubted.

True Bill was found against the duke on 30 November, and he was brought to trial by his peers in Westminster Hall on 1 December.[111] The court was no more packed than was usual on such occasions, about two-thirds of the available adult peers having been drafted to serve. The king took a keen but rather detached interest, and on this occasion his journal is informative. There were five main charges: conspiring to raise men in the north; gathering men at his house for the purpose of attacking and killing the Earl of Warwick; resisting arrest; plotting to raise London and attack the gendarmerie; and conspiring to attack and murder the council. Most of this Somerset denied point-blank, impugning Palmer's integrity and rejecting Crane's testimony as unsubstantiated. 'My Lord Strange's confession; he swore it was untrue, and the Lord Strange took his oath it was true.'[112] He had done nothing in the north, and as for attacking the gendarmerie, it would have been madness with only 100 men. Presumably he denied the complicity of Vane, or the reality of his 2,000 men, or both: they are not mentioned. He had not intended to kill either Warwick or Northampton, and those who had testified of his intention to raise London had been nowhere around at the time. He did, however, make two crucial admissions. He had spoken of an intention to kill Warwick, and he had gathered some of his own men in London – allegedly in self-defence.[113]

What basis there may have been for the charge of resisting arrest is not apparent, because there are no references to any such resistance before the trial. The lawyers argued long and hard: to raise any part of his power without authority was treason; to conspire an attack upon the council was felony; to resist arrest was felony; to attempt to raise London was treason. Northumberland admitted that a plot to kill himself was not treason, and their lordships took a sharp and well-informed look at the statutes that had been alleged. The Act against unlawful assemblies did indeed make such an action treason, but only after the company had been ordered to disband and had refused to do so.[114] No such order had been issued to Somerset, and therefore his action had not been treasonable. Similarly, they did not take seriously the charges relating to the raising of London. Consequently they took the (almost) unprecedented step of finding the duke not guilty of treason. News of this escaped with amazing speed, and provoked noisy rejoicings in London. The reaction was premature. Although it was not treason to gather men unlawfully, it was felony, and that Somerset himself admitted doing. Similarly, although it was not treason to plot the death of a councillor, that also was felony, and the duke's limited confession in that respect was enough. He was convicted of felony and sentenced to be hanged; the sentence, in respect of his status, was modified to beheading. As far as Northumberland was concerned, that would do just as well – 'stone dead hath no fellow'.

In August 1553, when his own life was on the line, Northumberland confessed to having fabricated the case against Somerset, but in a sense he confessed more than the truth. Somerset had discussed a counter-coup with the Earl of Arundel and others, and may even have raised the pos-

sibility of doing away with his rival. What was fabricated was the translation of these rather nebulous words into a serious intention to act. In
that sense there was no plot against the council. Similarly, the intention
to raise London and attack the gendarmerie seems to have been made up,
either by Palmer or by Northumberland himself. What was not made up
was the fact that Somerset had raised an unlawful assembly of men, and
his plea of self-defence was not allowable in law. Although his conviction and execution for such an offence might be considered unjust and
opportunistic, it was not unlawful. A month later four of his alleged
accomplices were executed on similar charges. On 26 February Michael
Stanhope and Thomas Arundel were beheaded and Ralph Vane and
Miles Partridge hanged.[115] How Edward reacted to all this is difficult to
say. After recording some detailed points of Somerset's trial, the note of
his execution on 22 January is laconic and uninformative. On the other
hand, at least one witness, who may have been close to events, thought
that the king's apparent indifference was occasioned by the fact that 'it
[was] not agreeable to his majestie openly to declare himself', and that
privately 'he would often sigh and let fall tears'.[116] However, nobody else
seems to have noticed these lamentations, and as we have seen, there are
other explanations for the somewhat frenetic festivities of the court that
Christmas. The writer was clearly sympathetic to Somerset, and believed
that the king should have lamented him.

By the end of 1551, Northumberland was in complete control. The
only senior officer in either court or state who was not an ally or a protégé of his was the chancellor, Lord Rich, and Rich was forced to resign
just before Christmas. At the end of September he had returned a royal
letter of instruction on the grounds that eight council signatures were
insufficient. Presumably he suspected Warwick of manipulating the procedure, but the response from Edward himself was indignant.

> We think our authority is such that whatever we do by advice of our
> council attendant, although much fewer than eight, has more strength
> than to be put into question. You are not ignorant that the number of
> our councillors does not make our authority . . .[117]

Edward was fourteen, and this may well have represented his own feelings, but it was also consistent with the line that Warwick had been pursuing since early 1550. On 10 November the council sent an instruction

to Rich that in future any authorisation for the Great Seal which bore the king's signature was to be accepted 'as was accustomed in the King's Majesty's time late deceased', irrespective of whether it bore councillors' endorsements or not. In this important respect, Edward was to be treated as though he was of full age. Rich resigned rather than be party to what he considered to be an abuse.[118]

It is perhaps not surprising that by the spring of 1552, when his influence over the young king was at its strongest and most assured, that Northumberland was becoming widely distrusted, even hated. It had not only been in London that rumours of Somerset's acquittal had caused rejoicings. Similar scenes were repeated as far away as Bath. Even when the truth was known there were hopes for a reversal of fortunes: 'Thou shalt see another worlde ere Candlemas,' one optimist had declared, 'the Duke of Somerset shall cumme forth of the Tower, and the Duke of Northumberland shall goo in.'[119] Rumours were spread that he was minting coin carrying his own badge of the bear and ragged staff. That Northumberland ever had any designs on the crown can be dismissed as part of his 'black legend', but he was constantly alert to strengthen his political position. The Earl of Arundel, who had been imprisoned and interrogated for his supposed involvement in Somerset's plot and could legitimately have been charged with misprision, was released without charge, as was Lord Strange. The gentle treatment of the latter was clearly aimed at preserving the fragile entente which Northumberland had reached earlier with the Stanley and Talbot families. He was acutely aware of his own lack of 'estimacion' among the older peerage families, and their support, however lukewarm, was highly valued.[120] No such consideration protected Lord Paget. He was charged, not with any part in Somerset's 'plot', but with peculation in his office as Chancellor of the Duchy of Lancaster. He confessed the offence and was heavily fined, remaining in prison until the summer. More significantly, he was stripped of the Garter on 23 April, on the grounds that he was 'no gentleman'.

Over its last few months, the king's journal consists mainly of brief notes on matters of public policy: the coinage, the repayment of loans, the affair of the bishopric of Durham, the ongoing war between the emperor and the French. Even his last progress is recorded mainly in notes of the removing days. We know from other sources that he wrote

papers, and discussed business with his council, but of the daily life of
the court after the ending of his formal education we know very little.[121]
Sir William Pickering delivered a diamond token to his betrothed,
Elizabeth of Valois, in January 1552, but after that there is no further mention of his marriage. England's refusal to become involved in the war
seems to have cooled relations, and even Mary's mass had ceased to be
an issue. It seems clear that Northumberland had achieved a balance
between the king, himself, and the council which he considered to be satisfactory. As Lord President he controlled the council, and as Lord Great
Master he controlled the court. However, events were to show that this
ascendancy was to some extent an illusion, because it depended entirely
upon the king. Edward was not likely to change his mind about the duke,
but by the spring of 1553 his health was giving cause for serious concern.

Notes and references

1 *APC*, vol.2, pp.343–4. Cecil seems to have been held at first by Lord Rich,
and did not reach the Tower until November. He was released on 25
January. In view of his good relations with Warwick, both before and after,
there is a certain mystery about his imprisonment. PRO, SP10/9 no.48.

2 *The Chronicle and Political Papers of King Edward VI* (London, 1996), ed.
W.K. Jordan, p.18.

3 Ibid., and notes.

4 J. Loach, *Edward VI* (London, 1999), p.95. On 4 May 1550 the king noted
that Clinton had been appointed Lord Admiral, which carried membership
of the Privy Council, but he makes no specific mention of the Privy
Chamber. *Chronicle*, ed. Jordan, p.29.

5 D.M. Loades, *John Dudley, Duke of Northumberland* (Oxford, 1996), p.145;
Chronicle, ed. Jordan, pp.57, 58.

6 On the Protector's popularity, and its possible consequences, see Ethan
Shagan, *Popular Politics and the English Reformation* (London, 2002),
pp.281–5. Somerset's appeal for popular support in early October was a
threat of unknown proportions.

7 The office of Protector was abolished by statute in January 1550.

8 Loach, *Edward VI*, p.94; Loades, *John Dudley*, pp.140–1.

9 *CSP Spanish*, vol.9, pp.462–3.

10 D.E. Hoak, *The King's Council in the Reign of Edward VI* (Cambridge, 1976),

pp.245–6. It was believed that Arundel was destined for the office of Comptroller of the Household when Paget (who held that office) became Lord Chamberlain. The Comptrollership did not, however, carry *ex officio* membership of the council. *CSP Spanish*, vol.9, pp.469–70.

11 For a discussion of this episode, see Hoak, *King's Council*, p.246. The later opinion that 'there were divers catholikes called in to counsel at that instante for the lady maryes sake she hoping to have bine Regent' appears to have been mistaken.

12 BL, Add. MS 48126, fol.15.

13 *APC*, vol.2, p.354.

14 Loades, *John Dudley*, p.142. Richard Hilles to Henry Bullinger 17 November 1549, in *Original Letters Relative to the English Reformation*, ed. Hastings Robinson (Parker Society, 1847), vol.1, p.268.

15 'The Letters of Richard Scudamore to Sir Philip Hoby', ed. Susan Brigden, *Camden Miscellany*, 30 (1990), pp.95–6.

16 Ibid., p.98.

17 BL, Add. MS 48126, fol.15; Hoak, *King's Council*, p.255.

18 The assumption that there was a clear-cut division between 'catholics' and 'protestants' in the council at this stage should be resisted, but it seems to be clear that the supporters of the Earl of Warwick slightly outnumbered his opponents. Either Wriothesley ignored this balance of power, or the main account misrepresents his intentions.

19 BL, Add. MS 48126, fol.16; Loades, *John Dudley*, p.144.

20 Loades, *John Dudley*, p.144.

21 *CSP Spanish*, vol.9, p.489; Hoak, *King's Council*, pp.255–6.

22 *Tudor Royal Proclamations*, ed. P.L. Hughes and J.F. Larkin, 3 vols. (New York, 1964–9), vol.1. pp.285–6.

23 *Chronicle*, ed. Jordan, p.19; Loades, *John Dudley*, p.146.

24 The king simply recorded the political comings and goings of these weeks without comment and (as in this case) with a straight face. We have no idea how much he actually knew.

25 *Chronicle*, ed. Jordan, p.19; 'Letters of Richard Scudamore', ed. Brigden, p.108.

26 He had actually been appointed to the presidency of the council in October 1549, but it only became effective when he had secured his ascendancy. The Lord Great Mastership he received on 20 February 1550. *APC*, vol.2, pp.347; *CPR*, Edward VI, vol.3, p.189.

27 See above, Ch.3.

28 Bibliothèque Nationale, MS Ancien Saint-Germain Francais, 15888, fols. 214–215; cited in Hoak, *King's Council*, p.123.

29 Loades, *John Dudley*. p.234. There is some evidence to suggest, however, that Edward was occasionally asserting himself, particularly over the diocese of Durham, which Dudley wanted to disendow but which was in fact divided and re-endowed.

30 *Chronicle*, ed. Jordan, pp.29–30.

31 Ibid., pp.32–3.

32 Ibid., pp.25–6. The terminology used here is confusing, because this is the only suggestion that there was actually a distinction between the 'inner' and 'outer' Privy Chamber, unless by 'inner' is simply meant the four knights (or principal gentlemen), and by 'outer' the rest.

33 PRO, LC2/4, i.

34 *Chronicle*, ed. Jordan, pp.57–8; *CPR*, Edward VI, vol.4, p.138; Loades, *John Dudley*, pp.179–80.

35 *Chronicle*, ed. Jordan, pp.75, 77; PRO, LC2/4, i.

36 *Chronicle*, ed. Jordan, p.113; D.M. Loades, *The Tudor Court* (London, 1986), pp.89–90.

37 PRO, LC2/3, I, fol.108; *Handbook of British Chronology*, ed. E.B. Fryde *et al.* (London, 1986), pp.167–8.

38 *Chronicle*, ed. Jordan, pp.102, 119. This seems to have related to the enforcement of the Prayer Book, rather than 'a brawling matter', as stated in the chronicle.

39 On Henry's use of his Privy Chamber as emissaries, see David Starkey, 'Intimacy and Innovation: The Rise of the Privy Chamber, 1485–1547', in *The English Court from the Wars of the Roses to the Civil War*, ed. Starkey (London, 1987), pp.71–119.

40 *The Literary Remains of King Edward VI*, ed. J.G. Nichols (Roxburgh Club, 1857), vol.1, p.86. *Chronicle*, ed. Jordan, p.144.

41 Ibid., p.145.

42 Ibid., pp.31–2.

43 Ibid., pp.59, 62–3.

44 Loach, *Edward VI*, p.108. This move had been planned for some time, because Elizabeth's portrait had been sent to the English court the previous December. *CSP Foreign*, 1547–53, p.109.

45 *Chronicle*, ed. Jordan, p.75–6. It is not quite clear where this substantial sum came from, but it was presumably the Privy Coffers.

46 Ibid., p.74; *CSP Foreign*, 154–53, pp.107, 109. For a discussion of the negotiations, see W.K. Jordan, *Edward VI: The Threshold of Power*, (London, 1970) pp.128–31.

47 *Chronicle*, ed. Jordan, pp.79–80.

48 D.M. Loades, *Mary Tudor: A Life* (Oxford, 1989), pp.134–70, contains a full description of Mary's resistance, and her brother's reaction.

49 *Chronicle,* ed. Jordan, pp.93–4.

50 Ibid., p.116. Although Edward noted a copy of a letter to this effect 'in the study', no such letter has been found, or any other written record of the decision.

51 Ibid., pp.46–50. The council, of course, moved with the court, as is apparent from its register.

52 For a list of all Tudor royal residences, see Loades, *Tudor Court*, pp.193–202, which is based on H.M. Colvin, *The History of the King's Works, IV, 1485–1660* (London, 1982), pt2, pp.1–367. A peak of 68 houses had been reached in the latter part of Henry VIII's reign.

53 *Chronicle*, ed. Jordan, p.33.

54 Ibid., p.36.

55 Ibid., p.123.

56 Ibid., p.137. *APC*, vol.3, 23 July 1552. For the sake of comparison, 18,000 horses accompanied the court of Francis I of France in 1526: R.J. Knecht, *Francis I* (Cambridge, 1982), p.97.

57 *Chronicle*, ed. Jordan, p.137.

58 *Literary Remains*, ed. Nichols, vol.1, p.80. 'A goodly house ... where we were marvellously, yes, rather excessively, banqueted.'

59 *Chronicle*, ed. Jordan, pp.138–9.

60 Ibid., p.139. The king wrote some particulars of his visit to the town in a letter to Barnaby: *Literary Remains*, ed. Nichols, vol.1, p.81.

61 PRO, SP10/14, no.68. In fact he was alarmed unnecessarily: Frances was to outlive him by several years.

62 *Chronicle,* ed. Jordan, pp.139–43.

63 *APC*, vol.2, pp.300–2; W.K. Jordan, *Edward VI: The Young King* (London, 1968), p.445; Loades, *John Dudley*, p.120.

64 *Chronicle*, ed. Jordan, p.17.

65 PRO, SP10/9, no.47.

66 *Chronicle*, ed. Jordan, p.24. For Tudor attitudes towards noble retainers, see P. Williams, *The Tudor Regime* (Oxford, 1979), pp.124–5; Loades, *John Dudley*, pp.125–79.

67 W.K. Jordan, *Edward VI: The Threshold of Power* (London, 1970), pp.56–69.

68 See below for examples of Somerset being deployed in the service of public order.

69 'Sir Thomas Wyatt's treatise on the militia', in D.M. Loades, ed., *The Papers of George Wyatt* (Camden Society, 4th ser., 5, 1967).

70 *Chronicle*, ed. Jordan, p.37.

71 For a full account of this bizarre episode, see Dubois to Mary of Hungary in *CSP Spanish*, vol.10, pp.124–35; Loades, *Mary Tudor*, pp.153–6.

72 *Chronicle*, ed. Jordan, p.40.

73 Ibid., p.39. This would suggest that the king must have had his own 'band', in addition to those provided by his nobles, but that is nowhere made clear.

74 Ibid., pp.41–2. Mary was (understandably) extremely defensive about the whole episode. Loades, *Mary Tudor*, pp.153–6.

75 *Chronicle*, ed. Jordan, pp.41–2.

76 Norwich Municipal Archives, Depositions taken before the Mayor and Aldermen of Norwich [1550], in *Tudor Economic Documents*, ed. R.H. Tawney and Eileen Power, 3 vols. (London, 1924), vol.1, pp. 47–53.

77 *Chronicle*, ed. Jordan, p.50.

78 Ibid., p.55. There were rumours at this point of a conservative conspiracy which would have involved Mary going westward to link up with the Earl of Shrewsbury. Loades, *Mary Tudor*, pp.162–3.

79 *Chronicle*, ed. Jordan, p.56.

80 Ibid. Sir Clement Smith was 'chided' for the same offence.

81 Ibid., p.58.

82 *CSP Foreign*, 1547–53, p.122; *Chronicle*, ed. Jordan, pp.66–7,69; Loades, *Mary Tudor*, p.163.

83 Loades, *Mary Tudor*, pp.165–6; *APC*, vol.3, p.347.

84 *Chronicle*, ed. Jordan, p.80. *CSP Spanish*, vol.10, pp.356–64, 12 September 1551.

85 See above, Ch.3.

86 *Chronicle*, ed. Jordan, p.86; Loades, *John Dudley*, pp.180–1; PRO, SP11/4,

no.21; BL, Add. MS 6113, fol.129, which is a detailed description of the ceremony.

87 *Chronicle*, ed. Jordan, pp.86–8. For the depositions and other statements relating to Somerset's alleged conspiracy, see PRO, SP10/13, nos.57, 58, 64, 65, 66, 67.

88 *Chronicle*, ed. Jordan, pp.88–9.

89 Ibid., p.100.

90 Ibid., pp.102, 107, 109.

91 Ibid., p.123.

92 Ibid., p.145. The explanation for this decision no doubt lies in the 'Brief declaration of principal military and naval charges' drawn up sometime during September, and the 'Memorandum of the King's debts' of 3 October. PRO, SP10/15, nos.11, 13.

93 Loades, *John Dudley*, pp.172–3.

94 Jordan, *Edward VI: The Threshold of Power*, pp.70–81.

95 *Chronicle*, ed. Jordan, pp.41–2.

96 Ibid., p.78. If summary executions were carried out as suggested, a proclamation of martial law would have been the only way of achieving that. There is no record of such a proclamation.

97 *APC*, vol.2, p.291; Loades, *Mary Tudor*, pp.144–7.

98 Loades, *Mary Tudor*, pp.167–70.

99 Loades, *John Dudley*, pp.145–6, discusses the legislation of January 1550, particularly the statutes 3&4 Edward VI, c.3, c.5, c.15 and c.23.

100 *Chronicle,* ed. Jordan, pp.87–9. Some of these charges appear to have harkened back to his time as Protector: BL, MS 48126, fols.1–4.

101 *Chronicle*, ed. Jordan, pp.86–7.

102 Ibid., p.88; PRO, SP10/13, no.65.

103 *Chronicle*, ed. Jordan, pp.88–9. The circumstantial detail suggests that Edward was particularly interested in these proceedings.

104 Ibid., p.89. Palmer was a thoroughly unreliable witness, and the fact that he was not charged, and was back in service the following year, strongly suggests that his testimony was fabricated.

105 PRO, SP10/13, nos.66, 67.

106 Ibid., no.65

107 *Chronicle*, ed. Jordan, pp.93, 99. Strange's testimony does not seem to have survived.

108 Loades, *John Dudley*, pp.169–75.

109 PRO, SP10/13, no.57.

110 Scheyfve to the emperor, 18 October 1551, in *CSP Spanish*, vol.10, pp.384–6

111 *Fourth Report of the Deputy Keeper of the Public Records*, App. 11, p.230; Jordan, *Edward VI: The Threshold of Power*, pp.94–5.

112 *Chronicle*, ed. Jordan, pp.97–100; BL, Harley MS 1294, fols.19–20.

113 Ibid.

114 Statute 3&4 Edward VI, c.5, ¶2, *Statutes of the Realm*, ed. A. Luders *et al.*, 11 vols. (London, 1810–28), vol.4, pt.1, p.105.

115 Loades, *John Dudley*, pp.189–90. No explanation was offered for the difference in treatment.

116 BL, Harley MS 1294, fols.19–20.

117 PRO, SP10/13, no.55.

118 *Chronicle*, ed. Jordan, p.101.

119 *APC*, vol.3, p.462, 24 January 1552.

120 Loades, *John Dudley*, *passim*.

121 *Chronicle*, ed. Jordan, pp.137–45, 176–84.

CHAPTER 5

· · · · · · · · · · · · · · ·

The succession crisis of July 1553

U ntreated pulmonary tuberculosis is a cruel disease, because its remissions hold out so many false hopes of recovery. Edward had become ill in January, with what seemed at first like a bad cold. By the beginning of March he was too unwell to open parliament in the normal way, and the members had been constrained to come to him. However, he did not become progressively worse. On some days he was bad, his servants shook their heads, and Jehan Scheyfve wrote despatches saying that his life was despaired of.[1] Other days he was better, and optimists about him spoke of speedy and complete recovery. As late as the beginning of June the Duke of Northumberland was quoting his physicians to that effect.[2] And then, about the second week in June, he suddenly became much worse. Physicians who only the previous week had been talking of recovery now declared that his death was not only certain but imminent.

It is important to understand this timetable, because so much disinformation was subsequently circulated in the creation of Northumberland's 'black legend'. Robert Wingfield, for example, a zealous supporter of Mary in the crisis that followed, declared that Edward died 'wasted away with a long and lingering disease', and reports circulated soon after that he had been slowly poisoned by the infamous duke.[3] His death had certainly been expected when it came, but the notice had been relatively short. Scheyfve had predicted it months before, but that was because he desired it rather than because he had any real evidence. Northumberland at first refused to believe it, even when it was authentic, because Edward's demise spelled the end of all the hopes that had been building since 1549. He was the last man to want the king dead, although it was probably his desperate resort to quack remedies which fed the rumours. The more extended the timetable, of course, the easier it was to pin other charges on to Northumberland. When he married his son Guildford to Lady Jane Grey on 21 May, it could be made to look like a plot to secure the throne for his family. In fact there is no evidence that he knew of the king's 'Device' as early as 21 May, and the Grey marriage was a substitute for the Clifford match which he had been seeking, but which the Earl of Cumberland had declined. At the time even Scheyfve did not associate Jane with the crown.[4] By 12 June the ambassador was sure that some sort of plot was being hatched to deprive Mary of the succession, but he did not know what it was, and since he had informants within the Privy Chamber, it is pretty certain that nobody else did either.

Exactly how and when the king's 'Device' was unearthed and applied to this emergency is not clear. As we have seen, it was probably written not later than January 1553 as a kind of school exercise on a hypothetical political problem. It may have simply remained in Edward's possession, or it may have been passed to William Thomas. It is unlikely that anyone else knew about it until early June. As it stood it was not much use, with its unborn male heirs and provision for a protectorship. However, either Thomas or Northumberland quickly spotted that one simple alteration would make it relevant. After any son born to Frances, Duchess of Suffolk, the Device provided for the crown to pass to 'the heirs male of the Lady Jane' (her eldest daughter). By altering that to read 'the Lady Jane and her heirs male', the whole effect of the document could be changed.[5] Whoever had this idea – and it may well have been Northumberland – both the king and the duke quickly became enthusiastic. Edward knew Jane well, liked her and approved of her piety. If a woman had to succeed, she was the best choice. She was also, of course, Northumberland's daughter-in-law, and her succession would secure his own future as well as would the king's survival. To Robert Wingfield, who was not close to events but appears to have had good sources, it appeared that the sick and helpless boy was bullied into making this grotesque provision by the self-seeking and overbearing duke. However, Wingfield, who by the time he wrote was playing the zealous catholic, was also anxious to gloss over the fact that Edward had also been a heretic, an inclination which it was much more difficult to attribute to the influence of his mentor – and in any case, he was being wise after the event. Contemporary evidence suggests that once Edward had become convinced that he would not live long enough to see a male heir, the drive to implement this scheme for the succession came from him.[6]

It was announced that the new order would be laid down in the king's will, which would be confirmed by parliament in September. The Law Officers and many of the council were horrified by these developments. The lawful succession had been laid down by statute in 1543, and confirmed by Henry VIII's will in 1547. Only if both Mary and Elizabeth had died, or had married without the council's consent, could Jane be considered the heir. It was not even certain that Edward, who was still a minor, could make a valid will at all, let alone dispose of the crown in this cavalier fashion.[7] However, when the king summoned his council and required them to take an oath to uphold his wishes, even the most reluctant realised that it would be high treason to refuse the monarch's explicit command. Eventually, perhaps advised of the legal limitations, the king did not entrust his intentions to a will, but instead instructed Letters Patent to be drawn up. This was done, but since the Letters did not pass either of the seals, they ceased to have any legal force once Edward was dead; a matter of some significance, as we shall see. Robert Wingfield reproduced a highly circumstantial account of the king's supposed oration to his council on the subject of the succession:

> my resolve is to disown and disinherit her [Mary], together with her
> sister Elizabeth, as though she was a bastard and born from an
> illegitimate bed. For indeed my sister Mary was the daughter of the king
> by Katherine the Spaniard, who before she was married to my worthy
> father had been espoused to Arthur, my father's elder brother, and was
> therefore for this reason alone divorced by my father. But it was the fate
> of Elizabeth, my other sister, to have Anne Boleyn for a mother; this
> woman indeed was not only cast off by my father, because she was more
> inclined to couple with a number of courtiers, rather than reverencing
> her husband, so mighty a king, but also paid the penalty with her head –
> a greater proof of her guilt . . .[8]

He then added, apparently as an afterthought,

> *For if our sister Mary were to possess the kingdom (which Almighty God prevent), it would be all over for the religion whose fair foundations we have laid ...*

Such orations were a well-established classical trope, and there is no reason to suppose that the words used were authentic. Other sources do not suggest that religion was explicitly mentioned (although everyone understood its importance to Edward), for fear of appearing to impose a confessional test, which would not have been acceptable to Cranmer or the other mainstream protestant thinkers of the time.[9] However, it is reasonably certain that both Mary and Elizabeth were rejected on the grounds of illegitimacy. Wingfield, who wished to represent Mary as the lawful heir by birth, simply ignored Henry's statute and will, but it is reasonably certain that both were considered by the council at the time. We do not know what arguments were actually used for setting them aside, but it would have been legitimate to argue that statute had no power to alter the status of legitimacy which had been laid down by the laws of God. That would have been contrary to received practice, but the relationship between statute and divine law was a grey area; so that Edward's argument of double bastardy was probably the strongest available to him. In the last few days of the king's life it appeared that everybody who mattered, at court, in council or in the City of London, had accepted his decision and sworn to uphold it.[10]

Mary's imperial connections were only too well known, and the newly arrived French ambassador, Antoine de Noailles, dropped a broad hint to Northumberland that his master would support any attempt to keep her off the throne. In an interview shortly before Edward's death, however, the duke had assured him 'that they had provided so well against the Lady Mary's ever attaining the succession, and that all the lords of the council were so well united, that there is no need for you, Sire, to enter into any doubt on this score'.[11] Noailles did not press the point, and it is possible that Northumberland's words were prompted less by over-confidence than by the thought that the involvement of French troops would be the surest way to ruin his cause, and that of Jane.

Charles V's special envoys, who reached England only hours before the king died, came to the same conclusion. Their sympathies were entirely with Mary, but they were under strict instructions not to intervene. Simon Renard, who was the brains of the mission, quickly assessed the situation. Northumberland, he believed, had strong forces mustered in the London area, and had control of the Tower armouries, the Treasury and the fleet. 'The actual possession of power', he wrote, 'is a matter of great importance, especially among barbarians like the English ...'[12] In any contest between force and justice, force would win every time, and therefore Mary had no chance. The emperor believed his envoys, and since his main concern was to avoid giving the French any excuse to intervene, he simply instructed them that they were to do business with the victorious party – and not to ask inconvenient questions. Consequently, when Edward died on 6 July, there seemed to be every prospect that Jane would be accepted as his successor.

Mary, however, was not intimidated. Like Scheyfve she had good sources of information close to the king, and being warned that Edward's end was approaching, on 5 July she set out from Hunsdon, where she had been living for some time, and headed for the heart of her own estates, at Kenninghall, in Norfolk.[13] As soon as Edward was dead, Northumberland moved to secure her, but he was too late. Realising that she had left Hunsdon, the council believed that she was heading for Flanders, and alerted the fleet to intercept her. However, nothing was further from her thoughts. She was the heir, by the laws of both God and man, and she was determined to claim her right. Northumberland, misled by some hysterical displays from her in the past, made the serious mistake of underestimating her determination on this occasion. On 8 July Jane was proclaimed in London, to an ominous lack of enthusiasm. Even the most protestant city in the kingdom did not believe in confessional tests for the succession.[14] Away from the court, Mary was safe, but at a disadvantage. Whoever her informant was, he was not present at Edward's deathbed, and it was two days before she received confirmation that her brother had indeed departed. Word actually reached her on the 7th, but she could not trust the source, and feared that she might be entrapped into making a premature claim. Of course, to have claimed the throne while Edward was still alive would have been high treason, and in such circumstances even her own affinity might not have backed her, so she had to be sure. By 9 July the news had been confirmed, and she had herself proclaimed at Kenninghall.[15]

she caused her whole household to be summoned, and told them of the
death of her brother Edward VI; the right to the Crown of England had
therefore descended to her by divine and by human law ... Roused by
their mistress's words, everyone, both gently born and humbler servants,
cheered her to the rafters and hailed and proclaimed their dearest
princess Mary as queen of England.

The same day she wrote to the council in London, claiming their allegiance.[16]

Meanwhile, the council was going through the motions of a normal succession. The Lord Mayor and Aldermen of London were sworn to Queen Jane, and letters were sent out to sheriffs and justices of the peace announcing her accession and requiring them to suppress any tumults or disorders. Mary was declared to be in flight towards the coast, either to pass into Flanders or to await imperial support. On the 9th Bishop Ridley of London preached at Paul's Cross, explaining that both Mary and Elizabeth were bastards, and that their unmarried status threatened the danger of foreign domination. The citizens were openly unsympathetic, and hardly needed reminding of Mary's claim.[17] On the 10th, the same day that Mary's letter reached the council, Jane made her formal entry to the Tower, accompanied by an ominous silence from the onlookers. Mary's determination may well have taken the council by surprise, but they had as yet no means of assessing the seriousness of her challenge; they rejected her claim, urging dutiful submission to Jane. However, it soon became clear that their confidence, if such it was, was misplaced. Over the next two days the news of Mary's gathering power, no doubt exaggerated in the telling, had become ominous enough to require urgent action. Robert Dudley's small following in Norfolk had been brushed aside, and a military campaign of some seriousness was urgently required.

By 13 July Northumberland was in a dilemma. He was the best soldier, and he was feared in East Anglia, so he stood the best chance of defeating the princess, whose force still lacked leaders of skill and experience. On the other hand he was concerned lest his departure from London might encourage some members of the council to break ranks, which would be as bad as a military defeat.[18] The Marquis of Northampton had demonstrated his uselessness as a commander in 1549, and the only other possibility was Jane's father, the Duke of Suffolk.

According to one source he declined the mission, while another states that Jane refused to allow him to go.[19] Whatever the truth, Northumberland eventually took the mission on himself, and set out on 14 July with about 1,500 men and a small artillery train, intending to link up with Lord Clinton and the Earl of Oxford as he moved north.

Unknown to Northumberland, by the time that he left London the first cracks in the council's united front had already begun to appear. According to Simon Renard's report, on the 12th Lord Cobham and Sir John Mason, on behalf of the council, had waited on the ambassadors to inform them that their credentials (to King Edward) had now expired and that they should remove themselves.[20] They were clearly thought to be behind Mary's unexpected resolution. Renard was pained. They had no such instructions. They could, however, assure their visitors that the French had nefarious intentions, and should they become involved would endeavour to place Mary Stuart on the English throne. It is hard to imagine that the council would not have thought of this possibility, but Renard clearly believed that he had scored a bull's eye. For whatever reason the instruction to leave was withdrawn, and replaced with an invitation to meet a larger group of councillors the following day. Northumberland was not informed.

The duke was paying the price of a risky strategy. In order to widen the ostensible base of Jane's support, he had hastily rehabilitated the Earl of Arundel and Lord Paget, and readmitted them to the council shortly before Edward died. Both had signed the instrument in favour of Jane, but neither had any gratitude to, or affection for, Northumberland, who had bullied and humiliated them remorselessly.[21] For a short while the issue hung in the balance. The councillors who met the imperial ambassadors on the 13th were non-committal, and as late as the 16th Renard still believed that the duke would prevail. On the strength of that belief, the ambassadors ignored an appeal from Mary the same day. It was probably the most helpful thing they could have done, because the princess had been ostentatiously entrusting herself to her loyal servants and subjects, and had it been known that she was reverting to her old habit of relying instead upon the servants of Charles V, it would not have done hor cause any good. As it was, her reputation remained unsullied. The critical shift in the balance of power probably came on 16 or 17 July, and cannot be accurately pinpointed. Lord Clinton joined Northumberland at

Cambridge, but with a smaller force than had been expected, and the same day came the serious tidings that the Earl of Oxford had defected to Mary. Oxford himself was a lightweight of no particular ability, but he had a great deal of influence in that part of the country. His change of allegiance was more symbolic than effective, but it reflected the extent to which confidence was slipping away from the duke. [22]

It is easy to see this, as Wingfield was inclined to do, as evidence of a spontaneous and irreversible surge of popular feeling, inspired (of course) by God. However, it would have counted for nothing without developments in London. Just what prompted the critical change of mood which took place between the 16th and the 18th we do not know. It is unlikely to have been Renard's 'revelation', and may have been the persuasive voices of Paget and Arundel. By the 18th the council had divided into those who were irretrievably committed to Jane, like Suffolk and Northampton, and those who were beginning to reconsider their positions, like Pembroke and Winchester. The latter group met on that day at Pembroke's London residence, Baynard's Castle, and appear to have decided upon their course.[23] On the morning of the 19th Jane's core supporters, including Suffolk, Cranmer and Goodrich, signed a letter to Lord Rich in Essex, informing him of the disaffection of the Earl of Oxford, and requiring him to remain loyal to Jane. Later in the day there must have been a showdown between the two groups, and the Marians emerged as a clear majority, because before the day was out Mary had been proclaimed in London, Suffolk had informed his daughter that she was no longer queen, and the whole council had signed a letter to Northumberland instructing him to disband his forces and await Mary's pleasure.[24] If we believe Wingfield, or Henry Machyn, there were few enough left to disband: 'ys men forsook hym', as the latter wrote. However, that is not quite the whole story. Most of the Household troops who had accompanied him from London stayed with him to the end, and his decision not to make any kind of stand was political rather than military. He could have made a considerable nuisance of himself if he had chosen; but he did not choose because in the light of the council's decision there was no longer any ultimate prospect of success.[25]

It was now a question of *sauve qui peut*. On 12 July, still anticipating a fight, Mary had moved her base from Kenninghall to the more defensible stronghold of Framlingham Castle, and it was there, on 20 July, that

Paget and Arundel arrived, bearing a cringing and hypocritical letter from the politicians whose belated change of mind had nevertheless delivered to Mary her bloodless victory.[26]

> we your most humble and obedient subjects, having always (God we take to witness) remained your highness's true and humble subjects in our hearts ever since the death of our late sovereign lord and master your highness's brother, whom God pardon ... have this day proclaimed in your City of London your majesty to be our true natural sovereign liege lady and queen.

They abased themselves, and sought pardon, as they were bound to do, but the problems were not all on one side. With a few exceptions, Mary's earliest and most loyal supporters had little experience of office. However dear they were to her, she could hardly have run the country with the aid of Robert Rochester, Francis Englefield or Edward Waldegrave. Even the Earls of Bath and Oxford were not very promising in that respect. Mary needed some, at least, of those experienced administrators and statesmen who only days earlier had been ordering the justices of the peace to support Queen Jane. The new queen was quite shrewd enough to see that, and quite human enough to resent it, because it meant that as she constructed her government, there were built-in fault lines of suspicion and mistrust.[27] To the core of Mary's household servants many of those who were now to be accepted and promoted were little better than traitors and heretics, while to the seasoned politicians who passed the new tests, the aforesaid servants were mere backwoodsmen.

There were eventually three main groups in the council as it was assembled between mid-July and the end of August. First there were the 'Framlingham' councillors – those recruited before 28 July. These were either Mary's existing household officers, such as Robert Rochester, or very early adherents like Sir Henry Bedingfield and the Earl of Bath. They were not selected for any particular skills they possessed, but for their loyalty, and because the queen needed a council from the moment of her first proclamation. They not only shared a personal attachment to the queen, but also a stronger than usual devotion to the old religion. Altogether there were about twenty of them.[28] Secondly, there were those of Edward's council whom the queen chose to recruit, usually men of long experience who had not been particularly close to Northumberland. This group included people like Paget and Arundel, the Earl of Bedford, Sir John Baker and the Marquis of Winchester. There were fifteen or six- teen of these, most of them with many years of service, and they had a much more chequered religious record.[29] Finally, there were those who had served Henry VIII but had been excluded and imprisoned by Northumberland's regime – the Duke of Norfolk, Cuthbert Tunstall, Bishop of Durham, and Stephen Gardiner, Bishop of Winchester. By early September the council numbered nearly 40, significantly larger than that of Edward at any time during his reign, and very much larger than the last council of Henry VIII. The number of councillors alone was not a serious problem, or rather it was a problem which could be coped with, but deep divisions of opinion over policy soon began to appear along the natural fault lines, and they were to cause the queen endless headaches. Worse, two of the most senior and talented members, Stephen Gardiner and William Paget, disliked and distrusted each other for sufficiently good reason, and tended to gather like-minded groups around them.[30]

By the time that Mary reached London on 3 August, the council was fully functional, and had already addressed quite a lot of important busi- ness. The court, however, remained in limbo, and Mary's magnate house- hold seems to have continued to function until she took up residence at the Tower. Such rearrangements as were deemed necessary were then made between that date and the coronation, which took place on 1 October. The first relevant issue which had to be addressed was that of Edward's funeral. Although the full extent of Mary's intended religious policy was not yet known except, perhaps, to a few intimates, she was a famous upholder of the traditional rites of the church, particularly the mass. She was also totally incapable of understanding that men and women could hold genuine religious convictions which differed from her own. As far as she was concerned, so-called protestants were mere hypo- crites and timeservers, concerned mainly to plunder the property and jurisdiction of the church. In the face of all the evidence, she had there- fore continued to believe that her brother was a mere child, manipulated by his unscrupulous mentors. If he had achieved his majority, and begun to make his own decisions, he would have shared the same faith as she did. This meant that it was her Christian duty to see him interred with traditional rites, and to ensure that his soul was prayed for in the ancient fashion.[31] Nobody else shared this view. When the imperial ambassadors heard of her intention, they were horrified. Edward had lived and died a professed heretic, consequently all intercession would be useless and misplaced. Moreover, they did not share Mary's dismissive attitude towards protestant opinion. So far the heretics had mostly supported her, or at least accepted her, and such a gesture would alienate them quite unnecessarily. In a secret *consulta* of 2 August they advised her to allow him to be publicly interred with reformed rites; custom would in any case excuse her from attending. She could then hold whatever private ceremony her conscience might dictate.[32] Whether she consulted her own council at this stage is not clear, but they would almost certainly have given the same advice. The queen bowed to this pressure of opinion, and given that there were already mutterings among the yeomen of the guard about the proposed traditional ceremony, it was clearly a wise decision. On 8 August, the day of the funeral, Renard reported that 'with the consent of her whole council', she had accepted their advice.[33]

Although the 1552 burial rite, over which Archbishop Cranmer presided, is liturgically bleak, the other ceremonies were carried out in full:

> The viii day of august was bered the nobull kyng Edward vi, and the vii yere of ys rayne; and at ys bere[ing was] the grettest mone mad for hym of ys deth [as ever] was hard or sene, boyth of all sorts of pepull, wepyng and lamenting; and furst of alle whent a grett company of chyldreyn in ther surples, and clarkes syngyng; and then ys father['s] bedmen ...[34]

There then followed the full heraldic panoply, concluding:

> [After him went a goodly horse, covered with cloth of gold unto the ground, and the master of the horse, with a man of arms in armour, which] was offered, boyth the man and the horsse. [There was set up a go]oddly hersse in Westmyster abbay with banar-[rolls] and pensells, and honge with velvet a-bowt.

From what we know of Edward in his lifetime, he would certainly have appreciated this show. On the other hand, he would probably not have appreciated the sermon. John Scory had been ousted from the see of Chichester within days of Mary's accession and without any recorded legal process, being replaced by the previously deprived conservative George Day. Day was Mary's characteristically insensitive choice of a funeral preacher. We do not know what he said, but since one tradition- alist witness described it as 'goodly', we may presume that it would have been offensive to Cranmer – to say nothing of Edward himself.[35]

The company which gathered to honour the king's passing was that which had served him in life (with the exception of Day), not that which was currently serving the queen. The list, however, is of those who were entitled to attend, and for whom issues of livery were approved, rather than of those actually present.[36] In spite of their imprisonment, the Dukes of Suffolk and Northumberland were included, whereas it is clear that many others who were still in prison or out of favour following the events of July were not. We know that those pensioners who were absent from the court on 14 July, and thus avoided accompanying Northumberland on his ill-fated mission, petitioned for their right to attend this ceremony, and the list of names roughly corresponds. This means, of course, that it was precisely those yeomen and gentlemen who had been most supportive of Edward's intentions who were denied the right to attend his obsequies.[37] The list is full of problems and apparent inconsistencies. The Privy Chamber is headed by the Earl of Worcester, who is not otherwise known to have served in that capacity, and includes Will Somers, the fool, who was not a gentleman by anyone's standards. Moreover, the Stable establishment is headed by Sir Edward Hastings, who was Mary's Master of the Horse, not Edward's. Nevertheless, there are also many familiar names who would not have been congenial to the queen: Sir Thomas Wroth, Sir Anthony Cooke, Thomas Cotton and Barnaby Fitzpatrick. In spite of her inappropriate choice of preacher, Mary allowed her brother to be interred in a style which was appropriate to a protestant prince, and there appear to have been few complaints from either side. A few days later, for her personal satisfaction, she caused the Bishop of Winchester to celebrate a solemn requiem mass in the chapel of St Peter ad Vincula.[38]

Having won a bloodless victory, which she attributed to direct divine intervention, Mary was not inclined to be severe. Northumberland, his sons and a few of his principal henchmen remained in prison awaiting trial, but most of those who had been rounded up were soon released. Two of the gentlemen pensioners, Clement and John Paston, who had been 'out' with the duke, were sent down into Norfolk on 30 July to remain in their father's custody, and both were excluded from Edward's funeral, but they were back at court by 1 October and Clement received an annuity of £20 in November.[39] Of all the pensioners who had been in trouble at the beginning of August (and were still alive), only Sir Ralph Bagnall was still excluded at the coronation. This seems to have been typical of the Chamber servants in general. Most of the head officers changed. The Marquis of Northampton was displaced, both as Lord Great Chamberlain and as Captain of the Gentlemen Pensioners, and the Earl of Oxford recovered an hereditary right which his father had lost to Thomas Cromwell in 1540. Darcy was displaced as Lord Chamberlain in favour of Sir John Gage, and Sir John Gates as Vice-Chamberlain by Sir Henry Jerningham. Sir William Cavendish, however, remained as Treasurer, a position which he had held since 1546.[40] A few of Mary's long-serving personal attendants, such as Randall Dodd, were given positions, but most of the existing sewers, ushers and other gentlemen servants remained undisturbed. A rather similar pattern was followed in the Household below stairs. The main change was that Cromwell's reform of 1540, which had seen the Lord Stewardship discontinued in favour of a Lord Great Mastership on the French model, was reversed, and the Earl of Arundel was appointed Lord Steward. The four Masterships of the Household which had been introduced at the same time (and two of which were vacant) were also ended. Sir Richard Cotton was replaced as Comptroller by Mary's long-serving and faithful steward Robert Rochester; but Sir Thomas Cheney continued as Treasurer, and apart from a few supernumeraries brought in from Mary's earlier household, the particular departments remained undisturbed.[41]

Altogether, Mary is known to have given about twenty positions at court to those who had served her before her accession, plus six or seven offices outside the Household.[42] A few of these, like Rochester and Jerningham, were high profile, but the majority were comparatively humble: George Tyrell (Gentleman Usher Daily Waiter), Robert Eton (Sergeant of the Pantry) and Thomas Palmer (Groom Porter) are typical. Given that the Chamber and Household together consisted of some 200 servants, and that these provisions were made at various times during her reign, it cannot be argued that Mary carried out any kind of purge, either political or religious. Occasionally her tolerance was not well rewarded.

Several yeomen of the guard at different times got drunk in local taverns and made opprobrious remarks either about their mistress or (more usually) about her consort. Edward Lewkenor, a groom porter, died in prison for his involvement in the Dudley plot of 1556, and Edward Underhill, one of the gentlemen at arms, was interrogated for a 'seditious pamphlet' in the early days of the reign.[43] Underhill was a notorious protestant, and *persona non grata* with all the officers of the court, but repeated attempts to dismiss him were unsuccessful, until he eventually withdrew of his own accord. We have it on his own evidence that there was no better place 'to shift the Easter tide' – that is, to avoid taking the sacrament – than Queen Mary's court.[44] This laxity must have been well known to those who were responsible for the spiritual well-being of the Household, but nothing was ever done about it. Whereas members of Henry VIII's Chamber, and even of his Privy Chamber, were occasionally incinerated (or saved from incineration) following outbursts of clerical zeal, the equally zealous clergy who surrounded Mary do not seem to have adopted similar tactics. The Dean of the Chapel and all the royal chaplains were inevitably replaced, but even within the chapel the clerks and choristers seem to have remained undisturbed.

However, at the most intimate level of service a complete transformation was effected. In place of the lords, principal gentlemen, gentlemen and grooms, a total of about 40 of whom who had served Edward in his later days, there appeared five ladies, about fifteen gentlewomen, and four 'chamberers'. There was a chief gentleman (John Norris), a few gentlemen ushers, to guard the doors, and one or two grooms to do the heavier manual work, but the Privy Chamber became a female sanctuary.[45] Several of these ladies had been in Mary's service for a number of years, and it can be assumed that here, at least, strict tests of religious orthodoxy would have been applied. The ladies of the Privy Chamber took it in turns to share the queen's private prayers, and John Norris was described (by Edward Underhill) as a 'rank papist'. One of the consequences was that the strong links between the Privy Chamber and the Privy Council, which had existed since 1540 and been particularly strong since 1550, were broken. Two or three of the ladies (but none of the gentlewomen) were the wives of Privy Councillors, but that was not at all the same thing as the extensive overlap of membership that had still applied in June 1553. For most purposes the Privy Chamber was taken out of the political arena. The exceptions were patronage, where the ladies continued to intercede for their menfolk, and marriage, which for a few months at the end of 1553 was the most important issue of all.[46]

The Duke of Northumberland was arrested at Cambridge by the Earl of Arundel on 24 July. As the council had instructed, he had duly proclaimed Mary, and awaited events. On the 25th he was escorted to the Tower, along with his brother, three of his sons, the Earl of Huntingdon and several other followers. On the 26th they were joined by the Marquis of Northampton, Robert Dudley and Sir Edward Montague, and on the 27th by the Duke of Suffolk, Sir John Cheke and others. Jane and Guildford seem simply to have been transferred from the royal apartments to the prison.[47] All these prisoners were interrogated by the council in the first week of August, and the Duke of Norfolk, days after his own release from the same prison, was appointed High Steward for the trial of the noble defendants. No further action was taken against the Duke of Suffolk or the Earl of Huntingdon, and both were soon after released, but Northumberland, Northampton and the Earl of Warwick were tried on 18 August. All were charged with offences committed only after Edward's death, and inevitably all were convicted. Warwick and Northampton offered no defence, but Northumberland claimed that he had acted only on instructions under the Great Seal – and that in any case half his judges were as guilty in that respect as he was. The second point, at least, was valid, but he was wasting his breath. He requested the privilege of a noble-man's death, and asked to speak with four of the council about 'secret mat-ters of state'.[48] He also asked to confess to 'a learned divine'. The council must have smelled a coup, because the divine they selected was none other than his old enemy Stephen Gardiner. We do not know what passed between them, but Northumberland let it be known that he was prepared to renounce the protestant faith which he had professed with apparent zeal for the last five years. His execution was postponed, and instead he was paraded to mass in the presence of a distinguished audience and accompanied by his brother Andrew, Northampton, Sir Thomas Palmer and Sir Henry Gates. The other prisoners were apparently less compliant. At the end of the service the duke addressed the assembly, saying:

> *'Truly, I profess here before you all that I have received the sacrament according to the true catholic faith, and the plague that is upon the*

realm and upon us now is that we have erred from the faith these
sixteen years . . .'[49]

The queen was delighted, and Renard declared that the people had been more edified than by a month of sermons. Whether this submission was a genuine consequence of defeat and disillusionment, or a desperate bid to bargain for his life, we do not know. Its impact at the time was considerable, and confirmed Mary and Gardiner in their low opinion of protestant integrity. In due course, when the wheel had turned another circle, it also ensured that his reputation would never be rehabilitated. On the evening of the 21st, Northumberland wrote an abject letter to the Earl of Arundel, whom he had so gratuitously humiliated, begging for his intercession, so it seems likely that he had a bargain in mind.[50] If so, it did not work, and he was duly executed on the 22nd, along with Palmer and Sir John Gates, making in the process an extremely correct scaffold speech:

> 'I confess unto you that I have been an evil liver, and have done
> wickedly all the days of my life . . . Do you think, good people, that we . . .
> be wiser than all the world besides, even since Christ? No, I assure you,
> you are far deceived . . . '[51]

Beneath the panoply of power, and in the face of death, Northumberland was a simple man, not unintelligent, but quite unintellectual. He may well have drifted into protestantism by way of political opportunism, and it had little hold upon him because he had no theological understanding. God had destroyed him to teach the people a lesson, and that was what they had all come to hear. Genuine protestants, like his daughter-in-law Jane Grey, were dismayed, but it soon became clear that they were well rid of the company of a man so deeply compromised and unpopular.

The good fortune that had so conspicuously smiled on Mary during July continued during August. However, a few signs began to appear that with hindsight look ominous. She began to consult privately with Simon Renard, and by the end of the month had established a confidential relationship with him which threatened to disrupt her dealings with her own council.[52] Also, in spite of issuing a bland and apparently tolerant proclamation on religion on the 18th, she announced to her council that it was her intention to restore papal authority, and she began to apply ruthless pressure to her sister Elizabeth to attend mass.[53] Elizabeth was as protestant as her brother had been, and like most fellow believers had declared firmly for her sister in the crisis of July. She had even greeted Mary at the head of 2,000 horsemen before she entered London. Such support had been very valuable in the circumstances, but Mary clearly felt no sense of obligation. Her victory, she had become convinced, was the work of God and not of any human agency – which was more than a little unfair to her loyal friends. It also distorted her perception of her own position in a manner that was eventually to be seriously debilitating. On the whole her very obvious intention to restore the old faith was popular, but a catholic sermon by Gilbert Bourne at Paul's Cross on 13 August was so badly received by a noisy mob that the preacher feared for his life. As Renard hastened to point out, a certain caution and tact might be required in the pursuit of so noble a cause as the restoration of true religion.[54]

By September, Mary's council and official appointments were substantially complete. On 5 August Stephen Gardiner was appointed Lord Chancellor. On the 10th the Duke of Norfolk and the Earl of Shrewbury, Lord President of the North, joined the council. On the 13th the Earl of Pembroke was sworn, and the Marquis of Winchester, the latter retaining his office as Lord Treasurer. On the 14th, the aged but eminently respectable Bishop of Durham, Cuthbert Tunstall, was admitted, in spite of the fact that his see had been abolished by statute earlier in the year, and on the 17th this round of appointments was completed with the recruitment of Edward Stanley, Earl of Derby, and William West, Lord La Warr.[55] Tunstall, Norfolk and West were all over 80, and should be seen as testimonies to the queen's sense of justice rather than as working councillors. During September only one further addition was made, when Nicholas Heath, the Bishop of Worcester, was sworn on the 4th. Of this very large group over half attended less than 20 per cent of the meetings to which they were summoned. The core of the working council numbered about eighteen, and the average attendance at meetings was no more than a dozen.[56] So when the imperial ambassadors complained of 'numbers' causing great confusion (which they had started doing as early as September 1553), they were really complaining about disagreements over policy – and particularly over the council not doing what they wanted it to do. Their reports in this respect, as in many others, need to be used with caution.

Mary's coronation was somewhat delayed. This was partly caused by debates over whether parliament needed to be summoned to confirm her title first, partly because of uncertainties over the protocol of a ruling queen (which was an unprecedented situation), and partly, it would seem, because Mary herself insisted upon obtaining 'uncontaminated' chrisom oil from the Low Countries before she was prepared to proceed.[57] To one of her sensitive conscience, the whole ceremony presented problems. It was easy enough to ensure that the traditional rite was properly followed, although even that had to be modified to take account of her sex, but the realm was in schism, and that was a situation which could certainly not be remedied in a few weeks. There was also the problem of who was to perform the ceremony. Both Cranmer and Holgate of York were heretics, and Cranmer was in the Tower by 14 September, having made a public protest against the reintroduction of the mass.[58] The highest-ranking prelate was Stephen Gardiner of Winchester, her Lord Chancellor. Gardiner had been imprisoned for his opposition to the Edwardian reforms, but like everyone else (including Mary herself) he was out of communion with the Church of Rome. Hence the importance of the chrisom. Should any fault be found with Gardiner's right to conduct such a ceremony, it was hoped that the use of the proper oil would cover the deficiency. It was the best that could be done at short notice.

As the regime prepared to put itself on show, there was much to be put right. During the first half of August it was all change in the London prisons, and even observers close to the action were confused about what was going on. The Earl of Pembroke was rumoured to have fled to the country, then he was under house arrest, then he was sworn of the council. Similar reports followed the Marquis of Winchester and Sir John Baker.[59] There were better-founded reports that Lord Russell and Lord Ferrers were under arrest. Mary was reported to have reached London accompanied by her sister Elizabeth and the Dowager Marchioness of Exeter, and followed by 10,000 horsemen.[60]

> It is credibly reported that the duke of Norfolke, Courtenay, the bushope of Winchester and my lady Somerset mette the queens grace at the Towre gate, and theare they kneeling downe saluted her grace, and she came unto them and kissed them and sayd 'Theis are my prisoners'.

> *Courtenay was made marques of Exeter the 4 of thes present, as the*
> *brute Goethe . . .*[61]

The rumour was mistaken. All these prisoners were released and re-instated within days, but Edward Courtenay was granted only the lesser honour of the earldom of Devon, and that not until 3 September. Edmund Bonner, the once and future Bishop of London, was released from the Marshalsea on 10 August, and his place was taken by Edward's old tutor, Richard Cox. By early September a pattern had been established. Northumberland and his chief henchmen had gone, while the rest of his conspicuous supporters were in prison awaiting trial. Lesser men, like the Paston brothers, could be released and reinstated. The court had been mildly shaken, but could prepare itself for the queen's big day without any sense of serious disruption.

We do not know just when the liveries of scarlet and other cloth were issued, but it must have been in time for the tailors and semp-stresses whose business it was to create the robes, to say nothing of the embroiderers, to complete their work.[62] Quite a number of the new queen's more intimate servants had been kept away from the court by their mistress's principled stand against her brother's church, and would have had to create all their finery from scratch. In London, preparations for the state entry which by custom preceded the coronation began about 12 September. Elaborate scaffolds and set pieces were built, with dragons, giants and choirs of children. There were about half a dozen separate pageants, spaced out along the route which the procession was to follow – one built by the Hanseatic merchants, another by the Genoese and a third by the Florentines. There were mounts, arches, conduits and fountains running wine, all of which must have taken both time and money to prepare.[63] A great deal of ingenuity went into some of these creations:

> *At the ende of Gracechurche [Street] there was another pageant made by*
> *the Florentynes, very highe, on the toppe wherof stode iiii pictures, and*
> *on the syde of them, on the highest toppe, ther stoode an angel clothed*
> *in grene, with a trompete in hande, and he was made with suche a*
> *device that when the trompeter, who stoode secretly in the pageant, ded*
> *blow his trompet, the angel dyd put his trompet to his mowth, as though*

it should be he that blewe the same, to the great marvailing of many
ignorant persons.[64]

When the great day came, on 30 September, the queen rode in 'a charett gorgeously be-sene'. John Hayward of the Chapel Royal, a famous court poet and entertainer, delivered a Latin oration, and the children of St Paul's school 'sang diverse staves in gratifying the quene', who paused and listened attentively to them. At one of the city pageants another child 'for the cyty' presented her majesty with a purse containing 1,000 pounds in gold 'which she most thankfully receyved'. Throughout this entry Mary seems to have conducted herself with great dignity, and to have responded appropriately, if somewhat passively. There is no mention of the interactive playacting which was to be such a feature of Elizabeth's corresponding entry just over five years later. It was not Mary's style. Lacking her sister's gift for histrionics, she was incapable of 'milking' the applause and genuine enthusiasm that greeted her, but nobody at the time thought that it mattered.[65]

On her coronation day Mary went by water to the old Palace of Westminster, and at about eleven o'clock walked to the Abbey 'apon blew cothe being rayled on every syde'. She was, we are told, escorted and pre-ceded by many bishops, in what must surely have been a calculated demonstration. In the Abbey she was duly proclaimed, and her corona-tion pardon issued, but the latter seems to have made rather a lot of exceptions: 'all prisoners in the Tower, the Flet, certayne in the Mershallsey, and such as had eny comandement to kepe the house, and certain other'. So who would have benefited, apart from a few debtors, is not very obvious.[66] The ceremonies of crowning were long and elaborate. She was 'ledde iiii or v tymes on the alter', so that it was almost four in the afternoon before she left the church, wearing her crown and carrying the orb and sceptre. The banquet which followed was very splendid, but marred by the disorderly behaviour of the crowd, who tore up the cloth and rails to carry off as souvenirs, and scrambled for the broken meats which were traditionally distributed as alms at the end of such feasts. Apart from the entry of the queen's champion, there seems to have been no entertainment offered, either at the banquet or afterwards. On 26 September the Master of the Revels had been instructed to deliver props and costumes to the gentlemen of the Chapel Royal 'for a play to be played before us at the feasts of our coronation, as hath in time past been accustomed'. What seems to have been intended was a conventional morality play, with characters called Reason, Virtue, Self Love and so on; but two days later the order was countermanded without explanation, the performance being postponed until Christmas.[67] Mary was also the only Tudor not to preside over a coronation tournament. The reason for this is similarly unknown. Perhaps too many of the knights and gentlemen who might have performed were out of favour, or it may have been that Mary considered such martial displays inappropriate for a woman. As we shall see, tournaments were held later in the reign, but the queen seems never to have attended. There was nothing of the Faerie Queen about Mary, and even her mother (who had frequently graced such events) might have been puzzled.[68]

At this point we should remember that Mary was England's first ruling queen. Matilda in the twelfth century had claimed the crown, and had fought for it, but had never been accepted or established. Since then the crown had passed from father to son (or in one case, grandson) in unbroken succession until 1399. Henry IV and Edward IV may or may not have been the lawful heirs, but their claims had been accepted as hereditary. It was only in 1485 that the normal order was obviously disrupted, because Henry Tudor's hereditary claim was remote, and he did not insist upon it. Had the later Tudor rules applied, it would have been his wife, Elizabeth, who inherited the throne. Had there been an even remotely plausible male claimant at the time of Edward's death, Mary might never have secured her inheritance. However, confronted by a young woman whose claim was obviously inferior to her own, and with yet a third woman, Mary Stuart, lurking obscurely in the wings, Mary had been easily victorious. Her coronation set the seal upon that success, but it did not solve any of the contingent problems. Was her authority equal to that of a king? What would happen when she married? And, most urgently of all, what images of power were available to her? Even the heraldry that decorated her coronation was military and masculine in origin. The church by which she set such store was totally male dominated. What was a woman to do to impose herself upon such a world?[69] In October 1553 she was greeted everywhere as England's dear sovereign lady, but no one – least of all Mary – knew exactly what that meant.

Notes and references

1 *CSP Spanish*, vol.11, pp.16–19, 32, 17 March and 10 April 1553.

2 D.M. Loades, *John Dudley, Duke of Northumberland* (Oxford, 1996), p.238.

3 'The Vita Mariae Angliae Reginae of Robert Wingfield of Brantham', ed. D. MacCulloch, *Camden Miscellany*, 28 (1984), p.244. Wingfield's source is thought to have been John Gosnold, the Chancellor of Augmentations, who was not a councillor, or a member of the Privy Chamber, but who had good contacts.

4 *CSP Spanish*, vol.11, p.46. Scheyfve described Jane as 'the duke of Suffolk's daughter, whose mother is third heiress to the Crown by the testamentary disposition of the late king'.

5 Inner Temple, Petyt MS xlvii, fol.316; *Literary Remains of Edward VI*, ed. J.G. Nichols (Roxburgh Club, 1857), vol.2, pp.571–2.

6 Loades, *John Dudley*, pp.240–42; W.K. Jordan, *Edward VI: The Threshold of Power* (London, 1970), pp.515–17.

7 Jordan, *Edward VI: The Threshold of Power*, pp.515–17. Henry VIII had created a precedent by seeking statutory approval for bequeathing the crown by will. The last occasion upon which the succession had been in dispute was 1483.

8 'Vita Mariae', ed. MacCulloch, pp.246–7.

9 The first English political thinker to impose a 'confessional test' upon the crown was Christopher Goodman, in *How Superior Powers Ought to be Obeyed* (1558). Cranmer was prepared to accept Mary as the lawful heir, but was persuaded to obey Edward's wishes.

10 *Literary Remains*, ed. Nichols, vol.2, pp.572–3. These oaths were sworn, and signatures applied, on 21 June.

11 Noailles to Henry II, 28 June 1553, in E.H. Harbison, *Rival Ambassadors at the Court of Queen Mary* (Princeton, NJ, 1940), p.43 (MS Aff.Etr., IX, fol.34).

12 Ambassadors to the emperor, 13 July 1553, in *CSP Spanish*, vol.11, pp.72–80.

13 'Vita Mariae', ed. MacCulloch, p.251. Kenninghall had been granted to Mary, along with most of the former Howard estates in East Anglia, in 1547, following the attainder of the third Duke of Norfolk. Much of the former Howard affinity transferred its loyalty to the princess at the same time.

14 *The Diary of Henry Machyn*, ed J.G. Nichols (Camden Society, 1848), p.35.

15 According to Wingfield, Mary was first told of Edward's death by 'her goldsmith, a citizen of London', but it was only when the news was confirmed by John [i.e.Thomas] Hughes, one of her physicians, that she decided to act. 'Vita Mariae', ed. MacCulloch, p.251.

16 John Foxe, *Actes and Monuments* (London, 1583), p.1406.

17 Ibid., p.1408; *Wriothesley's Chronicle*, ed. W.D. Hamilton (Camden Society, 1877), vol.2, p.88.

18 *The Chronicle of Queen Jane, and of the First Two Years of Mary*, ed. J.G. Nichols (Camden Society, 1850), pp.7–8; Loades, *John Dudley*, pp.261–2.

19 Wingfield ('Vita Mariae', ed. MacCulloch, pp.261–2) states that Suffolk made excuses to refuse the mission, while *The Chronicle of Queen Jane* (ed. Nichols, pp.5–6) says that Jane refused to allow her father to go.

20 Ambassadors to the emperor, 12 July 1553, *in CSP Spanish*, vol.11, pp.84–6.

21 Arundel had been imprisoned for his complicity with the Duke of Somerset and fined 6,000 marks, a penalty which had only been reduced and commuted on 10 May 1553. A month later he had been summoned to the council, and his fine remitted. Paget had originally been fined £5,000, and stripped of his arms. The penalty had been remitted in December 1552, and the arms restored the following March, but he did not forgive his humiliation.

22 'Vita Mariae', ed. MacCulloch, pp.263–4.

23 Francis Godwin, *Rerum Anglicarum Henrico VIII, Edwardo VI* (London, 1653), pp.366–8.

24 'Vita Mariae', ed. MacCulloch, p.266.

25 W.J. Tighe, 'The Gentlemen Pensioners, the Duke of Northumberland, and the Attempted Coup of 1553', *Albion*, 19 (1987), pp.1–11.

26 BL, Lansdowne MS 3, fol.26.

27 D.M. Loades, *The Reign of Mary Tudor*, 2nd edn (London, 1991), pp.18–57; A. Weikel, 'The Marian Council Revisited', in J. Loach and R.Tittler, *The Mid-Tudor Polity, 1540–1560* (London, 1980); G.A. Lemasters, 'The Privy Council in the Reign of Mary I', PhD diss., University of Cambridge, 1971.

28 For a nominal roll of Mary's councillors, see Loades, *Reign of Mary Tudor*, pp.404–11.

29 Ibid. All these men had accepted the Royal Supremacy, and the protestant reforms of Edward. Most were conservative by choice, but Richard, Lord Rich, had appeared at one point to be a strong protestant.

30 For a full discussion of the Gardiner/Paget rivalry and its consequences, see Loades, *Reign of Mary Tudor*, pp.57–95.

31 *CSP Spanish*, vol.11, p.134; D.M. Loades, *Mary Tudor: A Life* (Oxford, 1989), pp.193–4.

32 *CSP Spanish*, vol.11, p.156.

33 Loades, *Mary Tudor*, p.194.

34 *Diary of Henry Machyn*, ed. Nichols, p.39, which totally contradicts the imperial ambassador's statement that he was buried 'with scant ceremony'. What they clearly meant was 'without appropriate religious rites'.

35 R. Greenacre, 'A Controversial Sermon at a Royal Funeral', *Chichester Cathedral Journal* (1998), pp.4–12.

36 PRO, LC2/4, i., fols.1–10.

37 Tighe, 'The Gentlemen Pensioners'; PRO, E101/427/5, fol.29.

38 *CSP Spanish*, vol.11, p.156.

39 *CPR*, 1553–4, p.82.

40 D.M. Loades, *The Tudor Court* (London, 1986), p.204.

41 All these appointments are listed in Loades, *Mary Tudor*, pp.356–7.

42 For example, Francis Englefield as Master of the Wards (*CPR*, vol.1, p.249), Robert Strelly as Chamberlain of the Exchequer (ibid., p.193) and William Cordell as Solicitor General.

43 PRO, KB29/190, r.66d. Underhill's autobiographical 'narrative' (BL, Harleian MS 425) is reprinted in A.F. Pollard, *Tudor Tracts* (London, 1903), pp.170–99.

44 Underhill's narrative – see Pollard, *Tudor Tracts*.

45 PRO, SP11/1/15; LC5/49, fol.23.

46 Loades, *Reign of Mary Tudor*, pp.57–95. Renard several times expressed anxiety over the influence of the queen's ladies in respect of her marriage, but he ultimately won the support of the most important, Susan Clarencius. *CSP Spanish*, vol.11, p.344.

47 *Chronicle of Queen Jane*, ed. Nichols, pp.15–16; *Diary of Henry Machyn*, ed. Nichols, pp.37–9.

48 *Chronicle of Queen Jane*, ed. Nichols, p.17.

49 BL, Harley MS 284, fol.128; *The Chronicle of the Greyfriars of London*, ed. J.G. Nichols (Camden Society, 1852), p.83.

50 BL, Harley MS 787, fol.61. There is some doubt about the authenticity of this letter, which survives only in transcript, but it is consistent with the duke's other expressions of penitence.

51 BL, Harley MS 284, no.79, fol.127; W.K. Jordan, and M.R. Gleason, 'The Saying of John, late Duke of Northumberland upon the Scaffold', *Harvard Library Bulletin*, 23 (1975), pp.119–79.

52 This situation developed from a private audience as early as 29 July. On that day, after a public audience with the four ambassadors, Renard was authorised to speak to the queen alone, probably in response to a request from her. Ambassadors to the emperor, 2 August 1553, *CSP Spanish*, vol.11, pp.129–34.

53 *Tudor Royal Proclamations*, ed. P.L. Hughes and J.F. Larkin, 3 vols. (New York, 1964–9), vol.2, no.390; ambassadors to the emperor, 9 and 19 September 1553, in *CSP Spanish*, vol.11, pp.217, 220.

54 *Diary of Henry Machyn*, ed. Nichols, p.41; Renard to Mary of Hungary, 20 August 1553, in *CSP Spanish*, vol.11, p.175.

55 Loades, *Reign of Mary Tudor*, pp.404–11; based mainly on *APC*.

56 Ibid.

57 Loades, *Mary Tudor*, p.206. On this, and other aspects of the ceremonial of Mary's coronation, see D.E. Hoak, 'The Coronations of Edward VI, Mary I and Elizabeth I, and the Transformation of Tudor Monarchy', in *Westminster Abbey Reformed, 1540–1640*, ed. C.S. Knighton and R. Mortimer (Aldershot, 2003).

58 An English version of Cranmer's protestation survives in Corpus Christi College Library, Cambridge (MS 105, p.321). A Latin version, complete with a circumstantial account of its issuing, was published in Cologne in 1554 as *Vera expositio disputationis institutae mandato D. Mariae Reginae*. For an account of the episode and its consequences, see D. MacCulloch, *Thomas Cranmer* (London and New York, 1996), pp.551–3.

59 *Chronicle of Queen Jane*, ed. Nichols, p.15.

60 Ibid., p.14. Machyn (*Diary*, ed. Nichols, p.38) gives the same figure.

61 *The Chronicle of Queen Jane*, ed. Nichols, p.14.

62 PRO, LC2/4, ii.

63 PRO, SP11/1, no.15; *Chronicle of Queen Jane*, ed. Nichols, pp.27–30.

64 *Chronicle of Queen Jane*, ed. Nichols, p.29.

65 Mary had constant problems with her image, partly because she was very aware of her gender and the limitations it imposed but regarded any form of sexual display, however subtle, with horror. The issue is discussed below, and in Loades, *Mary Tudor*.

66 *Chronicle of Queen Jane*, ed. Nichols, p.31.

67 *Documents Relating to the Office of the Revels, Edward VI and Mary*, ed. A. Feuillerat (Louvain 1914), pp.149–50.

68 Catherine had taken it for granted that one of her duties was to play the gracious lady for the benefit of the courtly love displays associated with the royal jousts of the period 1510–25. Mary seems to have had no awareness of the opportunities these displays presented.

69 For a discussion of this dilemma, see Judith Richards, 'Mary Tudor as "Sole Queen"? Gendering Tudor Monarchy', *Historical Journal*, 40, 1997, pp.895–924.

. . . .

CHAPTER 6

The court of a *femme seule*

B y the time Mary was crowned, and her council settled, two urgent
policy priorities had been identified. Both were personal as well as
political issues. The first was the restoration of 'true religion' and the
second was her marriage. Her first public pronouncement on religion, the
proclamation of 18 August, indicated an immediate but cautious return
to the traditional rites. It promised a considered settlement after due con-
sultation, and said nothing at all about jurisdiction.[1] However, the
queen's personal agenda was far more radical than the proclamation
suggested. She had already indicated her intention to restore papal authority, and had struggled with her conscience over her brother's funeral.
There is no specific information as to when the mass was restored to her
own chapel and the clerical staff replaced, but it was almost certainly
with immediate effect. Thomas Thirlby, the dean, appears to have conformed, but Edward's chaplains had all disappeared by the time of the
coronation, just as most of the bishops who had replaced those deprived
by Edward's commissioners had been removed within a matter of weeks
by royal fiat.[2] The issue of marriage, on the other hand, did not as yet
have a public face at all. Mary was already 37, and given her chequered
medical history might reasonably have concluded that it was already too
late to be thinking of childbearing. As far as we know, no one close to her
uttered any such thought, and she herself declared that although she had
no personal desire for marriage, it was clearly a duty she owed to her
realm.[3] However, not only was she unmarried, she had never had even a
shadow of sexual experience – unlike her sister Elizabeth, who had been

caught by her outraged stepmother in the arms of Lord Thomas Seymour. During the first fifteen years of Mary's life, her marriage had been a lively diplomatic issue, but the only time she ever saw one of her suitors was in a brief interview with Philip of Bavaria, whom she instantly rejected as a Lutheran. Whatever qualms she must have felt, having made her decision the matter became one of urgency. By the middle of August 1553 it was no longer a question of whether, but who?

There were not many realistic candidates, because Mary would not have considered a French or German prince even if one had been available. The obvious front-runner from her point of view was the emperor, Charles V. They had been betrothed nearly 30 years before, and she had come to regard him during the troubled 1530s as her protector and champion, her 'true father' as she had put it at one point.[4] He was a widower and 53 years old. However, his health was poor, and he was already contemplating retirement. Much as a Habsburg/Tudor union appealed to him as a political coup, he declared himself to be a non-starter at a very early stage. A second possibility was Dom Luis of Portugal, the younger brother of the king. Luis had also bidden for Mary's hand in the past, and was now a man in his forties. The third possibility was Edward Courtenay, the son of Henry Courtenay, Marquis of Exeter, who had died on the scaffold in 1538. Edward was 26, eleven years younger than the queen, and had only recently been released after sixteen years in the Tower. And finally, there was Charles's son, Philip, Prince of Spain, who was also 26 years old.

Each of the three who were prepared to enter the lists had distinct advantages and disadvantages. All three were ostensibly loyal catholics, and Philip and Luis certainly were.[5] Courtenay had the enormous advantage of being English, and consequently would not attract the hostility that was bound to attend a foreign king. Moreover, his mother was a close friend of the queen, allegedly sharing her bed in the early weeks of the reign. When Courtenay was restored to the earldom of Devon at the end of August, many took it as an omen, and a strong party within the court and council espoused his cause. The political leader of this party was the formidable Lord Chancellor, Stephen Gardiner, and many of Mary's most loyal personal followers, such as Robert Rochester, were in the same camp. It was thought by some that their influence, allied to that of Gertrude, Courtenay's mother, would be found irresistible. Unfortunately,

Edward was a weak and rather feckless young man, bewildered by his unexpected turn of fortune, and there is no evidence that Mary ever seriously considered marrying him. Dom Luis was not feckless, but he seems to have had no very positive characteristics. He was a prince of royal blood but not the immediate heir to a throne, and he could reasonably have been expected to live in England and perform the functions of a king consort. However, he suffered from one major disadvantage: Charles V was totally opposed to his candidature, and he had enough influence in Portugal to frustrate it. That left only Philip. In spite of being rather young, Philip was already a widower with one son, and he was his father's choice. Given that Mary had declared years before that she would follow the emperor's advice when (or if) she came to marry, and had repeated that undertaking to his ambassadors within days of her accession, Charles's influence was always likely to be decisive.[6] However, Philip was his father's heir in respect of Spain and her empire, and he was likely to succeed sooner rather than later because of the emperor's declining health. He was purely Spanish by language, culture and upbringing, and the chance of his ever spending much time in England or according the country a high priority was remote.

There simply was no right answer. Both Edward and Luis laboured under fatal handicaps, and Philip suffered from serious disadvantages. However, given Mary's determination, and the forces that were working upon her, there was never much doubt as to what her decision would be. The only problem at first was that it was by no means certain that Philip was available. He was deeply engaged in a negotiation for the hand of the Portuguese infanta, and when the news of Mary's unexpected success reached Charles, he at first believed that that negotiation had gone beyond the point of no return. His first instruction to his ambassadors in England was therefore to stall, or rather to dissemble. The emperor's priority from the start had been to keep the French out of England, and if Mary had failed, his representatives had been under orders to make friends with the government of Queen Jane. Fortunately that was no longer necessary, but given his own disinclination and Philip's engagement elsewhere, it was much better that Mary should marry at home rather than choose a foreign prince who might turn out to be unfriendly. Moreover, he was at first sceptical about the security of her triumph, and well aware that one of the arguments her enemies had deployed was that she might choose a foreign husband and bring the realm into subjection. He therefore wrote almost at once, instructing his ambassadors to let it be known that the emperor would prefer the queen to marry at home: 'if they are reassured as to our intentions they may be less accessible to the schemes of the French and cease to dread having a foreigner, loathed as all foreigners are by all Englishmen, for their king'.[7] Only if the queen appeared to be secure and her regime stable were they even to hint at the possibility of 'a better solution'.

Reassured by the end of July that Northumberland (and the French) had really been defeated, Charles wrote a careful letter to his son in Spain. The English were notoriously touchy on the subject of foreign interference in their affairs, he declared, and if they could be persuaded to accept a foreign king at all, they would probably prefer himself. That, however, was no longer possible, and he therefore suggested infiltrating Philip's name into the discussions, preferably by means of a sympathetic English councillor. 'The advantages of this course are so obvious that it is not necessary to go into them', he wrote.[8] If his son was already committed, no harm would have been done, but if he could escape from his Portuguese entanglement, a great opportunity might be created.

Philip's cautious but positive response did not reach Brussels for some time, and in the meantime Simon Renard in London began to pursue the emperor's private agenda. He may well have been secretly briefed by Cardinal Granvelle, Charles's first minister, on this contingency plan before leaving the Low Countries. As early as 29 July he had delicately touched on the question of marriage, and discovered that Mary's general intention was to wed swiftly. She had also thanked the emperor profusely for his good offices in the past.[9] So far, so good. A few days later, after a private audience at Richmond, he reported that the queen distrusted her own subjects as 'variable, inconstant and treacherous' and was unlikely to marry within the realm. If he reported her words accurately, they did not bode well for her success, but in the immediate context they were very satisfactory.[10] Meanwhile, at about the end of the first week of August, Lord Paget mentioned the name of Philip. Whether he did this spontaneously or as the result of prompting, we do not know. Renard very much wanted such an initiative, and he wanted it to be spontaneous, so if he had prompted it he would have been unlikely to say so; and the ambassador's reports are our main source of information on this subject. At this very early stage most of Mary's council, and even the ladies of her Privy Chamber, seem to have been in the dark – the latter because the queen had no desire to disclose to her friend Gertrude in which direction her mind was moving. Antoine de Noailles, the French ambassador, whose reaction would have been totally predictable, kept discreetly out of the way after Northumberland's collapse, and did not even present his credentials to the new queen until 6 August.[11] By that time these initial and tentative moves had already been made.

There could, however, be no question of a negotiation until Philip's position was clarified. The prince's reply, dated 22 August, reached Brussels about the beginning of September, and the news was good. Far from being committed to the infanta, he had already decided to break off the negotiation, because he judged that the 400,000 crown dowry that was being offered was insufficient. Philip was duly gratified by Mary's success in England, and surprisingly complaisant towards his father's suggestion: 'I am so obedient a son that I have no will other than yours, especially in a matter of such high import ...'[12] He did not admit it, but in reality he knew very little about Mary or her kingdom. She was a lot older than him, and reputed to be a good catholic. The English were a cantankerous bunch of heretics, but it was an ancient and honourable crown. If the future was to be one of continued warfare with the French, it was much better to have the English on your side; and Mary's probable unattractiveness as a bride was a minor consideration to a man who would be king, and could have whatever woman he wanted – within limits. He committed the whole negotiation to his father 'to dispose as shall seem most fitting'.

With both parties having effectively commended themselves to the emperor's discretion, the whole issue should have been quickly resolved – but it was not. The problem, as Charles had anticipated, was with the English. Neither the emperor nor any of his servants really understood the dynamics of English politics. They knew about magnate factions and peasant revolts, but a gentry movement to uphold a law laid down by par- liament was quite outside their experience.[13] Renard, who knew that the previous regime had been thoroughly and effectively heretical, continued to believe that Mary's position was extremely precarious, in spite of all the evidence to the contrary. He was paranoid about the French, and saw heretics behind every bush. This served to conceal the fact that most of those who opposed a foreign marriage were perfectly happy with the queen's religious policy, and had not the slightest intention of serving French interests. Philip was unpopular for quite other reasons. He had spent two years in the Low Countries from 1549 to 1551 at his father's suggestion, to introduce himself to some of the people whom he would eventually rule. The exercise had been a public relations disaster. The prince was naturally a withdrawn and private person, not in the rather flamboyant tradition which the Netherlanders expected of their rulers; and he spoke only Spanish and Latin. This meant that he had surrounded himself with his fellow countrymen and with clergy, giving the impression that he regarded everyone else with an arrogant and aloof contempt. The burghers of Antwerp in particular hated him, and this emotion quickly travelled along the short and heavily frequented trade route which ran to London.[14] Renard's outgoing predecessor, Jehan Scheyfve, was quite correct when he told him early in September that 'the English did not at all want his Majesty or his Highness [Philip] but would prefer the King of the Romans [Ferdinand] or the archduke, partly because they dreaded the rule of Spaniards, and partly for religious reasons'.[15] This was very much a London sentiment, because English merchants had been remorselessly harried by the Spanish Inquisition since the breakdown of Henry VIII's relations with Catherine of Aragon, and there had been violent incidents as recently as 1545. The few English merchants who continued to venture to Spain were virtually under siege, and communications were few and hostile. Philip's unfortunate appearance in Brussels had confirmed and intensified those feelings.

Scheyfve's opinion in fact touched a sensitive spot because Charles, angered by the fact that the imperial diet had refused to include Philip in the imperial succession, had manipulated the constitution of the Low Countries to detach them from the Empire (which was his brother Ferdinand's inheritance) in order to bestow them upon Philip. Ferdinand naturally felt cheated, and relations at this point were strained. Consequently the thought that the younger Ferdinand (the archduke) might be a candidate for Mary's hand was extremely badly received.[16] It now seems clear that one of the emperor's main objectives in seeking this marriage for Philip was not to defeat the French but to frustrate any attempt by the Austrian branch of his own family to prevent the prince from succeeding him in the Low Countries. Renard knew

Henry VIII, by unknown artist, 1536
National Portrait Gallery, London

William Paulet, 1st Marquess of Winchester, date and artist unknown
National Portrait Gallery, London

Henry VIII and Will Somers, from Henry VIII's Psalter, by unknown artist
Copyright © The British Library, Royal 2.A. XVI, f. 63v

Edward VI, by an artist in the studio of William Scrots, 1546
National Portrait Gallery, London

Catherine Parr, by unknown artist, *c*.1545–50
National Portrait Gallery, London

William Cecil, 1st Baron of Burghley, attributed to Marcus Gheeraerts the Younger, after 1585
National Portrait Gallery, London

The Eve-of-Coronation Procession of Edward VI

The Society of Antiquaries of London

Philip II, King of Spain, by unknown artist, *c.*1580
National Portrait Gallery, London

Mary I, by Master John, 1544
National Portrait Gallery, London

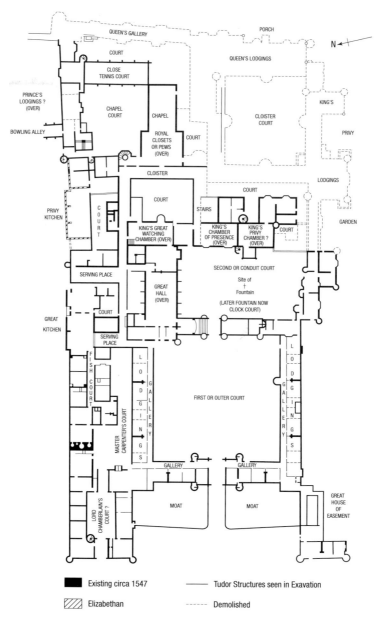

Ground Plan of Hampton Court
After p.131, Volume IV(ii) H.M. Colvin, *The History of the King's Works* (1982). Crown copyright material is reproduced with the permission of the Controller of HMSO and the Queen's Printer of Scotland.

The Darnley Portrait of Elizabeth I, by unknown artist, *c.*1575
National Portrait Gallery, London

The Family of Henry VIII: An Allegory of the Tudor Succession, attributed to Lucas de Heere, c.1572
National Museum & Galleries of Wales

this perfectly well, and in writing to Granvelle on 8 September he reported:

> It has been represented to the Queen that his Highness will have great difficulty in keeping possession of the Low Countries after his Majesty's death, for the King of Bohemia [Maximilian, Ferdinand's brother] is loved there, and his Highness and the Spaniards hated.[17]

Whether Scheyfve was deliberately trying to make his successor's life more difficult we do not know, but the suggestion that Mary might well find herself embroiled in a civil war in the Netherlands should certainly have given her pause. In fact, it seems to have had no effect at all. In early September Mary was in an exalted mood, and more concerned with identifying the will of God than with confronting practical problems. She resorted to prayer, and with hindsight it looks as if her decision was already made, but that was not actually the case. The rumours which leaked out of the Privy Chamber at this point were plausible, but premature, because Charles had not even got as far as a formal proposal. The unnamed English courtier, probably Sir John Leigh, who called on Noailles on the night of 6/7 September to warn him that such a proposal had been made was anticipating. Noailles wrote urgently to Henry II, warning him that such a match would mean perpetual war and suggesting an ultimatum. The French king was alarmed, but in no position to act, because if such a challenge were ignored it would only precipitate the situation he feared, and he could not afford to add England to his enemies while there was any chance of avoiding it.[18]

Mary was not the only person to be having problems. It was not until 22 or 23 September that Renard finally received instructions from the emperor to proceed with a full negotiation, and he immediately and naturally turned to Lord Paget as the ally he needed to give the proposal an acceptable English face. Although he favoured the match, Paget was frank about the difficulties. Philip spoke no English; he would soon have other realms to care for; the English had no desire to get entangled in another war with France; and they would be unlikely to entrust a foreign king with much real power.[19] Charles was not at all deterred by reports of these misgivings. It is clear from the subsequent treaty that war with France was not a priority, and he really did not care how much power

Philip had, as long as he was given the title and status of king. The other problems would have to be overcome.

Although Paget was in most respects a great asset to Renard's campaign, there was one sense in which he was a liability. Part of his motivation was to secure his own influence in court and council, and the Lord Chancellor was perfectly well aware of that. The two men were rivals, almost open enemies, and the queen's marriage became their battlefield. As soon as Gardiner discovered that Philip's name was under formal consideration, he moved to step up his campaign on behalf of Edward Courtenay. Renard became ever more anxious. Gardiner was a formidable politician, and had a lot of support, both in the court and in the parliament that assembled on 5 October. Aware of Gertrude Courtenay's peculiar position, the ambassador also feared that the 'perpetual chatter' of marriage among the queen's ladies would work in Courtenay's favour.[20]

Either Mary was being less than frank, even with her most confidential adviser, or she was still hesitating, in spite of her strong attraction to the Spanish marriage. She was probably hesitating, because another influential voice had by this time also joined the debate. This was Reginald Pole, legally an attainted traitor, but by this time Cardinal Legate to England. Pole was a prince of the Plantagenet royal blood, his grandfather having been the Duke of Clarence. He had fallen out fatally with Henry VIII over the latter's break with the church, and had remained in Italy, becoming a cardinal in 1535. He had obtained the English mission from Julius III as soon as news of Mary's success had reached Italy, and his priorities were quite different from those of the emperor. In several letters during August and September he urged Mary to make reconciliation with Rome her first priority. The very legitimacy of her government depended upon it.[21] Almost alone among the queen's advisers, he argued against marriage. Her age made it hazardous, and if she did her duty to God, he would provide for the succession. When the emperor found out about these letters, he was not pleased. Part of his plan was that the English reconciliation should follow the marriage – and that Philip should get the credit. The last thing he needed was Pole in London, instilling the advantages of celibacy into Mary's wavering mind. So he had the cardinal stopped at Dillingen in Bavaria as he made his way towards England, and kept him there for a frustrating twelve months, until the marriage was safely established.

By the end of October Renard's skill and persistence were at last paying off. The cumbersome colleagues who had accompanied him to England in June left on 27 October, giving him a clear run.[22] Susan Clarencius, Mary's long-serving and intimate confidante, came out strongly in favour of Philip – whether spontaneously or in response to inducements we do not know – and the queen fell out with the dowager marchioness in consequence. With Pole a distant figure and Gertrude out of favour, Mary at last made her decision. On 29 October, after anguished prayer and in the presence of the reserved sacrament, she swore a solemn oath that she would marry the Prince of Spain. It seems that only Renard and Susan Clarencius were present in the oratory at this dramatic moment, and they must have been bound by some promise of secrecy, because no one else in England seems to have known for some time.[23] When he reported this success to his master on 31 October, Renard made much of the queen's piety. She had declared that 'she felt herself inspired by God'. He also did not underestimate his own achievement: he had, he declared, 'almost caused her to fall in love with him [Philip]'. Unfortunately this was an understatement. The prospect of having her own man at last (and such a proper prince) had lit a small fire in Mary which she was quite unable to recognise, and attributed to divine inter-vention. The council, or at least a part of it, was notified on 8 November, although the emotional finality of the decision seems not to have been revealed, and a number of councillors retained the delusion that power-ful and rational arguments might still persuade her to change her mind.[24]

It is against this background that the parliamentary petition of 16 November must be seen. This had been drawn up in late October by Courtenay's friends, mainly in the House of Commons. Some council-lors had also been involved, including the Earl of Pembroke. The initiative may have come from Stephen Gardiner, and if so it casts no aspersion on his loyalty, because Mary's decision was not only unknown but unmade at that juncture. However, by the 16th things had changed. Not only did the council know, but it was also being reported on the streets of London. What was already gossip in the City must have been known at Westminster. On the other hand, parliament had not been officially informed, so the petition was perfectly in order. Mary was furious. She denounced the petitioners for presuming to meddle in matters which were none of their concern, and berated her Lord

Chancellor in public for preferring 'the will of the people' before her own.[25]

> *To force her to take a husband who would not be to her liking would be*
> *to cause her death, for if she were married against her will she would*
> *not live three months, and would have no children.*

It was an intemperate and unwise display, as well as being less than fair to Gardiner. Once they realised the strength of her commitment, the queen's councillors accepted her decision with a good grace, and turned their attention to striking a good bargain with the emperor. Others, however, reacted much more adversely. Courtenay sulked, publicly and foolishly, while a group of members and their friends began to consider what, if anything, could be done. According to the indictments later found, Sir Peter Carew, Sir James Croftes, Sir Nicholas Arnold, Sir William Pickering, William Winter, Sir Edward Rogers, Sir Thomas Wyatt, Sir George Harper and William Thomas met in London on 26 November to conspire the queen's overthrow.[26] These were not backwoods malcontents. All were substantial men in their local communities, and almost all had close connections with one or other of the Edwardian regimes. They had not, however, been involved in Northumberland's plot, and Wyatt and Carew had been among the first to declare for Mary in Kent and Devon respectively. That they were really protestants whose main concern was to halt the queen's religious policy is possible, but unlikely. They would have been extremely foolish if they thought they could reinstate the discredited Jane Grey, and although some of them may have been looking hopefully towards Elizabeth, their main intention was to force the queen to back down over her marriage.[27] We may now conclude that that could only have been accomplished by 'regime change', but the conspirators did not know, or believe, that at the time. Their concern was to mobilise an overwhelming demonstration of political will, such as even an obstinate Tudor could not ignore.

While these malcontents plotted, the council, and particularly Lord Paget, got on with the business of negotiating a marriage treaty. This proved to be remarkably easy, because the emperor had no mind to be difficult, and the whole process was completed in less than eight weeks. Philip was to be styled King, but was to exercise no government in England apart from the queen, and was not to appoint his Spanish servants to English offices. He was not to take Mary out of the realm without her own consent, and was not to involve England in the ongoing war with France. Any child of the marriage was to inherit England and the Low Countries, but to have no rights in Spain.[28] From an English point of view it was almost too good to be true, and the obvious suspicion was voiced in the House of Commons at the end of November. If there was no will on either side to accept these restraints, who would enforce the treaty?

> *In case ... the Bands should be broken between the Husband and the Wife, either of them being Princes in their own Country, who shall sue the Bands? Who shall take the Forfeit? Who shall be their Judges? And what shall be the Advantage?*[29]

Nor were doubts confined to England. Although he had committed the negotiations to his father, Philip was distinctly dissatisfied with the result when the draft reached him about 3 January. He considered that the position offered to him was an affront to his honour, and he was baffled by the clause excluding England from the French war – as far as he was concerned that was the main point of the treaty. He considered withdrawing from the whole project, but he did not want to quarrel with his father, and like the anonymous English MP, he thought that there might be ways around the restrictions. So he contented himself with filing a legal protestation that although he was signing the treaty, he had no intention of observing it![30] Fortunately for Mary, her subjects never found out about that.

The conspirators' plans, meanwhile, were taking shape. It was later claimed that they considered, and rejected, a proposal to assassinate the queen, but there is no confirmation of that. Their ranks were joined by the Duke of Suffolk and, more ambiguously, by the Earl of Devon.[31] A scheme for risings in Kent, Devon and Leicestershire, followed by a converging march on London, began to take shape. Noailles was sounded out, and French support was promised. Then things started to go wrong. On 14 January the terms of the marriage treaty were proclaimed, and they were so unexpectedly favourable that some of the heat was taken out of the discontent. At some point just after Christmas Gardiner succeeded in bullying the Earl of Devon into disclosing what he knew. This was not much, but it sounded an alarm. On 2 January Sir Peter Carew was summoned before the council, and after as long a delay as he dared, he sent his excuses.[32] Something was definitely amiss in Devon. Renard had picked up some scraps of the same information, and when he heard on the 18th that a French fleet was assembling on the Normandy coast, he put two and two together and made about twenty. He told the queen that she must take urgent steps to protect herself against a most dangerous insurrection.

The council did not do a lot, but because the conspirators' plans were so far from maturity, it did enough to snuff out the danger in Devon and Leicestershire – and to precipitate an open rebellion in Kent. No members of the Household were involved, either in the conspiracy or the rebellion, but the events of January and early February affected the court intimately. When the first news of the Kentish 'stirs' reached London about 19 or 20 January, several leading noblemen were absent. Renard claimed that they had feigned ill health as a pretext to withdraw, but since they included the Earls of Arundel and Shrewsbury, there was probably some more innocent explanation.[33] Their absence, however, meant that the queen could not immediately call upon their retinues for her own protection. There was confusion in the council, because Gardiner had concealed his knowledge of Courtenay's disclosures in an attempt to protect that foolish young man from himself. It was not quite clear, therefore, what was happening in Kent, and when the chancellor suggested sending a conciliatory message as a cover for an investigation, the idea was adopted. On 23 or 24 January Sir Thomas Cornwallis visited Allington Castle with an offer to negotiate. Sir Thomas Wyatt rebuffed him, and on the 25th raised his standard at Maidstone, proclaiming the exclusion of all foreigners – and loyalty to the queen.[34]

Over the next few days Wyatt raised a force of about 3,000 men, including some 30 gentlemen, with very little resistance from local loyalists. It became clear that a military response was urgently required, but the retinues were still unavailable, so a force of about 1,000 men was scraped together, consisting of the London trained bands and the yeomen of the guard. For some extraordinary reason the Duke of Norfolk, 80 years old and only just released from prison, was put in charge. Perhaps no more able-bodied nobleman was immediately available. On Sunday 28 January, this force set off against the rebels. The result was (or should have been) predictable. As they advanced on Rochester Bridge, the Whitecoats (the London militia) deserted en masse. The duke, with the

remnant of his force – mostly the yeomen of the guard – retreated precip-
itately. 'Ye shoulde have sene some of the garde com home', wrote one
eyewitness, 'ther coates tourned, all ruined, without arowes or stringe in
their bowe, or sworde, in very strange wyse …'[35] The Household troops
had remained loyal, but they were demoralised and partly disarmed; and
they were now the only force that stood between the queen and nearly
4,000 rebels with the scent of victory in their nostrils.

At Westminster there were divided counsels. Gardiner made a second
attempt at conciliation, and when that failed advised the queen to withdraw to a safer place. Renard told her that if she left her capital she would
lose her kingdom.[36] The Lord Treasurer set an example to his colleagues
by mobilising 500 foot and 100 horse. Mary was nothing if not cour-
ageous, and her instinct corresponded with Renard's advice. On 1
February, accompanied by her councillors and Household officers, she
went to the London Guildhall to appeal in person for the loyalty of the
citizens. Her speech was full of disingenuous promises, but it was rous-
ing and heartfelt; and the Londoners, who were deeply divided on the
issue, rallied to her sufficiently to turn the tide.[37] The City was put in a
state of defence, although no one could be sure, when it came to the
point, that the gates would not be opened to the rebels. Meanwhile, Wyatt
had delayed, mopping up pockets of resistance in Kent. When he reached
Southwark, on the same day as the queen's speech, he found London
Bridge held against him. This was probably the turning point. He stayed
in Southwark for five days, apparently awaiting a sign from across the
river, and when it did not come, on 6 February he decided to try a direct
attack. His troops by this time were beginning to desert, but he made a
rapid march upriver to Kingston Bridge, and early on 7 February he
approached London directly along the north bank of the river.[38]

By this time the balance of power had changed. The Earl of Pembroke
and Lord Clinton had returned to court with armed men at their backs,
and Pembroke as commander in the field had a sizeable force made up of
the retinues of his fellow peers. The court, however, was at St James, and
for the first and only time in the sixteenth century it came under direct
attack. An eyewitness account of this episode survives in the 'narrative'
of Edward Underhill, one of the gentlemen at arms.[39] When Wyatt
reached Southwark on 1 February, 'The Pensioners were commanded to
watch in armour that night at the court', but Underhill had been sent

home as an unreliable heretic, and he gives an amusing and circumstantial account of how he managed to get back into London, which was in a state of siege. When Wyatt 'came about' through Kingston on the 7th, 'notwithstanding my discharge' Underhill donned his armour and repaired to the court with all the rest of his fellows, mustering unchallenged in the Great Hall:

> Old Sir John Gage [the Lord Chamberlain] was appointed without the utter gate, with some of his Guard, and his servants and others with him. The rest of the Guard were in the Great Court, the gates standing open. Sir Richard Southwell had charge of the back sides, as the wood yard and that way, with 500 men. The Queen was in the gallery by the gatehouse ...[40]

However, when the attack came, the response was less than impressive:

> Then came [Anthony] Knevett and Thomas Cobham with a company of the rebels with them, through the gatehouse from Westminster: wherewith Sir John Gage, and three of the judges that were meanly armed in old brigandines, were so frighted that they fled in at the gates in such haste that old Gage fell down in the dirt and was foul arrayed: and so shut the gates, at which the rebels shot many arrows. By means of this great hurly burly ... the guard that were in the court made as great haste in at the Hall door; and would have come into the Hall amongst us, which we would not suffer. Then they went thronging towards the Water Gate, the kitchens and those ways ... With that we issued out of the Hall into the court, to see what the matter was; where there was none left but the porters, the gates being fast shut ...

The attack was not pressed, and after an interval the queen ordered the gates to be opened so that her pensioners could make a sally:

> 'But her request is that you will not go forth of her sight, for her only trust is in you for the defence of her person this day.' So the gates were opened, and we marched before the gallery window; where she spake unto us, requiring us 'As we were gentlemen, in whom she only trusted, that we would not go from that place.' There we marched up and down the space of an hour ...

After which news was received that the rebellion had collapsed.

Underhill was eventually forced to withdraw from Mary's court for religious reasons, and was writing in the relative tranquillity of the 1560s, so it might be supposed that his account was deliberately unflattering. However, a second eyewitness, whose position is not known, substantially corroborates it:

> *At Charinge cross ether stoode the lorde chamberlayne with the garde and a number of other, almost a thousand persons, the whiche, upon Wyat's coming, shott at his company, and at last fled to the court gates, which certayne pursued, and forced them with shott to shyt the court gates against them. In this repulse the said lord chamberlain and others were so amased that men cryed Treason! Treason! In the court, and had thought that the earl of Penbroke, who was assayling the tayle of his enemeys, had gon to Wyat, taking his part against the queen. There should ye have seene runninge and cryenge of ladyes and gentyll women, syting of dores, and such a scryking and noyse as yt was wonderfull to here.*[41]

An attack that was little more than a gesture produced panic and chaos. The pensioners were mostly veterans with serious military experience, but they numbered no more than 70 including the gentlemen at arms, and the performance of the guard raises serious doubts. Probably they were still suffering from the mauling they had taken at Rochester Bridge. The whole Household numbered about 700 or 800 men at this point, and there had been warning enough to arm the whole establishment from the Tower, but the government was still trying ten years later to trace and recover the equipment that was issued at this time.[42] What would have happened in the face of a serious attack must be left to the imagination, but it must be stressed that this was a unique incident, and we have no means of knowing whether the court of Henry VIII or Elizabeth would have responded any more effectively. Only the porters, who managed to shut the gates, emerge with much credit.

The tidying up after this insurrection took several months, and eventually some 750 men were indicted for their part in it, of whom half were tried and convicted, and about 100 executed.[43] Elizabeth was arrested, brought to court, interrogated, and eventually sent to the Tower. Edward Courtenay, whose indiscretions had eventually outstripped Gardiner's ability to protect him, shared the same fate.[44] Both were to remain in prison for many months. However, the problem of Philip's unpopularity did not go away. He was told about the rising only in general and dismissive terms, but he had problems of his own. Quite apart from the general reluctance that still lingered in his mind, he was Regent of Spain, and he had to make proper arrangements for the government in his absence. He was also short of money, and worried about the reaction of France. At the very least he would need a substantial escort to get to England, and that would be expensive. His father was pressing him to provide cash for the hard-pressed imperial exchequer to finance the war in the Low Countries. Mary had also decided that she would not marry during Lent, and all this added up to delays, and a breakdown of communication.[45] As a result, tensions were running high in the spring of 1554. Renard fought a running battle with Elizabeth's protectors in the council, trying to persuade Mary to have her sister executed. The queen disliked and distrusted Elizabeth, and had already made it clear that she wished to exclude her from the succession, but Mary's conscience would not permit her to execute anyone without clear evidence, and in this case there was only conjecture and malice.

By the end of March the ambassador had acknowledged defeat, but he felt bound to advise Mary that if she did not exercise more severity against her enemies, he would have to urge the postponement of Philip's visit, because 'his Highness could not bring forces to guard him, and must look to her for protection'.[46] He was very unimpressed by what he had seen so far. The mood of London continued to be volatile. The 70 or so Whitecoats who had been executed for their desertion at Rochester were better calculated to inflame opinion than to intimidate it, and Noailles, whose recall had rather surprisingly not been demanded, was screwing up the tension to the best of his ability. He was aware that an opportunity had been missed, and was trying to recover his ground.[47] 'It seems to me, Sire', he wrote on 17 February, 'that it would be very necessary for the prince of Spain and the nobles of his council to be assured of the ill-treatment which has been accorded here to his father's ambassadors, and which people are determined to accord to his own person if he comes here ...' Apart from a pelting with snowballs by London schoolboys, it is difficult to understand what 'ill-treatment' he had in mind, but it was his business to exaggerate. Philip had already decided that he could not set out, even if other matters had been settled, until the ceremony of betrothal *per verba de praesenti* had taken place in London. Unfortunately, he also decided not to communicate with his bride-to-be at all, or to send any token, and both Charles and Renard became acutely worried that this behaviour would make the already difficult task of winning hearts and minds in England absolutely impossible.[48]

By February the situation in the Low Countries was also desperate, and Mary of Hungary wrote to Philip that 'this country cannot hold out much longer unless it is supported . . .', by which she meant something in the region of a million ducats. The betrothal *per verba de praesenti* duly took place, with Count Egmont acting as Philip's proxy, but still no word came from Valladolid. The emperor was in a cleft stick. On the one hand it was necessary to make a success of the English marriage, but at the same time he desperately needed both Spanish money and his son's support in the Netherlands. How short a stay in England could the prince decently get away with? In England Renard resorted to increasingly desperate excuses, while in Spain Philip moved heaven and earth – or at least the Genoese bankers – to satisfy his father's financial demands.[49] Meanwhile the English council continued their hopeful preparations for his arrival. Philip had long since agreed, or so they thought, to come with a small retinue, and to rely on an English household for all but his most personal service. This had been urged by his father as a goodwill gesture, and was important if he was to present the 'face' of an English king. In the middle of February he had written to Renard to say: 'when I arrive, I shall have to accept the services of natives, in order to show them that I mean to trust myself to them . . .'.[50] However, there had then followed a prolonged silence, and April became May, and May became June before anyone in England had any clear idea of what was going on. In fact, Philip set out from Valladolid at the beginning of May, as soon as the English envoys arrived to confirm that the betrothal had taken place. As that had happened at the beginning of March, the delays were not all on one side, but it was the English who felt aggrieved. By the time the prince reached La Coruña at the end of June, an English embassy led by the Earl of Bedford had also arrived to escort him – or possibly to ensure that he did not dally any further. On 12 July he eventually sailed for England, accompanied not only by a sizeable military force, but also by a full Spanish household, even down to the cooks and stable boys.[51] A few days before he sailed he also received another urgent message from his father: Marienberg had fallen to the French, and he was to stay only a few days in England before joining Charles in the Low Countries. Fortunately this news was not communicated to the Earl of Bedford.[52]

Some time before Philip sailed, his English household had also been completed: some 350 lords, gentlemen and servants, covering every aspect of the chamber and the counting house except the chapel, where it was understood that Philip would make his own arrangements. It is clear from the fees calculated that the king's household 'below stairs' was only intended to be on a part-time basis. It was partly honorific, and partly intended to cover those times when the king and queen were apart, so presumably it would be summoned as required.[53] The chamber servants, and the yeomen of the guard, on the other hand, were intended to be in regular attendance. Most of them are little more than names, but the seven gentlemen of the chamber were all the sons of leading peers (or, in one case, grandson): Lord Maltravers, Lord Strange, Lord Fitzwalter, Lord Hastings, Lord Herbert of Cardiff, Lord Talbot and the Earl of Surrey. This was an honourable presence, and indicates a serious attempt to please. There were also three aides of the chamber, who were clearly intended to function as interpreters: Anthony Kempe, 'who has served the Queen of Hungary', Richard Shelley, 'recently at the court of the King of the Romans', and Francis Basset, 'a good man and a linguist'.[54] However, English enthusiasm was a little premature. Philip's harbinger, the Marquis de las Navas, reached Southampton on 11 June bearing the long-expected token, and on the 16th the queen set out from London to meet her betrothed. The weeks passed, and the king's household became distinctly restive. They were on Philip's payroll, and had so far received nothing. By the middle of July they were beginning to drift away, strictly against orders, 'speaking strangely of his Highness' as Renard reported unhappily.[55] It was not until 20 of July that Philip finally disembarked at Southampton. The journey, although unimpeded by the French, had been rough: they were all seasick, and it was pouring with rain.

Having disembarked his Spanish household and his noble entourage, Philip's fleet 'of vii score sail' then proceeded to the Netherlands bearing the money and reinforcements that were so urgently needed. Fortunately, the situation there had eased somewhat. The French had been unable to follow up their victory at Marienberg, and in the nick of time, just before Philip landed, Charles had cancelled his instruction for a brief stay in England. The prince could at least become properly acquainted with his wife. The lords of the council were there to greet him on his arrival, and the Earl of Arundel solemnly girded him with the Garter, both an honour and a symbol of his reception into the English system of chivalry.[56] Three days were allowed for recovery from the journey, and on the 23rd he proceeded to Winchester, suitably escorted by both English and Spanish nobles. The bishop received him at the cathedral, where he gave thanks for his safe arrival, and he proceeded to his lodgings at the Deanery. He had, indeed, much to be thankful for. Not only had the French not attempted to stop his journey, the riots and demonstrations which had been threatened in England did not materialise either, and the discontents caused by his long delays appear to have been forgotten also. Above all, the English never found out that until the last minute he had been planning to abandon his bride almost before the wedding banquet was cold. The omens, which had looked so bad in January, now seemed quite promising. On Tuesday 24 July, Philip finally paid his respects to the queen. So much hung upon their relationship that the eyewitnesses were agog with excitement:

> He ... entered the court, where all kinds of instruments played very melodiously, and came within the hal, where the queens maiesty was standing on a skafhold, her highness descended, and amiably receiving him, did kiss him in the presence of all the people. And then, taking him by the right hande, they went together in the chamber of presence, where after they had, in the sight of all the lordes and ladies, a quarter of an hour pleasantly talked and communed together, under the cloth of estate, and each of them merily smylyng on other, to the greate comforte and rejoising of the beholders, he toke his leve of her grace ...[57]

All the symbolic requirements had been met, and the wedding was set for the next day, St James's Day, in Winchester Cathedral.

Philip arrived with his retinue at ten o'clock, and Mary 'with all her council and nobilitie before her' at half past:

> And entering at the west dore of the said cathedral church ... her majestie ascended the foresaid steps, and came towards the quere dore;

where a little without the same dore was made a round mount of bordes,
ascending also five steps above the skafholde. On which mount, imme-
diatelye after her magestie and the king were shriven, they were married
by my lorde the bishop of Winchester . . . her magestie standing on the
right side of the said mount, and the king on the left . . .[58]

Mary's wedding ring, we are told, was of plain gold, 'because that was
how maidens were wedded in olden time'. Renard describes Mary as sitting throughout the ceremony with her eyes glued to the reserved sacrament, and after the wedding they proceeded to a solemn high mass, the
royal couple kneeling in front of the altar from the gospel to the conclusion. They did not, apparently, receive the sacrament.[59] The Bishop of
Winchester celebrated, assisted by the Bishops of Durham, Ely, London,
Lincoln and Chichester, and all the while 'the queens chappell matched
with the quire' to produce 'a sweet proporcyon of music' suitable to the
occasion. The ceremony was completed by the Lord Chancellor reading,
in both Latin and English, an instrument from the emperor creating his
son King of Naples and Jerusalem. The marriage was thus strictly
between equals, although Philip complained for a long time afterwards
that Charles showed no sign of handing over actual control of southern
Italy to him.[60] As they emerged from the cathedral the heralds proclaimed their style in Latin, French and English:

Philip and Marie, by the Grace of God king and queen of England,
France, Naples, Jerusalem and Irelande, Defenders of the Faith, Princes
of Spain and Secyll, archdukes of Austria, dukes of Milan, Burgundy
and Brabant, counties of Habsburg, Flanders and Tirol.[61]

A banquet followed in the hall of the bishop's palace, into which Edward
Underhill managed to insinuate himself in spite of the best efforts of John
Norris, the Chief Usher, to keep him out. 'We were the chief servitors', he
recorded, 'to carry the meat . . .' It was the custom at a royal wedding that
the second course should be given to the servitors in reward, and
Underhill describes how he made off with 'a great pasty of red deer',
which he sent to London to his wife and brother-in-law 'who cheered
therewith many of their friends'.[62]

In Winchester the celebrations continued, with dancing and other
'great cheer', for the space of ten days, and then on Tuesday 31 July the

royal couple removed to Basing, on 2 August to Reading, and on the 3rd to Windsor. This was the nearest Philip was ever to come to showing himself to the people of England; and Mary's trip to Winchester and back was the nearest she ever came to a progress. We do not know how they were received. There were clearly no hostile reactions, but the silence of the otherwise fulsomely loyal descriptions may be significant. At Windsor Philip was solemnly installed as a knight of the Garter. A few days later they moved on to Richmond, where they apparently waited for the preparations for their reception in London to be completed.[63] As these had required the removal of the remains of those executed for the January rebellion, as well as the creation of more orthodox pageants, there may well have been some apprehensions as to how the king would be received in the capital. Insofar as precautions were feasible, they were taken, and Philip and Mary reached Southwark on 17 August 'at ii of the cloke after none'.

Her wedding was obviously the climax of Mary's first year on the throne. On the whole it had been a successful year. She had defeated a small but determined rebellion, outfaced the French, and married the man of her choice. She had also made some progress in realising her other main priority, that of restoring the traditional church. Parliament had dutifully, even enthusiastically, brought back the mass with effect from 20 December, and in spite of a lot of noise and apprehension, there had been no resistance. Visitations conducted (paradoxically) under the Royal Supremacy had removed protestant bishops and incumbents. The prisons were full and many parishes were left temporarily unserved.[64] Elizabeth was safely under house arrest at Woodstock in Oxfordshire under the loyal and vigilant eye of Sir Henry Bedingfield.

Not everything, however, had gone according to plan. Reginald Pole was still fretting in Bavaria; and William Paget was in disgrace after a furious row with the Lord Chancellor in the parliament of April. This was partly the result of their old feud, and partly of mess and misunderstanding. Gardiner had lost influence over his initial opposition to the Spanish marriage, and he even found himself accused of complicity in the Wyatt rebellion. However, the defeat of that rebellion had restored him, because he succeeded in persuading the queen that it was an heretical conspiracy, and that severe measures against the protestants were the best answer. Not only was this advice congenial to Mary, but Gardiner was in the best position to implement such a policy.[65] The bishop then decided to capitalise on his favour. One of the reasons why he had opposed the Spanish marriage was that he had envisaged a connection between Philip's arrival and the restoration of papal authority. This he rightly feared would compromise the church with yet another foreign connection. It would be much better if at least the decision to return to the Roman fold could be taken before the marriage. So, although he had no mandate to negotiate on behalf of the papacy, or to settle the vexed question of the former church lands, he set out to secure a declaration of intent from parliament. For this he had the queen's authority, although the matter had not been discussed in council. Paget, realising what was afoot but not knowing about Mary's role, opposed him. As the main English promoter of the marriage, he was looking to the king for favours, and he realised through his connections with Renard and Granvelle that Philip wanted a role in the ecclesiastical settlement. The last thing the king would want was for the matter to be settled before he arrived, so Paget played on the fears of the House of Lords over church property to secure the defeat of the chancellor's proposal.[66] Mary was furious, and Paget fell so far out of favour that Renard dropped him like a hot potato. In an effort to protect his own influence, the ambassador began to draw closer to Gardiner, whom he had been denouncing only six months before, and even to hint that Paget was intriguing with the queen's enemies. So disorientated was the queen by these developments that she even authorised Renard to intercept Paget's mail in the search for evidence of his intrigues. Of course, none was found.[67]

In other respects, it was a quiet year. Parliament was summoned for 5 October, as soon as the coronation pageants had been dismantled, and Mary rode to Westminster again to open the assembly.

> Her grace rod in her parlement robes, and all the trumpeters blohyng a-fore them all; and so after her grace had hard masse, they whent to the parlement howsse al to-geyther, and the yrle of devonshyre bore the sword . . .[68]

Apart from the fact that some bishops walked out of the mass and ended up in prison, the two sessions which followed were relatively uncontroversial. Henry VIII's marriage to Catherine was declared lawful, and the queen (of course) legitimate in consequence. Virtually the whole of

Edward's ecclesiastical legislation was repealed, returning the church to the position of January 1547, but there were few objections to that. The most significant thing was that Mary decided to proceed by way of repeal, because Pole had been writing to urge that all schismatic and heretical laws were *ipso facto* null and void, and therefore not in need of repeal. The council wisely thought otherwise and the queen heeded their advice. This was not a matter upon which Renard could be expected to have an opinion – fortunately, because his influence was beginning to attract adverse comment.[69] The Convocation of Canterbury which accompanied the parliament was less tranquil, because there a group of protestant divines, led by John Philpot, staged a vigorous rearguard action against the reintroduction of the doctrine of transubstantiation. They were roughly handled and the leaders imprisoned, in spite of claiming that a free debate had been proclaimed and that the parliamentary privilege of free speech should extend to them. It was a sign of things to come.

Parliament was dissolved on 5 December, and the Christmas celebrations that followed were low key. The play originally prepared for the coronation, called *Humanum Genus*, may have been presented, but the costs were minimal.[70] The usual warrants were issued for the festive liveries of the courtiers, so presumably there was feasting and dancing, but nobody thought it worth recording.[71] It is not clear that there were any Shrovetide revels at all, but in the wake of the Kentish crisis that is perhaps not surprising. The fact that Sir Thomas Cawarden, the Master of the Revels, had been committed to the Tower on 27 January must have cast rather a blight over any efforts at jollity. It seems clear that Mary's favourite entertainment was a solemn high mass, and coming and going to such celebrations formed her most usual public appearances.[72] From the beginning she had a problem with her image which no amount of lavish entries and splendid processions could solve. There were no precedents for female images of power, and the desire to represent legitimacy and normality did not translate readily into striking visual forms. Mary's youthful prettiness was fading fast, and although she dressed lavishly, she had no taste in clothes. Above all, she set great store by 'shamfastness', and any kind of sexual display was strictly off limits. In spite of the affection in which she was held, it was difficult to know what to make of her; she was not even entirely English, although she was entirely royal. Perhaps a gentle and merciful princess releasing prisoners and going to mass was the best that could be done. In fact she could be remarkably tough, as her successful bid for the crown had demonstrated, and that was to show again in her appearance at the Guildhall in the face of Wyatt's rising; but toughness was not supposed to be a feminine characteristic, and confused the image problem further, rather than resolving it.[73] The queen probably believed that marriage, and hopefully motherhood, would solve the matter, merging her imperceptibly into the Queen of Heaven, but unfortunately that was not to be.

A second parliament had opened on 2 April. That had originally been summoned in February to Oxford because of security concerns, but the easing of the danger, and the outrage of the Londoners at the loss of profitable business, persuaded the council to use the usual venue. The queen again processed, accompanied by her bishops and lords. Again there was 'a goodly masse of the Holy-gost', and this time there were no dissenters. This parliament ratified the marriage treaty – a mere politic gesture since it had already been proclaimed – and more importantly extended the protection of the treason laws to the new king. This was not without controversy, but the objections seem to have come from those who wanted more generous terms, not less.[74] The main row was in the House of Lords over the chancellor's ecclesiastical measures, and that left a sour taste in a number of mouths, not least because it created the impression that the council was in a state of confusion, with the right hand not knowing what the left hand was doing. The session ended at the beginning of May, not having accomplished very much beyond signifying the queen's intention to take it seriously.

By that time Renard was not the only person who was anticipating trouble when Philip and his retinue arrived. The hostility was not all on one side:

> Ay Dios de mi tierra,
> saquesime de aqui!
> Ay que Inglaterra
> Ya no es para mi![75]

as one much repeated Spanish ballad had it. Even with the best of goodwill at the top, there was going to be trouble. Consequently it was common sense to make provision, and at about the time of the dissolution of parliament, the Earl of Arundel as Lord Steward issued a judicial commission, appointing an alcalde and a 'learned Englishman' to hear disputes arising between the two nations, 'consideration being had to the usages of the nation of the offender'. Briviesca de Munatones and Sir Thomas Holcrofte were later named to these somewhat thankless tasks.[76] The jurisdiction of this commission was not specifically defined, but it was clearly intended to operate within the court, because that was the limit of the Lord Steward's *ex officio* power. When, later, there was violence, much of it was outside the court, and was dealt with by the common law, as in all other cases; but the precaution was wise.

On 11 August, while he waited with Mary at Richmond for the preparations in London to be complete, Philip received news that the French had besieged Renty. No matter what his preoccupations in England never for a moment would the king be unmindful of his father's wars and needs. This news could have spelled the end of his stay in England, almost before it had begun, but it also created an opportunity, because Philip was aware of two things. First, he knew that having both an English and a Spanish household had been a mistake, and secondly, that he was surrounded by touchy Spanish grandees who were seeing insults and provocations on every side, and who were bound to become involved in serious conflict if they were not quickly restrained. Now virtually all of them petitioned to be allowed to go and join the emperor's army in the Low Countries.[77] Their requests could not have been more timely. Some of them were already writing home to complain what a dreadful hole England was, and how its barbarous people had no fear of God. 'We think of Flanders as a paradise', one declared, 'and are all longing to be off.'[78] They departed within a few days, leaving only a small number of senior advisers and personal servants with the king.

This undoubtedly spared Philip much embarrassment. Since arriving in England, he had behaved with a tact and self-restraint that nobody had expected. Charles had written secretly to the Duke of Alba, his son's majordomo: 'for God's sake, Duke, make sure that my son behaves in a suitable manner ...', no doubt mindful of the fiasco in the Netherlands four years earlier.[79] This time he need not have worried. Although he undoubtedly found his rapidly ageing wife less attractive than he would have wished (and some of his courtiers were quite scathing on the subject), he treated her with the most scrupulous courtesy and consideration. He bade her ladies 'Good night' in painfully learned English, and even managed to drink some beer. His bearing, his clothes, and his apparent kindness to Mary all attracted favourable comment, not only from his surprised fellow countrymen, but also from the sceptical islanders. Given the troubled background to the marriage, and the protests it had provoked, the situation in August 1554 was remarkably promising. Mary was probably happier than she had been at any time since her untroubled childhood, and it is not surprising that Simon Renard, who had worked so hard and suffered so much angst to get to this point, was inclined to hail another miracle.[80]

Philip and Mary arrived in Southwark by water from Richmond, landing at St Mary Overies amid what would now be described as very tight security. 'Every corner being so straight kept as no man could pass, come or go, but those that were appointed to attend their landing.' They stayed overnight at Suffolk Place, the former residence not of Henry Grey but of Charles Brandon, and entered the city the following afternoon.[81] They were received by the Lord Mayor, all the members of the Privy Council, and a large gathering of other peers and gentlemen, English, Spanish and 'other strangers', together with the ambassadors. The 'other strangers' were mostly members of London's resident merchant communities, many of whom would have been expecting to make a handsome profit out of England's new Habsburg affiliation. The Lord Mayor surrendered his mace to the queen, and received it again, preceding them into the City. They went in a mounted procession, with swords borne before them, the queen on the right and the king on the left – a careful reversal of the normal order of precedence. As the guns of the Tower fired a salute, they came to the first pageant, a 'fair table' borne aloft by the giants Corineus Britannus and Gogmagog, which contained a Latin verse beginning:

Unica Caesarem stirpis spes inclite princes
Cui Deus imperium totius destinat orbis ...

The narrator of this progress carefully translated this:

O noble Prince, sole hope of caesar's side
By God appointed all the world to gyuide ...

But it does not appear to have been translated in the original table.[82] This pageantry was aimed at Philip, as is clear both from the language and from the choice of flattery, and the less the ordinary citizens understood of what was being said, the better for all concerned. There was a presentation of the Nine Worthies in Grace Church Street, and at the Splayed Eagle a further pageant created by the merchants of the Steelyard,

> *Where emongest divers notable stories, there was in the top thereof a*
> *picture of the king sitting on horssbacke, all armed, verye gorgeously,*
> *and richly set out to the quicke. Under which picture were written in*
> *field silver with fayre Romaine letters of sable, these words followinge*
> *after this manner:*
> *Divo Phi. Aug. Max.*
> *Hispaniarum principi exoptatissimo . . .*

There were several other pageants with a similar theme: 'the four noble Philips' (Macedon, Rome and two of Burgundy), for example, with an exhortation to the fifth to emulate his noble predecessors. Orpheus played his harp in Cheapside, 'Anglia qua solo gaudet dicente Phillippo ...'. At the west end of the same street, Edward III, 'of whom both their majesties are lineally descended', displayed his genealogy; a scholar of St Paul's presented the king with a book 'which he receyved verye gentlie'; and they exited at Temple Bar with another lengthy Latin 'table'.

The account from which all this is drawn was official propaganda, published shortly after the event.[83] The author also represents the citizens 'in great number' rejoicing and shouting 'God save your graces'. Similar narratives were published in Spanish, Italian and German for the benefit of Habsburg subjects all over Europe.[84] Great care was taken to represent this marriage, and the subsequent entry into London, as a magnificent triumph for Philip. Even in the English version Mary is a very secondary figure, and in the other accounts she hardly features at all. An independent narrative, not published at the time, confirms the nature and subject of the pageants, but without comment, and notes that one of the Nine Worthies was Henry VIII bearing in his hand a book, clearly the bible, bearing the inscription *verbum dei*, an insinuation for which the artist was soundly upbraided by the Bishop of Winchester.[85] Henry Machyn, normally eloquent on the subject of 'goodly' display, passes the whole event by without mention, which is perhaps a fair comment on what most Londoners thought of what was being offered in their names. Machyn was by no means hostile to the regime, but his references to Philip are few and neutral in tone. The royal couple stayed about five nights at Westminster before moving on to Hampton Court, and 'during this period all the Lords of the Low Countries came over from Flanders to pay court to the king ...'. Philip was beginning as he intended to go on.[86]

Notes and references

1 *Tudor Royal Proclamations*, ed. P.L. Hughes and J.F. Larkin, 3 vols. (New York, 1964–9), vol.2, no. 390.

2 PRO, SP11/1/15. Day of Chichester, Bonner of London and Tunstall of Durham were simply received as bishops of their respective sees, ignoring the incumbencies of Scory and Ridley. Judicial commissions later declared their deprivations to have been invalid, which verdicts were themselves unsound unless the Edwardian laws had also been invalid – which was never alleged. Thirlby, who was also Bishop of Norwich, was one of several Edwardian bishops who accepted the return of catholicism.

3 Ambassadors to the emperor, 2 August 1553, *CSP Spanish*, vol.11, pp.129–34.

4 See the correspondence between Eustace Chapuys and Granvelle in October 1535: *Letters and Papers*, vol.9, p.596.

5 Courtenay's loyalty to the catholic church was problematical. He claimed to be a good catholic, and Gardiner seems to have accepted him as such, but there is circumstantial evidence to the contrary. Anne Overell, 'A Nicodemite in England and Italy: Edward Courtenay, 1548–1556', in *John Fox at Home and Abroad*, ed. D.M. Loades (Aldershot, 2004), pp.117–37.

6 Ambassadors to the emperor, 8 August 1553, *CSP Spanish*, vol.11, pp.155–8.

7 Emperor to the ambassadors, *CSP Spanish*, vol.11, p.60.

8 Emperor to Philip, 30 July 1553, *CSP Spanish*, vol.11, pp.126–7.

9 D.M. Loades, *The Reign of Mary Tudor*, 2nd edn (London, 1991), pp.58–9

10 *CSP Spanish*, vol.11, pp.155–8. It has to be remembered that Renard was inclined to tell the emperor what he knew he wanted to hear. He would not have ventured to invent this conversation, but he may well have put his own gloss upon rather different words. The original conversation was almost certainly conducted in French.

11 E.H. Harbison, *Rival Ambassadors at the Court of Queen Mary* (Princeton, NJ, 1940), pp.71–2.

12 *CSP Spanish*, vol.11, pp.177–8. Such a response could not have been taken for granted, as Philip was not reluctant to defy his father on occasion. See M. Fernandez Alvaro, *Corpus Documental de Carlos V*, vol.3, (Salamanca, 1977).

13 Harbison, *Rival Ambassadors, passim*.

14 Henry Kamen, *Philip II* (London, 1997), pp.40–9.

15 Renard to the Bishop of Arras (Granvelle), 9 September 1553, *CSP Spanish*, vol.11, pp.227–8.

16 In the middle of August the elder Ferdinand sent his Great Chamberlain, Martin de Guzman, to England to raise the possibility of such a marriage, but Charles succeeded in vetoing the proposal before it was ever made. At the end of October the King of the Romans tried again, but by then it was too late. *CSP Spanish*, vol.11, pp.163–4, 318–19.

17 *Ibid.*, pp.212–14.

18 Noailles to Henry II, 7 September 1553, in R.A. de Vertot, *Ambassades de Messieurs de Noailles,* 5 vols. (Louvain, 1743), vol.2, pp.144–5; Loades, *Reign of Mary Tudor*, p.65.

19 Renard to the emperor, 5 October 1553, *CSP Spanish,* vol.11, pp.265–72. Paget also told Renard that he thought Dom Luis would be preferable from an English point of view. He could afford to do that because he knew of the emperor's opposition to such a match.

20 D.M. Loades, *Mary Tudor: A Life* (Oxford, 1989), p.200; *CSP Spanish*, vol.11, p.189. Renard at first believed that Susan Clarencius was a 'second mother' to Courtenay, but afterwards acknowledged that he had been wrong.

21 Pole opened this correspondence on 13 August, the messenger being his Privy Chamberlain, Henry Penning. *CSP Venetian*, vol.5, pp. 384–7. Penning was entrusted with the difficult task of trying to persuade the queen to alter her priorities, in which he failed. Pole also tried to persuade the emperor, but without success: ibid., p.389.

22 Loades, *Reign of Mary Tudor*, p.70. They had ostensibly stayed for the coronation.

23 Renard to the emperor, 31 October 1553, *CSP Spanish*, vol.11, p.328.

24 Loades, *Reign of Mary Tudor*, pp.70–71. It seems that this meeting was attended only by those known to be sympathetic to the proposal, but no secrecy was enjoined, so the others soon found out. However, the strength of the queen's feelings on the matter do not seem to have been communicated to anyone except Renard.

25 Renard to the emperor, 17 November 1553, *CSP Spanish*, vol.11, p.364; D.M. Loades, *Two Tudor Conspiracies* (Cambridge, 1965), p.14.

26 PRO, KB27/1174, rex v.

27 Loades, *Two Tudor Conspiracies*, pp.20–4. The argument about how important religion was in motivating the conspirators continues. See

particularly M.R. Thorpe, 'Religion and the Rebellion of Sir Thomas Wyatt', *Church History*, 47 (1978), pp.363–80.

28 This was because Don Carlos, Philip's son by his first marriage, was the heir of Spain and the Indies. PRO, SP11/1/20; *Tudor Royal Proclamations*, ed. Hughes and Larkin, vol.2, no.398.

29 J. Strype, *Ecclesiastical Memorials*, 3 vols. (Oxford, 1822), vol.3, p.55.

30 *CSP Spanish*, vol.12, pp.4–6. Philip's original procuration is at Simancas. AGS, Patronato Real, 7.

31 The extent of the Earl of Devon's involvement remains uncertain. He seems to have been in touch with Carew, and to have promised some action, but he never did anything, and most of the evidence is hearsay. It is, however, safe to conclude that he knew things which as a good subject he should have disclosed, and by concealing them was guilty of misprision.

32 Declaration by John Priedeux, 24 January 1554, PRO, SP11/2/15.

33 Loades, *Two Tudor Conspiracies*, p.53. It was by no means uncommon for noblemen to go home for a while after their more or less compulsory attendance at court festivities, such as Christmas.

34 John Procter, *The Historie of Wiats Rebellion* (London, 1554, 1555), p.50.

35 *The Chronicle of Queen Jane, and of the First Two Years of Mary*, ed. J.G. Nichols (Camden Society, 1850), p.39.

36 Or at least, that is what he says he told her. Renard to the emperor, 5 February 1554, *CSP Spanish*, vol.12, p.78. At about the same time (31 January), the special envoys who had negotiated the marriage treaty beat a hasty retreat to Flushing.

37 There are two contemporary accounts of this speech, which agree in all essentials. See Procter, *Wiats Rebellion*, p.77, and *The Diary of Henry Machyn*, ed. J.G. Nichols (Camden Society, 1848), p.53.

38 *Chronicle of Queen Jane*, ed. Nichols, pp.43–4.

39 BL, Harleian MS 425; A.F. Pollard, *Tudor Tracts* (London, 1903), pp.170–98. Underhill was known to his contemporaries as the 'Hot Gospeller'.

40 Pollard, *Tudor Tracts*, p.190.

41 *Chronicle of Queen Jane*, ed. Nichols, p.49. This was written by an anonymous resident of the Tower of London, and is often called the Tower Chronicle. The author was not an enthusiastic supporter of the regime.

42 PRO, SP12/1, fol.53.

43 Loades, *Two Tudor Conspiracies*, p.116.

44 D.M. Loades, *Elizabeth I* (London, 2003), pp.99–103; Loades, *Two Tudor Conspiracies*, pp.89–95.

45 Loades, *The Reign of Mary Tudor*, pp.85–6.

46 Ibid., p.82.

47 Noailles to Montmorency, 17 February 1554, BN, Aff.Etr., IX, fols.137–8; Harbison, *Rival Ambassadors*, p.159.

48 *CSP Spanish*, vol.12, pp.73–6.

49 M.-J. Rodriguez Salgado, *The Changing Face of Empire: Charles V, Philip II and Habsburg Authority, 1551–1559* (Cambridge, 1988), pp.81–5.

50 Philip to Renard, 16 February 1554, *CSP Spanish*, vol.12, pp.103–5.

51 Fernando Diaz-Plaja, ed., *La Historia de Espana en sus Documentos* (Madrid, 1958), p.149.

52 *CSP Spanish*, vol.12, p.293.

53 The wages specified for most of the Household servants were either £2 0s. 0d. or £2 13s. 4d, irrespective of status. Yeomen, grooms and children were paid at the same rate, which suggests retainers rather than wages in the ordinary sense. In fact, these servants were hardly ever called on. Ibid., pp.297–9.

54 Ibid., p.297.

55 There were constant false alarms over Philip's arrival, and Flemish and English fleets were both at sea to provide escorts before the end of June. Both ran out of victuals, and the admirals quarrelled as the tensions of waiting increased. By the time that Renard wrote on 9 July a number of gentlemen, including Sir George Howard, designated as Chief Carver, had left pleading poverty. Ibid., pp.289, 307–10.

56 John Elder's letter 'sent into Scotland', published as Appendix X to *The Chronicle of Queen Jane*, ed. Nichols, p.139.

57 This was their first acknowledged meeting, but according to Elder, Philip had actually visited Mary secretly the previous evening, 'where her grace very lovingly, yea, and most joyfullye receyved him' – but he added, 'as I am crediblye informed'. Perhaps he thought that a quarter of an hour might seem a little perfunctory if it had really been their first meeting. Ibid., p.140.

58 Ibid., p.141.

59 None of the surviving accounts makes any mention of the couple receiving the sacrament, although one mentions them taking holy bread and holy water. This may have been because it was the custom to receive only at Easter, or it may have been out of respect for Philip's scruples. Although nothing was said openly, the English church was still technically schismatic,

and the king may have had doubts about its sacraments. *CSP Spanish*, vol.13, p.11; *The Chronicles of Queen Jane*, ed. Nchols, p.140.

60 Rodriguez Salgado, *The Changing Face of Empire*, pp.108–10.

61 Why the proclamation was made in French and not in Spanish is unclear. There is even doubt about what language the royal couple used in private. Philip's French was poor, and Mary understood Spanish but did not speak it. They may have used Latin, in which both were equally proficient. *The Chronicle of Queen Jane*, ed. Nichols, p.142.

62 Underhill's narrative, in A.F. Pollard, ed., *Tudor Tracts* (London, 1903), p.193.

63 *The Chronicle of Queen Jane*, ed. Nichols, p.145; *CSP Spanish*, vol.13, p.443, being extracts from the *Journal of the Travels of Philip II* by Jean de Vandenesse.

64 Loades, *The Reign of Mary Tudor*, pp.96–128. The queen abandoned the title 'Supreme Head' at Christmas 1553 because it offended her conscience. However, she went on exercising the powers for another year, a process which caused the catholic restoration to be known as 'the queen's proceedings'. Many protestants were held in prison, and a few were tried for treason, but ecclesiastical proceedings did not commence until the papal jurisdiction was restored in January 1555.

65 For a discussion of Gardiner's strategy in the aftermath of the Wyatt rebellion, see Glyn Redworth, *In Defence of the Church Catholic: The Life of Stephen Gardiner* (Oxford, 1990), pp.311–15.

66 Jennifer Loach, *Parliament and the Crown in the Reign of Mary Tudor* (Oxford, 1986), pp.91–105.

67 Queen Dowager Mary of Hungary to the Bishop of Arras, 14 August 1554, *CSP Spanish*, vol.13, p.26.

68 Machyn, *Diary*, ed. Nichols, p.46.

69 'No ambassador was ever so deep in the counsels of Kings or Queens of England as this one', an observation attributed to Lord William Howard. *CSP Spanish*, vol.12, pp.293–5.

70 *Documents Relating to the Revels Office in the Reigns of Edward VI and Mary* (Louvain, 1914), pp.149, 289–90.

71 There are no entries in the Revels accounts for the period between Christmas 1553 and All Hallows (17–21 October) 1554. PRO, LC5/49, pp.40–5 (warrants).

72 For example: 'The iii day of May (1554), at the cowrt of sant james, the quen grace whent a prossessyon within sant James with harolds and sarjants of armes, and iiii bysshops mitred, and all iii dayes thay whent her chapel a-

bowt the feldes, first day to sant Gylles and ther song masse; the next daye
tuwyse-day to sant Martens in the feldes, a sermon and song masse, and so
thay dronke ther; and the iii day to Westmynster, and ther a sermon and
then masse, and mad good chere; and after a-bowt the Parke, and so to sant
james cowrt ther ...' Machyn, *Diary*, ed. Nichols, p.61.

73 For a discussion of Mary's problems in this respect, see J.N. King, *Tudor Royal Iconography* (Princeton, NJ, 1989).

74 *CSP Spanish*, vol.12, p.221; Loach, *Parliament and the Crown*, p.98.

75 Diaz-Plaja, ed., *La Historia de Espana*, p.149.

76 PRO, SP11/4/10; *CSP Spanish*, vol.12, p.258.

77 *CSP Spanish*, vol.13, Appendix, p.443.

78 *Tres Cartas de lo sucedido en el viaje de Su Alteza a Inglaterra* (La Sociedad de Bibliofilos Espanoles, Madrid, 1877), Primera Carta, 91.

79 *CSP Spanish*, vol.12, p.185.

80 Ibid., p.185.

81 John Elder's letter, in *The Chronicle of Queen Jane*, ed. Nichols, p.145.

82 The surviving descriptions make no mention of any of these 'tables' being presented in English, the translations being supplied by the authors. S. Anglo, *Spectacle, Pageantry and Early Tudor Policy* (Oxford, 1965), pp.325–8.

83 *RSTC* 7552.

84 *La partita del serenissimo Principe con l'armata di Spagna* (Rome, 1555); *Viaje de Felipe II a Inglaterra* (Zaragoza, 1554); *La solenne et felice intrata delli serenissimi Re Philippo et Regina Maria d'Inghilterra* (Rome, 1555).

85 *The Chronicle of Queen Jane*, ed. Nichols, pp.78–9.

86 *CSP Spanish*, vol.13, Appendix, p.443.

CHAPTER 7

♦ ♦ ♦ ♦ ♦ ♦ ♦ ♦ ♦ ♦ ♦ ♦ ♦ ♦

King Philip

Philip's position in England was both unprecedented and uncertain. No man had ever held a crown matrimonial in England before, and there was a natural tendency simply to regard him as a king in the full and normal sense. This view appealed particularly to the English nobility, who tended to think of a king as being primarily a war leader, and were uneasy with the thought of a 'sovereign lady'.[1] They had been swept along by the momentum of Mary's campaign in July 1553, and none of them would have wanted to be thought disloyal; but it had been loyalty to the will and memory of Henry VIII that had mainly motivated them. Moreover, the English law of inheritance was unprepared for such an eventuality. There was nothing to prevent a woman from inheriting an estate, but if she married, that estate passed to her husband in what was virtually full ownership. He held it for his own lifetime, whether or not she predeceased him, and only after his own death could it pass to her other heirs, if any. The only restriction upon him was that he could not alienate the estate during her lifetime without her consent. The position of the *femme couverte* was thus weak in law. At the same time, most titles were entailed in the male line. Although a woman could be granted a title in her own right, and could transmit a claim to her male heirs, she could not normally inherit one herself.[2] The crown was not a title in the ordinary sense because it was not entailed – was it, therefore, an estate? If so, did the normal laws of inheritance apply? In the early weeks of 1554 Simon Renard had been much exercised over this question, because he did not know much about English law, and it was being represented to him by those opposed to the marriage that Mary had only a 'woman's estate' in the realm, and that it would pass to Philip when they married.[3] The treaty declared that if Mary predeceased her husband without heirs, the realm would then pass to the next heir by the laws of England,

> and in case that no children being left, the most noble lady the Queen doth die before him, the said Lord Prince shall not challenge unto him any right at all in the said kingdom, but without any impediment shall permit the succession thereof to come unto them to whom it shall belong and appertain by the right and laws of the said realm.[4]

The intention was clear enough, but the treaty had at that time no standing in English law, and in any case observing it would be little more than a matter of conscience on Philip's part. It could even be argued that he was the next heir by the laws of England, if normal inheritance applied

In order to provide against this, and to resolve some of the uncertainties, two statutes were passed in the parliament of April 1554. The first ratified the marriage treaty, thus giving it legal status.[5] Although this might not have been effective if the provisions had been seriously challenged, it is hard to see why else such an act should have been passed in respect of a treaty which had already been signed and ratified by both parties. The second was to confirm that the authority of the crown of England was the same, whether held by a man or a woman.[6] This removed the danger of a woman's estate, and countered any hypothetical argument to the effect that no statute could override the ancient common law. Like the Henrician Act of Supremacy, this statute did not pretend to create a new situation, but simply declared what was, and always had been – except that the question had never previously arisen. Although Philip had in his own eyes absolved himself from the need to observe the terms of the marriage treaty, no unilateral action on his part could alter the law of England, or the position he occupied in the eyes of his new subjects. How he could develop or exploit that position was therefore going to be one of the main issues of his rule in England. Such concerns were not pressing in August 1554. Both parties were in good health, and there might well be children, who would resolve the whole succession question very positively. There were, however, some related issues that were more urgent. What role was Philip to play as king of England? How was he to present himself? What were his priorities, and how could his honour be satisfied?

The question of honour was more important than the modern mind can readily appreciate. It had been because the treaty threatened a dis-honourable position in England, rather than for any more tangible politi-cal reasons, that it had so upset Philip in the first place. However, having decided to come, he was wise enough to play the game according to the rules. He took the left-hand side, leaving the more symbolically powerful right to Mary, and did not complain when the throne upon which he sat was a few inches lower than his wife's.[7] His servants, however, were less restrained. From their point of view the slights put upon their master were intolerable, and they were horrified at the lack of deference shown by the English to both their sovereigns. No less a person than Don Fernando Enriquez, the Admiral of Castile, created a panic in Valladolid by suggesting that their beloved prince was in actual physical danger. 'Neither the King nor the Queen have any authority over these lawless barbarians', wrote another of his colleagues. So alarming was the news from England that on 13 September one of the councillors whom Philip had left behind, Juan Vasquez de Molina, wrote anxiously, suggesting that a fleet should be despatched to rescue him, or at least that he should withdraw to the Low Countries until the English could be persuaded to treat him 'as becomes their King and Sovereign Lord'.[8]

A lot of the trouble was caused by the double household, or rather by the duplicate chambers. The redundant below-stairs servants could simply be stood down – or, in the case of the Spaniards, sent home – but the two chambers were competing for honour. Philip was quick to appreciate that this situation was potentially explosive, and he attempted to be both strict and fair. He laid down a general rule that in public he would be attended by his English servants, and in private by the Spaniards. He could hardly have done otherwise, given that he spoke no English and his English gentlemen, apart from the aids and Lord Fitzwalter, no Spanish. Inevitably, both sides complained. Renard, whose euphoria had quickly evaporated, commented at the beginning of September that 'very few Englishmen are to be seen in his Highness's apartments', and Lord Fitzwalter grumbled that he had no chance to practise his Spanish.[9] On the other hand, the Spaniards, many of whom had gone to great personal expense and inconvenience to follow their prince to England, felt slighted and redundant: 'we are all hanging about with nothing to do and might as well go and serve his Majesty in this war', as one of them wrote well after the first contingent had departed for Flanders. Philip let a few more go, but he had no intention of 'entrusting himself' to the English, as he had earlier promised. Instead, he tried to impose a rule of silence: 'his Majesty has commanded that while we are here no one shall say a word, but put up in silence with all the provocations of the English, so they ill treat us without fear', as one wrote indignantly.[10]

This tense situation was complicated further by the fact that several of the more senior Spanish courtiers had brought their wives – strictly against the emperor's instructions. Even soldiers, he had written, would be more likely to get on with the English than these touchy dames. The most senior was the Duchess of Alba, who arrived unannounced and threw the harbingers into a panic because there was no accommodation allocated to her at court. They provided her with lodgings, but not within the precinct (the defined location within which the court was situated), to her great chagrin. When the duchess presented herself to the queen, a comedy of competitive protocol developed which left them both sitting on the floor.[11] It must be wondered whether anyone had the courage to laugh. The duchess did at least see Mary. Others were less fortunate. One report of 17 August ran: 'Dona Hieronima de Navarra and Dona Franisca de Cordoba ... have not yet seen the Queen, and are not going to see her, for they have not joined the court because they would have no one to talk to, as the English ladies are of evil conversation.'[12] If this was a typical attitude, the emperor had clearly been right.

Ruy Gomez da Silva, the king's secretary, on the other hand, possessed a sardonic sense of humour: 'There are some great thieves among them [the English]', he reported at one stage, 'and they rob in broad daylight, having the advantage over us Spaniards in that we steal by stealth, and they by force.'[13] Senior courtiers on both sides behaved correctly enough, although with little real friendship. Apart from their wives it was their servants who caused most of the trouble. As early as 15 August there was a fracas of some kind within the court which caused the Privy Council to call on the Lord Steward to investigate, and sent the Spaniards rushing to their *alcalde* to complain – with what outcome is not known. Although Philip studiously ignored the fact, the English church was still in schism, and this created problems for his clerical entourage. The friars debated anxiously whether they should wear their habits in public: not only was the church out of communion, it was feared that the population would be hostile. Eventually they compromised, and wore their habits 'on duty', but not at other times. Such fears were not exaggerated, because in spite of the enthusiasm with which most of Mary's subjects had welcomed a return to the old ways, there was little affection for the regulars. On one occasion a crowd 'tried to tear their cloaks off the backs of Don Pedro de Cordoba and Don Antonio his nephew, who are *comendadores*, asking them what they meant by wearing crosses, and jeering at them'.[14] No one was killed, but it was an unpleasant incident.

As Philip felt his way cautiously towards some resolution of his household problems, he also had to decide how to conduct his political affairs. Within a few days of the wedding the council had decided to minute its proceedings in Latin or Spanish for his benefit, and on 13 August the Duke of Alba reported that 'only Castilian' was being used for matters of state.[15] He may have been referring to non-English business, of which there was plenty (and which would have had precedence in his mind), or he may have meant that Philip was using an interpreter. As no English officer of state spoke Spanish, his observation cannot be taken at face value, and may have been no more than a placebo designed to quieten the fears which were already being expressed both in England and in Spain. It is very unlikely that the king would have attempted to address his English council in Spanish, knowing their limitations. Most (but not all) of them had competent Latin, and Gardiner was an accomplished scholar, so it is much more likely that that was the medium of communication. Mary did her best to ease her husband into a practical role. An undated memorandum, which must have been written in early August, instructs the Earl of Bedford, the Lord Privy Seal, to 'tell the king the whole state of the realm'. As Bedford had travelled with Philip from Spain they must already have been well acquainted, so it was natural to entrust this task to him rather than to the chancellor, who might have been better qualified. Rather surprisingly, she also instructed the earl 'to obey the commandments of the king in all things'.[16] If followed literally, this instruction would have made Bedford his servant rather than hers, and there is no sign of that happening. At this early and enthusiastic stage Mary may have meant it literally, but Philip was far too wise to take advantage of it — if he ever found out.

The problem of the double household was solved during the early autumn, as more of the Spanish and Italian courtiers leaked away to the Low Countries, and those who remained became adjusted to the situation. The mutual hostility, however, did not go away. According to one Spaniard there was 'knife work' within the precinct, but there are no records of fatalities there, or even of bloodshed. Outside the court there were brawls, robberies and one or two murders which Henry Machyn commented upon with a touch of relish.[17] It is difficult to know just how bad the situation was because those who reported the incidents had their own agendas. Giovanni di Stroppiana, a special envoy from the Duke of Savoy, wrote a number of chatty letters from London during the autumn, and he claimed that the alarmist reports emanating from the Spaniards who had already withdrawn were grossly exaggerated. Antoine de Noailles, on the other hand, seized gleefully upon every report of animosity, and seems to have been doing his best to stir it up. In early September he reported a lurid plot to massacre all the Spaniards at London and Hampton Court, but nothing happened and he may well have invented the whole affair.[18] Apart from an understandable touchiness and apprehension on the Spanish side the main problem seems to have been caused by unauthorised entrepreneurs setting up stalls and booths in the vicinity of Westminster, in direct violation of local privileges. On 12 October Francis Yaxley reported to Sir William Cecil (keeping a low profile in Lincolnshire):

> the artisans Spaniards were commaunded yesterdaye to shutte up theyr shoppes, I think because by the order and lawes of the citie they may not open the same not being free denyzens.[19]

In spite of strenuous efforts by both Philip and Mary, who was allegedly very distressed by attacks upon her husband's fellow countrymen, the problem never went away entirely while the king was in England. On 14 September one Griffin Middleton was attacked near St Clement Danes and died of his injuries; Alonso Martine and Luis Mendoza were convicted of his murder.[20] The English were usually, but not always, the aggressors, and several robbers were hanged for plundering Spaniards. On 13 May 1555 there was a pitched battle in the city involving about 500 men which resulted in five or six deaths, and on Corpus Christi Day (13 June) a mob attacked a church where a number of Spaniards were worshipping, although on that occasion there seem to have been no fatalities.[21]

Philip did much better within the court than his servants and hangers-on managed to do outside it. This was partly because of his studious affection towards his wife. However disappointed he may have been (and there are several hints in reported court gossip to that effect), he successfully concealed the fact from her. In any case, Mary was not disposed to be critical: 'I daily discover', she wrote to the emperor, 'in the king my husband and your son, so many virtues and perfections that I constantly pray God to grant me grace to please him, and behave in all things as befits one who is so deeply embounden to him.'[22] By November Mary was convinced that she was pregnant, and the ballad writers began to celebrate the prospect of a prince to carry on the line.

The other main reason for Philip's success was money. Charles had already authorised one distribution of largesse by Renard as a sweetener, but it was on a modest scale because he did not want to dampen the impact of his son's generosity. Soon after his arrival Philip distributed gold chains of 100 or 200 crowns (£25–£50) in value to 22 named and about 200 unnamed courtiers and servants, most, but not all, of lower status. Then, on 23 August there was a major distribution of pensions, ranging from 300 to 2,000 crowns annually. The major beneficiaries were the Earls of Arundel, Shrewsbury, Derby and Pembroke, and Lord Paget. Thirteen other councillors and Household officers received smaller grants; and there was an expressed intention, which may or may not have been realised, to reward in some unspecified manner a further 47 individuals, including 24 of the queen's ladies.[23] The effect of this is hard to assess, because most of the recipients did not need this sort of inducement to remain loyal and do their jobs. It was also based upon the standard Habsburg judgement that all Englishmen were venal and would do anything for money, an attitude as likely to cause offence as gratitude. It is even possible that some men may have refused the king's generosity, because several names appear on the proposal list who did not receive anything – including the Lord Chancellor.[24] By October Ruy Gomez believed that the English council was divided into two factions, 'one for the Queen and the other for the King'. There is no reason to suppose that

this was connected with the pension distribution, but there were certainly a number of councillors, including Pembroke and Paget, who were
looking primarily to Philip for patronage and promotion, as well as a
number who shared the Spanish perception that there were 'matters
impertinent to women' which the king would have to deal with, no
matter what the marriage treaty might say.[25]

In spite of the aggressive tone adopted by his own councillors, in the
autumn of 1554 Philip was still looking for a role. One thing he had
achieved, perhaps unintentionally, was to put an end to the unique influence of Simon Renard. Ruy Gomez disliked and distrusted Renard, an
attitude which had more to do with the politics of the imperial court than
with anything that had happened in England, and he was generally
despised by Philip's Spanish councillors, for no better reason (apparently) than that he was not a Spaniard. They blamed him, quite unfairly,
for the problems over the double household, and sniped at the emperor
for employing about such important affairs 'one who gets everything into
a muddle', instead of entrusting them to a Spaniard.[26] When Philip, as
part of his household reshuffling, dispensed with the services of Sir
Anthony Browne as Master of the Horse, his English colleagues were
indignant, and it became 'an affair'. For some extraordinary reason the
Spaniards blamed Renard for that also, and by October he was relegated
to the diplomatic sidelines. Understandably, he asked to be recalled, but
Charles found him useful, even in reduced circumstances, and kept him
at his post for another year.

Very sensibly, Philip did not press for a larger part in ordinary English
affairs. He concentrated instead on keeping abreast of what was happening in Italy and the Low Countries, and on negotiating the return of the
English church to Rome. This latter project had been in the forefront of
his father's mind since the marriage was first mooted, and as we have
seen he had taken some care to ensure that it did not happen pre-
maturely. In the autumn of 1554 the time was ripe. The main problem
was not over doctrine, or over worship, but over property. To the protestants, of course, the pope was Antichrist, but they had already demonstrated the limited nature of their capacity (or willingness) to cause
trouble. Much more serious, as Renard had realised at an early stage, was
the fact that 'the catholics hold more church property than do the
heretics'. When the monastic lands had been sold off, mostly between

1540 and 1547, the purchasers and grantees had been noblemen, gentle-men and yeomen, for the most part of impeccable orthodoxy, at least from Henry's point of view. These men had welcomed the return of the 'old ways' in 1553, but the pope was a different matter. They had, for the most part, paid a full twenty years' purchase for their property, and they had no intention of losing their investments without a fight. Their title depended upon the statutes that had dissolved the lesser houses and con-firmed the property of the greater houses which had surrendered to the crown. Those statutes depended in turn upon the Act of Supremacy – in practice although not in theory. Whatever individual abbots and com-munities may have done, the church as an institution had never given up its claim to those lands, and if full ecclesiastical jurisdiction was restored that claim would return with it.[27] It had been fears of that kind, stirred up by Paget, that had scuppered Gardiner's plans in April. Philip understood those fears, and realised that a deal would have to be done. Mary would not make any compromise which touched the faith, and in any case she had no diplomatic connection with Rome except through Reginald Pole, who shared her views. It was therefore up to Philip; and since Mary raised no objection (because his actions did not touch her own con-science), he began to use the full weight of Habsburg influence in Rome to force Julius III into a deal.

Pole was useless for this purpose, and Nicholas Ormanetto, the papal datary who was acting as go-between, had already explained to the emperor that 'leaving all church property in the hands of the actual holders ... would make it look as though the apostolic see was buying back its authority in England with money'.[28] Charles was not impressed, because that was precisely what was required. In a *consulta* of August 1554 Renard, acting on the emperor's instructions, advised Mary to make no allusion to papal authority until parliament had been per-suaded to clear the way.[29] Unwelcome as this advice probably was to the queen, Philip concurred. Eventually, in the middle of October the king managed to persuade Julius to grant Pole a brief empowering him to absolve all holders of church property from canonical penalties. That was the critical breakthrough, but it remained difficult to persuade the cardinal legate to exercise his discretion in that direction. Renard visited Pole in Brussels in late October, and extracted from him a suffi-ciently explicit promise to enable the next step to be taken. On 5

November Pole was invited to return to England, and Lord Paget was
sent out at the head of an honorific mission to escort him. Pole travelled
by easy stages between 13 and 24 November, being greeted by nobles
and senior clergy at each stage of the journey. He arrived at Westminster
by river from Gravesend, thus avoiding the City of London, and was
greeted with high emotion, on both his part and the queen's. The salu-
tation on his side was an adaptation of the Hail Mary, and Renard later
reported that the queen's child had quickened in response to her emotion.[30] The cardinal's Henrician attainder had been repealed only days
before, and shortly after he also resorted to parliament, making a careful and conciliatory speech because he knew well enough that in spite
of the euphoria, the real work was still to do. Both Houses sought
pardon and absolution on their knees, which he granted on the formal
intercession of the king and queen – Philip being technically the only
person present not to need it.[31]

Jean de Vandernesse, looking back on these events four years later,
declared:

> This was a miraculous event, brought about by the hand of God, that a
> people and a kingdom which had been so misguided and so desolate
> should have been led back to union with the church, without
> bloodshed, by Divine Providence and the efforts of their Majesties and
> their Council ...[32]

However, even at this stage there were serious difficulties. Julius had
written to the emperor early in November, shortly after the decision to
admit Pole had been taken, to the effect that 'it would be far better for all
reasons human and divine to abandon all the church property [in
England] rather than to risk the shipwreck of this undertaking'; but the
cardinal was still not convinced. He had undertaken to absolve the 'pos-
sessioners' from canonical penalties, not from the actual sin of holding
stolen property. As far as he was concerned, the pope's dispensation
neither removed the sin nor conferred a legal title. The land still
belonged to the church, it was just that the holders had been given temporary permission to hang on to it. A campaign to persuade or force resti-
tution would now follow. Mary agreed, but this was not what the king
had in mind at all. As far as he was concerned, the pope's change of heart
signified the permanent transfer of the land in question to the new

owners and their heirs, with no strings attached; and that was certainly what the English aristocracy expected. Somewhat bizarrely, the debate focused on a proposal to include the full text of the dispensation in the statute which would be needed to repeal the Henrician Supremacy. A dispensation given by one pope could be withdrawn by his successor, but a law was a law and could only be repealed by parliament; so the effect of this inclusion would be to give the dispensation the status of law in England, irrespective of subsequent papal actions. In that respect it was rather like the ratification of the marriage treaty.[33] Philip, who probably had good English lawyers, supported this proposal; Pole and Mary opposed it. We do not know exactly what happened, but at some point during Christmas, the king talked his wife round, and without her support the cardinal gave way. The Henrician Acts were duly repealed in January 1555; the dispensation was enacted, and papal jurisdiction was restored. The immediate consequence was that the trial and execution of heretics commenced in February, a process for which Philip was immediately blamed, although he had nothing whatsoever to do with it. He had, however, brought back the jurisdiction that enabled the queen to fulfil her wishes.[34]

Philip does not have the reputation of being a cheerful man, but his impact on the social life of Mary's court was entirely positive. This was partly because of the effect he had on Mary. Although it must have been a traumatic experience for her, two days after her wedding night she was reported to be joyful and blooming. Reporting 'newes from the courte' on 12 October, Francis Yaxley wrote:

> *The Kinges and Queenes maiesties be in helthe and meary ... they*
> *daunsed together on Sunday night at the courte. There was a*
> *brave maskery of clothe of gold and sylver wherin the maskers were*
> *dressed as marryners, whereof the first was as I thynke my lord*
> *Admirall.*[35]

Mary had always been an enthusiastic dancer, and by the time of her accession it seems to have been her only form of exercise, but she did not dance when she was anxious or depressed. There are only minor saints' days during the second week of October, so these revels were out of the normal sequence, and the more significant for that. For the first time since the previous Christmas the Revels accounts show signs of activity. Between 17 and 21 October, instructions were issued for the new making of

> divers and sundry maskes both for men and women as playes set forth by [Nicholas] Udall and other pastimes prepared furnished and set forth out of the revels, to be showed and done in the Kings and Queens Majesty's presence from time to time as the same was commanded.[36]

It seems very likely that these included the masque to which Yaxley referred. On 1 November (All Hallows), instructions were again issued for a masque 'of viii marryners with their torchbearers, apparelled, furnished and prepared' at a cost of £4 6s. 8d. It is not clear whether this was simply a repetition of the celebration of 7 October or something new, but they were clearly not the same event.[37] None of this was entertainment on a grand scale, but it went on so late into the night that a special barge had to be hired to bring the props back from the court, which was then at Greenwich. At the end of the same month there was a further masque, 'of the vi Arcules [Hercules] or men of war, with vi mariners for their torchbearers', for which the props included 'viii headpieces ... like gryphons heds' and 'xvi lions faces', which suggests a large supporting cast. Again a return 'very late at night' was recorded, at an additional cost of 6s. 8d.[38]

At Christmas 1554, when optimism was running high at court, there was a positive orgy of frivolity. There was a masque of 'viii patrons of gallies, like Venetian senators', again with the ubiquitous mariners, and another of 'vi Venuses or amourous ladies with vi cupids' – which sounds more like Philip's taste than Mary's. An unspecified number of plays by Nicholas Udall were also performed, the actors probably being the gentlemen and children of the Chapel Royal, since no fees to professionals are recorded. The female masquers would almost certainly have been the younger members of the queen's Privy Chamber.[39] There do not appear to be any eyewitness accounts of these performances, which suggests that the ambassadors, who would almost certainly have been present, did not find them sufficiently remarkable to mention. The cost was a modest, but not miserly, £44 4s. 11d.[40] When we remember that the total recorded Revels expenses for the first year of the reign had been £24 14s., the £50 or so spent during the first six months of Philip's residence is an indicator of the significant change his presence had brought about. At Shrovetide (26 February) there were further entertainments, including 'a masque of vi Turkish magistrates' and another of 'women like goddeses'. The total revels costs for the year 1554/5 came to £254 11s. 9d., which was about normal although well short of the first year of Elizabeth (£602 11s. 10d.),[41] to say nothing of the last year of Edward VI (£717 0s. 9d.).

Although they seem to be explicit enough, we must also be cautious about using the Revels accounts as an exclusive guide to what was happening. In the first year, when only £24 is recorded, the expenses of the queen's coronation, wedding and other public appearances would not have been included. Nor indeed were the costs of the Chapel Royal or the Queen's Music, both of which were met through the normal Household and Chamber accounts. One estimate of 'musical and theatrical expenses' for 1553/4 goes as high as £2,233 17s. 6d., although how that figure was obtained is not clear. We should not therefore suppose that Philip and Mary spent no more than £250 amusing themselves during the king's long stay in England. Philip, after all, paid quite a few of the costs himself, apart from his expenditure on gold chains and pensions. He found the rewards, fees and wages for his own servants, which was a matter of grievance to some of his advisers, including the wages of the 100 archers of his guard. He also found the expensive liveries worn by the 'teams' in the various war games which he organised. His expenditure in England during the year 1554/5, exclusive of rewards and gifts, can hardly have been less than £5,000, and may have been very much more.[42] It must also be remembered that this sum had to be found out of his Spanish revenues. For some reason which has never been satisfactorily explained, Mary gave her husband no English patrimony or title other than that of king. The queen held the duchies of Lancaster, York and Cornwall and the earldom of Chester in addition to the crown, but Philip held no land in England. So although he was bound by the terms of his marriage treaty to employ English servants while in England, he was given no means with which to pay them. In the circumstances, he seems to have been remarkably generous.

Apart, perhaps, from the 'amourous ladies', Philip's main contribution to the entertainments of the court took the form of sporting combats of various kinds. These had an ulterior motive, because although they were ostensibly for recreation, Philip's real intention was to build bridges to the English aristocracy, partly by giving them a chance to show off their martial skills, and partly to win their respect by demonstrating his own. Mary's complete indifference to such demonstrations, and her supposed pregnancy for much of the year, gave him a free hand. He had a fair amount of experience in such matters, but not in the land of King Arthur and his knights, and his first effort revealed that he had a lot to learn. On 25 November 1554 he organised a *juego de canas* (cane game), a purely Spanish entertainment which was not at all to English tastes. We have no proper description of what was involved beyond Henry Machyn's rather sniffy account:

> [The xxv day of November] the wyche was Sonday, at afternoone, the Kynges grace and my lord [Fitzwalter] and divers Spaneards dyd ryd in divers colas, the kyng in red ... and with targets and canes in their hand, herlyng of rods on at unodui.[43]

According to Noailles, whose evidence on all such matters needs to be treated with extreme caution, there was a plot to assassinate both the king and the queen during these games, which failed because the sport came to a premature end.[44] This is the only time that the queen's presence at such an event is mentioned, and since it dates from many months later, even that may not be accurate. The premature end, however, seems likely enough. The English preferred more robust entertainments, and that was provided very soon after, because no sooner had the *juego* petered out than Don Ferdinando de Toledo, in the name of a group of noblemen both Spanish and English, issued a challenge to fight on foot at the barriers. It was proclaimed that

> [it] ... bene a custom that to the courts of kinges and great princes, knights and gentlemen of divers nations have made their repaire for the traill of knighthood and exercise of armes[45]

in what seems to be a conscious echo of the *Morte d'Arthur*.

The actual combat took place on 4 December, and Philip himself was one of the answerers, winning the prize for swordsmanship. The judges were both English and Spanish. That does not prove that Philip was really a champion swordsman, but it does indicate that – like Henry VIII in the lists – he was good enough to be able to take a prize plausibly if his honour was deemed to require it. Being slightly built, he was more suited to swordplay than tilting, and as far as we know he never ventured to joust on horseback – at least not in England.

By this time the king had got the bit between his teeth, and on 18 December there was another round,

> *a grett tryhumph at the court gatt, by the Kynge and dyvers lordes boyth Englishmen and Spaneards, [of] the which the kynge and his compene [were] in goodly harness ... and so thaye rane on fott with spayrers and swerds at the tornay.*[46]

On 24 January 1555 they were at it again, this time on horseback, 'grett ronnyng at the tylt at Westmynster, with spayrers, boyth Englys men and Spaneards' being recorded in passing by Machyn, who was really much more interested in the St Paul's Day procession which took place on the following day, and in which the king was also involved. A few days later, on 12 February, Philip honoured the nuptials of one of his English *chamberlones*, Lord Strange, with a tournament, banquet, masque and *juego de canas*. These were strictly private entertainments rather than court ones, but they took place at Whitehall and the king's involvement was conspicuous. His biggest, and most successful, effort was made on 25 March, 'the wyche was owre lade [day]' as Machyn recorded. Whether these 'gret justes' were intended in any way to honour either the Virgin or her royal namesake is not clear, but Mary, who was getting close to her confinement, did not appear. On this occasion the spectacle really did impress the onlookers at Westminster. Sir George Howard shared the challenge with an unnamed Spaniard, and 'ther was broken ii hundred stayffes and a-boyff', a total which had hardly been exceeded even in the great days of King Henry.[47] Philip had got it right at last! On 20 April another of his *chamberlones*, Lord Fitzwalter, got married, and the king again obliged with a foot tournament, obviously feeling that such an event was a proper part of any nobleman's wedding.

There was no close season for jousting, but that appears to have been Philip's last effort. At about that date Mary retired to her chamber, and a period of tense waiting began. Philip had been itching to leave for the Netherlands once he had finally settled the church in January, but he had been persuaded to stay for the expected confinement. Not only was it a kindness and a courtesy to Mary to remain within reach, but he might also have vital interests to protect if the child survived and the mother did not.[48]

The king invested time, effort, money and dignity in these sports, but whether they paid him a dividend is more difficult to assess. With a few exceptions, privy councillors did not joust: they were either clergy or men of gravitas whose military days (if they ever existed) were well behind them. So there was no immediate political dividend. However, among the younger courtiers, particularly those looking for military service to enhance their honour and material prospects, enthusiasm was generated. 'By such demonstrations', the Venetian ambassador observed, 'he from day to day gains the goodwill of all.'[49] Bearing in mind how short of goodwill the English had been when he had dropped anchor at Southampton, this was a considerable achievement. Among the beneficiaries of Philip's search for potential soldiers were the surviving sons of the Duke of Northumberland. The youngest, Guildford, had gone to the block in February 1554 and the eldest, John, Earl of Warwick, was mortally sick when he was released from the Tower early in October, and died on the 21st. However, the remaining three were released in January 1555 and pardoned soon after. Robert, and probably Henry, took part in the March jousts, which must have been on the king's initiative because they never obtained any favour from Mary.[50] In 1557 both, together with their elder brother Ambrose, were to serve in the king's expedition to St Quentin, where Henry was killed. Philip recruited quite a number of formerly disaffected gentlemen in this way, taking the pragmatic view that their former crimes had probably been due as much to idleness as to ideology, and that they would remain loyal to a reliable paymaster.

Philip never settled in England. Although he remained in the country for thirteen months he never made any serious attempt to learn English, and was therefore cut off from the vast majority of the people. Some petitions were addressed to him, usually by people who had been unsuccessful with the queen, but they used his remaining Spanish servants and councillors as intermediaries. One of the most successful, rather surprisingly, was the Duchess of Northumberland, who when she came to compose her will, shortly before her death in January 1555, acknowledged much kindness and help from that quarter.[51] Perhaps his councillors knew that their master already had his eye on her sons as potential recruits to his service. He did occasionally make public appearances on his own, as on 25 January when he attended high mass in St Paul's in the company of Reginald Pole. When he took part in the Garter celebrations at Windsor on 23 April, we are told that the queen watched from a nearby window. The royal couple were hardly ever apart. After their entry to London, they stayed for five nights at Whitehall before moving to Hampton Court on 23 August. On 28 September they returned to Westminster, and according to one itinerary remained there until 4 May following.[52] If this stay was really unbroken it would have been most unusual, and would have posed all sorts of problems for those who were supposed to keep the palace clean. Another source describes them as keeping their Christmas at Greenwich, and that is much more likely. It may be that the first author simply thought of both Westminster and Greenwich as 'London' and failed to make any distinction.

On 4 May 1555 the couple were reported to have moved again to Hampton Court, where arrangements were made for the queen's lying in. Over the next few weeks, while Mary was effectively out of action, Philip seems not to have done very much, and we do not know whether he was much in her company, or offered any real support.[53] When the queen had finally been forced to acknowledge that there was no child, on 4 August they removed to the small and relatively secluded palace of Oatlands, where Mary remained for about ten days to convalesce after her ordeal. During that time Philip went off and spent two nights on his own at Windsor. This is the only occasion on which he is known to have done such a thing, and the reason is obscure. He was as disappointed as Mary by the failure of her pregnancy, and far more profoundly disillusioned, so it may be that they quarrelled, or simply that they could not stand the sight of each other for a while. As even the usually chatty ambassadorial reports make no reference to a quarrel, and it would have been impossible to keep such a thing secret, they probably each felt the need of a little space.

On 10 August Philip went back to Oatlands, and on the 13th they both returned to Hampton Court, which was no doubt suitably refreshed and refurbished. By this time the king had decided that he had done his duty, and that he could no longer delay his withdrawal to the Netherlands, where his father's affairs were reaching a crisis. After a brief stay at Whitehall on 26 August they moved on to Greenwich, and there on the 29th they parted – with bitter regret and grief on Mary's part, and infinite relief on Philip's. The king spent one night at Canterbury and two at Dover, embarking for Calais on 3 September, 'from which place the

Emperor's troops conducted him safely. He came to meet the Emperor at Brussels, finding his Majesty weakened with illness . . .'[54]

Whether Philip's English household was ever mobilised during this period is not clear. It could hardly have been summoned to cover his two nights at Windsor, a decision which seems to have been taken on the spur of the moment; and as long as the royal pair were together they would have been served by a single set of departments. It may well be that those who were originally named to serve the king in a menial capacity were already servants in the queen's household, and their modest fees represented not so much part-time service as extra duties when these were called for.[55] Although he seems to have made considerable use of his chapel staff and secretaries, there are no details of Philip's daily routine. This is partly because much of it did not relate to England at all. He consulted with his Spanish advisers about imperial affairs, and Ruy Gomez made it his business to know what was happening in Brussels. Philip's dealings with the English council have not left much trace in the records, except in one interesting respect. Before July 1554 the ambassadorial despatches, imperial French and Venetian alike, are full of reports of quarrels and arguments, particularly between Gardiner and his allies and Lord Paget. By 1556 these reports were resumed, the protagonists being Paget and Cardinal Pole, but during the period of Philip's residence in England very little was said. In spite of his lack of English, the king had the capacity (which Mary lacked) of knocking heads together. Whether he played a more positive role in getting issues resolved, we do not know. On 11 June Giovanni Michieli, the Venetian ambassador, reported that the king was playing no part in the government, and that would seem to be confirmed by the absence of record, but he may also have derived his opinion from Philip's Spanish councillors rather than from direct observation.[56]

During the queen's abortive confinement there were many rumours about what Philip, or the emperor, would do if she were to miscarry, but the truth seems to be that they had no specific plans at all. In January, when it had extended the protection of the treason laws to him, parliament had also made provision for a regency in the event of Mary dying, and leaving a minor as heir. Philip had not been pleased, because in his view he was entitled to such a regency anyway, and parliament had no right to interfere. More positively, and something which Michieli seems not to have known about, by the middle of June and before it was clear what the outcome of Mary's condition would be, Philip was making provision for his next move. This consisted of the establishment of what was called a 'council of state'. The idea was to give some formal status to an inner ring of councillors – Gardiner, Thirlby, Paget, Arundel, Pembroke, Winchester, Rochester, Petre and Pole – which probably existed already. This group would form the king's council in England, which would keep him informed of affairs and which he would consult on matters that did not directly involve the queen.[57] Whatever way the confinement ended, the king was going to have to leave England to take up some of his responsibilities elsewhere; but England would remain his realm unless both the queen and her unborn child died, in which case he would have to decide whether to abide by his treaty commitments – or not.

Mary's pregnancy was the major non-event of 1555. When her condition had first been reported in October 1554 everyone, even the pessimistic Renard, had seemed pleased. 'Everything will now calm down', he had written. Philip's servants had been particularly pleased, believing – probably correctly – that the birth of an heir would greatly strengthen the king's hand and would make their own sacrifices, of both money and dignity, worthwhile.[58] In the unborn child they saw the passport to the 'true sovereignty' which by the terms of the treaty Philip so conspicuously lacked. The king himself said nothing, or at least nothing that has reached the record, but there is no reason to doubt that he considered her pregnancy to be genuine. Her physicians affirmed as much, and the changing shape of her body appeared to leave no doubt. Most English people shared this optimism. In spite of her bad taste in men, Mary was their beloved queen, and she was about to perform the universally respected feat of womanhood by giving birth. In spite of the fact that the child would be three-quarters Spanish by blood, he (hopefully) would also be the grandson of Henry VIII.

> Now singe, now springe, our care is exil'd
> Oure vertuous Queene is quick'nd with child

sang the loyal balladmongers.[59] In early January 1555 Mary was reported to be nervous and depressed by the possibility that Philip might leave before the birth. Renard, acting probably on the emperor's behalf, wrote a solemn letter to the king, advising him to stay put, and so he did. By the beginning of April the queen was supposedly into her seventh month, and tensions began to mount.

There is some doubt about when Mary's confinement actually began. Vandenesse, as we have seen, dated it to 4 May, but that is almost certainly too late. Other evidence points to 20 April, except that she is reported to have been at Windsor on the 23rd. The most probable date is either 24 or 25 April, because on 30 April there was a rumour flying around London that the birth had actually taken place:

> the last day of Aprell tydynges came to London that the Quen grace was delivered of a prynce, and so ther was grett rynyng thrugh London, and dyvers places Te deum laudamus songe: and the morrow after yt was torned odurways to the plesur of God. But yt shall be when it plese God, for I trust God that he wyll remember ys tru servands that putt ther trust in hym.[60]

At this stage the physicians were somewhat rashly predicting 9 May. However, beneath the hopeful expectancy lay more than one doubt. Protestants, who dreaded the prospect of a catholic heir – particularly one brought up by Philip – began to express scepticism. The queen was not with child at all, and there was a substitution plot. John Foxe later reported that one Isobel Malt had been approached by officers from the court to part with her newborn son – good terms and no questions asked; 'this much', Foxe declared, 'was told me by the woman herself'.[61] Whether Mrs Malt was telling the truth or not is another matter, but as May advanced and nothing happened it was not only protestants who began to have doubts. On the 22nd Ruy Gomez confided to Fransisco Eraso, the emperor's secretary, that he could see no sign of an imminent birth. When Mary walked in the privy garden 'she steps so well that it seems to me that there is no hope at all for this month'.[62] Her physicians rather foolishly continued to say that it could happen any day, but Ruy Gomez was right: apparently even the queen herself did not expect to give birth until June.

Meanwhile it was not only England that was holding its breath. A Franco-imperial peace conference, with English mediation, convened at La Marque between Calais and Gravelines on 23 May, but the problem of the English succession stalled the talks. If Mary gave birth to a healthy son, and particularly if she also survived the ordeal, Philip's position would be greatly strengthened. If neither the queen nor her child lived, it was generally expected that Elizabeth would succeed, and that she would favour the French.[63] There was no positive evidence of such an inclination, beyond the conventional assumption that anyone who opposed the Habsburgs must favour the Valois, but Elizabeth's position greatly intensified anxiety in the imperial camp, and must have affected Mary herself. Renard, who had done his best to get Elizabeth executed in the aftermath of the Wyatt rebellion, now urged the council to name her publicly as the heir in order to dampen down public speculation.[64] His advice was ignored, partly because Mary had already made it perfectly clear that she was not willing to recognise her half-sister, and partly because the Lord Chancellor and his friends were still hoping to find some means of formally excluding her. So no indication was given of what would happen if the queen 'miscarried', and that cannot have reassured anybody – least of all the delegates at La Marque.

At the time of Mary's confinement, Elizabeth was still under house arrest at Woodstock, where she had been since the previous May, when she had been transferred there from the Tower. Within a few days she was moved from Oxfordshire to Hampton Court. This was not, and was not seen as, release. The intention was to keep her under the closest possible surveillance as the crisis of delivery approached; although whether she would eventually find herself on a scaffold or a throne was not clear to anyone, least of all the princess herself. Some, among both her enemies and her friends, thought that she would be better off out of the country,[65] and Philip had been pursuing a marriage negotiation for her with the Duke of Savoy. The duke was willing but Elizabeth was not, and the matter was not pressed. If Mary were to die, the last place she wanted to be was the other side of the Channel, and it is possible that Philip was already thinking that he would have to come to terms with this clever young lady by whom the English seemed to set such store. Her friends, both at court and in the council (of whom she had many), made sure that no action was taken against her claim; and the uneasy wait went on.

At the end of May blank letters were prepared announcing the queen's safe delivery to all the courts of Europe, and rumours all over the country triggered premature celebration like that which had taken place in London a month earlier.[66] On 1 June it was reported that she was feeling some pain, although not enough to take to her bed, and the physicians shifted their predictions to 6 June.[67] However, that date also came and went, and still nothing happened. It was on 11 June that Isobel Malt claimed to have been approached, and the rumours began to be scandalous and alarming: the queen was bewitched, she was seriously ill, even dead. What was really wrong has never been entirely clear. Noailles had been told as early as March that the queen's condition was the result of a tumour, not pregnancy; but his interest in the matter was such that that may have been no more than wishful thinking. The stakes were certainly high, and Michieli was merely reflecting imperialist convictions in believing that a safe delivery would transform the king's relations with both his consort and her council.

The physicians began to take refuge in excuses: they had miscalculated the time. Renard continued to believe them. As late as 29 June he reported that the queen was definitely with child, and was as well as at any time during his stay.[68] However, by that time he was far from the court, and relying on dubious sources. The first to be undeceived were naturally the queen's ladies. Whatever sycophantic physicians might say, they knew that real pregnancies do not proceed in this protracted and indeterminate manner. By 10 July they had persuaded their mistress to emerge from her self-imposed seclusion and get some much needed fresh air. She began transacting business again. The court must have been a strange place at this time, because in spite of the fact that the symptoms were diminishing, Mary clung to the conviction that she was with child, instructing Sir John Mason, her ambassador in Brussels, to deny reports to the contrary in her name.[69] As late as 25 July some of those about her were continuing to support the delusion, perhaps because they did not have the courage to be more frank. By the end of the month, however, even Mary had given up hope.

Whether she was really suffering, as some medical historians have claimed, from cancer of the womb which had gone into remission, or whether her desperate longing for a child had caused her mind to betray her body – a so-called 'phantom pregnancy' – we do not know. What is clear is that early August 1555 was the turning point of the reign. The queen was physically and emotionally devastated by the setback, but refused to accept that it was more than that. In spite of the fact that she was now 39, she continued to believe that she would have a child. Philip did not. He recognised that the dynastic ambitions that had so far driven his marriage were now at an end. For the time being England remained critical to his plans, both in the Netherlands and in Rome, but the long-term prospects were clouded. He had only one son, and an ageing and barren wife would soon be a serious liability. Nothing was said, and given Mary's condition at the time nothing could be said; but from being a problem, Elizabeth suddenly began to look like a solution. She was quietly released and allowed to return to Ashridge to pick up the threads of her life as best she could.[70]

For the time being, nothing was going to change. The queen's life was not in danger, and although the king was obviously going away about his proper business, there was no reason to think that he would not come back. The most serious damage that the crisis had inflicted upon the regime was intangible. The queen was such a pious woman, and the church had invested so much spiritual energy in praying for her safe delivery – what had gone wrong? Why had God turned his back upon such virtuous efforts? Only the protestants had a clear answer. Far from being a pious and virtuous lady, Mary was a wicked tyrant who was persecuting the saints of God; and such punishment was not only to be expected, but was well deserved. Not many took such an extreme view, but rumours to the effect that the queen had been delivered of a foul monster, and that God was protecting England from the Spanish yoke, were vaguer expressions of a similar attitude. The real casualty was what we would now call 'credibility'. Few now believed that Mary would have an heir of her body. Elizabeth was the heir, and everyone knew that Elizabeth was a very different kind of person. Unless something quite unexpected happened, Philip's days as England's king were numbered by his wife's life. Nobody knew whether that would be long or short, but a regime which had seemed to stretch away for generations into the future was now measured by the life of one not very robust woman approaching 40. It was a drastically different prospect.

As we have seen, Philip took a brief retreat from 8 to 10 August, perhaps to get away from the gloomy atmosphere at Oatlands, but he then began to move resolutely towards his departure. By that time he had made his plans, including the establishment of the 'select council', but we do not know exactly what they were. Whether he really intended to be away for only a few weeks, or was merely trying to reassure his anxious and fretful queen, is not clear, but he left the bulk of his Spanish household, clergy and councillors in England, including his steward, Don Diego de Acevedo.[71] It had been decided to convene a parliament in October, and he spoke confidently of returning for it. At the same time he took his English *chamberlones* with him, as though the English connection retained a high priority in his mind. When he parted from Mary on 27 August, she had every reason to suppose that he would be back in about six weeks. She consoled herself for his absence by writing constant messages of affectionate enquiry and small news, giving an impression of emotional dependence which is in sad contrast with what we know of his own chagrin and disappointment. For consolation the queen turned to two things, business and Reginald Pole. The cardinal had been privately entrusted by Philip with this responsibility, which he found congenial and Mary found natural. He moved into residence at court, and although he did not become a councillor in the ordinary sense, he assumed the function of guide, philosopher and friend which the king had earlier discharged, and before him Simon Renard.[72] The queen's application to business was soon back to the level it had reached before the effects of her 'pregnancy' had begun to show, and Pole fretted that it was undermining her already slow recovery. Renard, whose duties finally came to an end when Charles handed over his responsibilities in the Netherlands to Philip, finally quitted England in September. Mary had already generously rewarded him for his work during the first year of her reign, and his departure was low key.[73]

As Philip travelled to meet his father at the beginning of September 1555 and begin the takeover of his major European responsibilities, he had to take stock of the English situation. Mary was emotionally dependent upon him, and he had allies in the council, particularly Paget and Pembroke. His status had been carefully recognised in all official acts of government, and he had created a fund of goodwill among those whom he might soon need as soldiers and captains. On the other hand, he had failed to get an heir, and he had failed to escape from the crippling restraints imposed by his marriage treaty. Even as they had extended the protection of the treason laws, the parliament had sought reassurance that he would employ no Spaniards or other strangers in English offices.[74] The bulk of his household remained within the English court, but it performed no function there and had little contact with the main establishment.

On 15 October Philip wrote to both the council and parliament explaining that he was detained by urgent business, and would not be able to return as planned for the opening on the 21st. He had, indeed, no desire to return. Having witnessed his takeover of power in the Netherlands from his father on 25 September, his English gentlemen were sent home in twos and threes over the next month.[75] If he was not allowed to employ his own servants in England, there was no way in which he was going to find employment for these men in his other dominions. At the end of October Don Diego de Acevedo and the remainder of Philip's household removed from Hampton Court to Whitehall, where they were instructed to await further orders. At the beginning of December they were summoned to join the king in the Low Countries, and they set off on the 20th. The remaining chaplains had already preceded them, and one of Philip's confessors, Alonso de Castro, unburdened himself to Federico Badoer, the Venetian ambassador in Brussels:

> he repeated a variety of foul language uttered by the English, indicating
> their ill-will towards his majesty and the Spanish nation [and says] that
> on seeing him and the rest of the royal attendants depart, they made
> great rejoicing well nigh universally; and [he also says] that the Queen's
> wish to see the king again is very great, nay boundless.[76]

Clearly, nothing had changed. Mary was very distressed by her husband's behaviour, and more so by hints that he intended soon to withdraw to Spain.

From Philip's point of view, it remained to be seen whether he could turn the queen's longing for his return to some political advantage. One possibility was to obtain a proper coronation in England. In spite of the loyal displays that had accompanied and followed his wedding, Philip had never been crowned. At first this had been regarded as a mere slight, and had not been made an issue of; now it became important. The reason seems to have been that the king was advised that coronation was taken very seriously in England as a confirmation of title; and now that there was unlikely to be an heir, he needed to strengthen his position in every way possible. As Mary's pleas for his return became more desperate, he started to suggest that a proper coronation was a condition of his compliance.

News of this got out – quite possibly leaked by unsympathetic members of the council – and there was a popular furore.[77]

In fact the formal act of coronation would have made no difference to Philip's legal position, but the situation was an unprecedented one, and no one could be sure. Rumours spread that the queen was proposing to 'give away her crown' and that pro-Habsburg nobles like the Earls of Arundel and Pembroke were in a conspiracy to aid and abet. 'Ye saye that the Quene hath the Power in her hands [and] that we must obey her', ran one tract.

> That is true in all such Laws as be already made and passed by Parlement. But whether ye may lawfully consent [contrary] to the Discretion of the whole Realm and nation of Englishmen [to the giving away] of the Crown, and disannul the authority that was given by parlement, I leave yt to your consciences. Yf the Crowne wer the Queens, in such sorte as she might do with it what she would, bothe now and after her death, ther might appeare some rightful Pretence in giving it over to a stranger Prince: But seeing it belongeth to the heirs of England after her death, ye commytt dedly synne and dampnation in unjustly giving and taking away the right of another.[78]

This was hardly sophisticated constitutional thinking, but it represented a powerful body of opinion. Whether Mary heeded this, or became resentful of her consort's attempts at political blackmail, we do not know; but she refused his request on the grounds that parliament would never allow it, and ignored his indignant protests that it was none of parliament's business.

Another possible point of leverage was to influence, or even dictate, appointment to key offices in England. This need not have involved any attempt to appoint Spaniards, which would certainly have been resisted, but rather Philip's own pensioners and sympathisers already within the English system. In an extraordinary and revealing advice of October 1555, the Duke of Alba wrote to Philip about 'two offices which your majesty has to control and be careful whom you install, that they are not the Queen's men'.[79] One of these posts was probably that of Lord Privy Seal, which had been vacant since the death of the Earl of Bedford in March. Which the other was is not apparent, because Gardiner did not die until 14 November. When the office of Lord Chancellor fell vacant, it appears that the king wanted to promote Paget, but the queen refused, wishing instead to install Thomas Thirlby. Eventually they compromised on Nicholas Heath, and Paget received the lesser promotion of Privy Seal.[80] This represented effective influence, but not quite the role of *señor absoluto* that Alba had in mind.

Philip may also have been behind the programme of shipbuilding which began in the autumn of 1555, when two new and large warships were laid down. He was certainly interested in the English navy, far more so than Mary, but the fleet had been well maintained since the beginning of the reign, and there was no sudden change of policy which could be ascribed to the king.[81] Someone in England certainly understood his aspirations, however, because about the beginning of 1556 he was presented with a treatise ostensibly about the Saxon and Norman invasions of England, but which was really a thinly veiled suggestion as to how he could increase his power. William I, the author concluded, 'left [the kingdom] in trust to his successors until the coming of the powerful and most merciful Philip, son of the Emperor Charles V. This I do not call change or alteration in the Kingdom, but legitimate succession.'[82] It has been suggested that this represents the last political thoughts of Stephen Gardiner, but since it was (apparently) written in English and presented to the king in an Italian translation, that seems unlikely. The king had little Italian, while both he and Gardiner were fluent in Latin.[83]

Mary was deeply ambivalent about Philip's return. Emotionally, she desperately wanted him back, but politically she was unable (or unwilling) to meet his demands for a greater share in government. For months she kept ships on standby to escort him back, and more than once reassembled his English household in response to false reports of his coming. In March 1556 she instructed Sir John Mason to ask whether the fleet should be kept on standby, adding on a more personal note that she longed for his coming, and that he should not despair of getting an heir.[84] It was delicately hinted that the queen's age (she was now 40) was a compelling argument for haste. The king responded with excuses, and bland professions of affection. His courtiers could afford to be more frank: why should he waste his time and money going to England to gratify a woman who had done nothing to gratify him? By April Mary was becoming exasperated. She is alleged to have hurled Philip's portrait across the room in fury at his callous indifference, and sent Lord Paget to make urgent representations about the needs of the kingdom. Paget, it was thought, enjoyed sufficient favour with Philip not to have to mince his words. By this time some of the king's own advisers were becoming anxious, and urged him not to provoke his wife too far.[85] At the same time the queen did for the last time what she had often done before: she appealed to Charles. He had by this time handed over both Spain and the Low Countries to his son, and was in virtual retirement, but he was still technically emperor, and he was still in the Netherlands.

> I thank you humbly for remembering me where the return of the king my husband is concerned, as I have seen not only from your letters, but also by the messages brought by Lord Fitzwalter ... I implore your Majesty most humbly for the love of God to do all that is possible to permit it. I see every day the end of one negotiation and the beginning of another. I beg your Majesty to forgive my boldness, and to remember the unspeakable sadness which I experience because of the absence of the king ...[86]

A month later she tried again, in a similar vein. Nothing happened because in fact Charles no longer had much say in what went on, and was certainly in no position to give orders to his son. The French began to speculate happily on the possibility of a total breakdown in relations. Mary, they believed, was living in daily fear of assassination, her palace filled with armed men. Only five women were sufficiently trusted to 'keep her chamber'; she was sleeping badly, and spending her days in 'tears, regrets and writing letters to bring back her husband'.[87] With the possible exception of this last, there is hardly a trace of any of this in the English records, and the reports were almost certainly wildly exaggerated. On 6 August, 'upon consideration of the state of things at this time', the council took steps to improve security at court, which was always a problem because of the varied needs for access. All the officers, yeomen of the guard and 'ordinary servants' were called together and asked 'what armure and weapon eche of them hathe'. The Household was then mustered, which was a very unusual event unless the monarch was proposing to go to war, but the cause was probably fear of disorders arising from two successive harvest failures rather than any specific anxiety about attacks on the queen.[88]

By 19 October things were looking up. Michieli reported that the king had renewed his promises, and this time had actually ordered some of his household to proceed to England. Mary immediately put his English servants on standby, and her spirits were noted to be markedly improved. Everyone still had a long wait, however, and it was 20 March 1557 before Philip finally landed at Greenwich, to a royal salute and shouts of 'God save the King and Queen'. The bells of London rang out, and every church was commanded to sing *Te Deum* for the king's safe return.[89]

On 23 March the king and queen again rode through the capital from Tower Wharf to Whitehall, with the sceptre born before them and the livery companies lining the route. Compulsory rejoicings were the order of the day, because, as Henry Machyn noted with a hint of alarm, three shiploads of Philip's Spanish servants had followed him before the sound of the *Te Deum* had died away.[90] However pleased Mary may have been, this visit was not prompted by her needs, but by Philip's. The truce with France, negotiated early in 1556, had broken down, and the king needed England's support in his renewed war. He argued that because of the truce, this was not the same war from which the marriage treaty had excused England. The English council disagreed. A truce was not a peace, and in any case England could not afford to go to war. It was at this point that Philip's investment in aristocratic goodwill three years before paid off. A minority party in the council favoured war, and ambitious soldiers supported them. With their aid, and the help of a mysterious raid on Scarborough which was blamed on the French, the king and queen overrode the majority in the council, and war was decided upon.[91] During May and June an expeditionary force was mustered, and on 5 July Philip was able to return to the Low Countries at the head of an English army – for which he was paying.

On this occasion the tensions that had run throughout Philip's first period of residence in England seem to have been largely absent. Perhaps he brought fewer Spanish servants with him, or perhaps they were better disciplined, but there appear to have been no incidents of the kind that had marred 1555. Most of the time he stayed at Whitehall, and the chapter of the Garter was held there rather than at Windsor for his benefit on 23 April. Three new knights were elected and one of them, Lord Fitzwalter, was probably on his nomination. The other two were Lord Grey and Sir Robert Rochester, Mary's old and loyal servant.[92] Evensong afterwards was enlivened by the exotic presence of Duke Nepeja, the ambassador from Ivan IV, who had presented his credential on 25 March.

At some point, probably during May, Philip put in some hunting at Hampton Court, and it seems that Mary accompanied him. On 4 May he also witnessed a tragic accident in the privy garden at Whitehall, where Sir Jacques Granado was killed while giving a demonstration of horsemanship: 'the bridle bytt did breke, and so the horsse ran aganst the wall'.[93] On 25 April a masque was provided for his entertainment, in which he is reported to have taken part, but no details, apart from the general instructions to Cawarden, survive.[94] There were no tournaments or other war games, possibly because that battle was won, and the men of war were preparing for a real campaign. On Ascension Day, 27 May, the king and queen rode from Whitehall to mass in the newly restored Westminster Abbey, 'with the lordes and knyghtes and gentylmen, and ther ther graces whent a prossessyon abowt the cluwster'.[95] Philip had by this time given up pressing for a coronation, and even for a larger part in the government. Involving England in his war was achievement enough for the moment, and very necessary for his honour. Six months later Mary believed herself to be pregnant again, so their personal relationship must have been restored, but the king was under no illusions, and politically he had more or less given up on England. His last serious attempt to influence the course of events was to renew his pressure for a marriage between Elizabeth and the Duke of Savoy. This time he called upon the support of his widowed half-sister, Margaret, Duchess of Parma, and Christina of Denmark, the widowed Duchess of Lorraine. Both these formidable ladies spent a month at the English court in May–June 1557 and attempted to exercise their powers of persuasion upon the 23-year-old princess – entirely without success.[96] Philip could, of course, have simply carried Elizabeth off with him when he returned to the continent, but he was not prepared to be heavy-handed. Elizabeth represented the future, and no one knew how far off that might be. For the time being, Mary was happy with his presence, and greatly depressed when he again departed. This time there were no promises, and she was never to see him again.

Notes and references

1 Glyn Redworth, '"Matters Impertinent to Women": Male and Female Monarchy under Philip and Mary', *English Historical Review*, 112 (1997), pp.597–613.

2 Margaret Pole had been created Countess of Salisbury in her own right in 1513, and Anne Boleyn Marquis of Pembroke in 1532. Both were attainted, and the titles died with them, so the transmission was not tested.

3 The best near-contemporary discussion of property law as it affected women can be found in *The Lawes Resolution of Women's Rights or the Laws Provision for Woemen*, by E.T. (London, 1632).

4 *Tudor Royal Proclamations*, ed. P.L. Hughes and J.F. Larkin, 3 vols. (New York, 1964–9), vol.2, no.398.

5 Statute I Mary, st.3, c.2. *Statutes of the Realm*, ed. A. Luders *et al.*, 11 vols. (London, 1810–28), vol.4, pt1, p.222.

6 Ibid., Statute I Mary, st.3, c.1.

7 BL, Add. MS 71009, fols.31–32.

8 Juan Vasquez de Molina to Philip, 13 September 1554, *CSP Spanish* vol.13, p.47; D.M. Loades, *The Reign of Mary Tudor*, pp.160–1.

9 Renard to the emperor, 3 September 1554, *CSP Spanish*, vol.13, p.45; ibid., p.50. Fitzwalter was complaining generally about the unwillingness of the Spaniards to attempt any communication with their English colleagues.

10 *Tres Cartas de lo sucedido en el viaje de Su Alteza a Inglaterra* (La Sociedad de Bibliofílos Espanoleo, Madrid, 1877), Primera Carta, p.91; *CSP Spanish*, vol.13, p.32.

11 *CSP Spanish*, vol.13, p.33. This arose because neither was prepared to allow the other to take a lower seat.

12 Ibid. This comment was intended as an aspersion on their morals rather than their conversational ability – and was so taken.

13 Loades, *Reign of Mary Tudor*, p.161. On Ruy Gomez and his special relationship with Philip, see M.-J. Rodriguez-Salgado, *The Changing Face of Empire: Charles V, Philip II, and Habsburg Authority, 1551–1559* (Cambridge, 1988), pp.15–16.

14 *CSP Spanish*, vol.13, p.33. *Comendadores* were members of the military orders. On the problems of the friars, see Redworth, '"Matters Impertinent"'.

15 *Epistolario del III Duque de Alba*, ed. 17th Duke of Alba, 3 vols. (Madrid, 1952), vol.1, p.64.

16 BL, Cotton MS Vespasian F.III, no.23.

17 *The Diary of Henry Machyn*, ed. J.G. Nichols (Camden Society, 1848), pp.69, 72, 79.

18 Noailles, Advis au Roi, 5 September 1554, in E.H. Harbison, *Rival Ambassadors at the Court of Queen Mary* (Princeton, NJ, 1940), p.197. There was also a French-inspired rumour that Philip was planning to seize the Tower.

19 BL, Lansdowne MS 3, fol.92.

20 We know about this only because Medina was subsequently pardoned. *CPR Mary*, vol.2, p.243. Martine was presumably hanged.

21 Michieli to the Doge and Senate, 27 May and 1 July 1555, *CSP Venetian*, vol. 6, p.85.

22 *CSP Spanish.*, vol.13, p.28.

23 The list of proposed gifts and pensions is held in the Vienna Staatsarchiv (E.V.5). It is not dated, but is ascribed to July 1554. *CSP Spanish*, vol.12, pp.315–16.

24 Archivo General de Simancas, CMC laE, 1184.

25 *CSP Spanish*, vol.13, p.35. A Venetian commentator wrote of Paget that it was from the king that 'all favours shown to him proceed, nor does he fail to seek them by all means and with all his might'. *CSP Venetian*, vol.6, pp.415–16.

26 This was a view held strongly by the influential Ruy Gomez, but shared by others, such as Juan de Figueroa. *CSP Spanish*, vol.13, pp.49, 58; MS Bib.Pal. Real (Madrid), II – 2285, fols.70–1.

27 Paul IV finally surrendered the church's legal title to all former monastic lands, and canonically extinguished the dissolved houses, by the bull *Praeclara* of June 1555. The Marian foundations were thus new houses, not continuations. M.C. Knowles, *The Religious Orders in England*, vol.3 (Cambridge, 1959).

28 *CSP Spanish*, vol.13, p.14.

29 Ibid., pp.28–30. Described in the *Calendar* as being addressed to Philip, it seems clear from the content that Mary was the intended recipient.

30 J. Loach, *Parliament and the Crown in the Reign of Mary Tudor* (Oxford, 1986), pp.105–9; D.M. Loades, *Mary Tudor: A Life* (Oxford, 1989), pp.238–9.

31 Biblioteca Vaticana, Rome (MS on microfilm at the Bodleian Library, Oxford): Vat.Lat. 5968, fol. 348; J. Collier, *An Ecclesiastical History of Great Britain*, vol.2 (London, 1714), pp.372–3. Rullo to Seripando, 1 December 1554; Carlo de Frede, *La Restaurazione Cattolica in Inghilterra sotto Maria Tudor* (Naples, 1971), p.57.

32 *Journal of the Travels of Philip II*, trans. and calendared in *CSP Spanish*, vol.13, Appendix, pp.443–5.

33 Statute 1 & 2 Philip and Mary, c.10; Loach, *Crown and Parliament*, pp.107–15.

34 The driving force behind the persecution was the queen. Foxe tells the story that Philip put up his confessor (Alonso de Castro) to preach against it in the spring of 1555, but that is unsubstantiated. Philip certainly believed in burning heretics on principle, but may have thought that it was politically unwise at that time. Loades, *Mary Tudor*, pp.323–4.

35 BL, MS Lansdowne 3, fol.92.

36 *Documents Relating to the Revels Office in the Reigns of Edward VI and Mary*, ed. A. Feuillerat (Louvain, 1914), pp.159–60.

37 Ibid. On 11 November Lords Maltravers and Lumley wrote to Cawarden to borrow costumes for a masque of Almains. But this may have been for a private entertainment. Ibid., p.249.

38 Ibid., pp.159–60.

39 Spanish observers were rude about Mary's ladies, describing them as 'neither young nor beautiful', but that was not true of Jane Russell or Jane Dormer, and it was a long-standing custom for the queen's ladies to perform in these masques.

40 Ibid., p.161.

41 D.M. Loades, 'Entertaining Philip and Mary' (forthcoming); *Documents Relating to the Office of the Revels in the Reign of Queen Elizabeth* (Louvain, 1908), pp.79–108.

42 The pension list alone represented an annual commitment of 22,600 crowns (about £5,600), and the tournament liveries must have added nearly another £1,000. AGS, CMC la, 1184, fol.64; D.M. Loades, 'Philip II and the Government of England', in *Law and Government under the Tudors*, ed. C. Cross *et al.* (Cambridge, 1988), pp.177–94.

43 Machyn, *Diary*, ed. Nichols, p.76.

44 Advis au Roi, 18 June 1556, Harbison, *Rival Ambassadors*, p.198. These details emerged during the interrogation of suspects in the 'Dudley conspiracy' of that year. See the confession of Thomas White, 30 March 1556, PRO, SP11/7, no.47.

45 R.C. McCoy, 'From the Tower to the Tiltyard: Robert Dudley's Return to Glory', *Historical Journal*, 27 (1984), pp. 425–35.

46 Machyn, *Diary*, ed. Nichols, p.79.

47 Ibid., p.84

48 *CSP Spanish*, vol.13, p.131; Loades, *Mary Tudor*, p.235.

49 *CSP Venetian*, vol.6, p.58; Loades, 'Philip II and the Government of England', p.193.

50 McCoy, 'From the Tower to the Tiltyard'.

51 On her deathbed she besought such powerful friends as the Duke of Medina Celi and Don Diego de Mendoza: 'for God's sake continue ... good lords to my sons in their needs'. A. Collins, ed., *Letters and Memorials of State* (1746), vol.1, p.34.

52 Vandenesse, *Journal*, *CSP Spanish*, vol.13, p.443.

53 Probably not, although through no negligence of his own. The custom was that only women were admitted to a queen's presence during such a period.

54 *CSP Spanish*, vol.13, p.444.

55 Redworth, '"Matters Impertinent"', suggests that all the servants allocated to Philip were already employed in the Household. However, five, including the Clerk of the Greencloth (John Dodge), were paid full fees, and were presumably retained on a full-time basis, whether the king was in England or not. Dodge was paid £44 6s. 8d. a year. Loades, 'Philip II and the Government of England', p.187.

56 *CSP Venetian*, vol.6, pp.106, 173.

57 BL, Cotton MS Titus B.II, fol. 160; Redworth, '"Matters Impertinent"'.

58 Loades, *Reign of Mary Tudor*, pp.163–4.

59 Ibid., p.164. See also *A new ballade of the Marigolde by William Forrest Priest* (Broadsheet 36 in the Library of the Society of Antiquaries).

60 Machyn, *Diary*, ed. Nichols, p.86.

61 John Foxe, *Actes and Monuments* (London, 1583), p.1596, 'concerning the childbed of Queen Mary, as it was rumoured among the people'.

62 Loades, *Mary Tudor*, p.249. Noailles was even more emphatic: the queen was spending long hours sitting on the floor in her chamber, and thus could not possibly be carrying a child: Avis au Roi, 29 May 1555, in R.A. de Vertot, ed., *Ambassades de Messieurs de Noailles*, 5 vols. (Louvain, 1743), vol.6, p.89. The ambassador did not disclose the source of this intriguing piece of information.

63 The fullest discussion of these negotiations is in Harbison, *Rival Ambassadors*, p.245.

64 *CSP Spanish*, vol.13, pp.165–6.

65 D.M. Loades, *Elizabeth I* (London, 2003), pp.109–11. Lord William apparently visited the princess in an attempt to persuade her to petition for licence to leave the country.

66 Foxe, *Actes and Monuments* (1563), p.1141.

67 Loades, *Mary Tudor*, pp.249–50. In the queen's chamber a cradle awaited, 'very sumptuously and gorgeously trimmed'.

68 Ibid., p.250.

69 Some of her councillors apparently privately dissented, and so informed Mason, who must have been placed in a very difficult position. Badoer to the Doge and Senate, 21 July 1555. *CSP Venetian*, vol.6, pp.138–9.

70 On 4 August, when the court moved to Oatlands. Loades, *Elizabeth I*, p.110.

71 Loades, 'Philip II and the Government of England', p.190.

72 PRO, SP11/6, no.16; Loades, *Mary Tudor*, pp.318–19.

73 She presented him with 1,200 oz. of plate on 23 September 1554, in gratitude for his service. BL, Cotton MS Titus B.II, fol.162.

74 Loach, *Crown and Parliament*, pp.117–20.

75 Loades, *Mary Tudor*, p.255. Badoer commented at the same time that the Spanish household left in England was merely a blind – and events proved him right. *CSP Venetian*, vol.6, pp.167, 173, 199.

76 Ibid., p.285.

77 PRO, SP11/16–21, 82, 83. Some of Philip's replies also survive in BL, Cotton MS Titus B.II, fols.114–16.

78 John Bradford, *Copye of a letter ... sent to the Earls of Arundel, Darbie, Shrewsbury and Penbroke* (London, 1556); John Strype, *Ecclesiastical Memorials*, 3 vols. (Oxford, 1822), vol.3, pt2, no. xlv; D.M. Loades, *Two Tudor Conspiracies* (Cambridge, 1965), pp.139–40.

79 Alba, *Epistolaria*, vol.1, p.320.

80 Redworth, '"Matters Impertinent"'.

81 D.M. Loades, *The Tudor Navy* (Aldershot, 1992), pp.159–60.

82 Fol.135r–v. P.S. Donaldson, *A Machiavellian Treatise by Stephen Gardiner* (Cambridge, 1975), pp.149–50.

83 The ascription to Gardiner was challenged almost at once by Dermot Fenlon, in the *Historical Journal*, 19 (1976). See also P.S. Donaldson, 'Bishop Gardiner, Machiavellian', *Historical Journal*, 23 (1980), pp.1–16.

84 *CSP Venetian*, vol.6, p.376.

85 Ibid., pp.401–2.

86 Ibid., pp.260, 271.

87 Giacomo Soranzo, Venetian ambassador in France, to the Doge and Senate, 14 April 1556, *CSP Venetian*, vol.6, p.410; Vertot, *Ambassades*, vol.5, pp.361–3. Noailles received and passed on rumours to the effect that Philip was negotiating in Rome for an annulment.

88 *APC*, vol.5, p.320.

89 Machyn, *Diary*, ed. Nichols, p.129.

90 Ibid.

91 On 23 April an English adventurer named Thomas Stafford appeared off Scarborough with two French ships and a band of fellow exiles. They seized the castle, which was virtually undefended, and Stafford proclaimed himself protector of the realm. They were soon overpowered, but the incident was made to appear like French provocation. Nicholas Wotton to Sir William Petre, PRO SP69/10, fol.588; Surian to the Doge and Senate, 29 April 1557, *CSP Venetian*, vol.6, p.1026; Loades, *Reign of Mary Tudor*, pp.305–6.

92 Machyn, *Diary*, ed. Nichols, pp.132–3.

93 Ibid., p.135.

94 *Documents Relating to ... Edward VI and Mary*, ed. Feuillerat, p.302.

95 Machyn, *Diary*, ed. Nichols, p.137.

96 Loades, *Elizabeth I*, p.120.

CHAPTER 8

• • • • • • • • • • • • • • • •

The declining years, 1555–8

With Philip's departure at the end of August 1555, Mary was for most practical purposes on her own again. The months from March to July of 1557 marked an Indian summer of happiness for the queen, but this should not disguise the fact that a steady decline had set in. The royal nursery, constructed with so much hope in the spring, remained empty, and the ornate cradle was put away unused. Physically, Mary recovered slowly and by the end of October was not noticeably weaker or more depressed than she had been before her marriage; but the times were difficult and Pole fretted about her ability to cope. She felt beleaguered, and not without reason. The harvest had been disastrous, so the price of bread was bound to go up, and that often meant sporadic riots. However, a few riots did not constitute a crisis. More serious was the persistent hostility to the Spanish connection, which did not abate with the king's departure. There were fewer violent incidents because there were fewer foreigners around to be confronted. Indeed some ardent spirits regretted Philip's going for precisely that reason: it was much more difficult to arouse a mob by crying 'no Spaniards' if there weren't any Spaniards around.[1] However, the pamphlet war did not calm down, and a number of extremely virulent attacks were launched in the autumn of 1555 and early 1556. Some of these were protestant assaults provoked by persecution, such as *A supplicacyon to the queens maiestie* and *A shorte treatise of politike power*, which lamented that the English church was under the heel of Antichrist.[2] Others, including some of those most abusive to Philip personally, did not mention religion at all. *A warnyng for*

Englande invoked the 'plague that shall light upon the English nobility yf the Kyng of Spayn obtaine the dominion of England', while the *Copye of a letter* cruelly mocked Mary's lack of physical attractiveness, claiming that Philip was solacing himself with 'bakers daughters and other poor whores' in Antwerp while his wife attempted to retrieve him with political favours.[3] The king may not have had a taste for the low life, but he did have a taste for sexual adventures. There were guarded references to a certain Madame d'Aler, and to the need to protect the queen from news of her husband's amusements 'because she is easily agitated'.

The political agenda behind these anti-Habsburg tracts was the fear of what Philip might do in the event of Mary's death, and concentrated, as we have seen, on the issue of coronation. However, the queen was not obviously ailing, and the agitation has a somewhat contrived air. More serious and immediate was the death of Lord Chancellor Gardiner on 12 November. Gardiner's relationship with the queen had been up and down. At first she had regarded him as a champion of the true faith, but when he opposed her marriage plans she remembered that he had served her father and implemented the break with Rome. After the collapse of the Wyatt rebellion he had recovered her confidence by blaming it on the protestants and suggesting a congenial policy of fierce religious repression. His position had been further strengthened by Paget's ill-judged campaign in the parliament of April 1554, and by the role which he was called upon to play in the queen's marriage.

Philip had taken the Lord Chancellor as he found him. There was no hostility, nor any marked cordiality, in their relationship. Philip had been sceptical about the religious persecution from the start, not because he was averse to killing heretics but because he regarded it as a mistaken strategy in English circumstances.[4] After a few months, Gardiner came round to the king's point of view. Defiant protestants going resolutely to the stake was not at all what he had envisaged, so in the words of John Foxe he 'gave over as utterly discouraged'. That is an exaggeration, but he became less proactive and began to advocate alternative tactics. However, neither his change of heart nor the king's departure made any noticeable difference, because the real driving force was Mary and the main agent was Pole. Gardiner's death, however, left a big gap, and seriously compromised the management of the third parliament. For about six or seven weeks the Great Seal was in commission. The subsidy, which Gardiner had spent his last energies in promoting, was duly passed, in spite of French-backed attempts to sabotage it in the House of Commons, but a bill to confiscate the property of religious exiles was defeated, as much on account of inept government tactics as strength of feeling.[5]

After what appears to have been a tussle between the king and the queen, Nicholas Heath, the Archbishop of York, was appointed to the chancellorship in January 1556. He was a man of ability and integrity, and a good bishop, but he was not a statesman of Gardiner's stature. By the end of 1555 the only man of first-rate political ability left in government was Lord Paget, and on 31 December, the day before Heath's promotion, he became Lord Privy Seal. If Heath was (perhaps) the queen's man, Paget was the king's.[6] Perhaps for that reason he was not allowed to fill Gardiner's shoes. It was largely thanks to him and his Cromwellian training that the council functioned so well at an administrative level, reforming the Council for Marine Causes and farming numerous lesser councillors out to committee work and the commissions of the peace, but he had little personal influence at court.

Apart from Pole, who was operating at a tangent to secular politics, it is not easy to see who did. Mary had no flamboyant favourites of the type of Robert Dudley or Robert Devereux later, and no trusted adviser of great ability, like William Cecil. Her favourite among the councillors seems to have been the faithful but totally undistinguished Robert Rochester, and her chief confidante after the departure of Gertrude Courtenay was the long-serving Susan Clarencius. An anonymous courtier poet, who signed himself 'R.E.', at some point in the middle of the reign wrote some verses in praise of eight of the queen's ladies, but Susan was not among them. She was probably too matronly, and too close to her mistress, to feature in an amorous and light-hearted ditty:

> Thes eight nowe serve one noble Quene but if power were in me
> for bewtise prayse and virtues sake eche one a Quene showld be ...[7]

One who did feature, however, was Jane Dormer, to whom we will return.

Susan Clarencius was by this time a woman of about 50. Her date of birth is uncertain, but it was soon after the turn of the century. Her proper name was Susan Tonge, 'Clarencius' being derived from the fact that her husband, Thomas Tonge, had been Clarence herald for two years before his death in 1536. She seems to have entered Mary's service before that time, because when the princess's household was reconstituted after she was restored to favour in that year, she requested the continuation of Susan's attendance in view of her good record 'since [she] came into my company'.[8] She had been born Susan White, the daughter of Richard White of Hutton Hall, South Essex. Her mother was a Tyrell, and she retained close links with that family – notorious in Mary's reign for their ardent catholicism. Clarencius appears to have had no children of her own, or at least none that survived infancy, and for about 25 years she devoted herself to Mary. In 1553 she became Mistress of the Robes, an unprecedented position which seems to have combined the duties of Yeoman of the Wardrobe with those of Groom of the Stool.

Susan was always ranked as a gentlewoman, never as a lady, but in terms of intimacy her position was unique, and was often referred to by Renard and others who did confidential business with the queen. Although given no title, she received generous grants of land in Essex, and held a number of wardships. She was literate, but hardly any letters or other documents in her hand survive, and we know of her close relationship with her mistress only through the testimony of observers.[9] According to John Foxe, 'Mr. Rice' (Rhys Manxell) and Susan were the two who attended Mary at her death, information which he claimed to have had from Manxell himself. By December 1558, when Jane Dormer finally married the Count of Feria, who had been seeking her hand for some time, Susan had joined the household of the new countess. With the aid of her friend Sir Francis Englefield she bestowed her English properties upon the sons of her brother Richard, and quitted England with Jane in August 1559. She remained an intimate, and seemingly much loved, member of the Feria household until her death, which seems to have occurred in the autumn of 1564.[10]

Although we know so little about her, Susan Clarencius was at the heart of Mary's distinctive court. She did not officially hold the Privy Purse, but seems to have received and disbursed modest cash sums for such matters as alms offerings and gambling debts. Before Mary's accession, she can occasionally be observed doing the princess's shopping, and that may have continued during the reign, although we have no record of it. The queen was a frequent gambler – it seems to have been her only vice – and Susan was a regular gaming partner. In her earlier days Mary had lost (of all things) a breakfast in a bowling match, but during her reign she seems to have confined herself to cards and 'pass-dice'. Sir William Petre's accounts show him borrowing 13*s*. 4*d*. from one of the grooms of the Privy Chamber when he was unexpectedly called upon to play dice with the queen, and he also on one occasion lost money to Susan Clarencius, who seems to have been deputed to keep him amused while he waited for an audience.[11] Edward had also enjoyed a flutter, although the practice was frowned upon by his puritanical mentors and his stakes never seem to have exceeded a few pence. Towards the end of her father's life, Mary had been losing between 12*s*. 6*d*. and 40*s*. a month in this way, but no similar figures survive for her reign. Such losses do not necessarily mean that she was either unfortunate or inept, because winnings were not similarly recorded: what they do show is that she either played frequently or for moderately high stakes. Because a courtier's life inevitably involved spending a lot of time waiting in antechambers, often with nothing very useful to do, gambling was pervasive. Edward Underhill, before he saw the light of the Gospel, confessed to being a great gambler, and one of a 'fast set' in Edward's court that also included Sir Ralph Bagenall.[12]

The daily routine of Mary's Privy Chamber can only be conjectured from scraps of evidence, because the diplomat who most regularly reported the affairs of the kingdom had withdrawn by the end of 1555. There was no imperial ambassador resident in England after Simon Renard's recall, and the Venetian was not close enough to the court to be very informative. A French embassy remained until the outbreak of war in 1557, but neither of the Noailles brothers, who were successively ambassadors, had any access except on the most formal of business. What does survive is a *vade mecum* for the duties of a gentleman usher put together by John Norris at the end of Mary's reign, perhaps for the guidance of his successors.[13] Most of the individual items date from the middle years of Henry VIII's reign, but the fact that Norris included them suggests that they were still relevant. The court was notoriously conservative in its habits, and Mary was more conservative than most, so she may well have followed her father's practices wherever that was possible. There are, for example, detailed descriptions of 'the order of the kings worship' for each of fourteen major festivals of the church's year, setting out the exact procedure for his going to chapel, who was to accompany him, and who performed what parts of the ritual. Henry 'toke hys rites or howsell', that is, received communion on Easter Day, Corpus Christi Day, the Feast of the Assumption of our Lady, All Hallows Day and Christmas Day, and each of these, with the exception of the Assumption, was also an 'offering day'.[14] We do not know whether Mary's devotions followed the same pattern, because unless she made a public demonstration there was no observer to comment. Henry Machyn, for example, noted that on 4 September 1555 'the Quene grace and my lady Elsabeth and all the court, dyd fast from flesh, and toke the Popes jubele and pardon granted to all men', but he does not mention either All Hallows (1 November) or Christmas. His chronicle contains a long description of the obsequies for Stephen Gardiner between 14 and 21 November that year, when 'durge [was sung] in evere parryche in London, and a hearsse and ryngyng, and the morrow masse of requiem', but there is no reference to the queen or her courtiors participating.[15] In February 1556 there was a further commemoration, and then Sir Robert Rochester 'and divers others' did appear, but we have no knowledge of how Mary mourned her most distinguished servant.

It seems that the queen did not appear very much in public while her husband was away, and although she must have made routine moves with the seasons, they were seldom noticed. An exception occurred on 21 July 1556 when the court moved from St James to Eltham by way of St George's Fields and Lambeth. The cardinal rode with her, we are told, and 'a-boyff x M pepull' turned out to see her pass. On 19 September she moved back to St James by the same route, but if there was similar enthusiasm, it was not commented upon.[16] On 20 December the queen attended evensong at the newly restored Westminster Abbey, probably as a gesture of support for Abbot Feckenham and his community. This was a state visit, with the sword borne before her, and 'my lade Montyguw bare up her quen ['s train]'. Two days later she moved from St James, which seems to have been her favourite residence, to Greenwich to keep the Christmas. None of this was very remarkable, but on 20 January 1557, when the court had been stirred into life by the news of Philip's impending reappearance, Mary held a muster of her pensioners in Greenwich Park. There were 50 gentlemen, and each was accompanied by 'iii men in grene cottes'. The whole troop paraded around the park with standards displayed and 'trumpeters blohing'. Mary stood on a dais by the park gate, accompanied by Pole and divers other lords and ladies, and 'took the salute'. A tumbler then appeared who 'played mony prate fettes' and caused great hilarity.[17] It seems to have been something of a carnival, and whether it had any serious message for the 10,000 or so spectators who (it was claimed) attended is not very clear. If a display of force was intended, it was much less impressive than Edward's gendarmerie, and the probability is that a stylish entertainment was the main purpose. Someone had convinced the queen that she had been invisible for too long.

In February there was another notable spectacle when Ossip Nepeja turned up 'out of Scotland' as ambassador from Tsar Ivan IV. He had barely survived shipwreck on the Scottish coast, but that does not seem to have cramped his style.[18] The Russians were greeted both by the Lord Mayor and by a delegation from the court 'in gorgyous aparelle', but it was their own exotic gear that attracted the main attention. This was an important embassy, and one which was to have significant results, so presumably Nepeja was received in audience by the queen, but no account of their meeting seems to have survived. He was received by Philip after the Garter ceremonies on 23 April, when the guard was turned out for his benefit, but beyond the fact that he attended evensong in the chapel at Whitehall, we do not know what passed between them. Nor do we know what Western language Nepeja may have used; it is unlikely to have been either English or Spanish. As we have seen, Philip and Mary appeared together on a number of occasions during his second visit, but when he left on 5 July there was no ceremony: it was merely noted that he had taken ship at Dover.[19]

Ten days later Mary removed to Richmond, dining with Pole at Lambeth on the way, but thereafter she quietly disappears from the record. The court turned out in force for the funeral of Anne of Cleves on 3 August, but Mary was represented by Lord Howard, and did not appear in person. Her long-serving comptroller, Robert Rochester, also died on 4 December and was buried at Sheen.[20] This must have been a heavy blow to the queen he had served so faithfully, but we have no means of knowing how it affected her. In March 1558 the gentlemen pensioners were again mustered, but this time the Earl of Rutland took the salute and there is no reference to Mary's appearance. By that time war and the influenza epidemic had both taken their toll, and there is no hint of the carnival atmosphere of fifteen months before. Although she was not yet seriously ill, and must have attended the opening of parliament on 20 January, the queen seems to have appeared very little during the last year of her reign, and this was not without its effect upon the climate of the Household. Paradoxically, the court actually cost more during this last year than in any other year of the reign. Vigorous economy measures had reduced the £66,000 spent in Edward's last year to £46,000 by 1556–7, but in 1557–8 over £75,000 was disbursed.[21] There must have been some change in accounting procedures, perhaps surreptitiously shifting military costs on to the Household, to account for this, because there was certainly no increase in the normal activities of the court – rather the reverse.

Norris's memoranda include a description of the queen's marriage in July 1554 which adds little to the other, more contemporary, accounts except an intriguing statement to the effect that Mary was 'given away' (in accordance with custom) by 'the Duke of Alvey'. This must have been Alba, because the only duke in England was Norfolk, and what right he may have had to represent the realm of England is not explained.[22] Norris also says that Philip took an oath to observe 'the Covenant that was made' in the course of the ceremony. This must refer to the marriage treaty, and is interesting in the light of his earlier (secret) disclaimers. Norris claimed to have been the Master of Ceremonies, not only for the wedding itself, but also for the subsequent progress and entries.

> John Norris gent. Usher ... had all the doings for that marriage, and for his [Philip's] receaving at Hampton, and in all other places where any grett ceremony was to be don, as at Pauls or Wyndsor touchyng the Order of the Garter, and in all other cathedral churches during his abode in England ...[23]

If this is true, it prompts questions as to what the Lord Chamberlain, the Chancellor of the Order, and all the other senior officials who were supposed to bear those responsibilities were doing – to say nothing of Philip's officers. Norris's memory of these events was only four years old at the time of writing, but should be seen more in terms of the claims he wished to establish for his office in connection with the next royal wedding than as an authentic record of what had happened in 1554. It is highly unlikely that Sir John Gage would have allowed a mere gentleman usher to have controlled such important events.

More interesting in view of the paucity of the information that is otherwise available is his description of the 'order of the queens privie chamber', which appears to date from the latter part of the reign. Men were strictly forbidden,

> other than such as her highnes shall from tyme to tyme call or command or such as her highnes hath now taken into her privie chamber, wch was iii gentlemen theare names followinge: Mr.Risse, Mr.Bassate, Mr. Kempe: iii gentlemen ushers, Mr.Ligons, Mr.Norrisse, Walter Earle: iii gromes George Bridman, Steven Hadnoll, Christopher a lande, being in all the number of x persons [sic] . . .[24]

The duties of these men were either formal or manual. The grooms moved furniture and other heavy objects, did the cleaning, and fetched and carried. The gentlemen ushers guarded the doors, making sure that no one entered uninvited, and the gentlemen escorted and accompanied those who were admitted to the inner sanctum on business. It seems likely by analogy with an earlier period that they worked a shift system, and that no more than two or three of the nine would have been on duty at any one time. Norris clearly did not know what the ladies did behind the doors for which he was responsible. Apart from their guard duties, these gentlemen were Mary's link with the outside world, and one which became increasingly important as she appeared less in public.

One of the main domestic rituals in which they were involved was the service of meals, and here we are told that Mary 'had her borde of state in her privie chamber', as distinct from her father, who had kept his 'board of state' in the Great Chamber. In earlier days the monarch had dined on great occasions in his Hall, surrounded by his servants, and had retreated to his Chamber for normal meals, where only his Chamber servants would have been in attendance. Henry VIII had virtually abandoned the Hall, dining on formal occasions in the Chamber and informally in the Privy Chamber. By the latter part of her reign, Mary seems to have retreated entirely:

> there her meale was set & one of the ordinarye servants without dyd go for yt when he was commanded by a gentleman usher & brought yt to the dore & there the ladies and gentlemen dyd feche yt . . .[25]

So presumably at least one of the gentlemen waited on the queen at meal times, but they were strictly private, small-scale occasions. Not even the

Privy Chamber servants dined there unless they were in attendance or specifically summoned. All the others, according to Norris, dined 'with Mistress Clarencius in her chamber' or in another chamber set aside for the purpose. Susan received two 'messes', which would have fed about a dozen people, and the grooms 'that dyd not wayte' one further messe between them. Some of this pattern may have been due to a desire for economy, because the queen's own food was prepared in the Privy Kitchen, and was of superior quality. There was a lot of competition to get on the list of those fed from the Privy Kitchen, and a good deal of waste which constantly exercised the Board of Greencloth;[26] but Norris gives the impression of a woman who preferred to be with a small and intimate company, and was reluctant to emerge into the turbulent (and male-dominated) world of the court at large.

Although the revels of the court did not continue at the level that Philip had inspired, neither did they return to the minimal activity of the first year. There were no more tournaments or war games, and Mary did not go hunting, but the regular seasonal festivities were observed. There were no entertainments during the autumn of 1555, but Christmas was suitably kept, and between 11 December and 8 January £45 6s. 9d., was disbursed, which was actually somewhat more than the previous year.[27] We do not have any particulars, which probably means that nothing new was created, but there were certainly masques and plays during that period, probably performed 'in house' as no specific fees are mentioned. Some £25 7s. 1d. was expended at Candlemas 1556, and £28 0s. 3d. at Shrovetide, although again we do not know what was created.[28] The costs for the whole year 1555–6 amounted to £195 0s. 1d., which was not much less than the previous year, and given the difficulties which the government was experiencing represents a valiant attempt to keep up appearances.

We have a full record of the New Year gifts exchanged in 1557, and that certainly suggests a court in full working order. Twenty-nine peers, 53 'ladies', 19 bishops and 27 knights appear on the list, together with no fewer than 170 male and female courtiers of lesser rank, and numerous acceptable hangers-on.[29] This represents a much larger number than the staffs of the Chamber and Privy Chamber combined, and is a fair reflection of the range of the queen's favour. Many of the gifts received were in cash, to the tune of about £1,300, with innumerable garments, handkerchiefs, and other small articles of use or ornament. The queen's gifts were almost all in the form of plate, and the goldsmith's bill must have come to at least £1,500. The Countess of Bedford was included, although her husband was a fugitive in Germany at the time. Rather surprisingly, no one seems to have represented the king at this central ceremony of the courtly year. Philip sent no gift, nor (apparently) was any sent to him. The only diplomatic representative was the secretary to the French ambassador, who presented four books in French and received a 13 oz. gilt jug.[30]

The Christmas that had immediately preceded this New Year was also suitably celebrated. This time there were new props, because the carvers who created masks and other images were paid for nine days' work, and one of them, Robert Trunkwell, was given a special reward. Unfortunately, we do not know what they created. The total expenditure for the holiday came to a respectable £40 17s. 7d., of which the special barge used for late-night recovery cost no less than 33s. 4d.[31] There were Candlemas and Shrovetide celebrations in 1557, but nothing is known about them beyond the fact that they took place. Philip's return in March stimulated further activity at the unusual season of St Mark's Day, 25 April, when there was a 'Greate Masque of Allmaynes, pilgrims and Irishmen' at Whitehall. Whether this was one performance or several is not clear, but it seems an odd combination if they were all together. Several documents relate to this event, including a warrant to the Great Wardrobe to provide Cawarden with the necessary materials, and an instruction from Jerningham to make the preparations.[32] The Master of the Revels clearly had qualms, because Jerningham felt it necessary to use some gentle cajolery:

> Mr Carden I have declared to the Queen's highness how that you have no other masks then such as has Byne shewed already before the King's highness, and for that he hath seen many fair and rich beyond the seas, you think it not honourable [but] that he should see the like here. Her highness thinks your consideration were good [but] notwithstanding such hath commanded me to write to you saying to me that she knows right well that you can make a shift for need, requiring you so to do, and that you shall deserve great thanks ...

Philip's reaction is not known, but it is to be hoped that he appreciated the effort. A fair sum of money, as well as a lot of effort, seems to have been expended, because the total for an otherwise unremarkable year came to £151 17s. 7d., making 1556–7 the third costliest year of the reign.[33] There may have been some entertainment immediately before his departure, but nothing was recorded in the Revels accounts, so we have no idea what form it took.

Although the last year of the reign was in many ways a gloomy one, the court put on a brave face. Entertainments were prepared for Christmas (11 December 1557–10 January 1558), Candlemas and Shrovetide, and the annual 'airing' of the props and costumes took place as usual in early June.[34] On New Year's Eve 'ther cam a lord of mysrulle from Westminster' into London, with trumpets and drums and a company of revellers 'dysgyssyd in whytt', but they seem to have raised only a ripple of curiosity, and there is no record of what 'feates' they may have performed.[35] A few days later news was received of the fall of Calais, and that cast a blight over the rest of the holiday, because for the next week the city was busy with musters as the government struggled to mount a counter-attack. The Revels expenditure for the year 1557–8 was £113 7s. 4d., well down on the two preceding years but still more than 1553–4. However, it must be confessed that there are some problems with these accounts, and they may not tell the whole story, even of the Revels Office itself, let alone of court amusements in general. In 1559, when petitioning for his account to be taken, Sir Thomas Cawarden wrote:

> the charges for the making of maskes cam never to so little a some as they do this year, for the some did ever amount as well in the Queenes highnes time that now is as at all other times heretofore to the some of £400.[36]

The recorded expenditure for 1558–9 was about £600, which was well in excess of any year of Mary's reign, and almost equal to Edward's last extravagant fling. Apart from that year (1552–3), even Edward did not regularly spend £400, so the basis of Cawarden's comment is hard to find – but he was in an excellent position to know.

Apart from her exhortation to Cawarden to do his best for Philip, we know very little of how Mary reacted to the entertainments that were provided for her. She danced with Philip, and perhaps with other partners when he was not around, but of a sense of humour there is no trace. A few of Henry's jokes have come down to us, and we know that Elizabeth laughed uproariously, particularly at bawdy stories. Even Edward left one or two snatches of humour behind, but for Mary we have no clue. What we do have, however, is a record of gentle humanity which is quite consistent with the affection and loyalty that she generated among her servants, although totally at odds with her more general historical reputation. She had a fool called Jane. Jane was what was then called an 'innocent', a person who as an adult had retained many of the qualities of early childhood.[37] An innocent had to be looked after, and provided with a minder, and in return usually performed simple and amusing antics. Nothing is know of Jane's background, but she appears in Mary's service for the first time in 1537, and there is some suggestion that she may have been taken over from Anne Boleyn, who is known to have entertained a similar, but unnamed, woman.[38] Mary then proceeded to care for Jane until her own death over twenty years later. Her accounts show gifts of clothing, horses and other things, and constant expenditure on medical care for Jane's repeated ailments. What kind of services she provided in return we do not know. She was *compos mentis* enough to take part in the St Valentine's Day lottery, and seems to have been paired with Will Somers on some state occasions, but whether she was a jester in any conventional sense, or simply someone on whom Mary had taken pity, is not clear. It seems quite likely that she was a surrogate child, a substitute for the son or daughter the queen wanted but was unable to bear. Even Renard never mentioned her, and their relationship can only be reconstructed through such things as wardrobe accounts, but it casts a gentle light on Mary's character. What happened to Jane after her protector's death is not known. Will Somers was able to spend what was left of his life at court, or at least under Elizabeth's protection, and it is to be hoped that Jane did the same.

The chances of mortality brought about a number of changes among the officers of the court between 1555 and 1558. In April 1556 Sir John Gage, Mary's Lord Chamberlain, died, and his funeral took place, with suitable pomp, on the 25th.[39] The position remained vacant for more than a year and a half, and it was not until Sir Robert Rochester died in early December 1557 that a number of new appointments were made, or at least became public knowledge. Sir Edward Hastings, the Master of the Horse, was then promoted to the vacant Chamberlainship; Sir Henry

Jerningham, the Vice-Chamberlain, was moved sideways to become Master of the Horse; and Sir Henry Bedingfield took over the Vice-Chamberlainship. At the same time Sir Thomas Cornwallis was appointed to Rochester's former office.[40] A month later Sir Robert Freston, the Cofferer, also departed. William Cavendish, the Treasurer of the Chamber, had died in the previous October, and neither of these positions seem to have been filled immediately. Sir John Mason took over as Treasurer before the end of the reign, but it is not known exactly when. The Earl of Arundel served as Lord Steward throughout the reign and well into the next, while Sir Thomas Cheney had been Treasurer of the Household since 1539, so there was continuity as well as change. No one commented upon the cause of these deaths, and Gage was an old man by the standards of the time, but the decease of Cavendish, Rochester and Freston in the space of three months can probably be attributed to the influenza epidemic, which was at its height at that time.[41] Mortality in the country as a whole was very high, and neither the court nor the city was exempt. Machyn records the funerals of an unusual number of citizens and their wives, but comments only upon the number of banners and the size of the dole. The winter of 1557–8 was a hard and difficult one, but Mary was nursing a secret. When she made her will in March, it was because she again believed herself to be pregnant and facing the hazards of childbirth.

The queen's second phantom pregnancy is even more of a mystery than the first. She seems to have convinced herself of her condition during the Christmas holidays, and since Philip had left in early July, that in itself is sufficiently remarkable. About the middle of January she wrote to the king, giving him the good news, and explaining the delay by saying that this time she wanted to be completely certain before making any public announcement.[42] He naturally expressed the warmest satisfaction, but it is probable that he shared the general scepticism with which the news was greeted in Europe. Three years earlier every observer had commented upon the queen's body shape, and the opinions of her physicians had been widely canvassed. On this occasion, nobody had said anything, or given any suspicion that Mary might be five months pregnant. When the news reached the Cardinal of Lorraine in February he observed sarcastically that they would not have to wait so long in anticipation since it was eight months since her husband had left.[43] His arithmetic was faulty, but his sentiment was generally shared. At the end of March, at about the time that Mary was writing her will, a rumour reached the Constable of France that she had been delivered of a son. If that had been true it would have been bad news for France, but he had difficulty in keeping a straight face. It is not even clear whether Mary's own courtiers took her seriously. In 1555 a nursery had been prepared, the queen had gone into confinement, and for weeks the court had talked of little else. In 1558 there was an eerie silence. This is partly due to the shortage of well-informed commentators, but messengers were passing regularly to Brussels, and councillors were keeping up a normal level of correspondence. However, there were no eagerly anticipated bulletins, no speculation about the happy day, and apart from the one which reached France, no false reports of a birth. The only possible conclusion is that it was generally thought that the queen was again deceiving herself (she was by this time 42) but that no one had the heart to tell her so. When the symptoms disappeared, if they did, or if there were any visible symptoms at all, we do not know. When Mary became seriously ill in the following October, it was reported that she was suffering from a 'dropsy', which has been interpreted as a cancer of the womb, and perhaps that is the most likely explanation.[44] It is also possible that it was a mere ploy to tempt Philip back to England for a notional 'lying in', but if so, it failed completely. The king gave no indication of any intention to visit his wife, no matter what her condition; and if he had really believed that a child was a possibility he would almost certainly have come, for the same reason that he had delayed his departure in 1555. A child, and most particularly a son, would have transformed the political prospects in western Europe, but Philip was not tempted.

Mary's health was a matter of nagging concern from the summer of 1555 onwards. She had never been particularly robust, and the stresses of a turbulent adolescence had taken their toll. She had a long history of menstrual disorders, and the failure of her first pregnancy – and the manner of it – had rung alarm bells. This fact, together with her childlessness and the conspicuous toughness of her younger half-sister, created a fragile political situation. If Mary had been sufficiently ruthless to have executed Elizabeth when she had the chance in the spring of 1554, this could have been avoided. But Mary was not ruthless (except in her treatment of heresy), and the princess had influential protectors.

Consequently, as soon as it appeared likely that the queen's chances of childbearing had evaporated, Elizabeth began to emerge as a serious contender, and conspiracies began to weave around her.[45] The most serious was the one that is conveniently known by the name of Henry Dudley, but in which he was only one, and not the most important, of the players.

The plan, as it eventually emerged, was for an invasion from France to link up with a major gentry-led rising in the West Country. The objective was to depose and exile Mary and to place Elizabeth on the throne in her place.[46] There were three critical elements in this plot: first, the English exiles in France, who numbered about 200 and were mostly fugitives from the Wyatt conspiracy of January 1554; second, the King of France, Henry II; and third, a disaffected group of important gentlemen, many of them members of parliament, led by Sir Anthony Kingston. In the second half of 1555 Henry was anxious to destabilise England by any means that were to hand, as a means of distracting the emperor and his son without committing any further resources to the war. He did not wish to make a pre-emptive strike himself, because that would only extend the war, but he was prepared to support the exiles with money and to allow them to hire ships and mercenary soldiers. He had no particular desire to support the pretensions of Elizabeth because he had an equally good claimant under his control in the person of Mary of Scotland, who was betrothed to his son, Francis, and had been brought up at the French court.[47] The disaffected gentry are a shadowy bunch, not because we do not know who they were but because we do not know how deeply they were involved. Half a dozen of them were arrested, including Sir John Perrot, Sir William Courtenay and Sir John Pollard, and several were indicted in general terms, but none were tried and all were eventually pardoned.[48] Some of the conspirators may have been covert protestants, but that was never even alleged by the government to be the mainspring of their action. According to their own statements (and these were reasonably consistent), their main objective was to free England from the threat of Spanish domination. They were concerned about Philip's demands for a coronation, but also more generally anxious to put an end to the Habsburg connection, which they rightly perceived to be only feasible by removing Mary. Neither her childlessness nor her questionable health reassured them, because they clearly did not trust Philip to resign his interest in the kingdom should Mary die in possession of the crown.

The first beginnings of this plot can probably be traced to some suspicious gatherings in London in the middle of July 1555, just after the collapse of the supposed pregnancy. There was no parliament in session, the law term was over, and most gentlemen were attending to their business in the country. Both Renard and Michieli identified these suspicious characters as friends of Elizabeth, and claimed that 'the Dudley's were amongst them', although which Dudleys is not clear.[49] Noailles was also alert to the possibility of causing the government some embarrassment, and when he was told that 50 English gentlemen had sworn to recover their liberties by the end of August, he was naturally interested. His informant, a certain Edward Randall, was soliciting French assistance for some kind of action, but it is not clear what, and his king instructed him not to be drawn.[50] However, a few weeks later a parliament was summoned, and it was generally reported that a subsidy would be demanded. Mary had so far managed without asking parliament for money, and no war was in prospect, so rumours immediately began to circulate that this taxation was for Philip's benefit – a sweetener, perhaps, to bring him back to England. Parliament eventually met on 21 October, and as we have seen, Philip did not appear. The usual efforts had been made to secure the return of 'wise, grave and catholic' men, and there was nothing unusual about the composition of the House of Commons, but it turned out to be unusually fractious.[51] This probably had more to do with a bad harvest and the unpopularity of the subsidy than with anything more sinister, but the council was nervous from the start, and within a few days had taken the unusual step of closing down all the venues for public dancing and gambling in London on the grounds that they were hotbeds of political intrigue. The air was full of rumours, and it is difficult to tell how substantial they were, because London was always a magnet for the discontented and the unemployed. Nevertheless, former supporters of Wyatt, who were supposed to be in France, like Edward Randall, William Staunton and Henry Dudley, were reported to have been seen, along with notorious pirates like Francis Horsey and Edmund Tremayne.[52] Through the agency of the French ambassador these adventurers began to make contact with the malcontents in the Commons; there were meetings at Arundel's tavern and in the thronged passageways at St Paul's. 'With gret willfullness', it was later alleged, 'they intended to resiste such matters as should be spoken of in the parliament other than liked them . . .'[53]

The impact of all this on the work of parliament should not be exaggerated. For all Noailles's efforts the subsidy passed without great difficulty, and even a controversial proposal to restore first fruits to the church was accepted, although in that case its opponents did succeed in forcing a division, which was unusual.[54] Only towards the end of the session did the government suffer a significant reverse, when a measure to confiscate the property of those who had gone abroad without licence was defeated, again on a division. There were strong feelings about interference with normal property rights, even by statute, and it was that rather than any exile conspiracy, combined with the inept tactics of the responsible councillors, that brought about this reverse.[55] The queen was annoyed, and the ringleader of the opposition, Sir Anthony Kingston, was imprisoned for a few days when the session finished, but it was not thought to be a serious defeat. It was, nevertheless, a symptom of something rather more sinister, because Kingston was the 'link man' between the malcontents in the Commons, the French ambassador and the adventurers noticed before.

Shortly before the 'Exiles bill' was brought to a vote, Henry Dudley had managed to set up a meeting between Kingston and Jean Berteville, a French soldier of fortune who had been in Noailles's pay for about two years. Berteville reported this interview directly to Anne de Montmorency, the Constable of France, saying that Dudley was minded to do the king some service.[56] Montmorency was cautiously supportive, and committed the management of the business to Noailles. The ambassador's response, sent on 16 December, after the parliamentary session had finished, was enthusiastic. Dudley was a good soldier, and reliable; moreover, he was in touch with a network of other unemployed gentlemen soldiers who were ripe for an 'enterprise'. Berteville said much the same thing. If Dudley decided to serve the King of France 'they will turn French whenever he pleases'. He also seems to have had an inflated opinion of Kingston: 'he can assuredly raise more than six thousand men in his district', he wrote. This was twice as many as Wyatt had managed, and if true would have made him a force to be reckoned with. However, Kingston's 'country' was Gloucestershire and the Welsh borders, and although he was a substantial landowner with strong court connections, there is no reason to suppose that he could have mobilised a private army on that scale.[57] According to Berteville, Kingston 'hated the Spaniards mightily', but there was no reason why that sentiment should have been strong in Gloucestershire, where no Spaniard had set foot. Sir Anthony was liberal with promises: if Dudley were to lead an invasion, 'I will go with you with all my forces' to drive the foreign tyrants out of England.[58]

It would be easy to dismiss this as so much hot air, but there was some substance behind it. Dudley reckoned that he would need an invasion force of about 3,000 to trigger a sympathetic rising of any size. That was far in excess of the number of English exiles presently in France, but not impossible to recruit in the south of England by using his network of contacts – provided that the French supplied the money. A number of 'gentlemen servants', such as John Danyell, John Bedell and John Throgmorton, joined the conspiracy. In themselves they were not powerful men, but they also had their networks, and Bedell and Throgmorton were on the fringes of the court. They 'rode about to provide men', and some were shipped over to France, but we do not know how many and there are no reliable facts about their operations. The most important recruit to the project was Richard Uvedale, the captain of Yarmouth Castle on the Isle of Wight. Uvedale was not himself a man of great 'substance', but his office gave him influence, and was strategically important.[59] If a force had landed on the Isle of Wight, it should have been his responsibility to deal with it; if instead he had joined it at the head of his garrison, it would have significantly boosted the credibility of the invasion. Uvedale also provided channels of communication between the exiles in France and the agents operating in England. Another ran through a French denizen at Winchelsea.

Shortly after his release from the Tower, Kingston began his own round of conferences, particularly with Christopher Ashton at Fifield in Buckinghamshire. Ashton was also a man with court connections and a friend (it was alleged) of Elizabeth.[60] Like some of the others, he had influence, but he appears to have been a wild character, and hardly to be relied upon if things got difficult. They talked, it was later claimed, about the need for up-to-date French weaponry, 'vii or viiiC of the best hagbuttes in all France', and such things did not come cheap. By the end of the year they had got to the point where a large sum of money was needed to turn aspirations into deeds – provided that promises could really be transmuted in that way.

At that point, in January 1556, the conspiracy appeared to break at its weakest point. Henry Dudley returned to the French court only to find that the political climate had changed. The king was in the process of signing the Truce of Vaucelles with Philip, and had no desire to upset that negotiation by provocative action. He could have provided Dudley with money surreptitiously and denied it in public, but he chose not to do so, perhaps thinking that a measure of goodwill was worth more than the political advantage. Before Christmas Dudley had been welcomed with apparent enthusiasm; by early February he was being dismissed with empty words.[61] This was made more serious by the fact that there were (or were alleged to be) far more substantial backers in England than Kingston and his mates, but these men had made it clear that they would only declare themselves if the French gave the movement large-scale and effective backing. The identity, and even the existence, of this group is a matter of conjecture. People like Courtenay and Pollard may have been meant, but the suggestion at the time was that senior courtiers and members of the council were involved. No action was ever taken that could suggest their names. Even Elizabeth, who had been severely handled in 1554, was this time merely admonished that certain evil men had taken her name in vain. However, several of her confidential servants, including Katherine Ashley, were dismissed, and the reliable Sir Thomas Pope was temporarily placed in charge of her household.[62] Henry's withdrawal should probably have stopped the conspiracy in its tracks, but Dudley had developed a certain momentum, and had created expectations. There were other possible sources of money, and a second plot developed to steal the money that the French would no longer supply.

To be accurate, there were two subsidiary plots, but the first was merely a rumour based on a conjecture. It was believed that the enormous sum of £200,000 was about to be sent out of England to Philip in the Low Countries. This was presumably the subsidy then being collected, the supposed destination of which had caused trouble in parliament. In fact, nothing like £200,000 had been collected, and there was no intention of sending it to Philip anyway, so the plot to seize it in transit was even more insubstantial than usual. Nevertheless, 'a grete many ... gentlemen', including Sir Thomas Cawarden, the Master of the Revels, were alleged to be implicated. Cawarden had enemies, probably because of his suspected protestant sympathies, and they had attempted to ensnare him in the Wyatt conspiracy two years earlier. He was arrested in March 1556, and may have been examined, but the case against him was as insubstantial as the plot itself, and no action was taken.[63]

Much more serious was an attempt to seize the £50,000 in silver bullion that was actually in the custody of Nicholas Brigham, one of the Tellers of the Exchequer. Brigham himself was a man of unimpeachable integrity, but he was vulnerable, not least because this very large quantity of silver appears to have been stored in his own house, which had a garden running down to the Thames. A friend of his, William Rossey, the Keeper of the Star Chamber, proved amenable to bribery or persuasion, and he had some kind of a hold over Brigham's wife. A sordid intrigue may be suspected, but was never alleged. Rossey persuaded Mrs Brigham to obtain an impression of her husband's keys. The conspirators gained access to the vault, but then discovered that the chests containing the bullion were too heavy for them to move. They decided that they would have to break open the chests and move the silver piecemeal to a crayer moored at the bottom of the garden. The vessel was hired, and everything ready, when the plot was betrayed.[64] Ostensibly, a minor conspirator named Thomas White went to Cardinal Pole in the first week in March and confessed everything he knew. There was then a major round-up on 18 March when about twenty arrests were made. Only a handful of the plotters made good their escape.

All this information is derived from later confessions, and sounds both too tidy and too fortuitous. Consequently it is hard to judge whether the plot ever had any real chance of success, but Dudley and his associates clearly believed in it, because they continued with their preparations. An illicit mint was established near Dieppe to turn the bullion into counterfeit English coin, and a skilled moneyer named Andrew Pomeroy was recruited to run it. This venture outlasted the plot, and may have been unconnected with it. It was eventually shut down in August by the French authorities after representations from Nicholas Wotton, Mary's ambassador in France.[65]

During the second half of February and into early March, recruits to the exile army continued to trickle across the Channel. We have a description of Christopher Ashton's departure from Southampton with sixteen men, but there is no means of knowing how many others went. When the plot collapsed they seem to have crewed the pirate ships which Ashton was operating in the Channel during the summer, so there are unlikely to have been more than a hundred or two of them. Uvedale had ambitious plans to subvert the garrison of Portsmouth, believing that the invasion force would indeed number some 3,000 men. There was talk of then leading two medium-sized armies, one from Hampshire and one from the West Country, to converge on London, where a sympathetic rising was also expected. Reading these testimonies, it all sounds quite plausible, but in fact success would have depended not only on the bullion heist succeeding, but also on the shadowy backers declaring themselves.[66] In the event, nothing happened. The London prisons were full of frightened and confused men, and several hundred doubly disgruntled adventurers were left stranded in France.

The investigations were intensive and prolonged.[67] Implausible as the conspiracy looks in retrospect, both the queen and the council took it very seriously. One of the reasons for this was the identity of some of the plotters. Henry Peckham was the brother of Sir Robert, a long-serving Privy Councillor, 'master Henneage of the Chapel' was a kinsman of Sir Thomas, Richard Uvedale held a position of trust, and Sir Thomas Cawarden, although only suspected, was an important courtier. Sir Anthony Kingston died, apparently of natural causes, after being interviewed only once, and the real problem was that no one knew how far the infection had spread. Although the Earl of Devon was in exile in Italy and the queen professed to believe him innocent, some of his servants were certainly involved, and a plausible case has recently been made for his own sympathy and support, which would still have been a matter of some significance in his 'country' in spite of his exile.[68]

By July, the investigation had run into the sand, and the sound and fury died away. Nearly 100 people had been arrested and interrogated. Of those, about half were released without any charges being brought, and there are 36 recorded indictments, at least sixteen of men who were safely out of the country. Thirteen were eventually tried, and eight executed, including Henry Peckham and Richard Uvedale.[69] As a sequel, a squadron of the English navy caught up with Ashton's pirate fleet in the Channel in July, and destroyed or captured most of the ships. Ashton himself escaped, but Peter Killigrew, one of the plotters, was taken. In spite of his delinquencies he was pardoned in 1557, along with Sir Ralph Bagenall and thirteen of the other suspects. Edward Lewkenor, a groom porter of the court, who was responsible for the supply of playing cards, died in prison, and there were rumours that some yeomen of the guard had been involved, but no action was taken against them.

By the end of 1556 it was getting difficult to know what constituted disaffection. Both the church and the court were full of 'grey patches'. Protestantism was underground, and might reasonably be associated with opposition to the regime, but there were a great many noblemen and major gentlemen who were less than enthusiastic about the proactive papalism of the queen and the hierarchy. There was no ambiguity about official statements, or officially sponsored literature, but events in the parliament of 1559 were to reveal that there were two rather different varieties of catholicism. Elizabeth restored the Royal Supremacy with very little dissent from the lay community, but she had a real fight to persuade them to accept a protestant settlement.[70] Similarly, Mary had restored the 'old religion' in 1553 with scarcely a dissenting voice, but had an uphill battle before she could abolish the Supremacy in 1555. All the evidence suggests that 'Religion as King Henry left it' was more popular in Mary's reign than either protestantism or 'proper' catholicism; but to have expressed such views openly in 1556 would have been to court trouble with the Legatine Commission, or the Privy Council, or both.

This situation was complicated further by the overt anti-Habsburg sentiments of Pope Paul IV, who was elected in May 1555. Paul started off by denouncing all agreements whereby church property had been secularised, thus apparently reneging upon his predecessor's undertakings to England. However, under pressure from both Pole and Mary he exempted England, and by issuing the bull *Praeclara*, tided away the legal status of the dissolved English houses.[71] He made supportive noises towards Pole's mission, and all seemed to be well. However, by September 1556 he had provoked Philip into open war in Italy and placed him under the ban of the church. England never became involved in war against the pope, but when Philip came to England in March 1557, it put Pole in a very difficult situation. As Archbishop of Canterbury he was the king's subject, but as Legate of the Holy See he could do no business with an excommunicate.

This problem was resolved untidily during Philip's stay. Paul was forced to withdraw from the war and suspend his alliance with France not long after England became involved on the Habsburg side. He also cancelled the commissions of all his legates in Habsburg lands, including

Pole's, and shortly after recalled the English cardinal to Rome to face investigation for heresy.[72] The king and queen would not allow him to go, protesting that they had full confidence in his orthodoxy. This left the archbishop in limbo. He could now discharge his proper functions and advise the king; on the other hand, his links with Rome were cut. He was in disfavour and his contact, Cardinal Morone, was under arrest. Mary made urgent representations to get him restored, and indignantly refused to accept his replacement, William Peto. Relations with Rome remained strained for the rest of the reign, so much so that Paul was pleased by the news that Pole and Mary had died almost simultaneously in November 1558.[73] This did nothing to strengthen the hand of those in England who believed that the unity of the catholic church was of crucial importance, and left the queen's most loyal adherents confused as to where their ultimate allegiance lay

This affected the court only when Philip and Pole were playing hide and seek. Much more significant in that context was the problem of the succession. Mary remained deeply antagonistic to her half-sister, and anyone who spoke up for Elizabeth risked severe displeasure. So averse was Mary to the thought of Elizabeth as heir to the throne that she tried to promote the cause of Margaret Douglas, the Countess of Lennox. Margaret was the daughter of Henry VIII's elder sister by her second marriage, to Archibald Douglas, Earl of Angus. She was almost unknown in England, and had absolutely no support, but she was a good catholic.[74] The real alternative to Elizabeth was Mary Stuart, but she was virtually a French princess, and was absolutely unacceptable to Philip. The king knew perfectly well that Margaret was a non-starter, and by the summer of 1556 he had concluded that any attempt to press his own claim in the event of his wife's death would involve him in a civil war in England. His attitude to Elizabeth therefore changed, and it was by his strongly expressed wishes (instructions would not be too strong a word) that no action was taken against her in the wake of the Dudley conspiracy.[75] At the beginning of June 1556, Mary consequently sent Sir Edward Hastings and Sir Francis Englefield to Ashridge with a gift, and smooth professions of regret at the disruption to Elizabeth's household, because Katherine Ashley had just been discovered in possession of protestant and anti-Spanish literature. No blame was attached to the princess herself. Elizabeth replied with equal smoothness, expressing gratitude for such sisterly solicitude.[76]

Not surprisingly, the two women seldom met, but the princess did visit the court from 28 November to 3 December 1556. This was an occasion replete with the hints and gestures beloved of courtiers. She rode into London accompanied by a retinue of 200 horsemen in red coats, 'to the infinite pleasure of the whole population', as Michieli reported.[77] She did not stay at court, but at her own residence at Somerset House, and the Venetian noted that although no one came officially from the court to greet her, many did so privately. She must have come on her sister's invitation, and the natural assumption is that she had come to 'keep the Christmas'. However, she stayed only five days. Whether her licence extended no longer, or there had been a falling out, we do not know; but she then retreated with the same pomp that she had displayed on her arrival.

Philip, as we have seen, wanted to marry Elizabeth to the Duke of Savoy, and logically that idea should have appealed to the queen, but apparently it did not. When she was in a particularly indignant mood, she described Elizabeth as the bastard child of a criminal (meaning Anne Boleyn), and even denied her paternity, saying that she closely resembled Mark Smeaton – which was manifestly untrue.[78] Mary was deeply hurt, not only by her subjects' apparent willingness to accept this heretically inclined bastard as their next queen, but even more by her husband's willingness to do the same. Elizabeth was not only unworthy of the crown, she was unworthy of an honourable marriage. According to Michel Surian, admittedly writing from France in the following year, Philip's confessor Bernardo de Fresnada briefly succeeded during the king's visit in 1557 in persuading Mary to accept the Savoy idea; but her acquiescence lasted less than two days, and thereafter she was implacable. 'Although it is dissembled', Michieli observed, 'it cannot be denied that she [Mary] displays in many ways the scorn and ill-will she bears her.'[79] It was an attitude that Elizabeth heartily reciprocated, but she was a better dissembler, and time was on her side.

When he returned to the Low Countries in July 1557, Philip was reasonably satisfied with what he had achieved in his wife's kingdom. Paradoxically, his decision not to press the Savoy marriage in the face of opposition from both women earned him a measure of goodwill from the princess which was to come in useful in due course. He also had a small but competent English army led by the Earl of Pembroke. This force fought well at the siege of St Quentin on 27 August, but it returned home in October, leaving him to foot the bill.[80] The king's Spanish household, which had been noticeably smaller than on his first stay, was withdrawn on 11 July, and only a token number of his English gentlemen, led by his Chamberlain, Lord Williams, remained at court.[81]

Mary may have been depressed by her husband's departure, but at least they now had a common cause to prosecute, and *Te Deums* were sung in all the churches of London to celebrate the victory of St Quentin. Philip, however, was rethinking his options in England. There was little he could do about Mary's childlessness, and as long as the war lasted he could not contemplate an annulment. He had a number of capable English soldiers in his service, and her fleet was at his disposal, but there was now much less point in maintaining a 'king's party' among the English nobility. He had got his war, and he was not going to contest the succession. Consequently, his English pension list ceased to be a priority, and got seriously into arrears. When his treasurer, Dominico de Orbea, took stock just after Mary's death, he found that the total debt on the English pensions was 45,462 crowns – about £11,365 – or rather more than two years' payments. Some were owed more, some less, but the most fortunate were twelve months behind.[82] To Philip's credit he eventually paid them down to the end of 1558, but Elizabeth would not allow her subjects to take any money from that source (with her knowledge), and it is perhaps not surprising that the Count of Feria, who was then Philip's representative in England, commented sourly that the English nobility were 'all as ungrateful to your Majesty as if they had never received anything from your hands'.[83]

During the last two years of the reign, Mary's courtiers consequently faced some problems of allegiance. As long as she was alive, their primary loyalty was to her, but beyond her, where should they look? Philip clearly intended to honour his treaty obligation and forgo any interest in the kingdom if (or when) the queen should die, but what should be their attitude to Elizabeth? She was the heir by law, and however little Mary may have relished the thought, there was no realistic alternative. On the other hand, the queen's attitude towards her half-sister was an open secret. Some, particularly the more zealous catholics, respected Mary's feelings more than their own interests, and maintained a chilly hostility. Others, more politically inclined, began to put out feelers towards Ashridge, or in some cases to develop connections that already existed.[84]

Not very much is known about Elizabeth's activities in 1557 and the early part of 1558. Sir Thomas Pope was relieved of the duty of running her household in October 1556, having (apparently) become rather too sympathetic to her, but Mary seems to have made no attempt to maintain the surveillance that he had represented. Elizabeth stayed at Somerset House again from 25 February to 4 March 1558, arriving and leaving with the same ostentation as before. Presumably she visited the court, but we do not know how she was received. We can only be certain that there was no cordiality.

After the brief satisfaction stimulated by the victory of St Quentin, the political news got steadily worse. In January 1558, in spite of warnings from Philip's intelligence agents, the Duke of Guise was able to surprise and take Calais, a prize which Henry had been seeking since before his accession. The blame for this disaster lay squarely with the English council, which had never wanted the war in the first place and was now endeavouring to economise at the expense of its garrisons. To make matters worse, an attempt was made to blame Philip before responsibility was less controversially settled on 'the heretics' who (it was claimed) had betrayed the city. The king was extremely annoyed, but he also made the situation worse by licensing his Flemish subjects to victual the French garrison while still ostensibly urging his English subjects to mount a counter-attack.[85] The English were angry in turn, and the king's agents in England had the grace to be embarrassed. As Philip was also doing his level best at this point to prevent London merchants from becoming involved in the lucrative Guinea trade, relations could hardly have been worse.

By May Mary was unwell, and Feria attributed her condition to the failure of her second supposed pregnancy. She was, he reported, weak and melancholy; but these were also 'her usual ailments' and there was no particular sense of crisis. In early June she was worse, but had improved again by the end of the month, when Philip wrote enquiring why she had not written for several days, which was evidently unusual. Even when she was sick – or perhaps especially then – she seems to have been in the habit of writing to him almost daily, although none of these small personal letters have survived. In August she caught a fever, but Pole assured Philip that she was taking good care of herself, and the symptoms had disappeared by the end of the month.

Mary was not the only one who was depressed. Feria, who had no time for the cardinal anyway, described Pole in March as being 'a dead man', meaning not one who was seriously ill, but one who has lost all animation and sense of purpose.[86] This was unfair, and we have other testimony to the effect that he was sticking to his task with admirable persistence; but whether he was any longer much consolation to the queen may be doubted. He had tried very hard to persuade Pope Paul to rescind the cancellation of his legateship. In August 1557, two months after his recall, he had penned a long and passionate apologia, professing his total allegiance to the church. It was never sent, because in a fit of despair he threw it on the fire, but a copy survives and some of the points were repeated in real letters over the next few months.[87] Paul did not respond, and Pole became increasingly despondent. Mary denied any intention of reopening the schism, but she absolutely refused to obey the pope over the matter of the legateship. As a result Edward Carne, her ambassador in Rome, could secure no audience, and English business, including the confirmation of episcopal appointments, was put on hold.

Feria was one of the very few Spanish nobles who had any liking for the English, or any rapport with the English court, and that was one of the reasons why Philip chose to send him to England in December 1557. The original reason was a wake-up call over Calais, but when that failed he remained in England, trying to coordinate the flagging war effort, and to placate the English over the Flemish activity in Calais and Philip's point-blank refusal to declare war on Scotland.[88] The latter was particularly irksome because Mary of Guise was pointedly threatening to do to Berwick what her brother had just done to Calais. In the event, Mary had her own problems and the threat turned out to be hollow, but that did not make Feria's task any easier, and it could not have been predicted in the spring of 1558. The count remained until July, and before he left he visited Elizabeth on the king's instructions. Mary was informed, but her reaction is not known. The nature of their discussions was never revealed: Feria described them as very satisfactory, and promised to disclose them to Philip when they met.[89] The queen's life was not thought to be in danger – indeed, her health had recently improved – so it is unlikely that they talked about the imminent prospect of her succession. From allusions made in later letters by Feria it seems likely that the princess made some professions of friendship, perhaps undertaking to continue the Habsburg alliance in the event of her coming to the throne. She almost certainly disclaimed any sympathy with the French, which she could have done with a clear conscience given the threat that Mary Stuart presented to her prospects.

Feria was replaced in England by Don Alonso de Cordoba and by the Brabantine councillor Christophe d'Assonleville. This represented a downgrading of the mission, and perhaps a response to Mary's improved health rather than a change of purpose and direction. By August there was talk of peace, but that could not be taken for granted. It seems that the king intended to come to England again in the autumn of 1558; but his father the emperor died at San Yuste on 21 September, and Philip, who had been King of Spain since January 1556, had to arrange the obsequies. Then on 8 October the peace negotiations started at Cercamp and his preoccupations multiplied.[90] Also, by early October the news of Mary's health was becoming alarming. This might have made a visit to England more pressing, but the king did not see it that way. Natural humanity might have prompted him to abandon his other concerns for the time being, but Philip was anxious not to be caught in England if Mary should die. In such circumstances, honour might require him to claim the crown, which he had no desire to do and which would have been a serious political mistake. By staying away he could decently avoid such a dilemma, and he had plenty of excuses to do so.

On 22 October, as the queen's condition became critical, Philip withdrew Cordoba and informed the English council that Feria would be returning in his place. There was then a short delay, caused by a false report of Mary's recovery, and Feria did not leave Arras until 5 November. He arrived in England on 9 November with instructions that if (or when) Mary died, he should ensure the smooth succession of Elizabeth, with as few obstacles as possible.[91] These instructions (which have not survived) he apparently showed to the princess, although whether Mary ever knew about them is not clear. As he was accompanied by his household, it was generally understood that he was under orders to sit out the crisis until the queen had either recovered completely or died and been succeeded by her sister. It is not quite clear whether he went straight to the court, although it would have been natural for him to do so. On the 14th he reported that he had found Mary's health just as he expected, and that there was therefore 'no hope of her life'.[92] She had been pleased to see him, and to have news of Philip, although she had been unable to read the letter he had brought. This raises the critical question of whether he told her anything directly of his instructions. According to his own account he conveyed the king's wishes to the council, but it is not clear exactly when he did that. D'Assonleville, who had remained at his post, wrote on 7 November that it had been on 'the previous day' that the queen had finally surrendered to the logic of the situation and named Elizabeth as her heir.[93] This was a bitter blow, and may well have hastened her end, but she appears to have come to that conclusion independently of Philip's wishes. There really was no option unless she wished to inflict unpredictable damage upon her country. As late as the end of October she had written a codicil to her will, finally acknowledging that an heir of her body was unlikely, but merely decreeing that the crown should pass to 'the next heir in law' without naming anyone.[94] It was, according to d'Assonleville, the council's insistence rather than Feria's arrival which forced her hand, so the count was spared what had promised to be his most intimidating task.

Virtually the whole council attended Feria's briefing session. Much of what he had to say related to the peace negotiations, and particularly to the king's determination to secure the return of Calais, but he also dealt forthrightly with the main domestic issue. Philip, he reminded them, had long since wished Elizabeth to be formally recognised as heir, but the queen had until now refused. He hinted that some councillors had been rather too willing to abet this negative attitude, knowing perfectly well that his words would go straight back to Elizabeth. '[Sir John] Mason was there and he is greatly favoured by Madame Elizabeth, and would report to her all that had passed between us.'[95] Feria also made haste to see Elizabeth herself, and most of his despatch is concerned with her attitude, plans and preferences. He was looking anxiously for some signs of gratitude towards the king for his intervention in the succession issue, but was reluctantly forced to concede that none was visible. Elizabeth was quite clear that her claim rested upon the law and the will of the people, and not upon any recognition by either Philip or Mary. The court, he reported, was tense and expectant:

*These councillors are extremely frightened of what madam Elizabeth
will do with them. They have received me well, but somewhat as they
would a man who came with bulls from a dead pope . . .*[96]

This was true of some, but not of others, because Mason was not the only
councillor to be in touch with the next queen. What was happening at
Ashridge at this time can only be deduced. Some sort of a 'shadow council' had come into existence, to which Sir William Cecil was central.
Messages were sent out to Elizabeth's affinity, which was by this time
very large, putting them on standby in case there was a disputed succession, but otherwise the princess was playing her cards very close.

By the time that Feria wrote his despatch no one believed that Mary
would recover, although a polite fiction was maintained to that effect. At
the same time Pole was very weak with a quartan ague, and the ambassador feared that he too would die. Exactly what was wrong with Mary we
do not know. No one described her ailment as an ague, so it seems that it
was not influenza. In the light of her medical history over the last few
years, some kind of cancer of the womb or cervix seems the most likely
explanation.[97] A number of stories are told of her last days: how she told
her councillors that much as she regretted Philip's absence, it was Calais
that would be found written on her heart. 'She comforted those of them
that grieved about her; she told them what good dreams she had, seeing
little children like angels play before her . . .' The first of these comes
from Rhys Manxell and the second from Jane Dormer, both of whom were
present, although their memories were written down long after.[98] The
mass was central to her last hours, as it had been to her whole adult life.
A day or two before she died, we are told that the host acted as a 'sacred
medecine', and she rallied briefly. It was just after making the responses,
at six o'clock on the morning of 17 November, that she died. Susan
Clarencius rallied the gentlewomen of her Privy Chamber to lay her out,
innocently burning some of Sir Thomas Gresham's accounts which had
been carelessly left lying around in the process of 'cereing' the body.[99]
The court went into mourning, and waited with bated breath to see what
would happen next.

Notes and references

1 The indictment of Sir Ralph Bagenall, *CPR Mary*, vol.3, p.318.

2 The anonymous *supplicacyon* was published in an unknown location in 1555, the *Shorte treatise* by John Ponet probably in Strasbourg in 1556.

3 *The copye of a letter*: 'Will ye crowne the king to make him live chast with his wife, contrary to his nature; peradventure his maiestie after he were crowned would be content with one woman, but in the mean time his Grace will have every night v or vi.'

4 D.M. Loades, *Mary Tudor: A Life* (Oxford, 1989), pp.323–4.

5 *CSP, Venetian*, vol.6, pt1, p.293; J. Loach, *Parliament and Crown in the Reign of Mary Tudor* (Oxford, 1986), pp.138–9.

6 G. Redworth, '"Matters Impertinent to Women": Male and Female Monarchy under Philip and Mary', *English Historical Review*, 112 (1997). See also above, p.204

7 BL, Cotton MS Titus A 24, fol.83*v*. For a discussion of this poem, see D.M. Loades, *The Tudor Court* (London, 1986), p.213.

8 Mary to Cromwell, probably 30 June 1536, *Letters and Papers*, vol.10 no.1186. For a short biography of Susan Clarencius and an assessment of her career, see J.A. Rowley-Williams, 'Image and Reality: The Lives of Aristocratic Women in Early Tudor England', PhD diss., University of Wales, 1998, pp.218–45.

9 Ibid., pp.233–4.

10 Henry Clifford, *The Life of Jane Dormer, Duchess of Feria*, ed. J. Stevenson (London, 1887).

11 F.G. Emmison, *Tudor Food and Pastimes* (London, 1964), p.81. This is drawn from the Petre household accounts, and is not separately referenced.

12 Frederick Madden, *Privy Purse Expenses of Princess Mary* (London, 1829); Underhill's narrative, in A.F. Pollard, *Tudor Tracts* (London, 1903), p.87.

13 BL, Add. MS 71009, ffols.10*r*–17*v*. Extracts from this document, edited by Fiona Kisby, are printed in *Religion, Politics and Society in Sixteenth Century England* (Camden Fifth Series 22, 2003), pp.1–33.

14 BL, Add. MS 71009, fols.22*v*–26*r*.

15 *The Diary of Henry Machyn*, ed. J.G. Nichols (Camden Society, 1848), pp.94, 97.

16 Ibid., pp.110, 114.

17 Ibid., pp.124–5.

18 Nepeja had been coming to England with Richard Chancellor when their ship was wrecked on the Scottish coast and Chancellor was drowned. For an

account of his mission and its consequences, see Sir William Foster, *England's Quest of Eastern Trade* (London, 1933), pp.16–17.

19 On this occasion, the queen accompanied him to Dover. Machyn, *Diary*, ed. Nichols, p.142; Loades, *Mary Tudor*, pp.291–2.

20 Machyn, *Diary*, ed. Nichols, p.160.

21 BL, Lansdowne MS 4, vii, fol.19; Cotton Titus B IV, fol.133; PRO, E351/1795, E101/427/20, E101/428/8, SP11/1/14.

22 BL, Add. MS 71009, fols.31–2.

23 Ibid.

24 Ibid., fols.60r–60v.

25 Ibid.

26 Loades, *Tudor Court*, pp.62–4.

27 A. Feuillerat, *Documents Relating to the Office of the Revels in the Reigns of Edward VI and Mary* (Louvain, 1914), pp.199–211.

28 Ibid.

29 BL, MS RP 294. Printed as Appendix 2 in Loades, *Mary Tudor*, pp.358–69.

30 Ibid., p.367.

31 Feuillerat, *Edward VI and Mary*, pp.218–21.

32 Ibid., pp.302, 345.

33 Ibid., pp.225–31.

34 Ibid., pp.235–42.

35 Machyn, *Diary*, ed. Nichols, p.162.

36 A. Feuillerat, *Documents Relating to the Revels Office in the Reign of Queen Elizabeth* (Louvain, 1908), p.108.

37 John Southworth, *Fools and Jesters at the English Court* (Stroud, 1998), pp.100–6.

38 *Letters and Papers*, vol.10, p.383; *Miscellanies of the Philobiblion Society*, 7 (1862–3), pp.2,16.

39 Machyn, *Diary*, ed. Nichols, p.105.

40 Ibid., pp.161–2. On Cornwallis, see R.C. Braddock, 'The Rewards of Office Holding in Tudor England', *Journal of British Studies*, 14 (1975), pp.29–47.

41 F.J. Fisher, 'Influenza and Inflation in Tudor England', *Economic History Review*, 2nd ser., 18 (1965), pp.120–30.

42 Surian to the Doge and Senate, 15 January 1558, *CSP Venetian*, vol.6, p.1427; Philip to Pole, 21 January 1558, *CSP Spanish*, vol.13, p.340.

43 Loades, *Mary Tudor*, p.302.

44 John Foxe, *Actes and Monuments* (London, 1583), p.2098.

45 D.M. Loades, *Two Tudor Conspiracies* (Cambridge, 1965), pp.176–217.

46 Ibid., p.177. 'If my neighbour of Hatfield might once reign, then shulde [I] have [my] landes again'. Indictment of Lord John Bray, *CPR Mary*, vol.3, p.396.

47 Mary was the granddaughter of Margaret Tudor by her first marriage to James IV of Scotland. She had been betrothed to the dauphin by the Treaty of Haddington in 1548, and had been at the French court since August of that year.

48 Loades, *Two Tudor Conspiracies*, Appendix IV.

49 Michieli to the Doge and Senate, July 1555, *CSP Venetian*, vol.6, p.137; Renard to the emperor, 10 July 1555, *CSP Spanish*, vol.13, p.227. On the one hand there were the three surviving sons of the Duke of Northumberland, Henry, Ambrose and Robert; and on the other hand there were their cousins, Henry and Edmund, the sons of John Sutton de Dudley.

50 Noailles to Montmorency, 15 July 1555, BN, Aff.Etr, IX, fol.489; Montmorency to Noailles, 27 July 1555, ibid., fols.498–9; E.H. Harbison, *Rival Ambassadors at the Court of Queen Mary* (Princeton, NJ, 1940) p.272.

51 Michieli's comment that the House of Commons 'is quite full of gentry and nobility ... and therefore more daring and licentious than former houses which consisted of burgesses and plebeians' has been shown to be mistaken. The House was indeed full of gentry, but it always had been. Loach, *Parliament and the Crown*, pp.132–3.

52 Loades, *Two Tudor Conspiracies*, p.179.

53 Examination of John Danyell, March 1556, PRO, SP11/8, no.35.

54 There was a long and animated debate, and the eventual vote was 193 to 126 – an exceptionally high level of attendance. *Journal of the House of Commons*, vol.1, p.45; *CSP Venetian* vol.6, p.270; Loach, *Parliament and the Crown*, p.137.

55 Loach, *Parliament and the Crown*, pp.138–41.

56 Berteville to Montmorency (no date), BN, Aff.Etr., IX, fol.660; Harbison, *Rival Ambassadors*, p.280; Montmorency to Noailles, 26 November 1555, BN, Aff.Etr., XVII, fols.212–14.

57 Estimates of Kingston's military potential were wildly exaggerated. Ashton said that he 'was able to bring a gret part of Wallis at his taile'. Henry Peckham was informed that he could raise 10,000 men in three days. Confession of Thomas White, 26 March 1556, PRO, SP11/7, no.37; Loades, *Two Tudor Conspiracies*, pp.189–90.

58 Loades, *Two Tudor Conspiracies*, pp.186–7; Harbison, *Rival Ambassadors*, p.280.

59 Interrogatories drawn by White, 9 May 1556, PRO, SP11/8, no.62. He was reputed to be 'sure' of the whole garrison of the Isle of Wight.

60 He had at one time been a gentleman usher of the Privy Chamber: Loades, *Two Tudor Conspiracies*, pp.202–4.

61 Nicholas Wotton to Mary, 12 April 1556, *CSP Foreign*, vol.2, p.222.

62 Michieli to the Doge and Senate, 16 June 1556, *CSP Venetian*, vol.6, p.484.

63 Cawarden seems to have been implicated by the actions of his servant John Dethicke rather than by anything he had done himself. Third confession of White, 30 March 1556, PRO, SP11/7, no.47; Loades, *Two Tudor Conspiracies*, Appendix IV.

64 Second and third confessions of White, PRO, SP11/7, nos.47, 48.

65 Wotton to Mary, 4 August 1556, *CSP Foreign*, vol.2, p.244.

66 Loades, *Two Tudor Conspiracies*, pp.176–217.

67 Ibid., pp.218–37. The originals of all these confessions are contained in SP11/7, no.12 through to SP11/8, no.81.

68 Anne Overell, 'A Nicodemite in England and Italy: Edward Courtenay, 1548–1556', in D.M. Loades, ed., *John Foxe at Home and Abroad* (Aldershot, 2004), pp.117–36.

69 Loades, *Two Tudor Conspiracies*, Appendix IV.

70 For a full account of these struggles, see Norman Jones, *Faith by Statute* (Cambridge, 1982).

71 This bull canonically extinguished all those houses that had been dissolved by Henry VIII or had surrendered to him. Mary's foundations were consequently new creations, not restorations.

72 Paul actually withdrew his legates from most of Philip's lands in November 1556, but Pole had then been excepted. Pole's legation was cancelled in April 1557, at which point he was recalled. Thomas F. Mayer, *Reginald Pole: Prince and Prophet* (Cambridge, 2000), pp.304, 309–10.

73 Loades, *Mary Tudor*, p.314.

74 *CSP Spanish*, vol.11, p.393. She was also the mother of Lord Darnley, later (briefly) King of Scots.

75 Redworth, '"Matters impertinent to Women"'.

76 *CSP Venetian*, vol.6, p.475. Katherine Ashley's interrogation is PRO, SP11/8, no.54. Later in the summer there was another attempt in Suffolk to proclaim Elizabeth, this time the work of a schoolteacher called Cleobury. On that occasion, the council simply informed the princess. BL, Cotton MS Titus B.II, fol.139.

77 Loades, *Mary Tudor*, p.288; Machyn, *Diary*, ed. Nichols, p.120.

78 Mark Smeaton was a court musician who had been executed for alleged adultery with Anne. Elizabeth not only had her father's colouring, she also resembled him in temperament. The story comes from Henry Clifford's *Life of Jane Dormer.*

79 *CSP Venetian*, vol.6, p.1059.

80 D.M. Loades, *The Reign of Mary Tudor*, 2nd edn (London, 1991), pp.312–14.

81 Loades, *Mary Tudor*, p.292.

82 AGS, CMC la E, 1184, fol.64; AGS, E 811, fol.124.

83 'Feria's Despatch of 14th November 1558', ed. M.-J. Rodriguez-Salgado and Simon Adams, *Camden Miscellany*, 28 (1984), pp.328–37.

84 For a view of Elizabeth's contacts at court during Mary's reign, see D.M. Loades, *Elizabeth I* (London, 2003), pp.120–2.

85 Duke of Savoy to Philip, 9 January 1558, and Feria to Philip, 22 February, 1558, *CSP Spanish*, vol.13, pp.323, 361–2. For a full discussion of this fracas, see Loades, *Mary Tudor*, pp.294–7.

86 Loades, *Mary Tudor*, p.304.

87 Mayer, *Reginald Pole*, pp.316–20.

88 Philip to Feria, 4 February 1558, and to the Privy Council, 31 January 1558, *CSP Spanish*, vol.13, pp.351, 348.

89 Feria to Philip, 23 June 1558, *CSP Spanish*, vol.13, pp.399–400.

90 Loades, *Mary Tudor*, p.306.

91 'Feria's Despatch of 14th November', ed. Rodriguez-Salgado and Adams.

92 Ibid.

93 Christopher d'Assonleville to Philip. He also mentioned that Mary had 'sent word' to Elizabeth, although there is no record of any response. *CSP Spanish*, vol.13, p.498.

94 BL, Harleian MS 6949; Loades, *Mary Tudor*, pp.380–83.

95 'Feria's Despatch of 14th November', ed. Rodriguez-Salgado and Adams, p.328.

96 Ibid., p.329.

97 Foxe described it as a 'tympany', and the recorded symptoms point to a cancer, but the matter is still under investigation by medical historians.

98 One by Foxe, the other by Henry Clifford. Jane's recollections were not written down until the beginning of the seventeenth century.

99 Loades, *Mary Tudor*, p.312.

CHAPTER 9

Elizabeth

The xvii day of November be-twyn v and vi in the morning ded quen Mare, the vi yere of here grace rayne, the wyche Jhesu have mercy on her sole. Amen

[The same] day be-twyne xi and xii a'for[noon the lady Eliza]beth was proclaimed quen Elizabeth . . .

The sam day at after-non, all the chyrches in London dyd ryng, and at nyght dyd make bonefyres and sett tabulls in the strett, and ded ett and drynke and mad mere for the newe quen Elsabeth, quen Mare syster . . .[1]

There was no delay in announcing Mary's death. Edward's passing had been concealed for two days, and Henry's for rather longer, but Elizabeth was proclaimed within hours. This may have been partly in order to forestall any counter-move, but it was equally an indication that the new queen was thoroughly prepared to take over the reins of power, and probably had been for some weeks before Mary had finally bowed to the inevitable.[2] Elizabeth is alleged to have heard the news while walking in the park at Hatfield, and to have uttered appropriate sentiments of thanksgiving to God. However, one of the problems in dealing with any narrative of Elizabeth's actions is that most of them were not described in writing until years later, when the queen's myth-makers were in full flow. She is supposed to have received a representative body of peers and councillors at Hatfield on 20 November, and to have uttered to Sir William Cecil the prophetic words:

*I give you this charge, that you shall be of my Privy Council and content
yourself to take pains for me and my realm. This judgement I have of
you that you will not be corrupted by any manner of gift, and that you
will be faithful to the state, and that without respect of my private
judgement you will give me that counsel that you think best . . .*

Unfortunately, the source for this famous judgement is a copy, and we do
not know just when it was written.[3] What Machyn tells us is strictly contemporary, so we may conclude that Londoners (or at least many of them)
received the news of her accession with joy, but that was not based on any
foreknowledge of how she would reign. Rather, it was relief at having
avoided a disputed succession, and particularly at having seen the last of
Philip. More remarkable is a tract which appears to have been published
before the end of 1558, and is therefore equally contemporary, entitled *A
Speciall grace, appointed to have been said after a banket at Yorke* . . . If
this oration was made as claimed, it was probably delivered on Thursday
24 November, the day upon which the news of Mary's death reached York.[4]
Most of it is a savage attack upon the Marian clergy of which John Foxe
would have been proud; but it is also more than that. The author
announces the death of the late queen but largely avoids criticising her,
describing her instead as 'a Ladie that of her owne inclinacion wisht all for
the best . . .'. It was her 'spiritual council' which got the blame for everything that had happened. Of course the author, who identifies himself only
as 'W.P.', was a protestant – that was what fuelled his indignation; but he
was also a reconciler. He assumes – extraordinarily enough given the presumed date – that the catholic clergy are now out of power and can do no
more harm. They must, therefore, be called to repentance and reconciled
to the new order. This he is confident Elizabeth will do. She is a prince 'of
no mingled blood, of Spaniard or stranger, but borne mere Englishe here
amongst us'. There is a fervent patriotism about this work, and an anticipation of so much that was to feature in the queen's policy over the next few
years, that we must wonder about 'W.P.' and his sources of information. It
was precisely her attempts to reconcile the old clergy that got Elizabeth
into such trouble with the 'hotter sort' of protestants, and yet not even
Knox himself was more savage towards the likes of Gardiner and Bonner.
As there are no grounds to doubt the date of publication of this tract, we
can only credit the author with an extraordinary prescience.

Although Elizabeth was busy from the moment the messenger knelt in front of her, she did not rush into London. On 23 November she quitted Hatfield, accompanied by more than 1,000 lords, ladies, knights and gentlemen, and proceeded sedately to the Charterhouse, where she remained five days. On the 28th she moved on to the Tower, through the City, similarly escorted, 'and next after her rod Robart Dudley, the master of her horse; and so the gard with halbards. [And] ther was shyche shutyng of gunes as never was hard a-fore . . .'[5] On 5 December she moved on again, to Somerset Place, 'and [brought] joye and comfort to all truw Englys-men and women, and to all pepulle'. Machyn, as we have seen, liked the old ways, and must have known Elizabeth's reputation as a 'heretic', but that was not the first thought in his mind. Here we find the same patriotic (or nationalistic) note that we find in W.P. Elizabeth was an English queen – her father's daughter – and she would restore her subjects' pride and independence, both political and ecclesiastical. She had, as Feria noted, an empathy with her subjects from the very beginning that Mary had never shown. The old queen had often, as both Renard and Feria himself had reported, expressed distrust of her own subjects, and had been widely blamed for 'loving another realm better than this'.[6] Not all that criticism was justified, and the imperial envoys exaggerated for their own purposes, but Mary had conspicuously lacked that sense of English identity which Elizabeth had – and which she exploited to the full.

By the time the queen reached Somerset House, both her court and her council had largely been reconstructed. In some ways this was very unconventional. The Great Seal remained in her hands, and there was not to be another lord chancellor for more than twenty years; at the same time, Lord Paget surrendered the Privy Seal, and no fresh appointment would be made until 1572. John Boxall was replaced as principal secretary by Sir William Cecil, and of the senior officers of state only the Lord Treasurer, the Marquis of Winchester, and the Admiral, Lord Clinton, remained in office.[7] The archbishopric of Canterbury was vacant by the death of Cardinal Pole the day after Mary, and that position was not to be filled for another year. Of Mary's somewhat inflated Privy Council of about 40 members, only ten were retained. All these moves indicated a completely different style of government, a government built around the Principal Secretary and his friend and ally Sir Nicholas Bacon, who became Lord Keeper. The archbishopric inevitably awaited a new religious settlement, and the one thing the vacancy at Canterbury indicated was that things were not going to carry on as before. To the councillors who had been retained, all of whom might be classed as conservative Erastians, ten others were added, all protestants although of different levels of intensity. Of the senior officers at court, only the Lord Steward, the Earl of Arundel, remained, although the Treasurer of the Household, Sir Thomas Cheney, was removed by death rather than dismissal.[8] Sir Edward Hastings was replaced as Lord Chamberlain by William, Lord Howard of Effingham, Sir Henry Bedingfield as Vice-Chamberlain by Sir Edward Rogers, Sir Henry Jerningham as Master of the Horse by Sir Robert Dudley, and Sir Robert Freston as Comptroller by Sir Thomas Parry.[9]

The closer a courtier or an officer of state had been to the old queen, the less likely he was to be retained by the new incumbent. When Feria was assessing Elizabeth's likely moves shortly before her accession, he reported that she was on good terms with Heath, Paget and Petre, and likely to favour Sir John Mason, Nicholas Wotton, Lord Clinton and Lord William Howard, but the last 'not as much as is thought'. Lord Grey, presently a prisoner in France, was also likely to be well received. She was not on good terms with the Earls of Arundel and Pembroke, nor with Thomas Thirlby, the Bishop of Ely, but her rancour was particularly reserved for Hastings, Freston, Boxall and Pole.[10] The ambassador had felt bound (or so he claimed) to defend the cardinal against the fierce attack she had launched against him during an otherwise relaxed dinner at Brocket Hall about 11 or 12 November. Elizabeth joked pointedly about Philip's attempts to marry her off, and rejected any suggestion that she owed an obligation to the King of Spain, but she also made it clear that she had no quarrel with him and expected to continue the existing alliance. Feria had made good use of his time, and assessed the prospects of several other men whom the princess had not mentioned. The Earl of Bedford, Lord Robert Dudley, Sir Nicholas Throgmorton, Sir Peter Carew, John Harrington, Sir Thomas Parry and Sir Ambrose Cave were all mentioned as likely to be favoured – but above all Sir William Cecil, who was destined for the Principal Secretaryship, 'an able and virtuous man, but a heretic'. Cave he believed to be 'a good christian', but Harrington was 'develish'.[11]

The ambassador was about 60 per cent right in his predictions. In spite of her apparent liking for them, both Heath and Paget were dropped, but Petre, Mason, Wotton, Clinton and Howard were all sworn of the new council, and Mason and Clinton retained their offices. Lord Grey was not, when he returned to England, singled out for any particular favour, and Pole was spared the new queen's animosity by his own death. In spite of her dislike, Arundel and Pembroke both remained councillors, and the former kept his position at court, but Thirlby, Hastings, Freston and Boxall all disappeared from public life, along with Bedingfield, Englefield and Jerningham.[12] Bedford, Parry and Cave were all appointed to the council, and Lord Robert became Master of the Horse, but Throgmorton, Carew and Harrington received only lesser preferments. About Cecil the ambassador was spot on. Wotton was the only member of the new council who was technically in holy orders, but he was a career diplomat rather than a functioning priest, and it is generally true that the climate of the new government was secular and well educated. Its religious complexion was protestant rather than catholic, but any ecclesiastical influence was conspicuous by its absence.

Apart from the change of comptroller, the Household was little affected by these sweeping changes. Elizabeth followed custom in placing a few of her own former servants in the departments 'below stairs', but the effect of this was far from revolutionary. Nor was the Chamber deliberately purged, except at the top. Groups like the gentlemen pensioners, the yeomen of the guard or the Queen's Music carried on very much as before, although a few of the more zealous catholic families withdrew of their own accord rather than face pressure to attend heretical services in the Chapel Royal. The Privy Chamber, however, was quite another story. At the time of her death, Mary had been entertaining seven ladies, led by Lady Ann Wharton, thirteen gentlewomen, three chamberers and some half-dozen gentlemen, gentlemen ushers and grooms.[13] This entire establishment, with its strong atmosphere of catholic piety, was swept away. In its place Elizabeth appointed four ladies of the bedchamber, seven or eight ordinary gentlewomen, three chamberers, and just two men 'in ordinary', one gentleman and one groom. The staff was thus apparently halved, but the appearance is deceptive. These were the people who received fees in addition to their keep (bouge of court). There were also seven 'ladies extraordinary', an indeterminate number of gentlewomen on the same basis, and several gentlemen and grooms. These received bouge of court when in attendance, but no fees, and came only when summoned.[14]

There was probably not much difference between the two regimes in outward appearance, and Norris's rule about excluding unwelcome males was strictly adhered to, but Elizabeth's Privy Chamber cost a lot less that her predecessor's. Its tone was also quite different, reflecting the quite different personality of the ruler. In place of Susan Clarencius, Elizabeth's chief friend and confidante was Katherine Ashley, a woman of much the same age as her predecessor, but highly educated and of strong protestant convictions. Katherine had been in Elizabeth's service since the latter's childhood, and had guided the first steps in her formidable intellectual training.[15] She had chaperoned – or perhaps failed to chaperone – her problematic relationship with Thomas Seymour, and had been peremptorily dismissed by Mary for leading her charge astray. The two women were remarkably close, and it was often noted that Elizabeth would hear no ill spoken of her favourite. Katherine's husband, John Ashley, was for many years the only ordinary gentleman of the Privy Chamber, and held that position until he died at an advanced age in the 1590s, although his attendance became less regular after Katherine's death.[16] The other three ladies of the bedchamber were Blanche Parry (the wife of Sir Thomas, her long-serving Cofferer), Elizabeth Norwich, and the queen's cousin Catherine Knollys (née Carey). Like their mistress and the other members of the new Privy Chamber they were educated far beyond the normal run of gentlewomen, and were firmly protestant in their faith and bible learning.

Katherine did not hold the Privy Purse, or apparently handle any money on the queen's behalf. The Purse had been a strictly private account since Mary's accession, although Elizabeth did occasionally use it for discreet political purposes – a faint echo of her brother's much larger-scale practice. The account was held by John Tamworth, the groom, but when it was being used for public causes, it was apparently topped up out of an obscure fund called the Queen's Coffers, which had also survived a sharp scaling down of its functions after Edward's death.[17] After 1558 it was controlled by the queen's personal secretary, who was also her principal secretary of state, Sir William Cecil. Cecil was the key man in the whole set-up of the new reign. Like Mary, Elizabeth accepted that her Privy Chamber was not, and could not be, a political forum. Her ladies had their own networks, and lobbied discreetly for men or causes they favoured, but they had no power, and no offices. Even Kate Ashley did not venture to cross into the public sphere; but that was precisely Cecil's job. As Private Secretary he was attached to the Privy Chamber, and enjoyed privileged access to the queen; as Principal Secretary he organised the business of the Privy Council, and usually acted as Elizabeth's voice because she was not in the habit of attending meetings in person. Cecil was 38 when Elizabeth came to the throne, and had already served as Principal Secretary under the Duke of Northumberland. She was 25, and looked on him as something between a father and an elder brother. She did not always take his advice, and sometimes was to drive him to distraction; but she always listened to him, and he came nearer than anyone else to understanding her powerful but idiosyncratic mind. This was probably because of their shared intellectual tastes and religious convictions rather than because of any general agreement on policy; but they were both totally committed to a vision of English independence and good government, and their partnership was to last until his death in 1598. It was to prove the longest, and most effective, such partnership in English history.[18]

Elizabeth liked to keep her private and public lives separate. Even more than in Mary's case, her Privy Chamber was a refuge from the world of masculine priorities and demands. There she could gossip, sew, play music, read, pray or daydream like any other woman without being intruded upon by aggressive and self-seeking males. However, in other respects the two women had quite different attitudes towards men. Mary had been brought up with a pious horror of sex, and regarded marriage as an unpleasant but necessary duty. She had had, as far as we know, no emotional relationship of a sexual nature before her marriage. That must have made her a very unsatisfactory partner, and so much can be discerned between the lines of Philip's letters, but she was too innocent to see any problem.[19] As a young woman she had been thought attractive, but such a concept seems to have been meaningless to her. Gender was something which God had seen fit to inflict upon her for his own inscrutable purposes. The portraits of her as queen, particularly that by Anthonis Mor, reflect that stoical indifference. She appears as a plain, rather grim-faced woman, splendidly dressed as became her status, but utterly without either majesty or charm.[20] By contrast, Elizabeth was an instinctive flirt – a characteristic which she inherited from her mother. Anne Boleyn had been a sexual adventurer with a steely political intelligence, and her daughter took after her. At the age of fourteen she had had the perilous but immensely gratifying experience of stimulating the lust of a much older (and married) man. Thomas Seymour's miscalculation cost him his head, but Elizabeth discovered many interesting and exciting things about herself.[21] It was to be ten years before she could return to that particular playground, but she did not forget the lessons learned. Because she had the power to excite men, she also had the power to manipulate them.

The style of Elizabeth's court quickly began to reflect that perception. Years later, when her physical charms had faded, this was to be reflected in *The Faerie Queene* and the cult of Gloriana, but the substance was there from the beginning. The game of courtly love was picked up where it had been dropped after Anne's execution, and the queen became the beautiful and unattainable damsel whom strong men served with adoring devotion and no thought of reward. Of course that was a fantasy, and everybody (including Elizabeth) knew it perfectly well, but it was fun, and more important it was a way of turning a gender disadvantage to good account. The queen deliberately blurred the lines between politics and entertainment, using her femininity to baffle and confuse her councillors by procrastinating decisions and wilfully changing her mind. This was her way of refusing to be dominated or taken for granted. She was the monarch, and eventually decisions of importance had to abide her will – a fact which she was constantly at pains to emphasise. In the last days of her reign, Sir John Davies was to celebrate this unique style in verse:

> *Since when all ceremonious mysteries*
> *All sacred orgies and religious rites*
> *All pomps and triumphs and solemnities,*
> *All funerals nuptials, and like public sights*
> *All parliaments of peace and warlike fights*
> *All learned arts and every great affair,*
> *A lively shape of dancing seems to bear.*[22]

This dance of state began in 1558, presided over by a young woman whose sexuality was as lively as her mind. A greater contrast with the staid austerity of the ailing Mary could hardly be imagined.

Elizabeth was also fond of posing and gesturing, often choosing to convey messages in those forms rather than by specific words. At first she said nothing, and would allow nothing to be said in public, about the repudiation of traditional worship. However, by walking out of the high mass on Christmas Day at the moment of elevation she made her views abundantly clear. Her coronation on 15 January 1559, and the entry into London which traditionally preceded it, formed a splendid theatre for such virtual policy statements. Machyn's account is circumstantial, listing the pageants ('a-nodur goodly pagantt of kyng Henry and kyng Edward the vith ...', etc.) but not commenting upon the queen's performance.[23] For that we have to rely, significantly perhaps, upon the official account published shortly after by Richard Mulcaster. According to Mulcaster, her entry was highly interactive: 'Her grace did declare herself no less thankfully to receive her people's good will than they loving offered it unto her.' To all those that cried 'God save' her, she gave thanks, and all was 'nothing but comfort'. At the Conduit was a pageant portraying the contrast between a flourishing and a derelict commonwealth, a none too delicate hint from the city as to where its citizens thought their future should lie, particularly in respect of the fear of God. At the Little Conduit she was presented with an English bible, which she received with ostentatious gratitude, and a little further on was confronted with the image of Deborah taking council for the people of the Lord, emblazoned with verses beginning:

> Jabin of Canaan King had long by force of arms
> Oppressed the Israelites, which for God's people went.
> But God minding at last for to redress their harms,
> The worthy Deborah as Judge among them sent.[24]

Although they were created and paid for by the city, all these pageants would have been carefully vetted by the council beforehand, and we can be sure that the messages they conveyed had been officially approved. Even the prayer which Elizabeth is supposed to have uttered before the ceremony commenced was most carefully worded:

> O Lord ... Thou hast dealt as wonderfully and mercifully with me as
> thou didst with thy true and faithful servant Daniel the prophet, whom

thou deliveredst out of the den, from the cruelty of the greedy and
raging lions; even so was I overwhelmed and only by thee delivered.[25]

There can be no doubt that the way in which all this was set down by
Mulcaster was intended to get the message across to those who had not
been within earshot, or had been too distracted by the crowds, or had
simply not been able to keep up with the action. Without any explicit
criticism of her sister, Elizabeth deliberately set out to sharpen the contrast between them. At the coronation itself the mass was sung by the
dean of the Chapel Royal, without elevation, Owen Oglethorpe, who performed the actual crowning, having refused to conduct the rite in that
form.[26] The catholic bishops were right to be apprehensive, and Feria to
fear that all the people about the new queen were the heretics and traitors of the old regime. Without encouraging any overt departure from the
established order, Elizabeth had written her intentions all over the walls
of London and Westminster. 'She is a very vain and clever woman', the
ambassador had written.

> She must have been thoroughly schooled in the manner in which her
> father conducted his affairs ... [also] it is evident that she is highly
> indignant about what has been done to her during the queen's lifetime.
> She sets great store by the people and is very confident that they are all
> on her side – which is certainly true ...[27]

The Spanish nobleman and the English schoolmaster, who had nothing
else in common, were in complete agreement about the nature of the new
regime in England.

Whatever doubts may have been cast by subsequent commentators,
Elizabeth was unquestionably a protestant. Quite apart from the theatre
of the coronation, her choice of private companions and the prayers and
meditations she committed to paper prove as much.[28] However, she went
about her business in that respect very differently from Mary. Mary had
encouraged her council to abandon the enforcement of the Edwardian
statutes long before they were repealed, so we have the bizarre situation
of the Lord Chancellor telling a common law judge (James Hales) that he
should pay more attention to 'the Queen's proceedings' than to the law.[29]
By contrast, Elizabeth made no declaration of her personal position, and
insisted that the existing laws be enforced unless (or until) they were

changed. Controversial preaching was prohibited, and even in the Chapel Royal the mass continued to be celebrated. A Venetian commentator noticed in December that the litany was said in English, and the epistle and gospel also read in the vernacular – significant moves, perhaps, but well short of reviving the Edwardian Prayer Book.[30] These adjustments were widely imitated, but the full Edwardian rite was reintroduced only clandestinely and in a few places. Just before the opening of parliament on 23 January, but after the end of the Christmas revels, a 'farce' was performed at court and in the queen's presence which presented 'crows in the habits of cardinals ... asses habited as bishops and wolves representing abbots'. At the same time the symbolic figure of St Thomas Becket in Cheapside was beheaded and thrown down (again – this time finally); and at the opening of parliament itself Elizabeth dismissed the monks of Westminster with the contemptuous words 'away with those torches, for we see very well'.[31] There can have been little doubt of the direction in which the queen was heading, but she declared no policy until the bills of Supremacy and Uniformity were presented to parliament.

The first of these again abolished the papal jurisdiction and restored her father's authority, albeit in a slightly modified form. The second resurrected her brother's church settlement. It seems clear from modern research that these bills represented Elizabeth's considered intentions, and were not either the result of pressure or kites flown to test the wind.[32] The radical protestants who were once thought to have formed a pressure group in the 1559 House of Commons are now known not to have been present. Most of them did not return from exile until later. The easiest course for the queen to have followed would have been to end the persecution but otherwise retain the status quo. That would have settled her foreign affairs, pleased her bishops and gratified the pope. It would have upset the protestants, but that would have been a small price to pay. However, nobody expected her to do that, least of all Feria, who would have been delighted if she had. Most of the serious advice she received, and which we know about, pointed to the restoration of her father's church.[33] That would have upset the pope, but Philip would have borne with it, and most of her subjects would have been pleased. However, that was never her intention, and only the most resolute opposition in parliament could have persuaded her to settle for Supremacy without Uniformity. Even if she had been inclined to do so, the attitude of the

Convocations which met alongside the parliament would have demonstrated the impracticability of such a course. Led by the bishops, they declared unequivocally for Roman obedience and the catholic rite.[34] There would have been, therefore, no respectable bench of bishops to serve a Henrician church; the events of the last ten years had killed it as a practical option. The choice was between the status quo and the Edwardian settlement, and Elizabeth went straight for the radical option.

The details of the struggle in parliament do not concern us here. A large majority in the Commons supported the queen on both bills. The Supremacy bill encountered opposition in the Lords, but not nearly enough to defeat it. The bishops were solidly hostile, but they were depleted by death and only thinly supported by the secular peers. Protestant uniformity, however, was much more contentious. On this the split in the Lords was even, and the government had to resort to some sharp practice to get it through by the narrowest of margins. These Acts received the royal assent on 8 May, and were implemented at once.[35] All officials were now required to take the Oath of Supremacy, and a royal commission was sent up to take the oaths of the bishops. With one exception they all refused and were deprived between June and November 1559. There is evidence that Elizabeth would have greatly preferred some of them (notably Heath and Tunstall) to have accepted, but they did not. This meant that although the church had no continuity, the queen was at least able to appoint an acceptable team of protestant bishops instead of having to put up with a number of lukewarm or hostile conformists, as both her brother and her sister had been constrained to do.[36]

The new bishops were intellectually at least the equals of their predecessors, but they had from Elizabeth's point of view one major drawback. Many of them had been in exile during her sister's reign and had brought back with them, particularly from Geneva, ideas which did not suit her intended polity. It was not that their protestantism was more sincere than hers, but it was different. They accepted the Royal Supremacy as a condition of appointment, but they were uneasy about it, believing that the only source of authority in doctrinal matters was the bible. That Elizabeth did not deny, but she also believed that God had given her a unique interpretative function which justified her role as Supreme Governor.[37] This was, of course, a political position, but it was not only political, and over the following years the queen was consistently to reject the attempts of the godly to prescribe a different role for her. Fortunately she was able to find a new Archbishop of Canterbury who had not been in exile, and whose view of the Supremacy was slightly, but significantly, closer to her own. Cecil was in touch with Mathew Parker as early as Christmas 1558, and he preached some sermons at court, but it was not until 18 July following that he reluctantly agreed to accept nomination.[38] He was consecrated in December, after the conservative bench had been disposed of, and his enthronement marked a new beginning for the church in England.

One of the consequences of these changes was that Mary's will became virtually a dead letter. The old queen had made only two requests of her successor, that she pay her debts and retain the catholic faith; and Elizabeth did neither. As far as we know, Mary's personal bequests – the jewel to Philip and the £2,000 distributed among her servants – were honoured. However, most of Mary's legacies were destined for the religious houses which had been established during her reign and which Elizabeth's first parliament dissolved.[39] Other significant sums were intended to pay for masses for the repose of her own soul and that of her mother, a practice which became illegal with the reintroduction of the Edwardian Prayer Book. The chief executor was Reginald Pole, who died only hours after the queen, and the remainder were able to carry out only a small part of their intended function.

Mary's body lay at St James's for almost a month after her death, which was about normal for a monarch and does not imply any disrespect or neglect. She was finally buried with full traditional rites in Henry VII's chapel at Westminster Abbey on 14 December, attended as she would have wished by Abbot Feckenham and his monks. The ceremonies were lavish, extending over two days, and cost the Exchequer £7,763.[40] The chief mourner was Margaret, Countess of Lennox, Mary's closest blood relation apart from Elizabeth – and Philip, who was not available. Bishop John White of Winchester preached the funeral sermon upon the somewhat unfortunate text 'Laudavi mortuos magis quam viventes'. Elizabeth's council understandably took exception to this, but the bishop was probably not intending to be provocative. Most of his sermon was a traditional panygeric: 'She was a King's daughter, she was a king's sister, she was a king's wife; she was a queen, and by the same title a king also ...'[41]

Mary was not only regretted by clergy fearful for their future, she was also genuinely mourned by many ordinary people who had never crossed her formidable conscience, and remembered only her kindness and humanity:

She never closed her eare to heare
The righteous man distrest,
Nor never spared her hand to helpe
Wher wrong or power opprest . . .[42]

Elizabeth said nothing. She had no occasion to mourn the woman who had spared her life, but had in other ways given her the most stressful five years of her career. On the other hand, she uttered no public word of reproach or resentment. Feria was not the only person who knew what she felt, but her public statements were strictly correct. Not all her councillors were equally discreet. As early as 21 November it was being said at Westminster that Mary had sent vast sums of money out of the country to support Philip's wars, and had ruined the Exchequer by her generosity to the church. It was even being muttered that Feria himself had spirited away over 200,000 ducats (£70,000).[43] Two of these reports were completely untrue, and the third, relating to the church, was grossly exaggerated. However, there are memoranda among the state papers (including some in Cecil's hand) which suggest that these stories originated at the highest level.[44] In spite of the queen's restraint, there was not only a will for change, there was also an intention to discredit Mary's cherished priorities by every means available.

Apart from the ecclesiastical settlement, Elizabeth's first political priority was her position in Europe. She was the most eligible bride in Europe, and everyone assumed that she would soon marry. Much would depend upon her choice of husband – not only the English succession, but the whole orientation of her country in a Europe which was becoming increasingly polarised. She was 25, and therefore the matter was not as urgent as it had been for Mary, but it was nevertheless an issue which would have to be addressed in the near future. On 21 November Feria wrote to Philip:

The more I think about this business, the more certain I am that
everything depends upon the husband this woman may take. If he is a

suitable one, religious matters will go on well, and the kingdom will
remain friendly to your Majesty, but if not it will all be spoilt.[45]

The Duke of Savoy, the king's preferred candidate – as he had been for
some time – was no longer interested and by the end of 1558 had firmly
declined to be considered. An Austrian archduke would not have been
ideal from Philip's point of view, for reasons of internal Habsburg family
politics, so he reluctantly decided to put himself forward. The idea that
he had been smitten by his attractive sister-in-law some time before is
romantic fiction. This was a strictly political offer, designed as much to
foreclose other options as to secure great benefits for himself. He knew
that he was cordially hated in England, and that he would be unable to
spend much time there. Altogether the prospect was a thoroughly dis-
tasteful one, and having made his offer, in January 1559, he described
himself to Feria as 'a condemned man awaiting his fate'. 'If it was not to
serve God', he continued 'believe me, I should not have got into this.'[46]
Fortunately, Elizabeth found the idea equally disagreeable. She did not
say so at once, and speculation continued for some weeks, fuelled partly
by the positive reaction of some London merchants and partly by the
ongoing negotiations for peace, which by then had moved to Cateau
Cambrésis. Elizabeth's chosen religious settlement would probably have
ruled out such a marriage anyway, but she left it to Philip to come to that
conclusion. Let them remain allies – even friends – but the queen had no
intention of sacrificing her precious popularity by picking up her sister's
relict.

The court, of course, was fascinated by the prospect of another royal
marriage. Matrimony was an almost unique point of contact between the
public world of parliament and the Privy Council and the private world
of the Privy Chamber, but there was at first very little to go on. Feria
reported that Elizabeth had joked about the pretensions of the Earl of
Arundel, who was a widower approaching 50, and old enough to be her
father, but he had picked up few positive clues.[47] Only Sir William
Pickering was mentioned very tentatively as the kind of 'proper man' she
might go for. At that point, just before Mary's death, Paget had expressed
the view that there was no suitable candidate in sight, either at home or
abroad; but his view was soured, both by illness and by his own experience. He had, he claimed with some exaggeration, arranged Mary's

marriage to Philip, and much good had it done him. The queen had 'turned against him'.[48] By April 1559 the King of Spain had agreed to marry Elizabeth of Valois as part of the peace settlement, but he had also persuaded Pope Paul IV to postpone any sanctions against the now clearly heretical queen pending the outcome of his own plans for her. These plans now focused upon an Austrian marriage. Family relations had improved since the beginning of the year, and the peace with France had eased a number of tensions. The emperor had in fact sent an envoy to England as early as February to sound out both the queen and her court, but it was not until Philip was safely betrothed in France that he deemed it expedient to make a formal proposal, which he did in April, putting forward the name of his younger son, Ferdinand.[49]

Early in February parliament had petitioned the queen to marry, and her response had been equivocal. She had, she declared, happily chosen 'this kind of life in which I yet live, which I assure you for my own part hath hitherto best contented myself, and I trust hath been most acceptable to God . . .'. However, she was graciously pleased to accept their petition, and 'whensoever it may please God to incline my heart to another kind of life, you may well assure yourselves my meaning is not to do or determine anything wherewith the realm may or shall have just cause to be discontented'.[50] This was the first shot in a war which was to go on for decades, but nobody knew that in 1559, and in the circumstances it was accepted that the queen needed to keep her options open. There was consequently a cautious welcome for the imperial initiative, although Feria remained sceptical. His doubts were on both sides of the equation. He did not believe that an Austrian marriage would improve the religious situation, and indeed foresaw serious difficulties in setting it up. At the same time, he was by no means convinced that it would serve Philip's interests. The more accommodating Ferdinand was to the English, the less happy the King of Spain was likely to be with the outcome.[51] There was also one snag with the original proposal: Ferdinand, it transpired, had already contracted a morganatic marriage which he refused to renounce. Consequently the candidate who was the subject of future negotiation was his younger brother, Charles. A new embassy arrived in May, by which time Feria had gone back to Spain. His pithy comments thereafter are lacking, but he had posted one shrewd observation before departing. Elizabeth, he wrote, 'is in love with Lord Robert [Dudley], and is never separated from him'. Dudley's wife was alleged to be ailing, and in the ambassador's view the queen was waiting for her to die so that she could marry her Master of the Horse.[52]

At court, and particularly in the Privy Chamber, it would seem, there was a strong preference for a domestic marriage. All the queen's ladies, as Feria had observed, were protestants, and a foreign marriage was only too likely to be a catholic marriage. However, there appeared at first to be no serious candidate. Pickering was a lightweight. The Duke of Norfolk and the Earl of Westmorland were canvassed by a few hopefuls, but never advanced their own claims. The Earl of Arundel was a joke – not least because he took himself seriously. In December 1558 he was reported to be borrowing money on the strength of his prospects, and using some of it to bribe the queen's ladies to support his cause.[53] What they thought of his manoeuvres is not on record, but can be imagined given Elizabeth's own hilarity at the thought. The rumours nevertheless persisted. In January 1559 it was being reported that he had exploited his office as Lord Steward to persuade the queen to attend lavish banquets which he had both arranged and paid for during the Christmas holidays. He gave her an expensive jewel as a New Year gift, and even eight months later, when she visited Nonsuch on her summer progress, some amused observers attributed the lavishness of his hospitality to his lingering matrimonial ambitions.[54] Arundel was a conformist in religion, and partly as a result was also a survivor. However, he was also a survivor because he was not sufficiently intelligent to constitute a threat to anyone. He had only his name and lineage to justify his pretensions, and Elizabeth, like Feria and the imperial diplomat Baron Bruener, was unimpressed.

Robert Dudley, on the other hand, was a different proposition altogether. The queen and he were of the same age and had known each other from childhood. They had also shared Mary's disfavour, although Robert had jousted and fought for the king in 1557.[55] At one stage the princess had apparently borrowed money from him, although he was not a rich man. It is quite surprising that his name was not linked with Elizabeth's earlier – except for the critical fact that he was already married. Amy Robsart, Lady Dudley, is a shadowy and tragic figure. She was the daughter of a Norfolk squire, Sir John Robsart, and they had apparently married for love in 1556. However, when her husband's fortunes began to rise steeply with the new reign, she never followed him to court.

Whether this was a result of her natural reluctance or choice on his part, we do not know, but Robert, who was extremely charming and personable, appeared at court as a single man. He had probably been creeping up on Elizabeth for some time before Feria noticed, and their relationship was to be the great talking point of the court for the next two years.

During the summer of 1559, the Habsburg negotiation made no progress. As Robert Dudley's name became more frequently mentioned, Cecil began to warm to Charles and started gathering information about him. What sort of a man was he? What did he look like? What was his religious position?[56] The secretary seems to have had no personal dislike for Dudley, and in many respects they were allies, but he deeply disapproved of the possibility of the queen marrying him – and even more of appearing to want to while his wife was still alive. Elizabeth, perhaps with the same thought in mind, blew cold on the emperor, declaring that she preferred her 'solitude and our lonely life'. As Ferdinand learned more of the English religious settlement, and more of Robert Dudley, he also lost his enthusiasm, and by September it appeared that the trail was completely cold. Feria's successor, Alonso de Quadra, who favoured the match, became increasingly despondent, but Cecil was not beaten. Using his contacts in the Privy Chamber, he succeeded in rekindling the embers. The ostensible reasons for this are shadowy. Deteriorating relations with France following the death of Henry II in July, a plot to poison both Elizabeth and Dudley, and a generally increasing sense of insecurity were alleged.[57] However, it seems more likely that Dudley was becoming apprehensive and was backing off, perhaps in the face of some fairly straight talking by the secretary. It was Dudley's sister, Lady Mary Sidney, who sought out de Quadra in late September and told him that the queen had decided to marry during the winter, and that the Habsburg negotiation should therefore be pressed.[58] Not only was this story confirmed by Elizabeth's old and trusted servant Sir Thomas Parry, but Dudley himself appeared to be encouraging the match.

Shortly afterwards, the queen herself sent for both the Spanish and imperial ambassadors, in an obvious attempt to get her suitor back on the trail. She could not possibly marry a man she had never seen, she said, but she would be pleased to welcome Charles if he could be persuaded to pay her a visit. By mid-October de Quadra believed that Elizabeth 'is really as much set on this marriage as your majesty is'.[59] He was deceiving himself. Elizabeth wanted the negotiating up and running again because she was contemplating intervention in Scotland and wished to deter the French from taking a hand. Also it is quite possible that Dudley's apprehensions were fuelled less by Cecil and his friends than by the queen's increasingly possessive behaviour. By November 1559, just a year after her accession, the court was full of talk of her infatuation. She was going to his rooms at unseasonable hours of the night as well as of the day; there were inevitably rumours that they were sleeping together; and the scandal threatened to be immense.[60] The queen, it appeared, was about to make a monumental fool of herself, but even in these circumstances she did not altogether lose contact with political reality. A revival of the Habsburg negotiation would not only placate Cecil, and possibly impress the French, it would also provide a distraction from her own behaviour. That she had any serious intention of marrying the archduke appears extremely unlikely.

Charles was not the only lightning conductor available. As early as March 1558 Gustavus Vasa, the King of Sweden, had sent an envoy to England to seek Elizabeth's hand for his son and heir, Eric. The envoy, whose name was Dionysius Beurreus, was inexperienced and bungled his mission by going straight to Hatfield instead of presenting his credentials to Mary.[61] Elizabeth swiftly corrected his mistake by referring him to the court (and thus saving herself further disfavour), but made no answer to his request. Beurreus remained in England, accredited to Mary, and was inept enough not to get his credentials renewed to the new queen. Consequently, when he sought to recommence his matrimonial quest in December he was left without any reply for several months until his position had been corrected and an approach could be made in proper diplomatic form.[62] It was thus not until 6 May 1559 that the council finally informed him that the queen would not agree to any marriage with Prince Eric.

Gustavus was not deterred, perhaps attributing Beurreus's failure to his own shortcomings rather than to the unattractiveness of the offer. In the summer of 1559 he sent a new mission, led by Gustavus Johansson, Charles Holgersson and Charles de Mornay. Unfortunately, they were equally maladroit, making a magnificent show with their splendid clothes and the jewelled hearts (symbols of passion) which they wore on their lapels, but attracting derision by their 'outlandish' manners.[63] This does not necessarily mean that they were uncouth, but that their customs and manners were different; similar things were said about the Russians. Again Elizabeth rejected their proposals, and it may have been during this mission that de Mornay apparently considered furthering their cause by having Robert Dudley assassinated. Nobody in England (least of all Lord Robert) knew about this, but it left some traces in the Swedish archives.

Even so, the Swedish king was still not beaten. In September 1559 he went a step further and sent his younger son, John, Duke of Finland, to plead Eric's cause. John was a different kind of ambassador altogether. He was a great prince, and as smooth as he was rich. He was courteous, charming and generous, and he made the most favourable impression.[64] Even his command of Latin was sufficient to attract commendation in a court that was conspicuously literate. He adjusted very easily to the English environment, and used his base in the Bishop of Winchester's residence in Southwark to keep open house. Not only did he lavish gifts on any courtier whose word seemed likely to carry weight, he was also very liberal to the poor, presumably on the grounds that there is no such thing as bad publicity. His only mistake was to become embroiled in a feud with the imperial ambassador, Baron Breuner, which invoked the queen's displeasure.[65] In spite of every effort, however, he was no more successful than his predecessors. Elizabeth rejected his proposals, and even refused to accept the valuable ring which he offered. John stood his ground – he seems to have enjoyed himself in England – and on 14 December he put forward a new formal proposal for a matrimonial alliance between England and Sweden. The terms were attractive. Eric was a protestant, albeit a Lutheran, so the religious adjustments would be minor, and a bridge would have been built to the Lutheran princes of north Germany with whom Elizabeth was keen to do business.[66] The Swedes were prepared to pay the expenses of Eric's household, to limit its size, and to allow him to live in England even after he had succeeded to the Swedish throne. The two countries would remain entirely separate, and it was accepted that Eric, although king, would have very little authority in England. None of the problems that had bedevilled Philip's rule would plague Eric. Nor was it likely that the union of the crowns would prove permanent, since the Swedish crown was elective and there could be no presumption that any child of the marriage would be acceptable in Sweden.[67] However, in spite of all this, and in spite of the fact that John had succeeded in convincing his hosts that Sweden was not a barbarous backwater, Elizabeth was not tempted, and again refused the proffered marriage. This was not the end of the story, because John stayed on and tried again in April 1560, at which point he returned to Sweden, still full of enthusiasm. By that time, however, Gustavus had had enough, and although the negotiation was not formally terminated, it had lost what little credibility it had ever possessed. Elizabeth's only chance for a protestant foreign marriage had gone without regrets – at least on her part.

Neither the Austrian nor the Swedish negotiation had much impact on the court. Duke John was unquestionably popular, but he did not create a following, and Charles remained a fairly distant hypothesis. It was quite different with Robert Dudley. His appointment as Master of the Horse signified favour, but not necessarily great intimacy, and at first there was little reaction. In December 1558 Feria advised his master that there was no point in continuing his existing English pension list beyond the end of the year, as hardly any of his existing pensioners had influence in the new regime. Thereafter 'a different course must be adopted' and pensions paid to the 'new men' – if the queen would permit it, which was by no means certain. He named Parry, Bedford, Dudley and (of course) Cecil.[68] It caused no surprise at court that the Dudleys should be rehabilitated: in addition to Robert's appointment, his brother Ambrose became Master of the Ordnance and his sister Mary one of the queen's ladies. There was, however, apprehension in some quarters because Robert in particular was thought to be seeking vengeance against his father's enemies. There is little sign of such motivation, but he was seeking to rebuild the Dudley affinity, and as his relationship with Elizabeth developed during 1559 that caused some tension. It is not, however, true that the court immediately became divided into Dudley and Cecil factions. Sir William was totally opposed to Robert's matrimonial pretensions, regarding him as a political maverick, but over most issues of policy they were in substantial agreement. It was members of the 'old nobility' such as Norfolk and Arundel who were most resentful of this parvenu – although his family had three generations of court experience. They also muttered maliciously that his father and grandfather had died as traitors, although that would also have been true of the Duke of Norfolk but for the merest accident.[69] The Earl of Sussex resented his increasing familiarity with the queen, and there are also signs that Kate Ashley was becoming alarmed, perhaps remembering the trouble that had ensued the last time her mistress had taken a fancy to a dashing man. Part of the trouble was that Robert and Elizabeth were in many ways rather similar. Both had great appetites for the good things of life – food, clothes, jewels, horses – and both were intensely physical. He was tall, handsome and a fine athlete, and she, although not a great beauty, had presence and her mother's allure.

As Master of the Horse Dudley was also something of a Master of Ceremonies. Elizabeth's initial journey from Hatfield to London was a triumphal procession, and since the court were all mounted it was largely his place to organise that.[70] It was the council's job to organise the coronation, but the queen (rather surprisingly for a person of such consistent piety) was anxious to chose an auspicious day, and wished to consult an astrologer. Lord Robert obliged, bringing to court his father's former dependant, and perhaps his own tutor, John Dee. Dee was already a famous mathematician, and had acquired a dubious reputation as a necromancer, so it is not surprising that his appearance created something of a stir, and caused some to whisper that Lord Robert was making his way with the assistance of the black arts.[71] Throughout December he was occupied about the movements of the court, and the entertainments to be provided for Christmas. Thomas Cawarden remained officially Master of the Revels until the following year, but at this stage Lord Robert seems to have done much of the 'leg work'. He was also responsible for organising the coronation procession, in which it was his right to ride directly behind the queen. On 16 and 17 January there were 'great justes' at court, as was customary at the time of a coronation, and these would also have been his responsibility, although it is not clear whether he took part.[72] All these were normal aspects of his court duty, but in one respect from the very beginning his position was exceptional. He became what we would now describe as Elizabeth's 'personal trainer'. This did not involve exercises in the modern sense, but a great deal of riding, hunting and hawking in which he habitually accompanied her, and dancing in which he was often her partner. He also appears to have lectured her regularly on the need for exercise as an antidote to too much paperwork, and this was advice which she was to follow for the rest of her life.[73]

As we have seen, Amy Dudley did not appear at court. This may have been due to poor health, but other evidence suggests that there was nothing visibly wrong with her, at least before the end of 1559. She was active about the management of her husband's affairs in the country, and keen on fashion and the latest gossip.[74] It is more likely that the queen deliberately kept her away from court because she did not want to be reminded of her existence, and she may well have initiated rumours about her poor health to disguise this rather unworthy reaction. There are signs that by August 1559 Amy herself was beginning to resent her exclusion, and to suspect the true reason for it. Her husband's stays at home were distressingly brief and infrequent, and he was 'sore troubled with weighty matters'.[75] A wife could hardly be in a more unpleasant predicament than having the queen as the 'other woman', and Robert's career depended upon maintaining the favour which he had obtained by his sex appeal! In April 1559 he became a Knight of the Garter on the queen's nomination, and by the autumn talk of their relationship had spread to all the courts of Europe. The Queen of England, Catherine de Medici observed contemptuously, 'is to marry her horsemaster'.

However, it was not quite like that. Elizabeth was a young woman under enormous pressure, and welcome as the haven of the Privy Chamber must have been, it was not sufficient for all occasions. The conventional wisdom was that a woman needed a man, not just for sexual relations but for guidance and support. She had not yet reached the stage of concluding that there were no 'matters impertinent to women', except perhaps leading an army, and that in terms of government all she needed was advice. In 1559 she was still finding herself, and Robert Dudley played an important part in that self-discovery. In an acquisitive and competitive environment, he was a relaxing and undemanding companion.[76] Elizabeth was still thinking about marriage, but she was already beginning to suspect that the price, in terms of her own control of both her person and of events, would be too high. It was probably not until the winter of 1559–60 that her relationship with her agreeable Master of the Horse shifted into that sexual overdrive that observers had been postulating for months. Someone had read the signals correctly before the queen herself knew quite what was happening. The real crisis of the relationship was not to come until Amy's death in September 1560, because that opened up for the first time the possibility that romantic dalliance could turn into marriage.[77] The result then was a huge scandal, and bitter controversy within the court, but that lies outside the scope of this study. As long as Amy was alive, Robert was a safety valve for Elizabeth's sexual frustrations; but she was a woman who took her chastity as seriously as her royalty. Her subsequent denials that there was ever anything 'improper' in their relationship were almost certainly true – but there is more than one kind of sexual relationship, and the observers were right in identifying the nature of her favour.

Elizabeth was full of energy, both physical and mental, and greatly relished both the trappings and the reality of power. It is often said that she was a superb actress, and in a sense that is true, but an actress can turn her hand to many parts, and Elizabeth's repertoire was very limited. At the age of fifteen she had earned applause for her 'damsel in distress', and had only had to adjust that role slightly to become the 'much maligned woman' of Mary's reign. In 1558, however, she had to transform herself and play the queen. This was a subtle and varied part, but it required an underlying consistency. In council she must be grave and prudent, at court by turns magnificent and charming – at one moment the coquette, at another *La Belle Dame sans mercy*. She needed to be at once intimidating and approachable, gentle and ruthless, quick to laughter and the coarse joke, but a student of philosophy and able to impress Italian diplomats in their own tongue.[78] Her range was truly formidable: from piety to extreme rage, from masculine oaths to feminine indecisiveness. No wonder it is so hard to determine which was the real Elizabeth and which the mask. No wonder either that she needed her refuges, and at first Dudley was one of those, until the gossip created a public curiosity about their relationship. Once the great crisis over the marriage that never was had ended, they were able to resume something of that original friendship, and the complicated dance between them continued until his death in 1588.[79]

Christmas 1558 reflected the spirit of the new reign. From 11 December onwards sixteen tailors, ten carvers, six painters and a hatmaker, with various assistants, were working flat out preparing for the masques, plays and other presentations, at a cost in wages alone of over £64.[80] Together with the special purchases and the extra boat hire, the cost of Christmas to the Revels Office was £205 1s. 6d. We do not know what the masques were apart from the pointed jibe at cardinals and bishops, but an expenditure of £135 on new materials suggests that they were not recycling old works. In any case Elizabeth's tastes, to say nothing of those of her friends, were very different from those of the old queen. The coronation and the Candlemas celebrations which followed prompted not only a lavish distribution of cloth from the Great Wardrobe, but further activity at the Revels, entailing another £82 7s. 3d. in wages to tailors and embroiderers. The coronation itself was separately costed, as were the jousts which followed, and must between them have cost approaching £10,000. Shrovetide followed hard upon: more painters, tailors and joiners at a cost of £150, so more new works. On 21 March there was a parade at Mile End, with 'all maner of artelere' and a 'grett gyant danssyng', after which the queen and her officers dined in public, before they all moved into the park, when there was 'shutyng and play-hyng at bowl', bear baiting and morris dancing.[81] In May of 1559, to honour the French ambassadors who came to ratify the peace of Cateau Cambrésis, there was a further masque of astronomers at Westminster, together with bull baiting and a 'gret dyner', at a cost (to the Revels) of £97 3s. 1d. Altogether the expenses of the office for the first year of the reign came to £602 11s. 10d., more than had been expended during the entire reign of Elizabeth's predecessor.[82]

The Revels accounts also show that Will Somers was still on the pay-roll in 1559, although he had died by the end of 1560, but Jane, Mary's 'innocent', disappears, and her fate is a matter of speculation.[83] They had no immediate successors, because Elizabeth did not keep either an inno-cent or a full-time jester. There were professional entertainers at court, both James Lockwood and Richard Tarlton, who had served before her accession and continued to appear from time to time. Indeed, Lockwood was called 'The Queen's man', but he was paid when his services were called for, and not on a regular basis. Later in the reign there was Jack Greene, who was also known as 'The Queen's fool' and was given cloth-ing out of the Wardrobe but was not a regular member of the court, and the mysterious Ippolyta, described as 'oure deare and welbeloved woman' in 1564. Ippolyta was also given clothing, but not in terms which suggest that she was unable to care for herself, and she was therefore not an innocent. Just what services she performed is not clear, and she does not feature in any of the descriptions of the court. It is possible that she was a dwarf and was kept mainly as a curiosity.[84]

Parliament ended on 8 May, and the full English Prayer Book service came into use in the Chapel Royal on the 12th. Sir Edward Carne had already been recalled from Rome – or rather, his mission had been terminated because he had declined to return, and Philip had had to persuade the pope not to take any hasty action against his erring daughter. The first six protestant bishops were named in June, and by then the religious and political climate of the new regime was becoming clear.[85] Within a few weeks, Mary Stuart would be Queen of France by marriage as well as of Scotland in her own right, and was already quartering the arms of England with her own in violation of the recent peace. Meanwhile, in Scotland her mother, Mary of Guise, was struggling to contain the protestant rebellion of the Lords of the Congregation, and the lords were looking hopefully towards England for help. So hopefully, indeed, that there was talk of James Hamilton, Earl of Arran, as a possible candidate for Elizabeth's hand, because they were 'mariable both and the chief upholders of God's religion'.[86] This proposal would be formalised in the summer of 1560, after the Treaty of Edinburgh had consolidated English influence in Scotland, and when the Scots were getting worried about Eric of Sweden, but Elizabeth never seriously entertained it.

It is an interesting question how serious Elizabeth ever was about marriage. When approached directly on the subject, she always expressed a preference for the single life, which was taken for (and probably was) mere rhetoric. She told parliament that she would marry, but only when the time (and the man) was right; and yet every negotiation ended in failure, even those which she appears to have initiated herself.[87] It has been suggested that her adolescent encounter with Thomas Seymour had put her off sex permanently, or that she knew herself to be incapable of childbearing. If the latter were true, it would, of course, have altered the equation dramatically, turning any possible marriage into a purely political calculation, but there is no reason to suppose that it was. She reacted to the birth of Prince James in Scotland by lamenting that she was 'a barren stock', but that should not be taken literally. Unlike her sister, she had no history of menstrual disorders, and when she was seriously embroiled with Dudley, Kate Ashley besought her with tears to take no risks. Kate knew her better than anyone, and may have been referring to the political risks and disparagement of marriage with a subject, but she might equally have been referring to the appalling risk of conceiving a child out of wedlock.[88] At the beginning of her reign Elizabeth was not a 'professional virgin', and her image as such was far in the future. At the end of 1559 it was still universally expected that she would wed, and the persistent chatter on that subject must have made the Privy Chamber less peaceful than it might have been. There were inevitably rumours that she was pregnant, as had already happened in 1548, or that she had borne a child, with Dudley as the best guess at the father. But they were all just that – rumours. Whether Elizabeth was really a virgin is an unanswerable question, but she probably was, and she was certainly never a mother.

By 1560 the pattern of Elizabeth's future courtships had already become established: politically motivated suitors, careful calculations of the potential risks and advantages, complex negotiations over religion, and, perhaps most important of all, the request for a visit of inspection. Ferdinand's refusal to allow his son to be scrutinised hastened the breakdown of the Habsburg discussions; Eric was willing to come, but was deflected first by bad weather and then by his own succession.[89] Only the Duke of Anjou actually came, and that was nearly twenty years later. It is possible that on each occasion Elizabeth was simply trailing her petticoat for diplomatic advantages, and yet the tone of much of the correspondence does not suggest that. The only man she ever loved in the physical sense was Dudley, but each negotiation was honestly meant. When it came to the point, it was not the thought of sex that deterred her so much as the unwillingness to surrender her independence. Elizabeth wanted to be in control, and she could not bring herself to play the 'woman's part'. That is clear from the very beginning in the way in which she assembled her council and handled her religious settlement. She would not be sidelined, and she would not be taken for granted. A modern marriage, as a partnership of equals, might have suited her very well, but that was not what was on offer in a sixteenth-century context. Mary had retained control over her kingdom, but her marriage had failed, and even then many of her councillors had looked to Philip rather than to her. If Elizabeth married, the same thing would happen. The succession might (or might not) be settled, but when it came to the point the price was always too high: not only a loss of political power, but the loss of control over her own body. Gratifying as it might be, a woman's sexual role was perceived to be submissive – and if there was one thing that Elizabeth was not, it was submissive. It is unlikely that she ever decided against marriage in principle, for any reason, but when it came to the point she could not face the surrender that contemporary matrimony required. It is not perhaps surprising that she once yearned to be a milkmaid: an ordinary woman could not only have the man of her choice, she also had comparatively little to lose.

The queen's famous aversion to matrimony in others is to some extent an optical illusion created by these misunderstandings about her own attitude. The court was a theatre, and a lot of hearts were worn on sleeves; but the queen soon began to learn that courtly love was the only kind she was ever likely to experience. For a woman of her vitality, that was a hard cross to bear; but a queen who could not control her passions was unlikely to remain a queen, as Mary of Scotland was soon to demonstrate.

Notes and references

1 *The Diary of Henry Machyn*, ed. J.G. Nichols (Camden Society, 1848), p.178.

2 Mary sent a verbal message to her sister, accepting her right to the throne, and Elizabeth replied in the same way. There is no written record of the exchange apart from diplomatic reports.

3 PRO, SP12/1/7. Printed in *Elizabeth I: Collected Works*, ed. Leah S. Marcus *et al.* (Chicago, 2000), p.51.

4 *A Speciall grace, appointed to have been said after a banket at Yorke, upon the good nues and Proclamation thear, of the entraunce in to reign over us, of our soveraign lady ELIZABETH, by the grace of God, Quene of England, Fraunce and Ireland, defendour of the faith, and in earth the supreme hed of the church of England, and also of Ireland, in November 1558*, RSTC 7599. Also BL, MS Royal 17.C. III. Elizabeth was not at that time (or ever) entitled to be styled 'Supreme Head'.

5 Machyn, *Diary*, ed. Nichols, p.180.

6 D.M. Loades, *Two Tudor Conspiracies* (Cambridge, 1965), p.143.

7 W. MacCaffrey, *The Shaping of the Elizabethan Regime, 1558–1572* (London, 1969), pp. 27–40.

8 He was buried on the Isle of Sheppey at the beginning of January 1559: Machyn, *Diary*, ed. Nichols, pp.184–5.

9 MacCaffrey, *Shaping*, pp.33–4 and n.

10 'Feria's Despatch of 14th November 1558', ed. M.-J. Rodriguz-Salgado and S. Adams, *Camden Miscellany*, 28 (1984), pp.331–2.

11 John Harrington had been imprisoned in 1549 for his involvement with Lord Thomas Seymour, and again between January 1554 and January 1555 for carrying messages between Wyatt and Elizabeth. By 1562 he was described as 'the Queen's servant', but he held no office of note. R.J. Haughey, *John Harrington of Stepney: Tudor Gentleman* (Columbus, Ohio 1971).

12 MacCaffrey, *Shaping*, p.73. Several of these Marian councillors and courtiers kept a slender connection with the court through Francis Yaxley, a Norfolk gentleman with a position in the Chamber.

13 PRO, LC2/4, ii.

14 PRO, LC2/4, iii; BL, Lansdowne MS 3, fol.88.

15 D.M. Loades, *Elizabeth I* (London, 2003), pp.41–2. Her maiden name was Champernowne; she married John Ashley in 1545.

16 Katherine died in 1565 and John married again, but he retained the queen's favour.

17 D.E. Hoak, 'The Secret History of the Tudor Court: The King's Coffers and the King's Purse, 1542–1553', *Journal of British Studies*, 26 (1987), pp.208–31.

18 Conyers Read, *Mr. Secretary Cecil and Queen Elizabeth* (London, 1955); *idem*, *Lord Burghley and Queen Elizabeth* (London, 1960).

19 E.g. Ruy Gomez to Francisco de Eraso, 27 July 1554, *CSP Spanish*, vol.13, p.2.

20 Roy Strong, *Tudor and Jacobean Portraits* (London, 1969), vol.1, plate 415. There are three autograph versions of this portrait. One is in the Prado in Madrid; a second, originally in the Escorial, was in 1969 at Castle Ashby in the collection of the Marquis of Northampton; and the third, which originally belonged to Sir Henry Jerningham, is in the Isabella Stewart Gardner Museum in Boston, Massachusetts.

21 Loades, *Elizabeth I*, pp.64–70.

22 Roy Strong, *The Cult of Elizabeth* (London, 1977), p.53.

23 Machyn, *Diary*, ed. Nichols, pp.186–7.

24 *The Passage of our most dread Sovereign Lady, Queen Elizabeth, through the City of London to Westminster the day before her Coronation*, in A.F. Pollard, *Tudor Tracts* (London, 1903), p.387.

25 Ibid., p.395.

26 Il Schifanoya to the Castellan of Mantua, 23 January 1559, *CSP Venetian*, vol.7, p.17. On the importance of the symbolism invoked in Elizabeth's coronation, and the care with which it had been worked out, see Dale Hoak, 'The Coronations of Edward VI, Mary I and Elizabeth I, and the

Transformation of Tudor Monarchy', in *Westminster Abbey Reformed, 1540–1640*, ed. C.S. Knighton and R. Mortimer (Aldershot, 2003).

27 'Feria's Despatch', ed. Rodriguez-Salgado and Adams, p.331.

28 W.P. Haugaard, 'Elizabeth Tudor's Book of Devotions: A Neglected Clue to the Queen's Life and Character', *Sixteenth Century Journal*, 12 (1981), pp.79–105. Several of these prayers are also printed in *Elizabeth I: Collected Works*, ed. Marcus *et al.*, pp.135–63.

29 W. Cobbett, *State Trials* (London, 1816), vol.1, p.714.

30 Il Schifanoya to Ottaviano Vivaldini, 31 December 1558, *CSP Venetian*, vol.7, p.2.

31 Il Schifanoya to Ottaviano Vivaldini, 28 March 1559, ibid., p.23.

32 The most thorough modern examination of these bills and of their passage through parliament is N.L. Jones, *Faith by Statute* (Cambridge, 1982).

33 Particularly the 'Discourse on the Commonwealth' attributed to Armigal Waad, the Clerk of the Council. Read, *Mr. Secretary Cecil*, p.124. See also MacCaffrey, *Shaping*, pp.45–6.

34 D. Wilkins, *Conciliae Magnae Brittaniae et Hiberniae* (London, 1737), vol.4, p.179; Philip Hughes, *The Reformation in England*, vol.3 (London, 1954), pp.22–3.

35 Hughes, *Reformation*, pp.29–35; Statutes 1 Elizabeth cap.1 and 1 Elizabeth cap.2, *Statutes of the Realm*, ed. A. Luders *et al.*, 11 vols. (London, 1810–28), vol.4, pp. 350–55, 355–8.

36 D.M. Loades, 'Mary's Bishops', in *The Church of Mary I*, ed. D.M. Loades and E. Duffy (forthcoming).

37 Elizabeth's view of her own responsibility for the church can be deduced from a number of speeches, but it emerges most clearly from her statement to the House of Commons in 1576: 'her Majestie doubteth not but that her people shall see that her majestie will us that aucthoritie which she hath to the encrease of th'nonour of God and to the reformation of th'abuses in the Churche'. T.E. Hartley, *Proceedings in the Parliaments of Elzabeth I* (Leicester, 1981), vol.1, pp.445–7.

38 V.J.K. Brook, *A Life of Archbishop Parker* (Oxford, 1962).

39 Statute 1 Elizabeth, cap. 24. Mary's bequests to the regular religious had amounted to over £3,000 a year.

40 PRO, SP12/1/32–3.

41 J. Strype, *Ecclesiastical Memorials*, 3 vols. (Oxford, 1822), vol.3, pp.536–50.

42 *The epitaphe upon the death of queen Marie* (*RSTC* 17559). Broadsheet 76 in the collection of the Society of Antiquaries.

43 D.M. Loades, *Mary Tudor: A Life* (Oxford, 1989), p.312.

44 PRO, SP12/1/57, 64. Memorandum 'to consider in what points the realm hath sustained great loss during the late Quenes reign'.

45 *CSP Spanish*, 1558–67, pp.1–4.

46 Archivo de la casa de Medinaceli, caja 7, legajo 249, nos. 11–12. Cited in G. Parker and C. Martin, *The Spanish Armada* (London, 1988), p.281.

47 'Feria's Despatch', ed. Rodriguez-Salgado and Adams, p.331.

48 Ibid., p.335.

49 Susan Doran, *Monarchy and Matrimony: The Courtships of Elizabeth I* (London, 1996), pp.26–7.

50 BL, Lansdowne MS 94, item 14, fol.29. Printed in *Elizabeth I: Collected Works*, ed. Marcus *et al.*, p.57. This is the same speech in which the queen spoke of living and dying a virgin.

51 Feria to Philip, 18 April 1559, *CSP Spanish*, 1558–67, pp.57–9.

52 Ibid.

53 BL, Add. MS 48023, fol.357; Doran, *Monarchy and Matrimony*, pp.21–2.

54 Machyn, *Diary*, ed. Nichols, p.206.

55 Derek Wilson, *Sweet Robin: A Biography of Robert Dudley, Earl of Leicester, 1533–1588* (London, 1981), pp.71–3; R.C. McCoy, 'From the Tower to the Tiltyard: Robert Dudley's Return to Glory', *Historical Journal*, 27 (1984), pp.425–35.

56 *CSP Foreign*, 1558–9, pp.70–71: Cecil's instructions to Christopher Mundt (in Germany).

57 Doran, *Monarchy and Matrimony*, pp.27–8.

58 8 September 1559, *CSP Spanish*, 1558–67, pp.95–6. Elizabeth was extremely anxious to avoid diplomatic isolation, and at the same time she was conducting a dialogue with the Lutheran princes of Germany. *Elizabethan England and Europe: Forty Unprinted Letters from Elizabeth to the Protestant Princes*, ed. E. Kouri (London, 1982).

59 De Quadra to Ferdinand, 2 October 1559, *CSP Spanish*, 1558–67, pp.98–104; de Quadra to Margaret of Parma, 29 October 1559, ibid., p.107.

60 'An anonymous mid-Tudor chronicle', BL, Add. MS 48023, fol.352; Bruener to Ferdinand I, 6 August 1559, cited in Doran, *Monarchy and Matrimony*, pp.41–2.

61 'The Lady Elizabeth's answer made at Hatfield to Sir Thomas Pope', 26 April 1558, BL, Harley MS 444, fols.20–9. Mary had been furious.

62 *CSP Spanish*, 1558–67, p.51; Doran, *Monarchy and Matrimony*, p.30.

63 Doran, *Monarchy and Matrimony*, pp.30–1.

64 Machyn, *Diary*, ed. Nichols, p.221; *CSP Venetian*, vol.7, p.659; BL, Add. MS 48023, fol. 354.

65 *CSP Foreign*, 1559–60, pp.75, 211; *CSP Venetian*, vol.7, pp.659–60.

66 Doran, *Monarchy and Matrimony*, pp.31–2.

67 Ibid.

68 *CSP Spanish*, 1558–67, p.4.

69 Edmund Dudley (Robert's grandfather) had been executed for treason in 1509, and John Dudley, Duke of Northumberland, in 1553. Henry Howard, Earl of Surrey (Norfolk's father), had been executed in 1547, and the third Duke of Norfolk (his grandfather) was reprieved by Henry VIII's death at the same time.

70 Wilson, *Sweet Robin*, pp.84–6; Machyn, *Diary*, ed. Nichols, p.180.

71 Wilson, *Sweet Robin*, p.85; N.H. Clulee, *John Dee's Natural Philosophy: Between Science and Religion* (London 1988).

72 Machyn, *Diary*, ed. Nichols, p.187.

73 M.M. Reese, *The Royal Office of Master of the Horse* (London 1976), p.159.

74 Amy Dudley to John Flowerdew (their Norfolk agent), 7 August 1559, BL, Harleian MS 4712.

75 Wilson, *Sweet Robin*, p.95.

76 For the most recent discussion of Elizabeth's relationship with Dudley, see Simon Adams, *Leicester and the Court* (Manchester 2002), pp.133–50.

77 Doran, *Monarchy and Matrimony*, pp.42–4.

78 Il Schifanoya noted that when he and his colleagues had audience, the queen had spoken graciously to them in their own tongue: *CSP Venetian*, vol.7, p.2. On Elizabeth's strategy of manipulation, see Loades, *Elizabeth I*.

79 Wilson, *Sweet Robin*, pp.300–10.

80 A. Feuillerat, *Documents Relating to the Office of the Revels in the Reign of Queen Elizabeth* (Louvain, 1908), p.84.

81 Machyn, *Diary*, ed. Nichols, p.191.

82 Feuillerat, *Documents ... Elizabeth*, p.105.

83 John Southworth, *Fools and Jesters at the English Court* (Stroud, 1998), p.106.

84 Ibid., pp.109–10.

85 Machyn, *Diary*, ed. Nichols, pp.200–1.

86 Throgmorton to Cecil, 28 June 1559, in Patrick Forbes, *A Full View of the Public Transactions in the Reign of Queen Elizabeth* (London, 1740), vol.1, p.147.

87 This was most notably the case with her last negotiation, with the Duke of Anjou, between 1579 and 1581: Doran, *Monarchy and Matrimony*, pp.154–94.

88 Breuner to Ferdinand I, in Victor von Klarwill, *Queen Elizabeth and Some Foreigners* (London, 1928), pp.113–14.

89 Doran, *Monarchy and Matrimony*, pp.30–5.

CHAPTER 10

. . . .

The eye of the storm

The Tudor court, like that of every renaissance prince, was the political focus of the realm. It had always been bigger, richer and more
glamorous than any of its aristocratic competitors, but by the time that
Henry VIII died in 1547 it was unique in England. This was largely
because the relationship between the king and his nobles had changed
dramatically over the previous century.[1] The granting of the senior titles
of nobility – anciently earls, but by the fifteenth century viscounts, mar-
quises and dukes as well – had always been a prerogative of the crown.
It was not until the reign of Henry V that baronies were created by patent,
and later still before a patent became necessary.[2] By this means the king
set boundaries. Only he could determine who was, or was not, a nobleman; and this status was confirmed by the issue of an individual writ of
summons to attend parliament. The eldest son of a duke was styled an
earl, and of an earl a baron, but only the king could decide whether to
summon these title holders in their fathers' lifetime. Moreover, the function of a nobleman had changed. Traditionally the aristocracy were war-
riors – the companions in arms of the king – with whom they shared a
code of honour. That was still the case in the early part of Henry VIII's
reign, but the Duke of Suffolk, who died in 1545, was the last of his kind.[3]
Henry still promoted men who were partly soldiers, like the Earl of
Hertford and Viscount Lisle, but they were also other things – particularly the king's servants to do his bidding. By the end of his reign, Henry
had destroyed most of the ancient noble families – Stafford, Percy,
Courtenay and Howard – and replaced them with new men – Clifford,

Parr, Seymour and Radcliffe. Woe betide the nobleman who placed the honour of his ancient lineage above his service to the king! Ancient families survived, such as FitzAlan, Stanley and Talbot, but they did so by conforming to the new model. These men were office holders and Privy Councillors, and claimed neither power nor honour that did not derive from the crown.[4] By 1547 English gentlemen had discovered (in the words of Laurence Stone) that the king was a better lord than the Earl of Derby. In 1560 English noblemen still had great wealth and influence, and many dependants; but they neither intended nor expected to lead those dependants against the crown. When the Duke of Norfolk consulted his affinity in 1570, they advised unconditional submission to the queen. When the Earl of Northumberland rose in 1569, only a small proportion of his *manred* followed him; and in 1601 the Earl of Essex did not even bother to try.[5]

This left the royal court without rivals. By 1558 Thornbury had gone, and Alnwick and Kenninghall were shadows of their former selves. The last rival court had been that of Cardinal Wolsey, as John Skelton sardonically noted, and that came to an end when Wolsey made Hampton Court over to the crown in 1525.[6] Paradoxically, the blight of the Tudors – the absence of sons – was in this respect a blessing. No Tudor had to face the rival pretensions of an adult heir or sibling. For about ten years the young Henry Fitzroy, Duke of Richmond and Somerset, held court at Middleham in Yorkshire, but he was illegitimate and never constituted the slightest threat to his father. So the king's court was unique as a theatre of power and wealth – and as a focus of politics, culture and fashion. This also reflected the Tudor style of government in another way. Edward IV had governed by conferring great power upon a small number of noblemen – notably his brother the Duke of Gloucester – whom he deemed to be loyal to him. Henry VII changed that pattern, not by dismissing the nobility but by bypassing them and delegating most of the routine functions of local government directly to the gentry by commission – notably the commission of the peace.[7] The effect of this upon the court was very noticeable, because Henry recruited members of these gentle families into his service and introduced them to the court, as sewers, ushers and other gentlemen servants. They thus became directly dependent upon the king, whose affinity became greatly expanded at the expense of the local nobility who had previously commanded this service. Every county thus had its representatives at court, and this might have nothing to do with the Earl of Shrewsbury or the Duke of Suffolk.[8] The court thus became a 'point of contact', not only between the king and his natural companions – his peers – but also between the king and the political nation generally. This change of emphasis was also signalled by the rise of the House of Commons, but it gave the Tudor court a representative function that had not been true of the Plantagenet court.

The concentration of power and wealth in the hands of the king, which had been commented upon before 1509, had become very evident by about 1530. For all his pretensions, Wolsey was very much Henry's creature, as was Cromwell. Insofar as they were significant patronage brokers, it was the king's patronage they were distributing rather than their own. The great nobles of the 1540s had significant patronage in their 'countries', but real power lay in controlling access to the king, which was why the Privy Chamber had become so important by that time.[9] Both the Duke of Somerset and the Duke of Northumberland provide significant pointers of a similar kind. Both have been described as 'overmightly subjects', as though they were reincarnations of the fifteenth-century Dukes of Buckingham or Earls of Warwick. In fact they were nothing of the kind. Their power lay in controlling the king and the court, and when that power was broken, they had no resources with which to protect themselves. In this respect the major change came not in 1547 but in 1553. Both Mary and Elizabeth were adults, and 'minders' were out of the question, but neither could control the male 'bonding networks' that had previously determined the pattern of politics. Elizabeth quickly developed her own gender-specific strategy of manipulation, and thus established a control as complete in its own way as her father's had been.[10] Her court was therefore no less central and powerful than his. Mary was rather different. She had no charisma, sexual or otherwise, and no sensitivity to political strategy. What she did have was a formidable sense of duty, and the residual power which her father and brother had bequeathed to her. In spite of his disabilities (from an English point of view) and other preoccupations, Philip was to some extent able to make good these deficiencies; but he was not in England long enough to make any significant difference.[11] It is an open question how important Mary's court was as a political focus, or how long it would have retained its central role if Mary had lived. Her resurrection of the ancient noble families of Howard, Courtenay and Percy, and her failure to develop the service nobility, raise questions about the direction in which she was heading; but she did not live long enough to bring about (or permit) any major reversal of her father's policies in this respect. In one respect she was perhaps more in control. There were no major patronage brokers in Mary's reign, and the grants and creations she made were very much her own. Men like Sir Thomas Cornwallis and women like Susan Clarencius became rich by her gifts; but they did not become powerful.[12] Apart from Philip, the most powerful men around her were individual favourites, like Simon Renard and Reginald Pole, who conformed to no rules and whose position at court was enigmatic.

The English court was much less peripatetic than most of its European counterparts, and its relationship with the country was therefore different. Charles V toured his many dominions, although he was mostly in Spain or the Low Countries, and Francis I toured France with a huge entourage; both drew in the provincial nobility and gentry as they went. Between 1540 and 1560 the English court scarcely moved outside the Home Counties. Henry went to York in 1541 and to Portsmouth in 1545; Edward also to Portsmouth in 1552; and Mary to Winchester in 1554 and to Dover in 1557. Apart from that it was the regular circuit of Westminster, Hampton Court, Greenwich and Richmond, with occasional forays to Oatlands or Guildford.[13] Anyone living outside the 'magic triangle' would only expect to see the monarch by visiting the court, wherever it was located. Mary even gave Nonsuch away to the Earl of Arundel. It was not until later that Elizabeth developed a policy of regular progresses, to show herself to her people. The enthusiasm that Machyn records for Mary's occasional appearances in and around London is sufficient evidence of how important that could be.[14]

In a way, this lack of mobility actually increased the attractiveness of the court to provincial gentry and nobility, because if anyone had a petition to present or a grievance to air, it could not await the monarch's next appearance in the relevant locality. The court was also convenient for the main business centres. As the role of central government slowly increased, provincial gentlemen were increasingly drawn to London: for sessions of parliament; to do business in the law courts; to borrow money; or to negotiate commercial deals.[15] Many such gentlemen had kinsfolk based at court to be visited and 'networked'. If the monarch was

at Richmond, or St James, or at Westminster itself, this was easy and convenient. Anyone who needed an ear to the ground noises of English politics needed to be at court, or to have reliable sources of information there.
An ambassador's usefulness to his prince depended at least as much
upon the quality of these contacts as upon the business he formally transacted with the council. In this respect, as in every other, ambassadors
varied. Some were close to the centre of events, others were remote.
Some had the resources to buy good information, others did not. Some
were experienced, others less so. None (as far as we know) spoke any
English, and this was a significant handicap. All had their own agendas,
as we have seen, and this, combined with their various limitations,
means that their despatches – which are often our only sources for court
politics – have to be treated with great care. Neither de Quadra, nor Feria,
nor Marillac, nor even Renard can always be trusted, any more than
Eustace Chapuys a generation earlier. Too much conventional interpretation is based upon their words, often in translation, but it is a hard pit-
fall to avoid.

The court was not the centre of government in the ordinary sense. The
central law courts, the Exchequer and the Chancery had all gone 'out of
court' many years before. The king and the Privy Council retained an
oversight of these departments, but seldom interfered in their regular
business. Similarly, local commissions were supervised and instructed
by the council and were answerable to the Lord Chancellor, but their
normal business would not have been transacted at court. The council, or
at least a council, sat wherever the monarch happened to be, but a
number of councillors also remained at Westminster to deal with business which did not require the personal intervention of the ruler.[16] It
therefore depended what kind of business a visitor wished to transact
whether he (or she) headed for Westminster or the court. There was no
system of regular judicial appeal, so if redress was sought for a miscar-
riage of justice, it could only be done by way of pardon, and that could
only be sought from the monarch. Inevitably there were many complaints
about the number of courtiers who had to be bribed to obtain access to
the royal person, and the staff of the Chamber in particular ran a profitable sideline of this nature. Some were more skilled than others, or had
better opportunities, and commanded higher rates, but even the porter at
the gate could exclude the casual visitor unprovided with a suitable

inducement. On the other hand, if the petitioner were a gentleman anxious to avoid a turn as sheriff, it would have been the Lord Chancellor whom he needed to approach, and he might not be at court.[17]

Altogether, the centrepetal attraction of London and Westminster was enormous, and much greater in mid-century than it had been 50 years before. This was largely thanks to the policies, and personality, of Henry VIII. Henry had built his court into one of the most magnificent and efficient in Europe, largely to satisfy his ego and his determination to play in the premier league of European politics – a status to which his resources did not entitle him. Much of that magnificence faded away under his two immediate successors, to be restored eventually and in a different way by Elizabeth. However, the function of the court did not diminish, because the system of government which Henry had created did not change. Remarkably, it survived a minority and two female rulers.

Because many decisions could only be made by the monarch in person, during a normal reign, whether the ruler was male or female, councillors and ambassadors had to dance attendance – and that meant being at court, because the court by definition surrounded the monarch. During a minority the situation was rather different, because the critical decision makers might not be at court.[18] However, the difference was not as great as might be supposed. The Duke of Somerset indeed did not spend much time in his nephew's company, and paid the price. The Duke of Northumberland did not make the same mistake. He knew that the young Edward's confidence and affection represented the future, and as we have seen he was in almost constant attendance after he secured the office of Lord Great Chamberlain. Edward may not have made many decisions himself, but after 1550 the appearance that he was doing so became increasingly important – and the appearance blended imperceptibly into reality.[19] If there was a hiatus in the importance of the court (and that is debatable), it came between 1547 and 1549. In spite of the king's minority, between 1549 and 1553 the court was as important as ever, although in a slightly different way. The monarch was central, even if more as a symbol than as a functioning ruler; but that was always seen as a temporary situation, and the scenery needed to remain in place if the adult king was not to be disparaged.

The court was always a place of intrigue, and inevitably it was fiercely competitive. Everything depended upon making a good impression, either directly, upon the monarch, or indirectly, upon the person (or persons) who happened to be highest in favour at any particular time. In his younger days, Henry VIII had been open to influence from many quarters. At first Catherine, his queen, had promoted many men and causes successfully, and Anne Boleyn, Jane Seymour and Catherine Parr later did the same.[20] Henry also filled his Privy Chamber with congenial souls like Charles Brandon, who not only did well for themselves but successfully promoted their clients – and the more successful they were, the more clients they had. However, he was also listening to his official advisers: at first Warham and Fox, later Wolsey, Cromwell, Norfolk and Gardiner. These were men whom he had advanced to high office precisely because he appreciated their talents and valued their advice. The stakes were high, and virtually all these networks were disrupted or destroyed by intrigue and conspiracy. The Privy Chamber was diminished by the council in 1519 because its influence was deemed to be excessive.[21] Catherine was eclipsed by Anne Boleyn, who in turn was destroyed by a conservative and imperial plot in 1536. Catherine Howard, Henry's fifth queen, represented the brief ascendancy of the Howard interest, and was brought down by the opponents of that interest.[22] Both Wolsey and Cromwell were destroyed by their enemies for having allegedly failed the king in important business. A similar plot, apparently intended to remove Catherine Parr, was frustrated. These were not (or not only) competitions for access to the royal largesse, but also for influence over royal policy. At first this was a question of peace or war, a Valois alliance or a Habsburg one. But later the competition also acquired an ideological dimension: was the king right to break with Rome, bastardise each of his daughters in turn, or interfere with the worship of the church? It was all about influencing Henry, but there were causes to be promoted as well as interests, and it should not for a moment be supposed that the king was either passive or biddable. John Foxe later represented him as a man at the mercy of good or evil council, but that is a considerable distortion.[23] It would be fairer to describe him as volatile, and latterly deeply divided in his own mind. He was not a compulsive womaniser, and apart from Anne Boleyn no woman had a decisive influence over him, even temporarily. He was, however, consistently determined to have his own way, and extremely dangerous when thwarted because he was also compulsively self-righteous.

In spite of the strong feelings that some of Henry's actions provoked, even within the court, these intrigues never amounted to treason, irrespective of what was claimed. Wolsey was accused of treason because of his dealings with the pope, but such dealings did not become treason by law until after his death;[24] Anne Boleyn was convicted of treason because of her alleged adultery, and her accomplices also, but such a crime, even if it was committed, was not aimed at removing Henry. Cromwell's 'treason' was even more specious, and the Howards were convicted for their alleged designs on the succession. Insofar as treason consisted of a settled intention to frustrate the king's declared policy, then it did indeed fuel some of these innumerable intrigues, but insofar as it involved an intention to kill or overthrow the king and replace him with someone else, it did not. Apart from anything else, there was no obvious alternative.[25] There was, therefore, no equivalent in Henry VIII's court of Sir William Stanley, his father's Lord Chamberlain who had countenanced Perkin Warbeck, or of the Duke of Norfolk who (perhaps) plotted to replace Elizabeth with Mary Stuart in 1570.

The last court battle of Henry's lifetime was for the control of his heir. The result was the destruction of the Howards, the downfall of Stephen Gardiner, and the triumph of the 'Evangelical party'. That outcome, however, was determined by the king and not by the parties, a position which could not be repeated in the circumstances of a minority. Edward was involved in intrigue, because he was a party to Thomas Seymour's bid for the hand of the queen dowager, but he had no say in the power brokering that went on around him.[26] Neither the fall of the Earl of Southampton in March 1547 nor the regime change in October 1549 owed anything to the personal intervention of the king, in spite of his close involvement in the latter events. Consequently, these should not really be described as court intrigues. The fall of Somerset had a major impact on the Privy Chamber, but that was after the event, and nothing that was happening there contributed to it. The issue was settled in the king's presence, and so was a court event, but it was generated in the council meeting in London, away from the court. The one thing that it proved was that control of the king's person was not necessarily a decisive advantage, and the decision not to prosecute the fallen Protector for treason was correct, because neither side had any intention of harming Edward.[27]

It is debatable whether the destruction of Somerset in 1551 can be described in terms of the court. The duke had his supporters – a great many of them – but they were not in the Chamber or the Privy Chamber. Indeed, it was more a conflict between an 'in' party and an 'out' party, where the excluded were trying to recover a position at court – rather in the way the Duke of York had striven to acquire access and control in the 1450s. There may have been implications for the security of the court, but that was because an attack from outside was feared – or so it was claimed – rather than because of any internal disruption. The decision of the peers not to convict Somerset of treason was thus correct, both in law and in politics.

The crisis that followed Edward's death was much more complicated. As long as the king was alive, it was treason to disobey him, no matter what his command might be, and the emergence of the 'Device' could well be described as a court conspiracy, although one directed against Mary rather than Edward.[28] However, once he was dead the situation changed. His wishes, being embodied neither in statute nor in any other legally binding document, had no status which required obedience. Anyone wishing to obey the law was bound to reject them. Nevertheless, the court was divided, and a significant proportion of the gentlemen pensioners and yeoman of the guard supported the Duke of Northumberland. We have no idea what most of the Chamber and Household servants thought about the issue, and they were probably only too glad not to have to declare themselves. The reign of 'Queen Jane' was too brief to have any impact, and she established no relationship with the court, and did not even have time to appoint a Privy Chamber. The battle was fought out partly in the council and partly in the country, and as a political entity the court was virtually in abeyance for two or three weeks after Edward's death. His body must have been tended, and daily life went on, but no pen or voice recorded it.[29]

Both Northumberland and Mary were confronted with numerous protests and conspiracies, but none of these had either root or flower in the court. This was not because access became in any sense less important. The duke distributed a lot of royal patronage to his friends, and no doubt there was competition for it, but there were no plots against his ascendancy once the Duke of Somerset had been disposed of. Mary distributed her own patronage, and although there was no doubt much jockeying for position, this did not result in faction. The passport to

Mary's favour was conspicuous devotion to 'the old religion', and anyone not displaying that, or known not to share it, need not bother to come to court. There was a good deal of religious dissent already present in the Household – which is not surprising, given that she made very few changes – but Mary never knowingly entertained anyone who was not a good catholic. It is more surprising that she carried out no purge, because her chaplains must have known what was going on; however, they may not have told the queen. In all public pronouncements by the regime, heresy was held to be synonymous with sedition; but pragmatically, Mary's senior Household officers accepted that protestant sympathies did not turn court servants into traitors, and their restraint was entirely justified.[30] There were intrigues and factions within the court, but as with her father and brother, these were never directed against her. Disagreements over her marriage led to the rustication of the Marchioness of Exeter and divided the council, but once her decision was made it was accepted by all those about her. Insofar as men like Robert Rochester and Francis Englefield were involved in factional disputes, it was as members of the council, not as courtiers. Neither Stephen Gardiner nor William Paget, whose quarrels the political commentators so zealously recorded, had any position at court beyond the access to which their offices entitled them.[31]

The advent of Philip of course changed this environment considerably. Although living in the same building, the two courts were never fully integrated, and whereas the king's English servants were virtually indistinguishable from the queen's, his Spanish servants kept to themselves. After Philip's purge in August 1554 they were comparatively few, and that increased their sense of isolation and vulnerability. None of them seems to have compromised by learning any English, and although tight discipline prevented serious disturbances, the tensions were never resolved while Philip was in England. Only the queen was upset when he withdrew the last of his household in December 1555.[32] Anti-Spanish plots and demonstrations outside the court must have increased the claustrophobic atmosphere, but the courtiers themselves (as distinct from their servants) never seem to have become involved in brawls. Both the Wyatt rebellion and the Dudley conspiracy involved those who had enjoyed court connections, and even offices, in the past; but the only current courtier who was compromised was Sir Thomas Cawarden, and as we have seen, no action was taken against him. In complete contrast with the court of Henry VIII, after the first few weeks there appear to have been no machinations for the control of Mary's ear, either for personal or political purposes. Perhaps her servants were uncertain how to influence the mind of a woman, or perhaps, given her celebrated obstinacy, they did not see much point in trying. There must have been considerable excitement in the spring of 1555 about the birth of an heir, and much competition for positions in the royal nursery, but we know very little about these things, and no nursery staff were ever appointed.[33] Perhaps there were more doubts about the queen's condition than were publicly admitted. In spite of the strictures of both Renard and Feria upon the divisions of the English council, and the Duke of Alba's comments about there being 'King's men' and 'Queen's men', Mary's court seems to have been remarkably free from plotting and faction, and completely free from anything that could be called treason – unless a willingness to accept Elizabeth as the heir could be placed in that category. Elizabeth's supporters constituted an 'invisible faction' through most of her sister's reign, and as that faction's prospects improved, it becomes increasingly impossible to evaluate.[34]

In spite of the war and the unresolved religious conflict, Elizabeth was fortunate in the circumstances of her accession. Like Mary, she was free to constitute her Privy Chamber as she chose, but unlike her, she also had a free hand with her council. Consequently, there were no natural fault lines, and much less talk of faction and division than there had been five years before. This does not mean that her councillors always agreed with each other; in fact, they offered very diverse advice, both on the religious settlement and over the Austrian and Swedish marriage negotiations.[35] That suited the queen very well, because it emphasised her own role as the decision maker; and as with Mary, once she had made up her mind they accepted the verdict with a good grace.

What divided Elizabeth's council, and her court, in these early days was Robert Dudley. He was a favourite of a sort that had not been seen before. He was not a member of the council, but a courtier pure and simple, and the nearest equivalent to the kind of influence he wielded had been that of Anne Boleyn in the early days of her power. There were from the beginning rivalries for patronage and office, and this involved a number of different councillors and courtiers with their own agendas, but

Dudley was always a factor – either a help or a hindrance to everyone else's ambitions.[36] He and Cecil were like two sides of the same coin, the one political, the other intensely personal. They overlapped and there was friction, but there was no polarisation of the court. It was not until several years later (in 1568–9) that there was a real court conspiracy against Cecil, in which Dudley was involved, and by then the circumstances had changed. He was Earl of Leicester, and a councillor, no longer the maverick of 1559. The nearest thing to a treasonable conspiracy in which any of Elizabeth's courtiers became involved was the Ridolfi plot of 1570–71. That certainly aimed to remove Elizabeth in favour of Mary, Queen of Scots, and Norfolk was certainly implicated; but it is uncertain to what extent he should be described as a courtier. He held no office, had received no particular favours, and had little following at the court.[37] On the other hand, he was a kinsman of the Lord Chamberlain (Lord William Howard), and remotely of the queen herself. In the first year of the reign there were pro- and anti-Dudley groups, but the latter were of no settled composition, and there was nothing remotely treasonable about any of them in terms of the queen's security.

Taking the period as a whole, intrigue was endemic for both political and personal advantage. Faction, in the sense of settled groupings pursuing consistent aims, was much rarer. It probably disappeared with the death of Henry VIII, although it could be argued that Somerset and Northumberland were faction leaders in 1551. Perhaps because of the rather different expectations entertained of a woman, the courts of Mary and (at first) Elizabeth were free from it. Of treason, in the normal sense of plotting the death or overthrow of the incumbent monarch, there was likewise nothing. Offences were committed which could be described as treason and brought within the statute law, such as those of Norfolk and Surrey (1546–7), Somerset (1551) and Northumberland (1553), but only a wild (and unsubstantiated) charge against Somerset accused him of trying to seize the crown for himself.[38] Under Mary in particular treason was plotted, and even partly executed, but never within the precincts of the court. Someone may have shouted 'Treason, treason' in February 1554 as the rebels advanced, but that was nothing worse than panic and incompetence.

At the same time, the court was the theatre of monarchy as well as its political context. 'Magnificence' was not a matter of exotic taste or self-indulgence, but a necessary means of making power visible and enforce-able.[39] Renaissance princes were fiercely competitive, and that competi-tion has to be seen in dynastic as well as in territorial policies. England, France and Scotland were in some sense nations, but that was not true of the Holy Roman Empire, nor of Venice, Milan or Navarre; but dynastic and territorial competition applied equally to them all. The Tudors no longer needed to compete with their own nobility, that battle was won, but they were locked in combat with France and the Empire, and this extended beyond warfare to every aspect of their dignity and image. Henry VIII played in the premier league, and although neither Edward nor Mary managed to maintain that, they were still important to the poli-tics of northern Europe.[40] Under Edward, England also had the premier protestant court of Europe, and was thus required to set a pace and example, and not to be eclipsed in any way by the 'papists'. It must also be remembered that renaissance princes lacked coercive power. The kings of France had a small standing army, but the Tudors had nothing beyond the gentlemen pensioners and the yeomen of the guard. For the preservation of domestic order they were almost entirely dependent upon the retinues raised by their nobles and gentlemen. This meant that voluntary obedience, however maintained, was crucial, and magnifi-cence – the power to overawe and intimidate – played an important part in that process. This was partly a question of imagery, partly of the sheer display of wealth. Great tournaments, splendid processions and entries, and lavish masques and other entertainments all played their part. There was also an element of *sprezzatura*, or effortless superiority, about all this.[41] The king had to be seen to have the time, energy and resources to indulge himself and his friends in this fashion: no element of parsimony or self-doubt must be visible.

Henry VIII was a master of this medium, and his young son could not be expected to keep up. Nevertheless, Edward had to find his feet in this medium as in every other. The Duke of Somerset was not particularly good in this respect, and the Scottish war also left him seriously short of money, but Northumberland, who freed himself from war and began a process of retrenchment, had different priorities.[42] The lavish expendi-ture of the Revels Office in Edward's last year has to be seen in this con-text. So also does the boy's much-promoted godliness. This, although no doubt genuine up to a point, was also a method of display, and a bid for leadership. The rites of the reformed church were relatively austere, but a king of precocious learning and piety was almost as useful for competitive purposes as a ruler of great pomp and ceremony – more useful, in some ways, because different and distinctive.

Mary's trademark was equally her piety, but in a much more traditional mode. The frequency of her private devotions and her celebrated reverence for the 'sacrament of the altar' prompted some sceptical Spaniards to describe her as a saint, but they did little to promote her image among her own subjects.[43] More valuable in that respect was ecclesiastical pageantry. Both Mary and Philip observed festival days with processional and solemn high masses at St Paul's or Westminster, and if Henry Machyn's enthusiasm is anything to go by, the effect was entirely positive. This to some extent compensated for the queen's total lack of self-promotional skills. Although she dutifully paraded herself when necessary, as on the eve of her coronation, after her wedding, and during her convalescence in August 1555, she had no charisma and no flair. Philip did rather better. He had no idea how to please the English (nor any great desire to try), but both his tournaments and his public displays of affection for Mary were well received.[44] When it came to entertainments, again the queen was dutiful rather than enthusiastic. She knew that she was expected to put on a show, but she seems to have suffered from an inferiority complex when comparing herself with the Habsburgs. This was unnecessary, because several of Philip's courtiers, expecting a simple and poverty-stricken establishment, were impressed in spite of themselves. The number and size of England's royal palaces, and the scale of the catering, astonished them.[45] Philip's normal household was not only much less lavish, it was much more tightly controlled. The royal couple, they noticed, were always served on bended knee, but apart from that there was a shocking lack of 'decorum', and the free manners of the ladies of the court repelled them almost as much as their (alleged) plainness. By comparison with its Spanish equivalent, the English court was huge, sprawling and undisciplined.

If Henry VIII cast himself as 'the great King', and Edward was cast by others as 'the Godly Imp', Mary's image is hard to identify. In spite of her well-displayed piety she did not take up her mother's practice of going on pilgrimage, and most of the medieval shrines which her parents had visited in their younger days remained desolate. She probably aspired to be seen as a royal wife and mother, but the former was an ambiguous role, and the latter was denied her. There was nothing in Mary to fire the imagination, and the poverty of her revels express that more eloquently than any commentary.

Elizabeth, on the other hand, delighted in display. She was not yet Gloriana, or the Virgin Queen; but she was Deborah, the Judge of Israel, and also The Englishwoman. Unlike Edward, she did not choose to make either learning or piety a 'trademark', although she could well have used either. Rather, she was the Queen of the May – young, beautiful, vibrant and alluring.[46] Her enthusiastic interaction with the crowd during her coronation entry was calculated and typical. No one knew quite what to make of her, and that was also deliberate. To be pigeonholed was to be controlled, and Elizabeth had no intention of being controlled by anyone except herself.[47] However, no one knew in 1560 that she was going to remain unmarried, or live another 44 years, and it is important not to read back into that first year the achievements of a lifetime. Her proud independence stirred emotions, but no one knew how she, or her church, would be affected by the expected catholic marriage. An unmarried woman was a fragile symbol around which to build a national myth of autonomy and 'special providence'. To John Foxe she may have been the New Constantine, but few expected her to prove so robust.[48]

From Paris, or Brussels, or Valladolid, the English court was the most visible part of the realm, and Tudor investment in it was immense. It is very difficult to say exactly what it cost, because the expenditure never passed through a single account, and at every stage of the century there are apparent discrepancies between specific and general statements.[49] Also, at the end of Henry's reign and in the early part of his son's there is the problem of the Privy Coffers, which were managed within the court but which were in effect a public spending department unrelated to it. The best-informed guesses are that the ordinary revenue of the English crown went up from about £100,000 a year in 1510 to about £150,000 in 1550, and to about £200,000 by the end of the century. An inflation of rather more than 400 per cent over the same period meant that real revenue declined by about half, which not only required stringent economy (for which Elizabeth became famous) but also increased resort to parliamentary subsidies. The subsidy – a form of taxation invented in the 1520s – had originally yielded some £150,000, more or less according to the terms and period of the grant, but it had declined to about half that in real terms by 1600. In 1560–61, when no subsidy was being collected, Thomas Weldon, the queen's Cofferer, accounted for an expenditure of £50,912, and Sir John Mason, the Treasurer of the Chamber, for £11,389.[50] At that point the court was absorbing about a third of the available income of the crown. For the sake of comparison, the year which spanned the last months of Henry VIII's reign and the first of his son's cost £49,187; the last full year of Edward VI (1552–3) cost £65,923; and the third year of Mary (1555–6) cost £75,043 (with a deficit of £10,140). By 1559 the accumulated deficit was estimated at £25,000.[51] Thereafter (although it falls outside the scope of this study) the Household costs were gradually reduced in real terms: in 1564–5 to £44,932, in 1582–3 to £54,904. This was achieved partly by economies, and partly by 'adjusting' the accounting procedures, but it meant that by the end of the century the proportion of crown income being spent on the court had declined to about 25 per cent.[52] This was still a great deal, and should serve to remind us that the Chamber and the Household provided far more than just housekeeping for the monarch. They were a vital network without which no aspect of policy, either foreign or domestic, could be carried out. Wherever the head of government and the head of state are the same person, the same phenomenon can be observed – today most obviously in the White House and the Kremlin.

The mid-Tudor court also displayed other features which were less overtly political. Henry, in competition with Charles and Francis, attracted artists such as Hans Holbein, cosmographers like Jean Rotz, and musicians such as Dominic Memo and the Bassano brothers. Edward patronised John Dee, Sebastian Cabot and William Scrots, while Mary's court was thronged with Spanish and Italian theologians and clergy who had come in the entourages of Philip and Cardinal Pole.[53] As we have seen, Dudley reintroduced John Dee to the court, and Elizabeth soon began to attract scholars and poets to what was surely the most intellectually distinguished environment in Europe. The Chapel Royal provided not only a litmus test for the religious policy of the government but also a theatre for preachers, singers and performers. Edward's chapel was famous for its sermons, Mary's for the magnificence of its liturgy, and Elizabeth's for the adaptation of good music to protestant worship, an influence of great importance in cathedral churches.[54] There were always complaints, of course, from those who tried their luck at court and came away disappointed:

> *I have been begging sixteen years in court,*
> *Am yet a courtier beggarly nor could*
> *Come pat betwixt too early and too late*
> *For any suit of pounds . . .*[55]

That was a feeling which grew sharper towards the end of the century, when even the queen admitted that she could not reward her servants according to their deserts. Mary cancelled many of her brother's annuities and replaced them with her own, but that was to be expected, and the aggrieved were in no position to complain.

The court witnessed the brokering of many deals, particularly marriage settlements, and both Mary and Elizabeth attracted eligible young ladies anxious to improve their matrimonial prospects, usually with the blessing and encouragement of their male kindred. In this highly charged atmosphere feuds could easily develop, like that between Dudley and the Earl of Sussex, or later between Sir Walter Raleigh and the Earl of Oxford, and these sometimes spilled out into violence on the streets of London, or in the 'country' of the principals.[56] Sexual intrigue was endemic, although severely discouraged by the equally puritanical regimes of Edward and Mary. Under both Henry and Elizabeth it was to some extent corralled within the conventions of courtly love, but not all the passionate romances were feigned. Young men and young women thrown together and with time on their hands did not set a virtuous example to the sober burgesses of nearby London, and it is not surprising that there was an anti-court literature, with its roots deep in the middle ages. The court was corrupt – a place for timeservers, flatterers and cheats of all kinds. Castiglione had portrayed an ideal courtier, wise, suave and talented – a worthy companion and councillor of princes, but everybody knew that such were the exception rather than the rule.[57] In other words, the court was a human institution, and the best that a pious prince like Mary could do was to make it dull and workaday rather than exciting and attractive – and that did nothing to improve its effectiveness.

Notes and references

1 Helen Miller, *Henry VIII and the English Nobility* (Oxford, 1986), *passim*.

2 Richard III formalised this system when he established the College of Arms in 1484. *CPR Edward IV, Edward V and Richard III* (1476–85) (London, 1901), p.422.

3 For a full discussion of Brandon's career and its implications, see S.J. Gunn, *Charles Brandon, Duke of Suffolk, 1484–1545* (Oxford, 1988).

4 G.W. Bernard, *The Power of the Early Tudor Nobility: A Study of the Fourth and Fifth Earls of Shrewsbury* (Brighton, 1985).

5 'When he [Norfolk] found no comfort among his own, and Heidon, Cornwallis and others of his traine perswaded him that if he were guilty, should flye to the Queenes mercy, he was almost distracted with sorrow.' W. Camden, *Annales* (1635), p.212. Cuthbert Sharp, *Memorials of the 1569 Rebellion* (1840), pp.xviii–xix, 191–2, 194. The Earl of Essex relied entirely upon the City of London and did not appeal to his affinity at all. Mervyn James, 'At a Crossroads of Political Culture: The Essex Revolt of 1601', in *Society, Politics and Culture* (London, 1986).

6 John Skelton, 'Why cam ye not to courte?', in Alistair Fox, *Politics and Literature in the Reigns of Henry VII and Henry VIII* (Oxford, 1989), pp.182–93.

7 D.M. Loades, *Tudor Government* (Oxford, 1997), pp.111–38.

8 D.M. Loades, *The Tudor Court* (London, 1986), pp.133–46.

9 David Starkey, 'Intimacy and Innovation: The Rise of the Privy Chamber, 1485–1547', in Starkey, ed., *The English Court from the Wars of the Roses to the Civil War* (London, 1987), pp.71–118.

10 D.M. Loades, *Elizabeth I* (London, 2003), pp.123–50.

11 G. Redworth, '"Matters Impertinent to Women": Male and Female Monarchy under Philip and Mary', *EHR*, 112 (1997), pp.597–613.

12 R.C. Braddock, 'The Rewards of Office Holding in Tudor England', *Journal of British Studies*, 14 (1975), pp.29–47.

13 These moves can be traced through *CSP Domestic* for Edward VI and Mary, ed. by C.S. Knighton (1992, 1998).

14 E.g. *The Diary of Henry Machyn*, ed. J.G. Nichols (Camden Society, 1848), p.93.

15 Laurence Stone, *The Crisis of the Aristocracy, 1558–1640* (Oxford, 1965), pp.335–80.

16 Loades, *Tudor Government*, pp.17–37.

17 See, for example, the lobbying of Philip Gawdy of Norfolk on behalf of his brother Bassingbourne: I. H. Jeayes, *Letters of Philip Gawdy of West Harling* (Roxburgh Club, 1906), p.131.

18 M.L. Bush, *The Government Policy of Protector Somerset* (Manchester, 1975).

19 D.M. Loades, *John Dudley, Duke of Northumberland* (Oxford, 1996), pp.180–229; J. Loach, *Edward VI* (London, 1999), pp.94–115.

20 D.M. Loades, *Henry VIII and his Queens* (Stroud, 1994), pp.63–111, 133–56.

21 Edward Hall, *The Union of the Two Noble and Illustre Famelies of York and Lancaster* (the *Chronicle*) (London, 1548; ed. H. Ellis, London, 1809), p.598.

22 Loades, *Henry VIII and his Queens*, pp.121–32.

23 D.M. Loades, 'John Foxe and Henry VIII', *John Foxe Bulletin*, 1/1 (2002), pp.5–12.

24 In the Act of Supremacy of 1534 (26 Henry VIII, c.1): *Statutes of the Realm*, ed. A. Luders *et al.*, 11 vols. (London, 1810–28), vol.3, p.492. More fanciful charges were also laid: 'some saied that he had the pockes, & notwithstanding presumed both to drynke of the kinges Cuppe which might be expownded treason, sith therewith the king might be infected . . .' *The Papers of George Wyatt*, ed. D.M. Loades (Camden Society, Fourth Series, 5, 1968), p.145.

25 A. Fletcher and D. MacCulloch, *Tudor Rebellions*, 2nd edn (London, 1998).

26 Deposition of John Fowler, PRO, SP10/6, no.10.

27 Loades, *John Dudley*, pp.147–50.

28 *The Literary Remains of Edward VI*, ed. J.G. Nichols (Roxburgh Club, 1857), vol.2, pp.572–3.

29 Even Robert Wingfield is silent on this aspect. The last dated state paper of Edward's reign, in a grant of 27 June (PRO, SP10/18, no.29), and the first of Mary's reign, is dated 20 July (SP11/1, no.2). There is one proclamation of Jane, dated 10 July.

30 This can be deduced, and read between the lines of Edward Underhill's narrative, but it was never admitted – for obvious reasons.

31 G. Redworth, *In Defence of the Church Catholic: The Life of Stephen Gardiner* (Oxford, 1990); S.R. Gammon, *Statesman and Schemer: William, First Lord Paget, Tudor Minister* (Newton Abbot, 1973).

32 *CSP Venetian*, vol.6, p.285.

33 In the circumstances, it is not surprising that no appointments were made, but it is surprising that there was (apparently) no discussion, and no names were canvassed.

34 For a discussion of this point, see D.M. Loades, *Mary Tudor: A Life* (Oxford, 1989), pp.274–314.

35 Susan Doran, *Monarchy and Matrimony: The Courtships of Elizabeth I* (London, 1996), pp.13–39.

36 Conyers Read, *Mr. Secretary Cecil and Queen Elizabeth* (London, 1955), pp.198–218.

37 Neville *Williams, Thomas Howard, Fourth Duke of Norfolk* (London, 1964). For a recent assessment of the Ridolfi plot and Norfolk's part in it, see G. Parker, 'The Place of Tudor England in the Messianic Vision of Philip II of Spain', *Transactions of the Royal Historical Society*, 6th ser., 12 (2003), pp.167–223.

38 BL, Add. MS 48126, fol.1.

39 Loades, *Tudor Court*, pp.1–8.

40 Even when it was comparatively weak, England occupied a key strategic position in the endemic wars between Valois and Habsburg – hence the international importance of Mary's marriage, and of those that were proposed for Elizabeth.

41 For an elucidation of this concept, and its significance, see B. Castiglione, *The Book of the Courtier*, ed. and trans. George Bull (London, 1976).

42 Loades, *John Dudley*, pp.180–229.

43 *CSP Spanish*, vol.13, p.11. Mary's piety was universally praised in sermons and ballads, but it seldom features in the comments of English observers.

44 Ruy Gomez to Eraso, 12 August 1554, in *Documentos ineditos para la Historia de Espana*, ed. M. Fernandez de Navarete (Madrid, 1842–95), vol.3, p.531.

45 *Tres Cartas de lo sucedido en el viaje de Su Alteza a Inglaterra* (La Sociedad de Bibliofilos Espanoles, Madrid, 1877), Tercera Carta, p.102.

46 *Elizabeth I: Collected Works*, ed. L.S. Marcus *et al.* (Chicago, 2000), pp.303–5.

47 Loades, *Elizabeth I, passim.*

48 The dedication of the first edition of the *Actes and Monuments* was to Elizabeth as 'the new Constantine'. This was withdrawn from the second edition of 1570, and not repeated thereafter.

49 Loades, *Tudor Court*, p.77.

50 PRO, E351/1795; E351/541, fol.40.

51 BL, Lansdowne MS 4, vii, fol.19; PRO, E351/1795; BL, Cotton MS Titus B IV, fol.133; Loades, *Tudor Court*, pp.77–8.

52 Loades, *Tudor Court*, p.79.

53 T.F. Mayer, *Reginald Pole: Prince and Prophet* (Cambridge, 2000); Redworth, '"Matters Impertinent to Women"', J. Edwards, 'Spanish Influence in Marian England', in *The Church of Mary I*, ed. D.M. Loades and E. Duffy (Forthcoming).

54 Stanford E. Lehmberg, *The Reformation of Cathedrals* (Oxford, 1988), pp.182–226.

55 William Shakespeare, *Henry VIII*, Act 2, Scene 3.

56 Stone, *Crisis of the Aristocracy*, pp.223–33.

57 Castiglione, *The Book of the Courtier*, ed. and trans. Bull.

The structure of the court

The English court in this period was divided into two main sections, or jurisdictions, the Chamber and the Household.

The Household was stable, bureaucratic and well defined. Its function was to provide services, and to ensure that they were paid for. The chief officer was the Lord Steward, who was normally a senior nobleman and was always a person high in the monarch's confidence. The other 'white stick' officers who served under him, and who were invariably knights or gentlemen, were the Treasurer, the Comptroller and the Cofferer. Together with the necessary clerks, these officers constituted the Board of Greencloth, or Counting House, which was responsible for supervising all the constituent departments of the Household, and for receiving their accounts. All money received into the Household, from whatever source, was distributed by the Counting House. Eighteen ordinary departments were responsible to the Counting House, each under a sergeant or clerk, who was of yeoman status. The staff of each department varied in size from three or four to over twenty (in the main kitchen), and were defined by status, either as yeomen, labourers, or boys (who were also known as grommits).

The kitchen might have up to four subordinate departments, including the Privy Kitchen (which prepared the monarch's personal food) and the Consort's Kitchen, if there was a consort. The departments (and subdepartments) were:

The Kitchen [Privy Kitchen, Wafery, Boilinghouse, Consort's Kitchen]
The Larder

The Acatry (which dealt with fresh meat and fish)
The Poultry [Scalding House]
The Pastry
The Scullery
The Woodyard
The Porters [Carttakers]
The Almonry (which distributed charity and broken meats)
The Ewery [Laundry]
Confectionery
Chaundry (which made and distributed candles)
Cellar [Buttery, Pitcherhouse, Spicery]
Pantry
Bakehouse [Privy Bakehouse]
Knight Marshall [Provost Marshall, Harbingers] (who handled accommo-
  dation and discipline)
Artificers (the maintenance and upkeep men)
Musicians

There was also one extra-ordinary department, the Great Hall. This had originally been a major set-up, with a large staff of sewers, cupbearers and sewers of the dresser which had catered for all the main meals. By 1540, and even more by 1560, its function had diminished because the monarch took public meals in the Chamber. The Chamber servants avoided the Hall (which served coarser food), and by this time it provided only for the ordinary servants.

The Household staff numbered (officially) between 200 and 250 people, nearly all of them men. There were also many unofficial hangers-on, some protected by the sergeants, others not. The latter were periodically cleared out by the Provost Marshall. Patronage over appointments in the Household was controlled partly by the 'White Stick' officers and partly by the departmental sergeants. There was also a recognised career structure. It was normal for sons to follow fathers and nephews uncles, and to be promoted in accordance with 'buggins turn'. The Household was little affected by political or religious upheavals (except at the 'White Stick' level), but it was subject to occasional cost-cutting drives by thrifty ministers. Thomas Cromwell had conducted one such in the late 1530s, and William Cecil was to struggle with the same problem throughout

Elizabeth's reign. The Lord Steward (or Lord Great Master) kept his own court, having *ex officio* jurisdiction within the boundaries (verge) of the court over all offenders of no matter what status, and the only appeal was to the monarch in person. The boundaries of the court were normally defined by the liberty boundaries of the palace concerned; but if the court was on the move, or in a minor residence, then the temporary boundaries were specifically proclaimed. Because the Household was almost entirely male, the Provost Marshall and the porters had constant trouble with prostitutes, who plied their trade with particular vigour at Westminster.

The other main section of the court was the Chamber, or *domus regie magnificencie*, which was the honorific setting of the monarch. Here ambassadors and subjects were received, entertained and impressed. This was much less clearly defined, and its staffing was much vaguer. The chief officer was the Lord Chamberlain, and there was also a Vice-Chamberlain and a Treasurer, but no equivalent of the Board of Greencloth. There were 'departments', but they were categories of staff rather than institutions. The main exception was the Privy Chamber, which was controlled by the Groom of the Stool, or Principal Gentleman/woman. Appointments to the Privy Chamber were made personally by the monarch, and the gentlemen, or ladies, were intimate servants and companions. There were also humbler servants, grooms (male) or chamberers (female), and pages who did the manual work. The total staff of the Privy Chamber numbered between 30 and 40, and it was politically highly sensitive. The Privy Chamber also embraced the Privy Wardrobes of the Robes and the Beds, which had small staffs.

The staff of the Chamber (or Great Chamber) were divided by function. There were chaplains, physicians, tutors, henchmen (or maids), who were young courtiers in training, the yeomen of the guard, the gentlemen pensioners, gentlemen waiters, sewers, cupbearers, knights and esquires of the body, and selected artists, scholars and quacks who happened to be in favour at that time. Most of the Chamber servants worked on a part-time or 'shift' basis, and were paid fees proportionate to the time they served: so there were 'quarter waiters', 'daily waiters', and so on. It was in theory a serious offence for a Chamber servant to either leave or arrive at court without the licence of the Lord Chamberlain, but in practice (unless they were resident) such lapses were normally winked at, except in the case of important noblemen. The Privy

Chamber servants, and a proportion of the Chamber servants, lived in the court when they were on duty and received what was called 'bouge of court' as part of their reward. This was the right to be fed at the royal tables, which by this time meant at one of the officers' tables kept in the Presence Chamber or a nearby room. There was, however, an increasing tendency for such servants to take rations to their own chambers and to have their own servants prepare them – a practice which was frowned upon for both economic and social reasons.

The Chamber was intentionally flexible in order to meet the fluctuating demands placed upon it, and whereas a consort would have only a minimal household, she (or he) would have a full Chamber staff as well as a Privy Chamber. All the major palaces were so organised that there were separate suites of rooms (and even separate gardens) for the king and queen, usually connected by private passages or 'privy stairs'. Whereas access to the monarch's private apartments was tightly controlled by the Privy Chamber staff, access to the Great Chamber was as open as it was to the court at large. Although the porters on the gates had strict instructions to exclude undesirables, and anyone who could not demonstrate legitimate business, the great palaces were all fairly porous, and fictitious 'servants' were cleared out on a regular basis from the Chamber as well as the Household. However, anyone needing or desiring access to the monarch, to present a petition, for example, could secure admission to the court for a modest bribe, and to the Chamber for a rather larger inducement to one of the gentlemen ushers. There were recognised times when the monarch was accessible to this sort of approach – Henry when he was about to go hunting, Mary when she was on her way to chapel, and so on. Chaos at such times was routine, and security impossible. Lord Thomas Seymour once notoriously observed that it would be easy to abduct Edward VI because access was so poorly controlled. However, in spite of what was to happen later in Elizabeth's reign, during this period no verifiable attempts were made on the person of the monarch. Only in one respect was security tight: no one, however exalted, might draw a weapon or resort to violence in the royal presence. The penalties for such lapses were draconian, although in practice they were hardly ever carried out.

With the exception of very occasional feasts, it was in the Great Chamber that the monarch dined in public, and where the chief officers of the court 'kept their tables'. This latter practice continued irrespective of the monarch's presence, and in fact dining in public became increasingly rare as the period proceeded. Both Edward's youth and Mary's supposed pregnancy were given as reasons, but in fact habits and tastes were changing. Privacy in the modern sense, however, was unknown. Monarchs of both sexes carried out even the most intimate of bodily functions in the presence of servants, and it was normal for a gentleman, or lady, of the Privy Chamber to sleep in the royal bedchamber unless the consort was present.

It appears to have been Thomas Cromwell's intention to reorganise the whole court on the French model, with the appointment of a Lord Great Master to control both the Chamber and the Household. Such an officer was appointed in 1540 in the person of Charles Brandon, Duke of Suffolk, and the office of Lord Steward was abolished. However, this happened only just before Cromwell's fall. The office of Lord Chamberlain was vacant from 1540–43, but then a new appointment was made (William Paulet, Lord St John) which undermined the whole reform. For about ten years the Lord Great Master was in practice the Lord Steward, but with an undefined superiority over his colleague. Mary brought this illogical situation to an end in 1553, when the Lord Great Mastership was abolished and the Lord Steward restored.

Nothing was tidy about the Tudor court, and there were quite a number of departments which were properly attached to it but which were subject neither to the Lord Chamberlain nor to the Lord Steward. The Master of the Horse was certainly an officer of the court, and kept his own table in the Great Chamber, but the stables were not part of either the Household or the Chamber, and accounted separately. The same was true of the hunting departments – the kennels and the toyles – although their officers were of lesser status. The chapel, with a sizeable staff of gentlemen and choristers, was run independently by its dean, and the Tents and Revels and the Great Wardrobe each had their own master, who accounted independently. There were also 'fringe' departments – the Jewel House, the Works, the Ordnance and the Royal Barge – which were in a sense part of the court but were never embraced within its organisation. In its widest definition, the court was a vast and rambling structure which absorbed something like a third of the crown's ordinary revenue. More narrowly defined, it was the monarch's immediate setting, staffed by some 500 servants of varying degrees, some full-time, some part-time, some paid wages, some fees, and some not paid at all. It merged into the government of the realm on all sides. The Privy Council met at court. All councillors were members of the Chamber, even if they held no court offices, and were entitled to 'bouge of court'. Ambassadors' diets, and even the costs of garrisons, were sometimes paid out of the Chamber Treasury. Everyone from the Lord Chancellor to the kitchen scullion was a servant of the monarch, and although the distinction between the person of the monarch and the state was beginning to emerge, it was embryonic in this period. The ambiguous use of the word 'Crown' still reflects that.

• • • • • • • • • • • • • •

The chief officers of the court

Lord Great Chamberlain

Thomas Cromwell, Earl of Essex	1540
Robert Radcliffe, Earl of Sussex	1540–2
Edward Seymour, Earl of Hertford	1543–9
John Dudley, Earl of Warwick	1549–50
William Parr, Marquis of Northampton	1550–3
John de Vere, 16th Earl of Oxford	1553–62

[Before 1540 this office, which was entirely honorific, had been hereditary in the de Vere family, to which it was returned in 1553]

Lord Great Master

Charles Brandon, Duke of Suffolk	1540–5
William Paulet, Lord St John	1545–50
John Dudley, Earl of Warwick	1550–3

Lord Chamberlain

Vacant	1540–3
William Paulet, Lord St John	1543–6
Henry FitzAlan, Earl of Arundel	1546–50
Lord Thomas Wentworth	1550–1
Sir Thomas Darcy	1551–3
Sir John Gage	1553–6
Sir Edward Hastings	1557–8
William, Lord Howard of Effingham	1558–72

Lord Steward

Discontinued	1540–53
Henry FitzAlan, Earl of Arundel	1553–64

Vice-Chamberlain

Sir Anthony Wingfield	1539–50
Sir Thomas Darcy	1550–1
Sir John Gates	1551–3
Sir Henry Jerningham	1553–7
Sir Henry Bedingfield	1557–8
Sir Edward Rogers	1558–9
Sir Francis Knollys	1559–70

Treasurer of the Chamber

Sir Brian Tuke	1528–45
Sir Anthony Rowse	1545–6
Sir William Cavendish	1546–57
Sir John Mason	1558–66

Treasurer of the Household

Sir Thomas Cheney	1539–58
Sir Thomas Parry	1559–60

Comptroller of the Household

Sir John Gage	1540–7
Sir William Paget	1547–9
Sir Anthony Wingfield	1549–52
Sir Richard Cotton	1552–3
Sir Robert Rochester	1553–6
Sir Thomas Cornwallis	1556–7
Sir Robert Freston	1557–8
Sir Thomas Parry	1558–9
Sir Edward Rogers	1559–68

Cofferer of the Household

John Ryther	1547–52
Thomas Weldon	1552–3
Sir Robert Freston	1553–7
Richard Ward	1558–9
Thomas Weldon	1559–67

Master of the Horse

Sir Anthony Browne	1539–49
Sir William Herbert	1549–52
John Dudley, Earl of Warwick	1552–3
Sir Edward Hastings	1553–7
Sir Henry Jerningham	1557–8
Sir Robert Dudley	1558–87

Master of the Revels

Sir Thomas Cawarden	1545–60

Master of the Great Wardrobe

Sir Ralph Sadler	1543–53
Sir Edward Waldegrave	1553–9
John Fortescue	1559–79

Dean of the Chapel Royal

Richard Sampson	1523–44
Thomas Thirlby	1544–54
[William] Hutchenson	1554–8
George Carew	1558–72

Select bibliography and list of sources

This list includes all works cited, and a selection of the other works consulted and of general relevance.

List of abbreviations used

The following abbreviations are used in the notes. Full details of the works cited here can be found in the Bibliography.

APC	*Acts of the Privy Council*
BL	British Library, London
BN	Bibliothèque Nationale, Paris
CPR	*Calendars of the Patent Rolls*
CSP Domestic	*Calendar of State Papers, Domestic*
CSP Foreign	*Calendar of State Papers, Foreign*
CSP Spanish	*Calendar of State Papers, Spanish*
CSP Venetian	*Calendar of State Papers, Venetian*
HMC	Historical Manuscripts Commission
Letters and Papers	*Letters and Papers ... of the Reign of Henry VIII*
PRO	Public Records Office, London
RSTC	*The Revised Short Title Catalogue of Books Printed in England, Scotland, and Ireland, and of English Books Printed Abroad*

Manuscripts

At the British Library (BL):
Cotton Titus B.I
Vespasian F.III

Add. MSS 48126, 4724, 71009, 48023
Harleian 5087, 1294, 284, 787, 6949
Lansdowne 3
Lansdowne Charter 14

At the Public Record Office (PRO):
LC2
SP10, SP11, SP12
KB27
E101, E351

Contemporary printed works

A Speciall Grace appointed to have said after a banket at York
  (London, 1558)
John Foxe, *Actes and Monuments of these latter and perilous dayes* ...
  (London, 1563)
John Foxe, *Actes and Monuments of matters most speciall and
  memorable* ... (London, 1583)
Francis Godwin, *Rerum Anglicarum Henrico VIII, Edwardo VI* (London,
  1653)
Richard Grafton, *A Chronicle at large and mere history* (London, 1568;
  ed. H. Ellis, London, 1809)
Edward Hall, *The Union of the Two Noble and Illustre Famelies of York
  and Lancaster* (London, 1548; ed. H. Ellis, London, 1809)
[Richard Mulcaster], *The Passage of our most dread Sovereign Ladie,
  Queen Elizabeth* ... *the day before her coronation* (London, 1559)
John Procter, *The Historie of Wiats Rebellion* (London, 1554, 1555)

Later editions

Acts of the Privy Council, ed. J.R. Dasent (London, 1890–1907) [*APC*]
B. Castiglione, *The Book of the Courtier*, ed. and trans. G. Bull (London,
  1976)
Henry Clifford, *The Life of Jane Dormer, Duchess of Feria*, ed. J.
  Stevenson (London, 1887)
J.E. Cox, *The Works of Thomas Cranmer*, 2 vols. (London, 1844, 1846)

'Feria's Despatch of 14th November 1558', ed. M.-J. Rodriguez-Salgado and S. Adams, *Camden Miscellany*, 28 (1984).

A. Feuillerat, *Documents Relating to the Office of the Revels in the Reigns of Edward VI and Mary* (Louvain, 1914)

A. Feuillerat, *Documents Relating to the Office of the Revels in the Reign of Queen Elizabeth* (Louvain, 1908)

W.D. Hamilton, *Wriothesley's Chronicle* (Camden Society, 1877)

S. Haynes and W. Murdin, *A Collection of State Papers … left by William Cecil, Lord Burghley*, 2 vols. (London, 1740, 1759)

Household Ordinances (Society of Antiquaries, 1790)

P.L. Hughes and J.F. Larkin, *Tudor Royal Proclamations*, 3 vols. (New York, 1964–9)

W.K. Jordan, *The Chronicle and Political Papers of King Edward VI* (London, 1966)

'The Letters of Richard Scudamore to Sir Philip Hoby', ed. Susan Brigden, *Camden Miscellany*, 30 (1990)

The Life and Raigne of Edward the Sixth by John Hayward, ed. B.L. Beer (Kent, Ohio, 1993)

L.S. Marcus *et al.*, *Elizabeth I: Collected Works* (Chicago, 2000)

J.G. Nichols, *The Chronicle of the Greyfriars of London* (Camden Society, 1852)

J.G. Nichols, *The Chronicle of Queen Jane, and of the First Two Years of Mary* (Camden Society, 1850)

J.G. Nichols, *The Diary of Henry Machyn* (Camden Society, 1848)

J.G. Nichols, *The Literary Remains of King Edward VI* (Roxburgh Club, 1857)

J.G. Nichols, *Narratives of the Days of the Reformation* (Camden Society, 1859)

A.F. Pollard, *Tudor Tracts* (London, 1903)

Statutes of the Realm, ed. A. Luders *et al.*, 11 vols. (London, 1810–28)

Tres Cartas de lo sucedido en el viaje de Su Alteza a Inglaterra (La Sociedad de Bibliofilos Espanoles, Madrid, 1877)

Tudor Economic Documents, ed. R.H. Tawney and Eileen Power, 3 vols. (London, 1924)

'The Vita Mariae Angliae Reginae of Robert Wingfield of Brantham', ed. D. MacCulloch, *Camden Miscellany*, 28 (1984)

Calendars, etc.

Calendar of the Patent Rolls, Edward VI, 5 vols. (London, 1924–9); *Philip and Mary*, 4 vols. (London, 1936–9); *Elizabeth, 1558–63*, 2 vols. (London, 1939, 1948) [*CPR*]

Calendar of State Papers, Domestic, Edward VI, ed. C.S. Knighton (London, 1992) [*CSP Domestic, Edward VI*]

Calendar of State Papers, Domestic, Mary and Philip and Mary, ed. C.S. Knighton (London, 1998) [*CSP Domestic*, Mary]

Calendar of State Papers, Foreign, Edward VI and Mary, ed. W.B. Turnbull, 2 vols. (London, 1861); *Elizabeth, 1558–65*, ed. J. Stevenson (London, 1863) [*CSP Foreign*]

Calendar of State Papers, Spanish, ed. Royall Tyler *et al.*, 13 vols. (London, 1862–1954) [*CSP Spanish*]

Calendar of State Papers, Venetian, ed. Rawdon Brown *et al.*, 9 vols. (London, 1864–98) [*CSP Venetian*]

Letters and Papers ... of the Reign of Henry VIII, ed. J. Gairdner *et al.*, 21 vols. (London, 1862–1910) [*Letters and Papers*]

The Revised Short Title Catalogue of Books Printed in England, Scotland and Ireland, and of English Books Printed Abroad, 1475–1640, ed. A.W. Pollard and G.R. Redgrave, rev. W.A. Jackson, F.S. Ferguson and K.F. Pantzer (London, 1976–86)

R.A. de Vertot, *Ambassades de Messieurs de Noailles*, 5 vols. (Louvain, 1743)

Secondary works

S. Adams, *Leicester and the Court* (Manchester, 2002)

S. Alford, *The Early Elizabethan Polity: Sir William Cecil and the British Succession Crisis, 1558–69* (Cambridge, 1998)

S. Alford, *Kingship and Politics in the Reign of Edward VI* (Cambridge, 2002)

S. Anglo, *Spectacle, Pageantry and Early Tudor Policy*, 2nd edn (London, 1997) (1st edn 1965)

Ian Archer *et al.*, eds., *Religion, Politics and Society in Sixteenth Century England* (Camden Fifth Series 22, 2003)

T.W. Baldwin, *William Shakespeare's Small Latin and Less Greek* (London, 1944)

K. Bartlett, '"The Misfortune that is wished for him": The Exile and Death of Edward Courtenay, Eighth Earl of Devon', *Canadian Journal of History*, 14 (1979)

G.W. Bernard, *The Power of the Early Tudor Nobility: A Study of the Fourth and Fifth Earls of Shrewsbury* (Brighton, 1985)

G.W. Bernard, 'The Downfall of Sir Thomas Seymour', in G. Bernard, *The Tudor Nobility* (London, 1992)

R.C. Braddock, 'The Rewards of Office Holding in Tudor England', *Journal of British Studies*, 14 (1975).

S. Brigden, *London and the Reformation* (Oxford, 1989)

M.L. Bush, *The Government Policy of Protector Somerset* (Manchester, 1975)

H.M. Colvin, *The History of the King's Works, IV, 1485–1660* (London, 1982)

P.S. Donaldson, *A Machiavellian Treatise by Stephen Gardiner* (Cambridge, 1975)

Susan Doran, *Monarchy and Matrimony: The Courtships of Elizabeth I* (London, 1996)

Susan Doran and T. Freeman, *The Myth of Elizabeth* (London, 2003)

M. Dowling, *Humanism in the Age of Henry VIII* (London, 1986)

G.R. Elton, *Thomas Cromwell* (Bangor, 1991)

G.R. Elton, *The Tudor Constitution* (Cambridge, 1982)

G.R. Elton, 'Tudor Government, Points of Contact: III: The Court', in *Studies in Tudor and Stuart Politics and Government*, vol.3 (Cambridge, 1983)

Alastair Fox, *Politics and Literature in the Reigns of Henry VII and Henry VIII* (Oxford, 1989)

Antonia Fraser, *The Six Wives of Henry VIII* (London, 1993)

S.R. Gammon, *Statesman and Schemer: William, First Lord Paget, Tudor Minister* (Newton Abbot, 1973)

R. Greenacre, 'A Controversial Sermon at a Royal Funeral', *Chichester Cathedral Journal* (1998).

S.J. Gunn, *Charles Brandon, Duke of Suffolk, 1484–1545* (Oxford, 1988)

Peter Gwyn, *The King's Cardinal* (London, 1990)

E.H. Harbison, *Rival Ambassadors at the Court of Queen Mary* (Princeton, NJ 1940)

W.P. Haugaard, 'Elizabeth Tudor's Book of Devotions: A Neglected Clue to the Queen's Life and Character', *Sixteenth Century Journal*, 12 (1981)

D.E. Hoak, 'The Coronations of Edward VI, Mary I and Elizabeth I, and the Transformation of Tudor Monarchy', in *Westminster Abbey Reformed, 1540–1640*, ed. C.S. Knighton and R. Mortimer (Aldershot, 2003)

D.E. Hoak, *The King's Council in the Reign of Edward VI* (Cambridge, 1976)

D.E. Hoak, 'The Secret History of the Tudor Court: The King's Coffers and the King's Purse, 1542–1553', *Journal of British Studies*, 26 (1987)

Philip Hughes, *The Reformation in England*, 3 vols. (London, 1954–6)

M.E. James, *Society, Politics and Culture* (London, 1986)

Susan James, *Kateryn Parr: The Making of a Queen* (Stroud, 1999)

N.L. Jones, *Faith by Statute* (Cambridge, 1982)

W.K. Jordan, *Edward VI: The Threshold of Power* (London, 1970)

W.K. Jordan, *Edward VI: The Young King* (London, 1968)

Henry Kamen, *Philip II* (London, 1997)

J.N. King, *Tudor Royal Iconography* (Princeton, NJ, 1989)

R.J. Knecht, *Francis I* (Cambridge, 1982)

J. Loach, *Edward VI* (London, 1999)

J. Loach, *Parliament and the Crown in the Reign of Mary Tudor* (Oxford, 1986)

D.M. Loades, *Elizabeth I* (London, 2003)

D.M. Loades, *Henry VIII and his Queens* (Stroud, 1994)

D.M. Loades, *John Dudley, Duke of Northumberland* (Oxford, 1996)

D.M. Loades, *Mary Tudor: A Life* (Oxford, 1989)

D.M. Loades, 'Philip II and the Government of England', in *Law and Government under the Tudors*, ed. C. Cross *et al.* (Cambridge, 1988)

D.M. Loades, *The Reign of Mary Tudor*, 2nd edn (London, 1991)

D.M. Loades, *The Tudor Court* (London, 1986)

D.M. Loades, *Tudor Government* (Oxford, 1997)

D.M. Loades, *Two Tudor Conspiracies* (Cambridge, 1965)

D.M. Loades, *Essays on the Reign of Edward VI* (Oxford, 2001)

W. MacCaffrey, *The Shaping of the Elizabethan Regime, 1558–1572* (London, 1969)

T.F. Mayer, *Reginald Pole: Prince and Prophet* (Cambridge, 2000)

R.C. McCoy, 'From the Tower to the Tiltyard: Robert Dudley's Return to Glory', *Historical Journal*, 27 (1984)

H. Miller, *Henry VIII and the English Nobility* (Oxford, 1986)

J.A. Muller, *The Letters of Stephen Gardiner* (Cambridge, 1933)

Anne Overell, 'A Nicodemite in England and Italy: Edward Courtenay, 1548–1556', in *John Foxe at Home and Abroad*, ed. D.M. Loades (Aldershot, 2004)

Conyers Read, *Mr. Secretary Cecil and Queen Elizabeth* (London, 1955)

G. Redworth, *In Defence of the Church Catholic: The Life of Stephen Gardiner* (Oxford, 1990)

G. Redworth, '"Matters Impertinent to Women": Male and Female Monarchy under Philip and Mary', *English Historical Review*, 112 (1997)

A.W. Reed, *Early Tudor Drama* (London, 1926)

M.-J. Rodriguez Salgado, *The Changing Face of Empire: Charles V, Philip II, and Habsburg Authority, 1551–1559* (Cambridge, 1988)

J.J. Scarisbrick, *Henry VIII* (London, 1968)

Ethan Shagan, *Popular Politics and the English Reformation* (London, 2002)

L.B. Smith, *Henry VIII: The Mask of Royalty* (London, 1971)

John Southworth, *Fools and Jesters at the English Court* (Stroud, 1998)

D. Starkey, *Elizabeth* (London, 2000)

D. Starkey, ed., *The English Court from the Wars of the Roses to the Civil War* (London, 1987)

L. Stone, *The Crisis of the Aristocracy, 1558–1640* (Oxford, 1965)

R. Strong, *The Cult of Elizabeth* (London, 1977)

R. Strong, *Tudor and Jacobean Portraits* (London, 1969)

J. Strype, *Ecclesiastical Memorials*, 3 vols. (Oxford, 1822)

M.R. Thorpe, 'Religion and the Rebellion of Sir Thomas Wyatt', *Church History*, 47 (1978).

W.J. Tighe, 'The Gentlemen Pensioners, the Duke of Northumberland, and the Attempted Coup of 1553', *Albion*, 19 (1987).

Penry Williams, *The Tudor Regime* (Oxford, 1979)

Derek Wilson, *Sweet Robin: A Biography of Robert Dudley, Earl of Leicester, 1533–1588* (London, 1981)

Alan Young, *Tudor and Jacobean Tournaments* (London, 1987)

Unpublished theses

Andrew Boyle, 'Henry FitzAlan, 12th Earl of Arundel: Politics and
  Culture in the Tudor Nobility', DPhil diss., Oxford University, 2002.

R.C. Braddock, 'The Royal Household, 1540–1560', PhD diss.,
  Northwestern University, 1971.

J.A. Rowley-Williams, 'Image and Reality: The Lives of Aristocratic
  Women in Early Tudor England', PhD diss., University of Wales
  [Bangor], 1998.

Index